Crimes, Follies, and Misfortunes

Crimes, Follies, and Misfortunes

THE FEDERAL IMPEACHMENT TRIALS

Eleanore Bushnell

UNIVERSITY OF ILLINOIS PRESS

URBANA AND CHICAGO

This book is printed on acid-free paper.

Library of Congress Cataloging-in-Publication Data

Bushnell, Eleanore.
  Crimes, follies, and misfortunes : the federal impeachment trials
/ Eleanore Bushnell.
      p.   cm.
  Includes bibliographical references and index.
  ISBN 0-252-01827-3 (cloth)
  1. Trials (Impeachment)—United States—History.   I. Title.
KF8781.B87   1992
345.73′0234—dc20
[347.305234]   91-8519
                                                                  CIP

Antoninus diffused order and tranquillity over the greatest part of the earth. His reign is marked by the rare advantage of furnishing very few materials for history; which is, indeed, little more than the register of the crimes, follies, and misfortunes of mankind.

—Edward Gibbon

Contents

Preface ix

Introduction 1

1. Aspects of the Impeachment Mechanism 9

2. William Blount 25

3. John Pickering 43

4. Samuel Chase 57

5. James H. Peck 91

6. West H. Humphreys 115

7. Andrew Johnson 127

8. William W. Belknap 165

9. Charles Swayne 191

10. Robert W. Archbald 217

11. Harold Louderback 245

12. Halsted L. Ritter 269

13. Harry E. Claiborne 289

Epilogue 307

Appendix 325

Notes 327

Bibliography 365

Index 375

Preface

This study of the federal impeachment trials, begun in the late 1960s, was undertaken at a time when the impeachment process at the national level appeared to have fallen into disuse. The most recent impeachment, that of Judge Halsted L. Ritter, had taken place in 1936. Its labored course, nearly three years of investigation followed by eleven days of trial, did not win much approval; many senators did not even bother to attend the trial. The Ritter case, coupled with criticisms of the purposes and procedures of some of the preceding impeachments and trials, seemed to indicate that the "weapon" had become outmoded. My study began as a historical analysis of an antique, possibly obsolete, mechanism. But when Watergate and subsequent revelations brought Richard Nixon's administration into disrepute in 1974, impeachment moved from the history shelves to the headlines. Then came Judge Harry E. Claiborne, impeached, tried, and convicted in 1986. In a relatively short span of time the ponderous impeachment procedure became again a subject of attention.

The chapter on James H. Peck appeared in the *Missouri Historical Review* in January 1980; the chapter on Harold Louderback was published in the *Nevada Historical Society Quarterly* in Spring 1983; and the chapter on Harry E. Claiborne was published in the *Nevada Historical Society Quarterly* in Winter 1989. These articles, although presented in a somewhat different form, were based on the relevant chapters in this work.

In constructing this book I relied mainly on the transcripts of the impeachment trials. But I owe debts to writers whose studies proved useful in testing the validity of the conclusions I drew from the trials. These debts are recognized throughout the book as well as in the bibliography.

In addition to help from other writers, many colleagues and friends gave me valued support. Helma Elizabeth Kuehn read the entire manuscript; her unflagging commitment to clarity and exactness improved both style and substance. My sister Margaret Mathison read several chapters with professional care and precision. My friends Mary and Clarence N. Stone and Liane and Robert Norman gave advice on four of the chapters. Caroline B. Fogle helped with certain chapters, particularly one and seven. Other friends who contributed significantly include James Wignall, E. Muriel Bennett, and Marian Norman.

Colleagues at the University of Nevada also shared their expertise. Michael J. Brodhead and Jerome E. Edwards of the History Department; Elmer R. Rusco, Allen R. Wilcox, Don W. Driggs, William L. Eubank, and Joseph N. Crowley of the Political Science Department; Anne Howard of the English Department; Robert Laxalt, former director of the University of Nevada Press; and James K. Shaw all made significant contributions.

Michael Les Benedict, an eminent scholar on the era of Reconstruction, helped clarify my treatment of Andrew Johnson's impeachment. A. Stephen Boyan, Jr., shared his knowledge of the Watergate period.

Research assistance was provided by Eslie Cann of the Nevada Historical Society; by the reference and government publications sections of the University of Nevada Library, especially Judy Sokol, Sharon Prengamon, Duncan Aldrich, Teri Conrad, and Joanne Guyton; by former Nevada senators Paul Laxalt, Howard W. Cannon, and Alan Bible, and particularly by Attorney General Frankie Sue Del Papa, formerly of Senator Bible's office; by Clara S. Kelly, Marie Case, and the library staff of the National Judicial College; and by the University of Nevada Graduate School, which provided funds for part of the typing. Judge Alfred T. Goodwin of the Ninth Circuit Court of Appeals gave invaluable assistance on the problems of attempts to modify the impeachment procedure. Melissa L. Root, an excellent typist, deserves my special thanks because of the uniformly fine work she did and her concern for the successful completion of the project.

I am grateful for the searching criticisms that I received from those generous friends and colleagues who read all or parts of this book. Any errors of fact or any unjustifiable conclusions can be laid entirely at my door.

Introduction

> The President, Vice-President and all Civil Officers of the United States, shall be removed from Office on Impeachment for, and Conviction of, Treason, Bribery, or other high Crimes and Misdemeanors.
> —Constitution of the United States
> Article II, Section 4

The national government's efforts to define and apply standards for measuring official misconduct began with the impeachment and trial of Senator William Blount from 1797 to 1799. This book describes the experiences of the twelve federal officers who were impeached by the House of Representatives and tried before the Senate during the period from 1799 to 1986, with a brief summary in the Epilogue of the trials of Judges Alcee L. Hastings and Walter L. Nixon, Jr., in 1989. The trials themselves form the cornerstone of this work.

My aim is to examine and weigh the evidence accrued from the trials against such questions as whether, in order to be impeachable, an offense must be a crime indictable in court, must be performed in the accused's official capacity, or must be proved to be willful misconduct. An additional and significant constitutional question arose in the case of Judge Harry E. Claiborne in 1984, Must a life-tenured jurist be impeached before being subjected to a court trial? If, like Claiborne, a federal judge is tried in court, found guilty, and sentenced to prison, has he been removed, if temporarily, from office by a procedure not sanctioned by the Constitution? This question will be examined in chapter 13 and in the Epilogue.

Although not subjects of impeachment trials and so not appraised in this book, three officers require at least passing attention because their experiences reveal substantial aspects of impeachment theory and practice.

The first of the three, Mark W. Delahay, a Republican, was appointed a federal district judge in Kansas by Abraham Lincoln in 1863.[1] The House of Representatives impeached Judge Delahay in 1873 for unsuitable personal habits and for questionable financial dealings. His impeachment originated in a resolution by Benjamin Butler (Republican, Massachusetts) in 1872 calling for an inquiry into the judge's conduct. The investigating committee reported to

1

Mark W. Delahay. *The Kansas State Historical Society.*

the House of Representatives that Delahay's "personal habits unfitted him for the judicial office . . . and that his sobriety would be the exception and not the rule."[2]

The House impeached him on March 3, 1873 without a record vote and before articles of impeachment had been drafted detailing his misconduct. Judge Delahay resigned following his impeachment, and the House of Representatives took no further action against him. Evidence that his resignation had been accepted derives from the fact that Ulysses S. Grant appointed another judge to his post on March 10, 1874.[3] Thus, although Mark W. Delahay was impeached, no documentary record in the form of impeachment articles exists in his case. He is significant in history as the only impeached officer against whom articles of impeachment were not drafted, and the first such officer to evade trial by resigning.

The second impeached official to escape trial by resigning, Judge George W. English, withdrew from his judgeship just a week before his trial was scheduled to open in the Senate. The House of Representatives had voted articles of impeachment against him on April 1, 1926, following a year of investigation of his conduct by a subcommittee of the House Judiciary Committee. The subcommittee reported that Judge English had (1) unlawfully disbarred two attor-

George W. English, second from left, accompanied by his attorneys E. C. Kramer (to Judge English's right), W. F. Zumbrunn, and William Acton. *Library of Congress.*

neys; (2) coerced public officials, jurors, and reporters; (3) shown partiality in making appointments in bankruptcy proceedings for his own enrichment; (4) arranged for deposit of bankruptcy funds in banks in which he held stock; (5) secured a position for his son in a bank receiving deposits of bankruptcy funds under English's control and increasing those deposits from $10,000 to $130,000 following his son's employment; and (6) habitually used profane and vulgar language.

English, a Democrat, had been appointed to the federal bench in 1918 by Woodrow Wilson. The judge's misdeeds, as chronicled in the articles of impeachment, had occurred from 1918 to 1925, thus extending throughout his career as a federal jurist and illustrating a persistent impeachment theme: habitual malperformance.

Explication of the complaints when they were debated in the House of Representatives plainly disclosed that the accusers had an easier time arguing their position than did George W. English's defenders. The House adopted a resolution to impeach by a vote of 306 to 62; an impressive 83 percent of the congressmen recorded on the roll call supported impeachment.[4] The sixty-two no votes came

Richard M. Nixon and Gerald Ford confer in the Oval Office shortly before President Nixon's resignation, August 1974. *General Services Administration, National Archives and Records Service.*

from twenty-one Republicans and forty-one Democrats, a division showing some preference of English's brother Democrats for not proceeding against him.

On May 3, 1926 Judge English, accompanied by his attorneys, came before the Senate sitting as a Court of Impeachment.[5] His response to the charges levied against him in the articles consisted first of asserting that nothing of an impeachable nature had been imputed to him and, second, that not one of the charges was true.

The Senate fixed November 10 for the opening date of the trial. On that day the House informed the Senate that English had resigned on November 4 and that Calvin Coolidge had accepted the resignation the same day. Upon request of the House of Representatives, the Senate terminated the proceedings by a vote of seventy favoring, nine opposing.[6] Therefore, the impeachment of George W. English came to an inconclusive end, one brought about solely by his own action of resigning. He stands out as unique in the annals of impeachment: the only federal officer to evade trial by resigning after articles of impeachment had been adopted against him.

4

The third of the defective officers to be a serious object of the impeachment mechanism evaded both impeachment and trial. Richard M. Nixon, a Republican elected to the presidency in 1968 and reelected in 1972, resigned after the House Judiciary Committee recommended his impeachment. The committee had adopted three articles accusing him of obstruction of justice, abuse of powers, and unlawful refusal to supply material subpoenaed by the House of Representatives.[7] Nixon resigned August 9, 1974, ten days after Judiciary Committee approval of the articles and on the eve of their nearly certain adoption by the House of Representatives. His resignation halted the impeachment process but did not expunge acknowledgment, even among most of his faithful supporters, that his presidency had been marked by flagrant abuses of executive power and had ended in disgrace.

More than twenty of President Nixon's appointees went to prison for perjury, conspiracy, burglary, illegal wiretapping, and other activities not ordinarily associated with presidential administration of government. Nixon, named an unindicted co-conspirator by a federal grand jury, escaped impeachment and trial by resigning and escaped court review of his conduct when his successor Gerald Ford bestowed a blanket pardon upon him on September 8, 1974.[8]

The articles of impeachment charged Nixon with unlawful employment of agencies of government to advance his private goals, allowing and authorizing illegal electronic surveillance of citizens, knowing that his agents had broken into the Watergate offices of the Democratic National Committee and thwarting subsequent investigations of that break-in, permitting payment of hush money to the Watergate burglars, and recommending or approving perjured testimony by his aides before congressional committees or in court. The break-in at the Watergate office and apartment complex made "Watergate" a synonym for political corruption.

On July 24, 1974, after seven months of extensive review of the allegations against President Nixon, the House Judiciary Committee began public televised hearings on proposed articles of impeachment. After six days of debate, the committee voted on the articles. Article 1, obstruction of justice, received twenty-seven yes votes and eleven no; all the no votes were cast by Republicans. Article 2, abuse of powers, was adopted by a vote of twenty-eight to ten; again all opposing votes came from Republicans. The last of the articles the committee adopted dealt with the president's disregard of a subpoena issued by the House of Representatives; the vote was twenty-one to seventeen, with two Democrats joining fifteen Republicans in voting no.[9]

Richard M. Nixon resigned a few days after the Judiciary Committee adopted the three articles of impeachment. His resignation, precipitated by candid appraisals by his Republican adherents that he would be impeached by the House and convicted by the Senate, was further hastened along by revelation of the "smoking gun." President Nixon had recorded many conversations in the White House, and the Supreme Court had ordered the president to release some of those tapes.[10] The "smoking gun" tape showed that, despite having repeatedly said he knew nothing of the cover-up of the break-in at the Watergate, the misuse of government agencies, and other abuses, the president had been fully involved from the beginning. One of Nixon's most loyal supporters, Edward Hutchinson (Republican, Michigan), said that the "smoking gun" tape "for the first time tied the President to the conspiracy [and] was his undoing. Those who had been defending the President were left without a defense.... Under the circumstances impeachment became a certainty and resignation the only viable alternative."[11]

Although not ending in impeachment and trial, Richard M. Nixon's downfall underlines the crucial contribution to good government made by the existence of the impeachment mechanism, a mechanism that forced a defective president to withdraw from office and that thereby preserved the nation from a serious internal threat.

In addition to the experiences of Judge Delahay, Judge English, and President Nixon, more than fifty federal judges have come close to being impeached.[12] Some were found to be unjustly accused or accused of actions or inactions not serious enough to merit impeachment. But most of them escaped further investigation solely because they resigned. The impeachment procedure was designed to provide a means for removing a deficient officer, not to punish for derelictions of duty or to substitute for a court trial. Therefore, it might seem obvious that no action need be taken when a suspect occupant removed himself from his position. However, a second, and rarely used, aspect of the process empowers the Senate to disqualify an official convicted under the impeachment provisions from ever again holding a national office of honor, trust, or profit. My analysis of the twelve trials leads me to conclude that the Senate has ordinarily considered a guilty verdict enough of a stigma to preclude the disgraced officer's seeking or acquiring another national post. Only Judge West H. Humphreys (1862) and Judge Robert W. Archbald (1913) received an order of disqualification. Impeachment history reveals, then, that resignation may be expected to terminate action against an allegedly malperforming officer, and the Senate has rarely applied, or even contemplated applying, a sentence of disqualification from further national office.

In appraising complaints brought against those officers who evaded either impeachment or trial by resignation, I found that the greatest number of accusations concerned abuse of power and securing kickbacks from persons the officers appointed to receiverships in bankruptcy proceedings. Other frequent charges include tyrannical or undignified conduct, alcoholism, neglect of duty, promotion of personal financial interests at the expense of public trust, and—rarely—violation of the law. The twelve officers surveyed in this work who were tried under the impeachment provisions of the Constitution displayed these same defects, only their instances of misconduct were usually more persistent and more conspicuous.

1

Aspects of the Impeachment Mechanism

To grasp the place of impeachment in the constitutional scheme, and its potential role for the future, we need better to understand the use to which it was put in the past.
—Raoul Berger

Impeachment has been rarely used at the federal level. In the period from 1799 to 1986, the House of Representatives impeached just fourteen national officers: eleven jurists, one senator, one cabinet member, and one president. Two of the fourteen who received this unwelcome attention, Judge Mark W. Delahay (1873) and Judge George W. English (1926), resigned before trial, and the process was abandoned. Five of the twelve tried before the Senate were convicted, all of them judges.

Jurists are prevalent in the roster of impeached officers. Eleven of the fourteen whom the House impeached, the five whom the Senate convicted, the six impeached in the twentieth century, and the two disqualified from holding further national office all belonged to the judicial branch. That judges have been the subject of 78 percent of the impeachments and 100 percent of the convictions has stirred sporadic congressional efforts to devise a less cumbersome procedure than impeachment for examining and evaluating allegations of miscreant judicial performance, especially malperformance by lower-court judges. These efforts have usually involved consideration of two possible plans: (1)establishing a special commission authorized to remove a judge found incapable of functioning either because of corruption or because of physical or mental inability to perform his duties; and (2) assigning the authority to remove a defective judge to the judicial branch.

However deeply Congress feels about the need to modify the procedure for evaluating federal judges, my analysis of constitutional stipulations on the subject, particularly the Framers' careful provision for an independent judiciary, leads me to conclude that

9

Congress must retain its sole power to impeach and remove judges. This position has been persuasively endorsed and persuasively rejected.[1]

In several instances in the discussion that follows I mention my wish that Congress would define "good behavior," a term the Constitution applies only to judges and the ground on which they retain their life appointments. An act of Congress defining "good behavior" and making its absence an impeachable offense would solve the problems that arose in several impeachments when the judge being tried had deliberately or inadvertently violated the standards by which the majority of judges conduct their public and private lives.

Not only have judges dominated impeachment history, it is also the case that all the subjects of impeachment and trial have been male. No woman officer has ever been impeached. Either because of unblemished virtue or because of failure to attain a sufficient number of offices to become corrupted, female officials have never starred in an impeachment.

An impeachment proceeding originates with criticisms of a national officer's performance raised in the House of Representatives and followed by an investigation of the criticisms. The House then votes on whether the facts developed in the investigation warrant impeachment. Should the majority decide that the accused officer's conduct merits impeachment, the House prosecutes him before the Senate. If the Senate finds the official guilty by a two-thirds vote, he is removed from his post. The Senate can also disqualify a convicted officer from ever again holding a national office of honor, trust, or profit.

An analysis of the major charges against the twelve men discussed herein puts financial greed and abuse of office in primary positions; alcoholism, senility, and incompetence also stimulated complaints. The same flaws also characterized, variously, the officers who escaped impeachment or trial by resigning. To quote Edward Gibbon, each official who came to trial fitted one or more of these categories: "crimes, follies, and misfortunes."

Reflection on the history and scope of the impeachment mechanism leads to questions, if not always to satisfactory answers. Why were only twelve officers impeached and tried in the almost two hundred years from 1799 to 1986? This nation cannot be so blessed as to have produced only about sixty serious malefactors: fourteen impeached, twelve tried, more than fifty on the brink of impeachment. Some part of the answer to the scarcity of impeachments lies in the process, a process deliberately complicated and time-consuming; some part, in the fact that resignations by actual or potential subjects have resulted in termination by the House of Representatives of actions directed toward exposing their conduct.

A second and more substantive question is this: What caused the employment of the impeachment procedure against the particular twelve men who came to trial? What did they do that was so extraordinary that the House of Representatives felt compelled to examine their conduct and then decide that they should be impeached? They must have displayed dramatic venality, must have performed so corruptly that the House of Representatives decided that their remaining in their posts could be tolerated only at the risk of peril to nation and citizen. Perhaps certain of the impeached officers were abhorrent to powerful political or business groups. All must in any case have displayed characteristics in conducting their duties that made their impeachment inevitable, characteristics not as conspicuously displayed by those malperforming officers who escaped detection, or at least escaped impeachment. Otherwise the twelve who came to trial would have sunk from public view along with the other inadequately performing officials who did not attract sufficient notoriety to be impeached.

The officers appraised herein threatened—or were thought to threaten—political stability; they were viewed as endangering public confidence in an institution of government. To assemble a melange of facts into some kind of sensible whole requires a standard against which the twelve men can be measured and against which a future defective officeholder could in turn be measured. A generalized portrait of the official likely to be a subject of impeachment shows him as satisfying one or more of the following criteria: (1) persisting misconduct; a long train of abuses too serious to permit continuance in office; (2) misuse of position for personal gain or power; (3) political estrangement from the dominant party in Congress or alienation from the official's own party; (4) behavior offensive to influential personages powerful enough to mount an impeachment inquiry; (5) recognition by his constituent public that he is dishonest or unqualified; (6) loser of, or never possessor of, a significant constituency; and (7) inability to perform his duties.

Of course no single impeached officer could be expected to exhibit all of the foregoing attributes. The person coming closest is Judge Harry E. Claiborne (1986), whose conviction in federal district court for deliberately underpaying his income taxes in two successive years displayed persisting misconduct that estranged him from his own political party (Democratic), from prominent congressmen of

11

both parties, from the judiciary, and from portions of the public. The person who least fits the pattern is the ailing and senile Judge John Pickering (1804), ousted from his post by impeachment and trial only because no other method existed for removing an incompetent judge.

The other officers all exemplify some of the characteristics listed previously. The dominant component of impeachment concerns partisan adherence. Table 1, summarizing the impeachment trials, shows that only two officers were impeached by a House of Representatives in which their political party held a majority: Judge Charles Swayne, a Republican (1905), and Judge Harry E. Claiborne, a Democrat (1986). The House voted no other impeachment against a member of the majority party, and in Swayne's case partisanship revealed itself when the Republican-dominated Senate declined to convict him. The only Senate verdict of guilty when the accused belonged to the majority party occurred in the case of Judge Robert W. Archbald (1913), a Republican, whose brazen misconduct assured the two-thirds vote required to convict. Accusations of party-centered bias levied against impeachment proceedings are generally sustained by the evidence; partisanship occurs in varying degrees of intensity in most of the impeachment experiences.

But manifestations of partisanship should not be considered as unexpected aberrations of the impeachment procedure. Impeachment is a political event and does not become activated in an environment of objectivity and neutrality. It is not designed to punish an errant officeholder, but only to determine if he should be removed from his post; punishment remains a province of the judicial, not the legislative branch. Furthermore, the requirement of a two-thirds Senate vote to convict protects against an exclusively party-centered impeachment and trial.

Although partisanship is plainly observable in the operation of the impeachment procedure and is, in some cases, the prime mover of the process, all the trials produced evidence of wrongdoing or suspected wrongdoing. The accusers, whatever their motivation, could be seen as trying to protect the public from a possibly defective officeholder, not just to harass an obnoxious political opponent.

Two outstanding impeachments and trials, those of Justice Samuel Chase (1805) and Andrew Johnson (1868), both marked with intense political animosity, did not result in guilty verdicts even though each man belonged to the minority party in the House and in the Senate. Partisan commitment cannot be viewed as decisive, particularly in the absence of a strong, well-reasoned prosecution, but can fairly be viewed as a major component of the impeachment pattern.

Impeachment trials have not established precedents in the same sense that past decisions exert control over subsequent rulings in courts of law. In the latter forum, courts follow precedent; when they do not, they ordinarily acknowledge that a formerly adhered-to judicial position is being overturned. But the force and continuity of earlier holdings do not characterize impeachment trials. Each one is essentially new and a product of the political environment in which it takes place. In the majority of trials, both sides have referred to earlier impeachments, claiming, variously, that a precedent substantiating a point the claimant wished to make had been established in a preceding trial. But it is almost entirely the persuasive skill of the speaker rather than any historically recognized precedent that is dominant in convincing the Senate that a particular position finds support in past cases.

Thus, impeachment trials have a history but have not proved to be part of an evolutionary process. From the first trial in 1799 to the last one surveyed herein some common threads can be found, but one cannot trace the course of impeachment practice in the same sense that swelling and diminishment of presidential authority or activism and passivity of the Supreme Court can be traced. The Senate has never ruled on the issues emerging in the trials before it; hence, no body of precedents exists to be sustained or discarded. One can readily locate Senate decisions—the final vote—but can locate only fleeting proof of the reasoning behind such decisions. The trials, then, have not supplied decisive precedents and are susceptible to widely differing interpretations, but they have been influential in succeeding trials and would prove so in future impeachment experiences.

Even though controlling positions gleaned from impeachment trials are scant, I have identified twelve examples, some of them arguable, of often-repeated principles emerging from United States impeachment history. The examples I consider to be either established, or correct if not established, are these: (1) impeachment is directed to political offenses that threaten good government, offenses that are possibly but not necessarily criminal. (2) The accused must have engaged in repeated misconduct. (3) The misconduct need not have been performed in the subject's official capacity. (4) If the subject is an elected officer, his performance must

Table 1. Summary of Impeachment Trials

Name	Attained Office	Party	House Political Composition	Senate Political Composition	Managers' Political Composition	Senate Vote for Conviction
Senator William Blount (1799) Tennessee	Election, U.S. Senate	Democratic-Republican	58 Federalists 48 Democratic-Republicans	20 Federalists 12 Democratic-Republicans	11 Federalists	Yes 11 (10 Fed.) No 14
Judge John Pickering (1804) New Hampshire	Appointed by President Washington	Federalist	69 Republicans 36 Federalists	25 Republicans 9 Federalists	11 Republicans	Yes 19 (All R.) No 7 [Fed.] (100% Party)
Justice Samuel Chase (1805) Maryland	Appointed by President Washington	Federalist	102 Republicans 39 Federalists	25 Republicans 9 Federalists	7 Republicans	Yes 19 No 15 (9 Fed.) [Art 8]
Judge James H. Peck (1830–31) Missouri	Appointed by President Monroe	Republican	139 Democrats 74 National-Republicans	36 Democrats 6 Whigs 3 Federalists 3 National-Republicans	4 Democrats 1 Federalist	Yes 21 (18 D.) No 22 (15 D.)
Judge West H. Humphreys (1862) Tennessee	Appointed by President Pierce	Democrat	105 Republicans 43 Democrats 30 Other	27 Republicans 14 Democrats 7 Other	4 Republicans 1 Unionist	Yes 39 No 0 (Disqualified)
President Andrew Johnson (1868) Tennessee	Succeeded President Lincoln	War Democrat	143 Republicans 49 Democrats	42 Republicans 12 Democrats	7 Republicans	Yes 35 (All R.) No 19 (D + 7 R.)

Office / Judge	Appointed by	Party	House vote	Senate composition	Managers / Committee	Senate vote
Secretary of War William W. Belknap (1876) Iowa	Appointed by President Grant	Former Douglas Democrat	169 Democrats 109 Republicans 14 Other (Unanimous vote)	45 Republicans 29 Democrats 2 Other	5 Democrats 2 Republicans	Yes 37 No 25 (only 3 voted directly not guilty) (Jurisdiction)
Judge Charles Swayne (1905) Florida	Appointed by President Harrison	Republican	207 Republicans 178 Democrats	58 Republicans 32 Democrats	4 Republicans 3 Democrats (1st majority same party as accused)	Yes 35 (29 D.) No 47 (45 R.)
Judge Robert W. Archbald (1913) Pennsylvania	Appointed by Presidents McKinley and T. Roosevelt; Circuit Appointment President Taft	Republican	228 Democrats 161 Republicans	51 Republicans 45 Democrats	4 Democrats 3 Republicans	Yes 68 No 5 (1 D.) (Disqualified)
Judge Harold Louderback (1933) California	Appointed by President Coolidge	Republican	220 Democrats 214 Republicans 1 Other	60 Democrats 35 Republicans 1 Other	4 Democrats 2 Republicans	Yes 45 (38 D.) No 34
Judge Halsted L. Ritter (1936) Florida	Appointed by President Coolidge	Republican	319 Democrats 103 Republicans 10 Other	70 Democrats 26 Republicans	2 Democrats 1 Republican	Yes 56 (7 R.) No 28 (10 D.) (exactly 2/3ds)
Judge Harry E. Claiborne (1986) Nevada	Appointed by President Carter	Democrat	253 Democrats 182 Republicans (Unanimous vote)	53 Republicans 47 Democrats	5 Democrats 4 Republicans (2d majority same party as accused)	Yes 87 (Art. I) No 10 (5 D.)

have been so conspicuously wrong that the public good demanded removal before expiration of his term. (5) Resignation will terminate the procedure; Secretary of War William W. Belknap (1876) provides the sole exception to this principle. (6) Corrupt intent on the part of the accused officer need not be proved. (7) A new session of Congress does not halt an ongoing impeachment. (8) A finding of guilty on one count among several charges suffices to convict. (9) The accused need not be present at the trial. (10) The Senate in an impeachment trial acts as a court. (11) Following Senate conviction, a vote to disqualify the subject from ever again holding a post in the national government requires only a majority of the senators present, not the two-thirds required to convict. (12) Members of the House of Representatives and of the Senate are exempt from impeachment.

Of these "precedents," I consider all except one to be historically and logically valid—the belief that members of Congress are not liable to impeachment. It crept into United States impeachment history as a consequence of the trial of Senator William Blount (1799), who had been expelled by the Senate before his trial. The record does not establish whether the Senate found Blount not guilty because he no longer held office, or because it believed that a senator could not be impeached. A case can be made for either possibility. No other historical evidence supports immunity of legislators from the impeachment process; but practical considerations, primarily the capacity of each house to expel an offending colleague, suggest that this precedent will endure.

The other more-or-less established principles listed have coherent reasons behind their adoption. That the malperformance need not be criminal will be discussed in many of the chapters to follow. I consider it a precedent, and a proper one, but recognize that it would be argued anew in any future trial.

That the subject display a pattern of misconduct is a sensible requirement. Except for Judge James H. Peck (1831), who faced only one charge brought by only one accuser, all the impeached officers have confronted impeachments engineered by several people or groups and consisting of between four and thirteen claims of misconduct. The charges brought against them alleged habitual corruption or incompetence, not merely a single foolish or misbegotten act.

Whether the conduct complained of must be a direct product of the office held has been debated in several trials. These experiences support my belief that a judge, for example, can properly be impeached for improprieties not commited while serving on the bench in his judicial capacity. Judges engaging in shady business transactions, or failing to pay income taxes, or accepting favors, have been impeached.

As to having to demonstrate bad motives on the part of the accused in order to convict, the record is murky, although perhaps no more so than in a court of law. In most of the trials, failure to prove evil intent has been argued by spokesmen for the suspect officer. Several impeached officials insisted at trial that they harbored no ulterior motives in committting the acts of which they were accused. It seems sound to analyze the consequences of an impeached official's conduct and to base judgment on it, as has been the Senate's custom.

It is safe to claim the following four impeachment practices as solidly accepted. First, the process does not stop following the end of the congressional session in which it began; no serious argument has been raised on this point. Second, it has not been asserted that the accused officer must be found guilty on every count; a two-thirds vote on any one charge results in a conviction. Third, no one argued that a two-thirds vote to disqualify was required in the cases of the only two officials suffering disqualification from further office, Judges West H. Humphreys (1862) and Robert W. Archbald (1913). Removal from office upon conviction is mandatory, but the Senate need not even consider whether to disqualify; and if it does, a majority vote suffices. Fourth, because the impeached officer did not attend his trial in four instances and the Senate nevertheless proceeded to hear the case, I consider it established that absence of the accused will not invalidate a Senate impeachment hearing. Thus, continuation of an impeachment in a following session of Congress, a finding of guilt on one charge as sufficient for conviction, a simple majority vote to disqualify, and validity of a trial without the subject being present have enduring qualities and may be considered as precedents.

In several trials, disputes arose over whether the Senate in an impeachment trial sat as a court and so was governed by the same rules concerning admission of evidence and a finding of guilty that obtain in courts. As might be expected, in these disputes the *managers*, the term used for members of the House of Representatives who serve as prosecutors in an impeachment trial, argued that the Senate acted as a parliamentary body subject only to its own rules. The impeached officials' lawyers conversely and understandably insisted that the usual rules of court procedure must be observed. The record supports a claim that the Senate sits as a court; it has always been called a court in impeachment history and has usually behaved like one.

Thus, although impeachment "precedents" seem elusive, their emergence in varying forms in discussions of the trials that follow yields information helpful to an understanding of how fitness for continuance in office has been tested in the past. These principles produce clues to the course that proceedings would be likely to take when another case arises.

Before analyzing the twelve examples of the impeachment mechanism it is worthwhile to look at the constitutional prescriptions for its employment. Impeachment procedures in the United States are based on English and colonial precedents and on the state constitutions of the formative period of the nation's history. The Founding Fathers relied mainly on their experiences in colonial and state governments as sources for the clauses they incorporated in the Constitution. As Hoffer and Hull observe, "American impeachment law shifted, at first inadvertently and then deliberately, from the orbit of English precedent to a native republican course."[2]

Article I of the Constitution assigns to the House of Representatives the sole power to impeach. It assigns to the Senate the sole power to try an impeachment and further stipulates that (1) a two-thirds vote of the senators present is needed to convict; (2) the chief justice presides when the president becomes the subject of the trial; (3) the Senate's judgment extends only to removal from office and disqualification from holding any other national office; and (4) a convicted official may subsequently be tried in a court of law. The executive article gives the president power to grant pardons except in cases of impeachment and further specifies that the president, vice president, and all civil officers of the United States shall be removed from office if impeached and convicted of treason, bribery, or other high crimes and misdemeanors. Article III, the judicial article, establishes trial by jury for all crimes except in cases of impeachment.

The Constitution limits impeachable offenses to a stringent few. The constitutional description of these offenses is clear except for the phrase "or other high crimes and misdemeanors." The two accompanying causes for impeachment—treason and bribery—are straightforward, readily identifiable crimes. Both have a common-law meaning, both have been defined in statutes, and treason is described, and narrowly, in the Constitution. Treason and bribery have figured only peripherally in past impeachments. The national officers against whom impeachment inquiries have been started

18

have rarely committed such gross and explicit misdeeds; those few who might have been charged with either of these crimes were instead accused of high crimes and misdemeanors.

This slippery phrase, then, one that has eluded any firmly accepted definition, has commanded attention in all the impeachment experiences. The major effort for the House of Representatives has been to convince the Senate that the conduct for which it brought the official to trial qualified as a high crime and misdemeanor. The meaning of the phrase has been argued exhaustively, but a precedent-setting interpretation has never been articulated. On the one side the phrase has been deemed to require a criminal act indictable in court, and on the other to require only proof that an official has behaved in a manner inimical to the public welfare and violative of his duty.

Each of the impeachment experiences recorded in the following chapters supplies varying, sometimes contradictory, definitions of high crimes and misdemeanors. Such definitions spring from a given speaker's desire to persuade the Senate to adopt his own analysis of the meaning of the phrase, from his interpretation of possible precedents from earlier impeachment trials, or from his conclusions about the intent of the Founding Fathers as revealed in such sources as *The Federalist*, Jonathan Elliot's *Debates*, Max Farrand's *The Records of the Federal Convention of 1787*, *Writings of James Madison*, or Joseph Story's *Commentaries on the Constitution*.[3]

But no settled interpretation of high crimes and misdemeanors can be firmly derived from these references or from the twelve cases appraised herein. The term's meaning has been argued in the pre-impeachment debates in the House of Representatives and in the Senate trials. Having acknowledged that the phrase enjoys no authorized definition, I nevertheless conclude that, based at least on historical usage, it does not restrict impeachable offenses to crimes but also extends to serious, probably persistent, misconduct that brings the office into disrepute. This conclusion arises from three facts or assumptions: (1) the drafters of the Constitution gave no indication that they intended impeachment to be confined to criminal acts; (2) they provided for trial in a court of law following conviction in an impeachment trial, evidence that the latter proceeding is not aimed at legal punishment, nor as an alternative to a court trial, but instead provides a remedy for unendurable political offenses by removing a convicted offender from office; and (3) the Senate in certain trials has accepted charges by the House of Representatives as appropriate for impeachment even though the charges did not include indictable acts, and in three such cases the Senate delivered a guilty verdict for noncriminal conduct. The origins and practices of United States impeachment sustain an argument that high crimes and misdemeanors refers to more than just criminal conduct. As Raoul Berger states, " 'high crimes and misdemeanors' appear to be words of art confined to impeachments, without roots in the ordinary criminal law and which, so far as I could discover, had no relation to whether an indictment would lie in the particular circumstances."[4]

One other clause in the Constitution bears on impeachment. Article III, section 1 states that federal judges hold life appointments "during good behavior," another term that has never been defined. But the impeachment trials of certain jurists have, in fact, hinged upon the jurists' bad behavior. Senility, incompetence, profanity, questionable business practices, and bringing the court system into disrepute have been influential factors in several trials. Such a distortion of constitutional prescriptions for impeachable conduct reveals a serious confusion: a de facto equating of bad behavior with high crimes and misdemeanors. The "good behavior" clause assumes adherence to principles stated in the *Code of Judicial Conduct*, such as dignified and conscientious performance of duty and the mental, physical, and ethical competence to perform that duty.[5] Twisting such defects as alcoholism or senility into high crimes and misdemeanors in order to remove an unfit judge exposes the need to describe good behavior and provide a method for employing the clause against a malperforming federal judge.[6]

Although unable to settle on a definition of good behavior and establish violation of it as a cause for removal, Congress did, in 1980, take a step toward correcting the problem of dealing with defective judges by passing the Judicial Councils Reform and Judicial Conduct and Disability Act.[7] The act provides increased accountability of federal judges by creating a complaint and disciplinary procedure. The judicial councils within each circuit are empowered to receive accusations from any person alleging that a judge has acted in a manner prejudicial to effective administration of the courts or has become unable to carry out duties because of mental or physical disability. If, after investigation, the complaint is found justified, the judge may be corrected informally, censured, issued a certificate of disability, asked to resign, or prohibited from hearing cases for a fixed period.

Although the act does not authorize removal of federal jurists, it creates a system similar to the judicial discipline commissions that have existed for several years at the state level. Failure by Congress to provide for removal of judges under authority of the act is attributable to arguments presented during various hearings that impeachment is the exclusive method for depriving a federal judge of his post, and Congress may not divest itself of its sole power to remove a judge by assigning the task to another body.

When the arduous impeachment route is followed, either for a jurist or for an officer of the executive branch, the procedure by which it is initiated and conducted begins, as noted, with a complaint directed to the House of Representatives; that body then undertakes an investigation of the official complained of. Investigations of the first three impeached officers were made by select committees. All investigations have been referred to the House Judiciary Committee since it was created in 1813.[8]

The suspect official has been allowed to appear before the investigating committee, to have counsel with him, to present witnesses, and to examine the witnesses against him. The committee reports its findings to the House of Representatives. If the House votes to impeach, it elects or appoints managers to conduct the prosecution. The largest group of managers, eleven, served in the first two impeachment trials, those of William Blount and John Pickering; the smallest group, three, prosecuted Judge Halsted L. Ritter in 1936.

Articles of impeachment specifying the charges against the accused, the *respondent*, are drafted, usually by the Judiciary Committee; sometimes the articles have been prepared before impeachment has been voted, sometimes after. The number of articles drawn against impeached officers ranges from one in the case of James H. Peck to thirteen in the case of Robert W. Archbald. In the majority of instances the House of Representatives has, to the detriment of its argument, used a scattergun technique in drafting the articles. Not content with focusing on major defects, the House has touched upon every conceivable misstep of the officer concerned and thus has diluted the crucial charges. This unfortunate habit has, in some impeachment trials, most notably those of Samuel Chase and Andrew Johnson, caused the serious allegations to drown in a sea of minor claims.

Another aspect of House construction of articles is displayed in the impeachment of Halsted L. Ritter. The managers failed to achieve a two-thirds guilty vote on any one of the specific charges against the judge but contrived to produce a vote of guilty on a potpourri article encompassing all the accusations of which the Senate had just found Judge Ritter innocent.[9] Thus, use of a cumulative article to secure a guilty verdict entered the annals of impeachment, an outcome damaging to the process and unfair to the respondent.

The House of Representatives notifies the Senate when it has brought an impeachment, and from that point on the Senate is in control. Its rules govern the proceedings. It judges the validity of the charges; it decides not only the guilt or innocence of the accused but also whether, if guilty, the officer should be disqualified from holding any further position of honor, trust, or profit in the national government. Courts of law will not overturn or even examine a Senate verdict of guilty; the Senate has the final word in an impeachment.[10]

The House of Representatives has considered dozens of cases that did not result in impeachment. In many such instances the suspect officer has resigned under fire and thereby evaded full and orderly appraisal of his behavior in office because the House dropped its investigation. Congressional appetite for impeachments and trials is meager; both houses have shown their desire to avoid further action when an official resigns. The only exception to congressional abortion of a resigned officer's impeachment occurred in the case of William W. Belknap, whose trial was continued after he had withdrawn from President Ulysses S. Grant's cabinet.[11] Other inquiries directed at alleged official misconduct were discontinued by the House of Representatives because it did not find sufficient grounds to warrant impeachment.

In addition to resignations and failure to find adequate cause to impeach, one other fact contributes to the scarcity of impeachments and trials: the unwieldiness of the procedure. Investigating, prosecuting, and sitting in judgment take a heavy toll in money and in legislative time. Senators are not always informed about the details of the charges levied against the impeached official; fail to, or cannot, give the time to become informed; and frequently do not even regularly attend the trial, although at the trial's conclusion they must make a decision affecting an officer's life and reputation. Legislative business comes nearly to a halt. The burden imposed by employing the lengthy and costly impeachment procedure, particularly when directed against a lower-court jurist, is severe. For this reason, the Judicial Conduct and Disability Act holds some promise of lessening the problem of the inadequately performing judge whose misconduct appears insufficiently horrendous to justify impeachment.

Despite its cumbersome nature and sometimes imperfect employment, the impeachment process has proved to be an essential element of government. Many resignations of erring officials have been brought about because impeachment existed as a real threat to their continued tenure. Without it, such flawed officers as Richard M. Nixon and Harry E. Claiborne would have retained their positions. Furthermore, the fact that they could be impeached may have kept some potentially defective officers within the bounds of acceptable public service. The impeachment mechanism has served its purpose as a protector of the general welfare.

William Blount. *The Tennessee State Library and Archives.*

2

William Blount

Fit for treasons, stratagems, and spoils. . . .
—*The Merchant of Venice,* Act 5, scene 1

The meaning and reach of the impeachment clauses of the Constitution and the potential weight of English, colonial, and state precedents in developing impeachment machinery at the national level did not undergo testing during George Washington's presidency (1789–97). His administration, which established enduring precedents in several categories, did not provide examples of either the theory or the practice of federal impeachment procedures.

Rifts of the kind resulting in the impeachment and trial of Senator William Blount (1797–99), of Judge John Pickering (1803–4), and of Justice Samuel Chase (1805) began to appear during Washington's second administration and lurked not far from the surface during his first. But calmness generally characterized his tenure, especially when compared with the turbulence and harsh political warfare of John Adams's administration (1797–1801).

President Washington disliked politics and wished to be viewed as being above partisanship; still, he did not entirely submerge his political instincts. He appointed only Federalists to the bench, thus establishing the judicial branch as a Federalist instrumentality and a political institution from its beginnings. His successor, John Adams, maintained the Federalists' dominion over the judicial branch. Presidents Washington and Adams thereby created the conditions that brought forth two of the first three impeachments: those of Pickering and Chase. When Thomas Jefferson became president in 1801, both he and the newly elected Congress faced an antagonistic and politically active judiciary. By the impeachment route the Jeffersonians tried to gain a foothold in the judicial branch, no other device for replacing a federal judge being available.

The first three impeachments and trials took place within a six-year period, with some participants being involved in all three proceedings and many in two of them. These early impeachments reflected the division between Federalist and Democratic-Republican (hereafter, Republican)[1] positions on the nature and purpose of government. The Federalists' implacable enforcement of the Sedition Act, a repression of speech or writing deemed to defame government officials, and their disposition to interpret political opposition as treason—particularly with respect to the schism between their support of Great Britain and the Republicans' support of France—all had a direct impact upon the course of impeachment history.

The nation's first impeachment, unrelated to the problems of a one-party judiciary but displaying some aspects of partisan hostility sketched above, was initiated by John Adams in 1797, just four months after his inauguration. Its subject was William Blount, a United States senator from Tennessee, a former Federalist, now a Republican. His case not only illustrated party division but also reflected the regional antagonisms that existed in the formative period of the republic. The outcome of his trial showed that senators from the West generally supported Blount, those from the East opposed him. Another aspect of the Blount affair concerned betrayals of the public trust extending over many years. Persistent misconduct, not just one mistake, forms a basis for impeachment, and such a pattern of habitual malperformance typified all the subsequent impeachments except one, that of James H. Peck in 1831. William Blount exemplified the persistent wrongdoer, although exposure of his disloyalties became lost in a thicket of legal technicalities when the Senate heard his case.

Senator Blount's impeachment and trial took place in the years 1797 to 1799, a time when the attachment of the Western territories to the newly created United States seemed uncertain; when England, France, and Spain were enmeshed in various plots to reverse the Revolution and seize control of parts of the weak and fledgling country; and when huge fortunes were being made and lost by speculation in Western lands.

A leader in the movement to separate the West from the United States, William Blount sought to create a new country beyond the Alleghenies. In pursuit of this scheme and of his own enrichment, he interfered with and tried to subvert arrangements made between the United States and the Indians. He trafficked clandestinely with England in an effort to secure and enlarge his land holdings, and he was a reckless and persistent plunger in the land speculation boom. These activities brought about his downfall as a national figure but in no way impaired his standing in the West, where John Adams and Federalist practices grew increasingly unpopular and where Blount's freebooting behavior did not offend the Western spirit.

Blount had an extensive career. He served in the Revolutionary War; participated with his family in speculating in commodities, debts, land, and money issues; and won election at the age of thirty-one to the North Carolina Assembly. Blount made unabashed use of his position as an assemblyman and later as a state senator to advance special legislation that furthered his family interests and income.[2] Blount's political career at the national level included service in the Continental Congress and participation as a delegate from North Carolina in the Constitutional Convention. President Washington appointed him governor of the Southwest Territory in 1790; he also acted as superintendent of Indian affairs for the territory. When Congress created the new state of Tennessee in 1796, the state legislature selected Blount to serve in the United States Senate.

Francis Wharton described Blount as having "attractive manners, and remarkable business tact . . . his religious and moral principles were of equal looseness with his political." Quoting William Cobbett "of the ultra-federal school," Wharton records that Blount had "acquired great weight, not only amongst the people of Tennessee, but amongst the Indians in the neighborhood of the State. This circumstance rendered him a dangerous man if in any case he should become disaffected to the United States."[3]

The capstone of Blount's career as an intriguer concerned his effort, while a United States senator, to promote a military expedition for the purpose of wresting control of the Floridas and Louisiana from Spain. At that time England and Spain were at war, and Blount plotted with the British, whose aid he expected but did not get, to secure these areas for England and so improve his own financial position. A letter he wrote to James Carey, an agent and interpreter for the United States to the Creek and Cherokee nations, indicated Senator Blount's complicity in this farfetched scheme.

The letter and certain other documents came to the attention of John Adams, who sent them, on July 3, 1797, to the Senate and to the House of Representatives. The House, composed of fifty-eight Federalists and forty-eight Republicans, a majority of 55 percent for the Federalists, wasted no time in acting on the material President Adams had supplied. On July 6, 1797 it debated impeaching Senator Blount.

Congressman Samuel Sitgreaves (Federalist, Pennsylvania) reported securing an opinion from two eminent Pennsylvania attorneys, William Rawle and William Lewis, who informed him that Blount's letter to the Indian agent constituted a crime and that a senator could be impeached.[4] Obviously anticipating that a senator's liability to impeachment could become a major point of contention should William Blount be impeached and tried, Sitgreaves stated that in his view legislators were among those subject to impeachment under the Constitution. A corrupt legislator, he argued, could be impeached because the process had been "calculated to reach State offenders, not otherwise amenable to punishment. [When a senator] shall endeavor to lead a foreign nation to commit hostilities on his country, it was certainly such a violation of his duty as would warrant an impeachment."[5]

Samuel Dana (Federalist, Connecticut) supported Sitgreaves's position and added to it his opinion that an officeholder could properly be impeached for conduct not directly connected with his office. He noted that should a judge be "guilty of treason . . . though this would be no breach of official duty, he might certainly be impeached for the offence [sic]."[6] Thus, in the nation's first impeachment experience, an assertion was made that the accused, to be found guilty, need not have committed the offense while performing official duties. This position has been supported and contested in several subsequent trials.

The following day, July 7, 1797, the House of Representatives, without debate or division on the vote, impeached Blount; no congressman spoke in explanation of, or support of, Blount's conduct. The House briefly considered whether Blount could be tried by the Senate if he failed to appear when summoned to do so but reached no conclusion on this matter. The Senate displayed a similar uneasiness concerning Blount's possible disappearance and required him to post bond to insure that he would be present for his trial.[7] Fears that Senator Blount would run away were fully justified; he decamped from the capital and did not attend his trial.

At the same time that the House began its consideration of Blount's conduct, the Senate also interested itself in his affairs. It assigned a committee to look into the matter of the letter to James Carey and the accompanying documents submitted by John Adams. The committee made brief preliminary reports on July 5 and 6, 1797. Blount, having asked to have counsel, informed the Senate on July 7 that Jared Ingersoll and Alexander J. Dallas would represent him.[8] He refused to tell the Senate whether he had written the letter to Carey. A motion was made in the Senate to postpone consideration of Blount's situation until the next session of Congress; it lost by a vote of nineteen opposed, seven in favor.[9] No Federalists and no senators from the northeastern part of the country favored postponement. Thus, the vote revealed a strong Federalist and a strong regional preference for proceeding to deal with Senator Blount.

The investigating committee, having been authorized to make its report, presented to the Senate the incriminating letter to Carey and produced evidence that the letter was in William Blount's handwriting. The committee stated that when it looked at Blount's

> attempts to seduce Carey from his duty . . . and to employ him as an engine to alienate the affections and confidence of the Indians, from the public officers of the United States . . . his insidious advice tending to the advancement of his own popularity and consequence, at the expense and hazard of . . . the treaties subsisting between us and them, your committee have no doubt that Mr. Blount's conduct has been inconsistent with his public duty, renders him unworthy of a further continuance of his present public trust in this body, and amounts to a high misdemeanor.[10]

The Senate, displaying outrage at Blount's perfidy, expelled him by a vote of twenty-five to one for "having been guilty of a high misdemeanor entirely inconsistent with his public trust and duty as a Senator."[11] The Senate responsible for the dismissal of Blount consisted of twenty Federalists and twelve Republicans, giving the Federalists a 62 percent majority. But the vote to expel revealed no determination by the Federalists to banish a political opponent nor by the Republicans to support one of their own. Henry Tazewell (Republican, Virginia) cast the lone dissenting vote; all the other Republicans showed their contempt for Senator Blount's conduct by voting for his expulsion.

His swift dismissal from the Senate caused Blount's place in history to change dramatically. In a matter of two days he had achieved two historic firsts: he became the first national officer to be impeached and the first United States senator to be expelled. Following his unseating Blount fled the capital. The nation's initial exposure to the impeachment process, therefore, concerned a person who did not appear in his own behalf at the trial in the Senate and who no longer held national office.

Even though Blount had run away and was no longer in office, the House of Representatives proceeded to construct a case against him; because removal from office was no longer an issue, the only reason to continue impeachment proceedings would be to activate the second aspect of the mechanism: disqualification from again holding a post in the national government.

On January 29, 1798, the House of Representatives, without recording the vote, adopted five articles of impeachment. The first charged the former senator with conspiring against Spain "contrary to the duty of his trust and station as a Senator of the United States, in violation of the obligations of neutrality, and against the laws of the United States and the peace and interests thereof."[12]

The second article accused Blount first of directly contravening a treaty between the United States and Spain in which both signatories had agreed that neither would permit the Indians to act hostilely against the other, and, second, of exciting the Creek and Cherokee nations to attack Spanish subjects and possessions to bring them under the control of Great Britain.

Articles 3, 4, and 5 charged Blount with (1) alienating the confidence of the Indians in a presidentially appointed agent, (2) securing the services of an Indian agent of the United States government in furtherance of Blount's own criminal designs, and (3) stirring up the Cherokees to discontent over the boundary treaties with the United States, hence conspiring to "diminish and impair the confidence of the said Cherokee Nation in the Government of the United States."[13]

The House selected eleven managers to conduct the prosecution of William Blount, all of them Federalists. Thus, the partisan connotations that cling to impeachment history displayed themselves in the nation's first experience with the process.

In the period following its expulsion of Blount the Senate had concerned itself with matters clustering around the coming impeachment trial. Many Federalists wanted to give the broadest possible interpretation to impeachment, extending it to all malefactors, officeholder or not. Vice-President Thomas Jefferson commented on his appraisal of the Federalist majority's goal, saying that he expected the Senate

> to declare a Senator unimpeachable, absolutely; and yesterday an opinion was declared, that not only officers of the State governments, but every private citizen of the United States are impeachable. Whether they will think this the time to make the declaration, I know not; but if they bring it on, I think there will be not more that two votes north of the Potomac against the universality of the impeaching power.[14]

The Jeffersonians, on the other hand, preferred strict construction of the impeachment clauses, a suitable position for the party against whom the Federalists might have taken action under their broad

interpretation of the impeachment provisions. These party positions were subsequently displayed in the arguments presented
during the trial and in the Senate vote on Blount.

Although the articles of impeachment had been presented to it
on February 7, 1798, the Senate did not form itself into a High Court
of Impeachments until December 17 of that year, with Jefferson
presiding. A year and a half had gone by since William Blount had
been both impeached by the House of Representatives and cast out
by the Senate.

None of the principals—the House managers, Blount's attorneys,
nor the senators sitting as judges—had had any previous experience
in federal impeachment procedures. And they faced an immediate
snag: the central figure of the impeachment did not come forward
when the sergeant at arms called his name. The managers showed
particular distress at Blount's failure to appear; their knowledge of
legal procedure caused them to believe that they should not go
ahead with the trial in the absence of the respondent.

When the managers brought their predicament to the attention of
the House of Representatives, several members said that in their
opinion the Senate, not the House, had the responsibility of untan-
gling the snag. Some House members pointed out that the Senate
formulated the rules under which the trial of an impeached official
would be conducted; therefore, that body should decided whether
the accused could be tried in absentia.

Congressman Samuel Sewall (Federalist, Massachusetts) thought
that a bad precedent might be established should Blount be tried in
his absence. Sewall feared that then an impeachment trial would
"become a mere farce or play to be acted before the public."[15] A
House resolution instructing the managers to continue with the
prosecution even if Blount did not attend failed of passage. The matter was left hanging in midair, and no more was heard about the
nonappearance of the central figure.

Meanwhile, the Senate granted permission to Jared Ingersoll and
Alexander J. Dallas to appear as Blount's attorneys. Both had acted
on his behalf when the House of Representatives considered the impeachment resolution. The first real beginning toward examining
the issues occurred December 24, 1798, when Ingersoll and Dallas
filed their response to the articles of impeachment and presented arguments in support of Blount's position.[16]

The attorneys argued that (1) because the Sixth Amendment required trial by jury, their client ought not to be compelled to reply to
impeachment charges before such a trial;[17] (2) impeachment lay

31

only against a president, vice president, or other civil officer; (3) Blount was not now and had not been a civil officer of the United States because senators could not properly be termed "civil officers"; (4) Blount had not been charged with any crime or misdemeanor in the execution of his office; and (5) the common-law courts in the states where the alleged crimes had been committed remained open and competent to hear the charges. And, the attorneys concluded, William Blount utterly denied all allegations and objected to answering the articles of impeachment.

On January 3, 1799 the House managers began the case that, although springing from Blount's misdeeds, proved to be a test of which officers the Constitution prescribed as subject to impeachment rather than a test of the respondent's guilt or innocence. The star performer of the nation's first impeachment was not the departed senator. Instead, attention focused on the contending attorneys as they conducted a technical duel over whether a senator could be classified as a "civil officer" and hence be subject to impeachment under the Constitution. If so, a second question arose, Could a *former* senator be impeached? The duel consumed three days.

James A. Bayard, chairman of the managers, gave the opening speech. He urged the Senate to accept jurisdiction and argued at great length that a senator must be regarded as civil officer. He analyzed the precedents from England supporting the contention that legislators had historically been subjected to impeachment. Futhermore, he said, the capacity of the Senate to disqualify a convicted official from ever again holding a national position made Blount's case deserving of a hearing. Forbidding Blount to hold future office in the federal government would be a substantial protection to the public against a repetition of the misdeeds that had brought him to trial. Manager Bayard asserted that impeachment extended to a one-time officeholder and to an offense not part of official duties.

Bayard observed that "impeachment is a proceeding purely of a political nature. It is not so much designed to punish an offender, as to secure the State. It touches neither his person nor his property, but simply divests him of his political capacity"[18] This comment merited careful scrutiny, far more than he gave to it. A discussion focused on impeachment as a political device created to protect the nation from a malperforming official could have had valuable consequences involving, as it would, men who had direct knowledge of the formation and purposes of the Constitution. The

Blount trial might, then, have produced an exchange of informed views on the scope of impeachment rather than produce the jurisdictional elaborations characterizing this first impeachment proceeding.

On the second day of the trial, Alexander J. Dallas replied on behalf of the respondent. He organized his reply around the three arguments that he and Ingersoll found compelling: (1) only civil officers could be impeached and then only for offenses committed in the execution of their public office; (2) a senator is not a civil officer; and (3) no crime or misdemeanor had been charged against Blount in connection with his senatorial duties.

In an effort to show that the Framers did not intend legislators to be included in the group termed "civil officers," Dallas analyzed various parts of the Constitution. He noted that congressmen had not been named in the Constitution among those liable to impeachment and reminded the Senate that the president, who is constitutionally empowered to appoint ambassadors, judges, and *all other officers* of the United States, obviously did not appoint senators and representatives. Finally, Dallas pointed out that the Constitution prohibited a person who held an office in the United States from being a member of either house, proof, he argued, that legislators were in a different category from civil officers. Toward the conclusion of his speech Dallas added that the general penal law "applying as much to Senators and Representatives, as to any other class of citizens, was competent to every purpose of punishment, as well as to warn the people against unworthy candidates for their favors."[19]

The third, and last, day of the trial, January 5, opened with a speech by Jared Ingersoll for the defense. He elaborated on the "what is a civil officer?" theme and argued that any alleged misconduct precipitating an impeachment must be a product of official activity.

Manager Robert Goodloe Harper, last speaker in the trial, followed Ingersoll and touched upon what would appear to be a central matter in Blount's case although it had scarcely been mentioned before. He observed that the respondent's attorneys had said it would be foolish to impeach, try, and convict a man who did not hold an office from which he could be removed. But Harper pointed out that, following the conviction of an impeached official, the Senate could disqualify him from holding any further national office: "a sentence of disqualification, pronounced by this honorable body, in the face of the whole American nation, and on a charge of high crimes and misdemeanors by the representatives of the American people, is a punishment; and as this punishment is applicable to persons who are not officers as well as to those who are, it follows that the power of impeachment, if its extent be measured by that of the power of punishment, is applicable to all persons whether officers or not."[20]

However, even if the managers had convinced the Senate of the impeachability of a former officer, their attempt to establish that impeachment extended to everyone, "persons who are not officers as well as to those who are," was not agreeable to many political figures, including some Federalists. The concept of universal susceptibility to impeachment, as it existed in English history, had not been welcomed in American experiences, colonial or state.[21]

Bayard had raised the issue of the application of impeachment to private citizens in his opening speech. Referring to the scope of impeachment as derived from the British experience, he observed that "all the King's subjects are liable to be impeached by the Commons and tried by the Lords, upon charges of high crimes and misdemeanors. . . . I do not conceive it would have been sound policy to have laid any restriction as to persons upon the power of impeaching."[22] Manager Bayard had also supposed a situation in which a citizen of great influence who aspired to become president joined with disaffected citizens or foreign intriguers in an effort to secure the presidency. "What punishment would be more likely to quell a spirit of that description, than absolute and perpetual disqualification for any office of trust, honor, or profit, under the Government; and what punishment could be better calculated to secure the peace and safety of the State from the repetition of the same offense?"[23]

Robert Goodloe Harper, in summarizing the managers' case, reverted to Bayard's opening day contention by repeating the point that impeachment might be an important mechanism to prevent dangerous people from obtaining office. The sweeping Bayard-Harper argument favoring preventive impeachment capable of being invoked against persons who did not hold office created a confusion that obscured the relevance of trying Blount as a former officeholder and disqualifying him from any further national post.

Dallas and Ingersoll consistently disputed the claim of universal impeachability. Dallas said that an effort to stretch the impeachment provisions to "include a jurisdiction over all persons, for all offences [sic] is . . . to overthrow all the barriers of criminal jurisprudence; for every petty rogue may be tried by impeachment before this High Court for every offense within the indefinite classification of a misdemeanor."[24] Ingersoll added that whereas the Constitution specifically made civil officers amenable to the impeachment clauses, it nowhere referred to impeaching anyone who did not hold an office. "The power of proceeding by impeachment under the Constitution, extends only to the civil officers of the United States," he observed.[25]

The position of Blount's attorneys was sounder than that of the managers. The notion of impeaching a disaffected or criminally inclined private citizen in order to stop him from seeking public office did not fit the American experience. James Madison, criticizing the claim raised in Blount's trial, found it "the most extravagant novelty that has been broached."[26]

In his final presentation to the Senate, Harper sought to demolish defense contentions that impeachment applied only to criminal acts committed in discharge of official duties.

> Suppose a judge of the United States to commit theft or perjury; would the learned counsel say that he shall not be impeached for it? If so, he must remain in office with all his infamy; for there is no method of removing a judge but by impeachment. . . . It seems to me, on the contrary, that the power of impeachment has two objects: first, to remove persons whose misconduct may have rendered them unworthy of retaining their offices; and secondly, to punish those offenses of a mere political nature, which though not susceptible of that exact definition whereby they might be brought within the sphere of ordinary tribunals, are yet very dangerous to the public.[27]

The central issues stayed in the background in the Blount trial, however, as contending attorneys debated the meaning of "civil officer" and whether a senator belonged in that category.

Following manager Harper's address, the trial ended. On January 7, 1799 the Senate considered a resolution affirming that William Blount had been a civil officer liable to impeachment; therefore, his plea alleging lack of jurisdiction should be turned down. The resolution failed after three days of debate. "The court proceeded . . . on the motion made on the 7th instant, and which had been under consideration every day since; and, on the question to agree thereto, it was determined in the negative —yeas 11, nays 14."[28]

Next, the Senate voted on a motion to dismiss the impeachment on the ground that "the Court is of opinion, that the matter alleged in the plea of the defendant, is sufficient in law to show that this Court ought not to hold jurisdiction."[29] The Senate adopted this motion by a vote of fourteen to eleven, exactly the same senators voting no on the first motion and yes on the second. No one could have been surprised by the result; the first motion asserted Senate jurisdiction over William Blount; the second disclaimed jurisdiction.

Because the Senate consumed nearly four days in debating the question of jurisdiction and because Blount's attorneys prevailed by such a narrow margin, the issue must have been intensely argued. But information about the nature and scope of the Senate's four-day debate remains undisclosed; it took place behind closed doors, and the result of the two votes became the only information made public. Of the twenty-five senators who voted, nineteen were Federalists and six were Republicans. Party division on the vote shows that ten Federalists, all of them from the North, favored trying Blount, and one Republican voted with them, James Lloyd of Maryland. Not only the sole Republican voting to accept jurisdiction, Lloyd was also the only senator of either party representing a southern or western state who made up the eleven-member minority holding that Blount had held a civil office and was, thereby, liable to impeachment.

Nine Federalists and five Republicans constituted the fourteen-member majority rejecting jurisdiction. Of the fourteen, nine were from the South or West, and five from the North; every senator from the West voted against accepting jurisdiction. Regional forces proved to be decisive in the voting. A composite portrait of the senator who wanted to assert Senate jurisdiction over Blount shows him to be a Federalist from the Northeast.

On January 14, 1799 Vice-President Thomas Jefferson announced that "The Court, after having given the most mature and serious consideration to the question, and to the full and able arguments urged on both sides, has come to the decision . . . that the matter alleged in the plea of the defendant is sufficient in law to show that this Court ought not to hold jurisdiction of the said impeachment, and that the said impeachment is dismissed."[30]

The arguments of William Blount's counsel won the day. Substantive matters concerning his conduct remained outside the trial, neither considered nor even introduced. Senate refusal to hold their erstwhile colleague answerable to impeachment makes it apparent that zeal to be rid of him as a senator did not include a desire to expose his misdeeds in a trial, to forbid his ever again holding national office, or, least of all, to establish a precedent that members of Congress could be impeached.

In addition, some Federalists' goal of dislodging Republicans in Congress via the impeachment route collapsed because of the

Blount finding. "Their efforts failed," according to Peter Charles Hoffer and N. E. H. Hull, "because the bulk of American impeachment precedent prevented them from using impeachment to censure and remove politically malodorous officials. It remained limited to provable offenses against incumbents." Because the Federalists controlled the national government, they had slight reason to pursue their Republican adversaries by using the impeachment device. "Instead of legislative removal, they curbed their opponents with judicial tools,"[31] a fact that created the Jeffersonians' antipathy for the judiciary.

William Blount's expulsion from the Senate, his impeachment, and his refusal to return for trial did not mar his local reputation; he returned to a hero's welcome in Tennessee after he had been thrown out of the Senate and won election to the Tennessee senate in 1798, less than a year after the United States Senate had ejected him.[32] As Wharton observed; "On his return to Tennessee, so far from being shunned as a disgraced man, he was received in triumph . . . and was only prevented by his sudden death [in 1800] from mounting, as if in defiance of the Federal Government, the gubernatorial chair."[33]

By declining jurisdiction, the Senate, obviously, did not determine William Blount's guilt or innocence. It also failed to determine three other issues, ones actually brought forward in the trial. The first concerned whether the requirement in the Sixth Amendment for trial by jury in all criminal prosecutions must apply to an impeachment in which the articles allege criminal conduct. Blount's lawyers raised this question, but argument on it proved inconclusive and desultory. Manager Bayard had the best of such argument as occurred; he pointed out that impeachment is a political action, not a criminal proceeding. Also the Constitution (Article III, section 2) states that "The trial of all Crimes, except in cases of Impeachment, shall be by Jury."

The matter arose in reverse form when Vice-President Spiro T. Agnew (1973) and Judge Harry E. Claiborne (1986) asserted, without success, that they were immune from court trial unless they were first impeached and tried. The Constitution does not state that impeachment must precede court trial of an official charged with a crime. Nor does the Constitution provide the contrary: that trial by jury must or may precede an impeachment based on a charge of criminal misconduct.

However, what is the consequence if a subsequently impeached life-tenured judge has been tried, convicted, and imprisoned prior to his impeachment? Has not his being in prison removed him from the bench by court action rather than by the legislative action prescribed by the Constitution? The problem did not arise in an impeachment proceeding until 1986, when Judge Claiborne, in prison for underpayment of income taxes, stood trial in the Senate (chapter 13).

William Blount's trial, then, produced an unanswered question but one to which the answer seems obvious: an impeached official need not be provided with a jury trial before being tried by the Senate.

The second unanswered question in the Blount trial received extensive attention but, again, failed to produce a reliable clue for future impeachments. It concerned whether the bad conduct alleged in the articles of impeachment had to be a product of the office, such as neglect of duty or bribery. The history of impeachment suggests that the Constitution encompasses more than misconduct in office as a basis for impeachment. As manager Robert Goodloe Harper pointed out, a judge who stole or who perjured himself might remain on the bench unless he could be impeached. Although exhaustively argued in the Blount trial and arising in trials to follow, especially those of Judge Charles Swayne (1905) and Claiborne, the issue of whether the deeds complained of must be committed during performance of official duties was not decided in Blount's proceedings and remains arguable to this day. However, it seems correct to view "high crimes and mismeanors" as designed to include the conduct of the officeholder in its entirety, not just while he transacts business as a public official.

William Blount's trial gives some help on the third of the unsettled issues mentioned: whether an impeached officeholder will be tried when he no longer retains his post. This issue was central in the trial of William W. Belknap, Ulysses S. Grant's secretary of war, whom the House of Representatives impeached in 1876 and whose trial was continued despite his resignation. The Senate found Belknap innocent, not because it believed the charges brought against him unproved but because it believed that it lacked jurisdiction over a person no longer holding office.

Impeachment proceedings against George W. English, a federal district judge in Illinois, were dropped in 1926 when he resigned from the bench after articles of impeachment had been filed against him and after a trial date had been set. The Senate's abandonment of Judge English's case and the House abandonment of Judge Mark W. Delahay's impeachment in 1873 upon his withdrawal from office indicate Congress's lack of interest in continuing proceedings after the allegedly corrupt official has left office. More than fifty federal judges have resigned while under investigation or after their impeachment had been recommended to the House of Representatives, and further action was not pursued against them.[34] In addition, Richard Nixon resigned when proceedings against him were moving toward certain impeachment, and all congressional activity ceased when he stepped out of office. Although the Blount trial, the Belknap trial, discontinuance of Judge English's trial, failure to complete proceedings against Delahay and other judges who resigned under fire, and cessation of activity directed toward Nixon's impeachment do not absoutely fix the argument that a resigned or expelled official will not be tried under the impeachment provisions, the origin and development of United States experience point in that direction.

Based on good sense and the results of impeachments that followed, three aspects of William Blount's experience can be considered as establishing enduring principles. The first concerns the no-longer-serious argument regarding impeachability of private citizens: they are not impeachable. The second settled principle came about because of Blount's failure to appear before the Senate; his case established that absence of the accused will not invalidate an impeachment trial. The third possible precedent, one disregarded only in the trial of James H. Peck, can be dimly discerned: only repeated malperformance by an official, not just one misstep, will bring him within the scope of the impeachment provisions.

Blount's trial exemplified what would become a preeminent characteristic of succeeding impeachments: partisanship. All the House managers were Federalists, and that party provided all but one of the Senate votes favoring accepting jurisdiction and trying Blount on the accusations brought against him.

The major aspect of Blount's experience is not included as a recurrent theme because the question of the susceptibility of national legislators to the impeachment process has never again arisen. Samuel Sitgreaves, and others who agreed with him before and during Blount's trial, did, however, advance the position that legislators should be subject to impeachment. The apparent exemption of members of Congress from the process is manifested by the refusal of the 1799 Senate to accept jurisdiction in Blount's case; but we do not know, because the Senate deliberated in private, whether it refused jurisdiction because it believed a senator could not be impeached or refused to try Blount because he no longer held his post as a senator.

Although the Blount trial provides only slight support for sustaining an argument that national legislators should be exempted from impeachment, political reality is likely to cause continuation of such exemption. Why would the House of Representatives choose to impeach rather than expel one of its own members who was misbehaving? How would senators, sitting as a court, treat House impeachment of a senator whom the Senate had not acted to expel? Would its failure to oust an allegedly erring brother presuppose a Senate verdict favorable to the accused?

The prickly sensitivities of each house in relation to the other make impeachment and trial of a member of Congress decidedly remote. However, those who believe that the threat of expulsion provides a sufficient safeguard against congressional misconduct must recognize that expulsion does not carry the additional possibility, as does impeachment, of barring the guilty official from ever again holding a national public office. Even so, Congress cannot, in truth, be expected to bring itself under the impeachment provisions.

Had the Senate acknowledged its authority to try William Blount, a peculiar difficulty would have presented itself. Could the former senator, in such circumstances, be considered to have been accorded a fair and impartial trial? Could the same body of men who had so recently expelled him by an overwhelming twenty-five-to-one vote now evaluate his conduct as if appraising it for the first time? If the Senate convicted Blount in such an impeachment trial, the verdict could scarcely be accepted as that of an impartial court. Contrarily, if it found him innocent, the verdict would invalidate the Senate's earlier expulsion of him; senators would be weighing the very same evidence that had caused them to find him unworthy of remaining in the Senate.

The question of whether the Senate must meet the same test of lack of bias as does a court became a significant aspect of Andrew Johnson's trial in 1868. Although not absolutely established in President Johnson's trial, the weight of the discussion tended toward recognition of the special role of the Senate in an impeachment trial, a role requiring it to perform its constitutional duty and sit in judgment despite the fact that many senators had expressed an opinion on the guilt of the accused. But even if this later revelation had been accepted in a possible trial of William Blount, his experience would have been unique in the annals of impeachment: being tried by the same people who had previously found him guilty and punished him for the very acts for which he now stood in judgment before them.

Another aspect of the Blount impeachment deserves passing mention: the time it consumed. Nearly one and one-half years elapsed between John Adams's referral of Blount's incriminating letter and the end of the trial; the trial itself covered twenty-five days. Thus, over a long period, William Blount's behavior occupied some part of House and Senate time.

The nation's first impeachment did not provide reliable and significant information on the nature of the impeachment mechanism although it has occasionally proved useful in some of the following trials as a source of quotable passages. As a stage-setter for the creation of a body of impeachment precedents it has only modest value except for its apparently having established that members of Congress are not subject to impeachment.

John Pickering, miniature portrait on ivory. *New Hampshire Historical Society.*

3

John Pickering

Whom the Gods would destroy they first make mad
—Henry Wadsworth Longfellow

Federal district judge John Pickering of New Hampshire became the second national officer to be subjected to the impeachment procedure, a process spanning thirteen months from 1803 to 1804. Like his impeached predecessor, Senator William Blount, Judge Pickering did not come forward in his own defense when the Senate sat as the High Court of Impeachments to determine whether his conduct justified removal from office. Indeed, he was too sick and confused to have helped his cause, except for the sympathy that his condition might have aroused among the senators had he appeared in person. Pickering had become senile and an alcoholic by the time of his trial, a pathetic relic of a once-honored and effective statesman.

John Pickering, born in New Hampshire, probably in 1738, was graduated from Harvard in 1761. He had a long and notable record of public service, distinguishing himself as a patriot of the Revolution, a representative in the New Hampshire legislature, a drafter of the New Hampshire constitution, a member of his state's ratifying convention for the national Constitution, chief justice of the New Hampshire supreme court, and, finally, a federal district judge, appointed to that post by George Washington in 1795.[1] By the time of his impeachment and trial, however, recognition of his impressive accomplishments had been dimmed by his abnormal behavior, brought on by senility and alcoholism. It was not just Pickering's political or personal opponents who accused him of having these defects; his family and friends also recognized and acknowledged his incapacity. Because of his afflictions he conducted himself on the bench in an immoderate and erratic manner and had clearly become unqualified to sit as a judge.

In addition to the physical and mental disorders besetting him and destroying his fitness for public office, John Pickering had yet another vulnerability: he belonged to the Federalist party. The Federalists had been turned out of the executive and legislative

43

branches by Thomas Jefferson's victory in the election of 1800. For the first time a Republican occupied the White House, and also for the first time Republicans controlled both houses of Congress. Brought into office in the 1800 election were five more Republican senators than had served in President John Adams's last Congress and twenty-seven more Republican House members. By the time of John Pickering's trial the Senate contained twenty-five Republicans and nine Federalists, compared with twelve Republicans and twenty Federalists when William Blount was tried five years before.[2] Only four senators sat in both the Blount and the Pickering trials— another clue to the great changes attending the Republican triumphs of 1800 and 1802.

But the electoral successes of the Republicans were menaced by Federalist control of the judiciary, a control threatening to deny the Jeffersonians the command of government policies that their success at the polls seemed to assure. Having inherited from Presidents Washington and Adams a totally Federalist bench, the Republicans smarted under the sometimes partisan actions of the entrenched judicial branch. Dumas Malone observed that "the national judiciary, one hundred per cent Federalist, amounted to an arm of that party." Jefferson commented that his foes "have retreated into the judiciary as a stronghold, the tenure of which makes it difficult to dislodge them."[3]

In addition to confronting a totally Federalist judiciary, the Republicans had endured the further goad of a last-minute enactment of the lame-duck Federalist Congress: the Judiciary Act of 1801. That act, passed in the waning days of President Adams's administration, created many new judgeships that the president speedily filled with Federalists. Enlargement of their opponents' grip on the judiciary after they had lost control of the executive and legislative branches infuriated the Republicans. The new Jeffersonian Congress repealed the act in 1802.

Then Republicans began searching for ways to get members of their own party into judicial office. Senator William Plumer (Federalist, New Hampshire) commented, "The removal of the Judges, and the destruction of the independence of the judicial department, has been an object on which Mr. Jefferson has long been resolved, at least ever since he has been in office."[4] John Pickering offered a convenient opportunity for forcing room for a Republican in the judicial branch. What better route for beginning a reduction in the number of Federalist judges than the removal, under dignified constitutional process, of a grossly defective jurist for whom no one would make a plea of competence, who was no longer qualified to be on the bench whether he belonged to the Federalist or to the Republican party? Hints that Judge Pickering should resign had not been heeded, in part because he lacked the soundness of mind to reach such a decision, in part because his resignation would have been politically unacceptable to the Federalists, who did not want to see him, or any Federalist judge, replaced with a Republican.

Pickering's handling of a case involving the ship *Eliza* triggered his impeachment. His misconduct in that trial formed the main complaint against him and was alleged to be typical of his behavior. A customs official at Portsmouth, a Republican, had seized the ship and its cargo for a legal violation. The *Eliza*'s owner, a Federalist, appealed to fellow-Federalist Pickering, who ordered the vessel released. At the subsequent trial to determine the rights respecting seizure of the vessel, Judge Pickering, "in a state of distressing intoxication,"[5] ruled for the owner and in denying an appeal from this decision used offensive language. Lynn W. Turner described the atmosphere of the *Eliza* hearing as attracting "a mob of sensation-seekers, and the courtroom had been a bedlam of confusion and laughter at the judge's maudlin behavior."[6] President Jefferson, in February 1803, sent to the House of Representatives criticisms of Pickering's conduct that had been collected by Secretary of the Treasury Albert Gallatin.[7] The main complaint concerned the judge's handling of the *Eliza* case.

The House of Representatives impeached Pickering the following month. Sixty-nine Republicans and thirty-six Federalists comprised the House in the 7th Congress, a majority of 65 percent for the dominant party. The vote to impeach carried forty-five to eight; all eight no votes were cast by Federalists,[8] meager support even among congressmen of Pickering's own party. The House chose a committee to inquire into the criticisms lodged against the judge and to prepare articles of impeachment.

On January 2, 1804, nearly a year after President Jefferson's complaints had been received, the committee brought in four articles of impeachment. The House of Representatives then elected eleven managers, all Republicans, to conduct the prosecution; Joseph H. Nicholson of Maryland served as chairman.[9] As in William Blount's trial, the prosecution reflected a totally one-party complexion.

The managers presented the articles of impeachment to the Senate on January 4, 1804. The first three articles dealt directly with the *Eliza* case, the fourth with intoxication. Article 1 described the allegedly improper return of ship and cargo to its owner; Article 2 claimed Judge Pickering's return of the ship to have been contrary to the law and a deprivation of revenue to the United States; Article 3 stated that his refusal to allow an appeal derived from his "wickedly meaning and intending to injure the revenues of the United States"; and the fourth article referred to Pickering's appearing in a "state of total intoxication, produced by the free and intemperate use of inebriating liquors, and [he] did then and there frequently, in a most prophane [sic] and indecent manner, invoke the name of the Supreme Being, to the evil example of all the good citizens of the United States."[10]

Between the filing of impeachment charges and the convening of the Senate as the High Court of Impeachments three months later in March, many discussions took place among the senators who had misgivings about the difficulties that faced them in the impending trial. The judge's manifest unsuitability for office could not be disputed. The problem, then, did not arise from any uncertainty about John Pickering's fitness to continue on the bench; the problem arose from doubts that his conduct justified action against him under the constitutional description of impeachable offenses. Could bizarre behavior, chronic alcoholism, senility, or evidence of mental illness be classified as treason, bribery, or other high crimes and misdemeanors?

The Senate could not in good conscience answer yes to this question. Its uncomfortable dilemma concerned the obligation to follow the Constitution and the need to displace an official no longer qualified for his post. After some parliamentary maneuvering, a majority of senators somehow managed to pull Pickering within the compass of the constitutional description of impeachment and convince themselves that they should hear the case. Several, however, were troubled by the decision. Senator William Cocke (Republican, Tennessee) for example, moved to delete the words "according to law" from the special impeachment oath that the Senate would take; he reported feeling uneasy about the capacity of the House managers to prove that Pickering had broken the law "for I understand the Judge is deranged—and *I know of no law that makes derangement criminal.*"[11] The motion lost, with only Cocke voting for it.

Senator John Quincy Adams (Federalist, Massachusetts) brought up another problem: three Republican senators had formerly been members of the House of Representatives and had voted in that body for John Pickering's impeachment. He offered a resolution to disqualify them from sitting as judges now that they were members of the Senate. "Accuser and judge are not, in my opinion, compatible characters," he observed.[12] The Senate took up Adams's resolution on March 2, the day the trial opened, and defeated it twenty to eight.

Senator Plumer, dining with President Jefferson several weeks before the trial, had obseerved that Judge Pickering was unquestionably insane and asked whether Jefferson considered this a ground for impeachment. Jefferson replied that "if the facts of his denying an appeal [in the *Eliza* trial] and of his intoxication, as stated in the impeachment are proven, that will be sufficient cause of removal without further enquiry."[13] Although Jefferson's reference to Pickering's deportment as a "sufficient cause of removal" makes sense, it does not transform that deportment into constitutionally impeachable conduct. The "good behavior" clause of the Constitution has never been described in a law establishing its absence as impeachable and thus a cause for removal of judges who do not, or cannot, perform in accordance with it.

John Pickering's trial opened in the Senate on March 2, 1804. Vice-President Aaron Burr, presiding in the first of two impeachment trials in which he would serve as chairman, excused himself late in the trial in order to campaign for the governorship of New York. The Senate chose Jesse Franklin (Republican, North Carolina) to replace Burr; Franklin, subsequently elected president pro tem of the Senate, served as presiding officer for the decision-making portion of the trial.[14] The Senate sitting in judgment of John Pickering contained twenty-five Republicans and nine Federalists, a 73 percent Republican majority.

Robert Goodloe Harper, who had been a manager in William Blount's trial, presented a statement from Judge Pickering's son Jacob describing his father's insanity. The managers objected because Harper had specifically announced that he was not appearing before the Senate as counsel for Pickering. Caesar Augustus Rodney, for the managers, noted that Senate rules for the trial restricted testimony to the accused, his agent, or his counsel and pointed out that Harper did not meet any of these qualifications. In addition, it seems clear that the managers had a further reason for protesting introduction of Jacob Pickering's information about his father's condition: they did not want to deal with a defense contention depicting *inadvertent* malperformance caused by physical or mental incapacity. The managers wanted to exclude evidence of Pickering's insanity from being brought up at the trial because they believed that they would have to demonstrate knowing and willful misconduct by the judge in order to secure a conviction.

From March 2 to 6 the Senate debated in closed session the question of accepting testimony on Pickering's mental condition. John Quincy Adams recorded in his diary that Senator James Jackson (Republican, Georgia) expressed opposition to the admission of any evidence on insanity because such evidence might prevent getting rid of Judge Pickering, insanity not being a constitutionally established reason for inquiry into an official's conduct. In addition to that concern, Senator Jackson noted that "the House of Representatives were at this moment debating whether they would not impeach another Judge, and by-and-by we would have Judge [Samuel] Chase's friends come and pretend he was mad."[15] That the House of Representatives had already begun to work on the impeachment of Supreme Court Justice Samuel Chase before John Pickering's trial was even under way supports the fear some Federalists had of Republican plans for sweeping Federalist jurists off the bench.

Another Senate diarist, William Plumer, commented on the lengthy private Senate debates. He remarked that Judge Pickering's difficulties created "an embarrassing case for the Democrats [Republicans], but still I fear just principles will not restrain them from removing the accused from office."[16]

Senator George Logan (Republican, Pennsylvania) proposed to the Senate, still meeting behind closed doors, that an insane judge could not possibly be found capable of doing his job and should be removed on that ground; others agreed with this interpretation.[17] Had this argument been thoughtfully developed and had it been accepted, Congress might have passed a law defining "good behavior," a definition that would include involuntary violation of the oath of office.

Following its sequestered debate, the Senate voted eighteen to twelve to accept evidence respecting Judge Pickering's insanity.[18] All Federalist senators who voted not guilty at the end of the trial voted in favor of accepting the testimony, as did eight Republicans, all of whom cast guilty votes at the conclusion of the trial.

This vote reflects antithetical views on the probable consequences of admitting testimony designed to reveal that the judge was insane. The two opposing groups who voted for accepting descriptions of Pickering's eccentric conduct voted as they did for entirely different reasons. To the Federalist senators, introduction of evidence documenting the judge's mental condition should result in a Senate verdict of innocent because insanity did not appear on the list of impeachable offenses and could not be classified as a high crime or misdemeanor. They believed that proof of Pickering's mental illness would save him from a guilty verdict. Conversely, to those Republican senators who favored admission of the testimony, evidence that Judge Pickering was insane should prove to the Senate that he must be convicted and removed from the bench before he could do further damage to the judicial system. Thus, several senators holding diametrically opposed attitudes on what the outcome of the trial ought to be voted together to admit testimony on John Pickering's mental condition: entirely different motives stimulated a bipartisan decision.

The day following the vote, March 6, 1804, the managers withdrew from the Senate chamber in order to get further instructions from the House of Representatives. Because their original assignment extended only to the articles as presented, not to arguments concerning insanity, the managers wished to confer with their colleagues concerning the proper response to the new element in the proceedings. They felt further displeased by what they viewed as another irregularity: the Senate's willingness to receive Jacob Pickering's statement describing his father's mental condition before the managers had presented the articles of impeachment. Joseph H. Nicholson, speaking for the managers, said that they objected to Robert Goodloe Harper's intrusion into the trial proceedings and "did not consider themselves under any obligation to discuss a preliminary question raised by a third person, unauthorized by the person charged."[19]

The Senate proceeded, despite the absence of the managers, to hear evidence respecting John Pickering's condition. Robert Goodloe Harper read Jacob Pickering's statement to the Senate explaining his father's circumstances: "for more than two years before, and ever since [he] has been, and now is, insane, his mind wholly deranged, and altogether incapable of transacting any kind of business which requires the exercise of judgment, or the faculties of reason; and, therefore, that the said John Pickering is incapable of corruption of judgment."[20]

Jacob Pickering argued that his father's poor physical and mental health excused him from any taint of culpability, and he insisted that Judge Pickering was not answerable to impeachment charges or to any kind of tribunal for his actions. Jacob supported his father's rulings in the case of the ship *Eliza*, and so sought to refute the first three articles of impeachment. Of the fourth, the charge of intoxication, Jacob Pickering said that it set forth a true and deplorable fact now accurately describing the judge but entirely unlike the man his father had once been. He said that were his father able to attend the trial and the senators could see him, they would understand the hopelessness of his present situation.

Harper next introduced depositions from physicians and other observers describing John Pickering's dilapidated condition. All depicted him as deranged, incoherent, and too feeble to attend the trial; but they described him as having displayed exemplary character and deportment before his present "mental insanity," as Dr. Joshua Brackett put it.[21]

Meanwhile, the managers, having reported to the House of Representatives their dissatisfaction with the order of the proceedings and with the admissibility of evidence relating to the judge's sanity, awaited the decision of the House on the proper response to these improprieties. An inconclusive discussion produced no new instructions for them, and they returned to the Senate the following day, March 7, 1804, to present the case for John Pickering's conviction.[22]

Manager Peter Early presented witnesses who detailed Judge Pickering's conduct while trying the case of the ship *Eliza* and who also described his intoxication on various other occasions.[23] These witnesses did not add any substantial information to what the senators already knew about the judge's behavior. One witness, John Samuel Sherburne, had been the prosecutor in the *Eliza* case. Just a few days after Pickering's conviction, President Jefferson appointed Sherburne to the office of federal district judge to fill the vacancy created by John Pickering's removal. Senator Plumer commented, "Thus is the man who advised and promoted as far as he was able the impeachment of Judge Pickering rewarded by being appointed his successor."[24] Because Plumer himself served both as a witness affirming John Pickering's insanity and as a judge in the same case, lines of separation between an adverse witness and his own self-interest and between a witness and a judge became badly blurred.

On March 9 Joseph H. Nicholson said that the managers would not give a summary of their case against John Pickering because they "considered the testimony offered in support of the articles of impeachment so conclusive and pointed, as to render it impossible for them to elucidate [further]. . . . they submitted the articles on the evidence offered, entertaining no doubt of full justice being done by the decision of the Senate."[25]

The next day, having heard the reports on Pickering's mental state and the managers' substantiation of the articles, the Senate considered a motion stating that the High Court of Impeachments could not make a final decision relying only on the evidence so far presented to it. Proponents of the motion pointed out that neither Pickering nor counsel for him had appeared in his defense and that his son, two senators, and "the affidavits of sundry persons whose integrity and veracity is unimpeached" supported the fact that he was insane.[26] Therefore, the High Court of Impeachments should hear Pickering in order to be able to act with understanding. The motion lost nineteen to nine.[27] All nine votes supporting the motion were cast by Federalists, who may have been motivated by a desire to delay the trial by this maneuver or who may have believed that the judge's appearance would arouse such sympathy as to preclude his conviction.

Then the Senate voted on John Pickering's guilt. The question was put in the form of asking whether the judge stood guilty as charged, not whether the acts of which he had been accused constituted high crimes and misdemeanors. This stratagem offended several senators. One who spoke in opposition, Jonathan Dayton (Federalist, New Jersey), said the Senate was

> simply to be allowed to vote, whether Judge Pickering was guilty as charged—that is, guilty of the facts charged in each article—aye or no. If voted guilty of the facts, the sentence was to follow, without any previous question whether those facts amounted to a high crime and misdemeanor. . . . The Constitution gave no power to the Senate, as the High Court of Impeachments, to pass such a sentence of removal and disqualification, except upon charges and conviction of high crimes and misdemeanors.[28]

Senator Dayton had no doubt that Pickering had been proved guilty of most of the acts described in the articles, but he did doubt that any one of them was impeachable. Five senators—Federalists Dayton and Samuel White (Delaware) and Republicans John Armstrong (New York), Stephen R. Bradley (Vermont), and David Stone (North Carolina)—withdrew from the court when the Senate agreed to put the question in the form of "guilty as charged." The two Federalists objected to irregularities in the proceedings and declined to be recorded on a solemn vote framed so improperly and not directed to the essential question of whether the charges did in fact describe high crimes and misdemeanors.[29] John Quincy Adams wrote that the three Republicans who withdrew probably also objected to the irregularities and, in addition, did not want to separate from their party by voting against Judge Pickering's conviction, a separation their consciences would apparently have required had they been obliged to vote.[30]

That the Senate would find John Pickering guilty was inevitable given his incompetence and the political rancor of the time. Nineteen Republicans voted to convict on all four articles of impeachment, and seven Federalists voted to acquit.[31] The Senate approved the motion that Pickering should be removed from office by a vote of twenty to six, William H. Wells (Delaware) moving from the Federalist side to join the majority in what had already become a fait accompli.

Obviously, party proved to be the controlling force in the vote; regional factors are reflected but to a somewhat lesser degree. All seven of the Federalists voting represented states in the Northeast: two from Massachusetts, two from Connecticut, two from New Hampshire, and one from Delaware. Thus, the composite portrait of the senator who supported Judge Pickering proves easy to draw: he was a Federalist who lived in the Northeast. Conversely, the typical senator who voted in favor of Pickering's conviction shows him to be a Republican who represented the South or the West.

The evasive form in which the question of guilt was put is a flaw in the proceedings against John Pickering, a flaw suggesting the Senate's recognition that the charges did not meet constitutional requirements for impeachable conduct. Yet another weakness in procedure arose from the fact that three Republican senators had been members of the House of Representatives that had impeached Pickering and had voted in favor of his impeachment. All three, having subsequently been elected to the Senate, voted as senators to convict.[32] The outcome would not have been affected had they refrained from casting a vote on Pickering's guilt. However, their abstention would have removed one of the disturbing aspects of the trial: the mingling of roles of prosecutor and judge.

The House of Representatives, the Senate, or both bodies were involved with matters concerning John Pickering during the eleven months that elapsed between President Jefferson's notification to the House of Pickering's reported misbehavior and the bringing of charges against him, the two months between filing of the articles and trial, and the eight days of the trial. Thus, removal of a plainly ineffective judge consumed some part of legislative time for more than a year.

Judge John Pickering goes into the history books as the first United States official on whose conduct the Senate accepted jurisdiction, and the first to be convicted and removed from office under impeachment. His conviction does not provide any constitutional precedent as might have emerged if Congress had faced the question of Pickering's incapacity head-on and decided what could be done in future instances when a judge should not be permitted to stay on the bench and yet had committed no impeachable offense. It is obvious, however, that Pickering, or any officer in similar straits, should not be immured in office beyond the reach of any established process of removal.

Life tenure, obviously, puts the federal judicial branch in a category distinct from the president, vice president, or congressmen, who serve for specific terms and are subject to dismissal by the voters at regular intervals. Congressmen are, in addition to rejection at the polls, subject to discipline or expulsion by the chamber to which they belong. The cabinet and some other executive officers are not only susceptible to impeachment but also can be removed by the president if found wanting. But only impeachment can dislodge defective jurists. As Raoul Berger has observed, "not for a moment, of course, do I suggest that impeachment is the ideal way of ridding ourselves of demented or incapacitated judges, but only that if impeachment, contrary to my view, is the exclusive means of removal, it should be construed to comprehend removal both of insane and incapacitated judges."[33]

Such a construction could be achieved by congressional description of "good behavior," a description that could make such incapacitating infirmities as senility, alcoholism, mental illness, or nonperformance proper subjects for impeachment without trying to twist the infirmities into high crimes and misdemeanors.[34] By establishing "good behavior" as a distinct aspect of the impeachment process, Congress would provide a respectable method for removing judges who, like Pickering, are for whatever reason unable to meet their obligations but who have not indulged in treason, bribery, or other high crimes and misdemeanors.

But in the absence of a statutory description of good behavior, the Senate in 1804 had little choice. Judge Pickering conducted his business in so outrageous a fashion that no one made a case for his continuance on the bench. It was apparent that somehow or other he had to be ousted, and probably the senators who voted him "guilty as charged" expected that few people would cavil at constitutional restrictions if it meant retaining a flagrantly defective judge. But in the annals of impeachment the Pickering trial stands as a distortion of constitutional principles. Although the public trust is as effectively betrayed by a disabled officer as it is by a crooked one, the general welfare cannot be served by wrenching the Constitution out of shape in order to be rid of such a one.

In President Jefferson and Senator Plumer's conversation about the impending Pickering trial, Jefferson, in a much-quoted comment, referred to his dissatisfaction with impeachment as the method of purging the bench of unfit jurists. He believed that judges should be subject to removal by the president on address by Congress. "This business of removing Judges by impeachment," he said, "is a *bungling way*."[35]

Plumer referred to the outcome of the Pickering case as exemplifying "a mode of removal . . . [not] a charge and conviction of high crimes and misdemeanors."[36] Congress did not attend to Plumer's "mode of removal"; if it had, Pickering's trial could have supplied valuable aid toward establishing an honorable and straightforward method of ridding the bench of defective occupants.

John Pickering's trial and conviction received mention in subsequent trials, particularly those of Samuel Chase and Andrew Johnson. Robert Goodloe Harper, a House manager in the William Blount trial, spokesman for Judge Pickering's son in the second trial, and later an attorney for Justice Chase in the latter's impeachment trial in 1805, said of the Pickering case that the "Court, by finding the defendant guilty, gave their sanction to the charges that his insanity proceeded from habitual drunkenness. This case therefore proves nothing further, than that habitual drunkenness is an impeachable offense."[37]

William Evarts, counsel for Andrew Johnson, commented during the president's trial in 1868 that "the accusation against Judge Pickering partook of no qualities except of personal delinquency or misfortune, and whose results give us nothing to be proud of, and to Constitutional law gives no precedent except that an insane man may be convicted of crime by a party vote."[38] Evarts's observation underscores the damage done to the impeachment process by the Pickering case. It underscores, as well, the specter haunting impeachment trials in general: decision making rooted in partisan politics.

Only four senators acted in both the Blount and Pickering trials, reminders of the extensive changes in the national government wrought by the Republican victories of 1800 and 1802. Republican electoral triumphs left the Federalists in control only of the judiciary, in which branch President Jefferson claimed, "the remains of federalism are to be preserved and fed from the treasury, and from that battery all the works of republicanism are to be beaten down and erased."[39] This view explains the Republicans' enthusiasm for the impeachment process as displayed in the Pickering affair and in the trial of Chase that was to follow it so swiftly.[40]

The trial of John Pickering stands in history with only slight value as a guide to the impeachment process. It will be remembered for the introduction of "guilty as charged" as a substitute for "guilty of high crimes and misdemeanors," an evasive locution requiring the managers only to prove the facts set down in the articles, not prove that the facts constituted impeachable offenses. It will be remembered also because it was a trial without official representation of the accused. It will additionally be observed that the judge was convicted on a straight party vote, including votes by three senators who, as members of the House of Representatives, had supported his impeachment.

The Pickering case is short on guidelines for appraisal of fundamental aspects of impeachment procedures. However, it did have significant value to the antagonists in the warfare between the Republicans and the Federalists. Pickering's removal signaled the Republicans' first victory via the impeachment route. Although a singularly unattractive victory, it led to a historically far more important impeachment trial, that of Samuel Chase.

Samuel Chase, ca. 1773. Oil on canvas, Charles Willson Peale. *Maryland Historical Society.*

4

Samuel Chase

He trusted with general success to his fearlessness to extricate himself from the disorders which his imprudence fomented.

—Francis Wharton

The impeachment and trial of United States Supreme Court Justice Samuel Chase in 1805 revealed quite a different story from that of either William Blount or John Pickering. The first two impeachments did little to clarify the impeachment clauses of the Constitution. No great principle was at stake in either instance; an absconded senator and an insane judge did not produce significant examples by which fitness for office could be tested. Not so the case of Justice Chase. His experience measured the impeachment provisions of the Constitution, especially with respect to the appropriateness of construing them to cover high-handed, partisan, and irascible behavior—hallmarks of the justice's public career.

Unlike either Blount or Pickering, Chase appeared in his own defense; unlike Blount, the justice remained in office and intended to stay there, and unlike Pickering, he was neither demented nor otherwise incapable of performing official duties. The third impeachment, then, had all the ingredients needed for a real test of the process: an active, participating respondent who was holding office at the time of his trial and not manifestly unqualified for his job.

Like his two impeached predecessors, Chase had participated extensively in public affairs. Born in 1741, he studied law in Annapolis, Maryland, was elected to that state's assembly, signed the Declaration of Independence, was politically active during the Revolutionary War, and served as a member of the Continental Congress. After the war he held a judgeship in the Maryland court system for eight years. The capstone of his public life came when President George Washington appointed him an associate justice of the Supreme Court in 1796.[1] Chase's pugnacity and talent for controversy were not tempered by his elevation to the Supreme Court. The continuation of his established pattern of behavior finally brought him to the bar of the Senate in 1805, the only member of the United States Supreme Court ever to be impeached.

Samuel Chase had had an earlier experience with involuntary removal from office when, in 1791, the Maryland legislature sought unsuccessfully to have him ousted from his state judgeship.[2] The fact that he became the subject of efforts to expel him at both state and national levels suggests something of the irritating, if not illegal, aspects of Chase's performance as a public official.

Even Justice Chase's admirers did not call him judicious. An active, vehement Federalist, attached to John Adams's branch of the party, Justice Chase was known for his fervent support of the Sedition Act.[3] He did not shed his Federalist raimant when sitting on the bench nor hide his partisanship to insure the appearance of a fair trial for a defendant with a political outlook different from his. Chase's dedication to President John Adams even caused him to abandon any pretense of judicial independence or separateness from party politics; in August 1800 he deserted his duties as a Supreme Court justice in order to campaign for Adams in Maryland.[4]

Some of Chase's contemporaries, and certain historians, provide observations on his courtroom behavior. Francis Wharton said that Chase had "a singular instinct for tumult."[5] Yet Wharton recorded the justice as personally amiable, a good lawyer, and a man of robust intellect. Charles Warren referred to the hatred that Samuel Chase aroused because of "his unnecessarily strenuous support of the Sedition Law, his prejudicial and passionate conduct of the trials of the two Republicans [Thomas Cooper and James Callender]. . . his arbitrary and unusual rulings in the trial of John Fries."[6] Albert J. Beveridge called Chase "Marshall's irascible associate on the Supreme Bench."[7] Federal district judge Richard Peters, whose judicial behavior the House of Representatives was scrutinizing simultaneously with its inquiry into Justice Chase's official conduct, said, "I never sat with him without pain, as he was forever getting into some intemperate and unnecessary squabble."[8] Even Senator William Plumer (Federalist, New Hampshire), who did not believe that Chase should be impeached and voted him not guilty on every article of impeachment, observed that Justice Chase had "in a few instances, been guilty of intemperate feelings and language, and of imprudence not becoming the character of a judge."[9] That he was impetuous, arrogant, and overbearing is well documented; but whether he had misused his office and committed high crimes and misdemeanors remained to be proved.

Samuel Chase appeared to be a splendid subject for the Jeffersonians' second venture with impeachment. Should that immoderate Federalist be convicted, the path to the impeachment of Chief Justice John Marshall would lie open and inviting. The Federalists believed, without any credible supporting evidence, the chief justice to be the real target if preliminary Republican assaults on the bench proved successful. Albert J. Beveridge noted that "for a long time everybody had understood that the impeachment of Chase was only the first step in the execution of the Republican plan to replace with Republicans Marshall and the four Federalist Associate Justices."[10] Whatever their long-range goals may have been, the Jeffersonians had already achieved one win in the trial of Judge John Pickering and at once undertook to secure another.

Most vehement of the Republicans in pursuing ways to remove Federalists from office was Senator William B. Giles, "a pugnacious partisan," as Dumas Malone described him.[11] Giles wanted, according to Senator John Quincy Adams (Federalist, Massachusetts), all of the Supreme Court removed except Justice William Johnson, President Jefferson's only appointee then on the court. As Giles bluntly put it, "*We want your offices,* for the purpose of giving them to men who will fill them better."[12]

Although other Republicans spoke in less extreme language than Senator Giles, their expectations for further use of impeachment to cleanse the bench of Federalists had increased when their triumph in winning the presidency and both houses of congress in 1800 had been underscored in the election of 1802. Seven more Republicans had been added to the Senate in that year, with a loss of five seats by the Federalists; admission of Ohio in 1803 had raised the number of senators to thirty-four by the time of Chase's trial. In the House of Representatives the Republicans had gained thirty-three seats to the Federalists' three; thirty-six new seats had been added to the House since the 1800 election. The Chase impeachment, therefore, was framed by a House of Representatives in which Republicans outnumbered Federalists 102 to 39, a 72 percent majority for the Jeffersonians. The trial was held before a Senate equally one-sided—twenty-five Republicans and nine Federalists, a 73 percent Republican majority.

On January 5, 1804, eight years after Samuel Chase's appointment to the Supreme Court and one day after the articles of impeachment against Judge Pickering had been presented to the Senate, formal action against Justice Chase began. Republican John Randolph (Virginia) moved for appointment of a committee of the House of

Representatives to investigate Chase's official conduct. By a vote of eighty-one to forty the House passed the motion, amended to inquiring also into the conduct of Richard Peters, a federal district judge in Pennsylvania.[13]

The committee of inquiry included John Randolph, Joseph H. Nicholson (Maryland), and Peter Early (Georgia), who were on their way to becoming professional impeachers; they would serve as managers for the House in Judge Pickering's trial and would also be managers in Chase's trial. Two months later the committee recommended that Samuel Chase be impeached for high crimes and misdemeanors, a recommendation accepted by the House on March 12, 1804 by a vote of seventy-three to thirty-two.[14] Judge Peters, dropped from the affair at the recommendation of the committee, wrote of his being briefly associated with Chase in the latter's impeachment: "If I am to be immolated, let it be with some other victim or for my own sins. . . . I narrowly escaped sharing in the consequences of his hasty measures, which I highly and decidedly disapproved."[15]

Eight months after it had impeached Justice Chase, the House of Representatives adopted, on November 30, 1804, eight articles of impeachment. The following week it elected seven managers, including John Randolph as chairman. All seven managers were Republicans. Thus, the one-party aspect of the prosecution that had characterized the trials of William Blount and John Pickering reappeared in the trial of Samuel Chase.

The eight articles of impeachment set down the following charges: Article 1 asserted that as judge in the treason trial of John Fries, accused of resisting a federal law, Chase (1) behaved in an arbitrary, oppressive, and unjust way by announcing his interpretation of the law on treason before defense counsel had been heard; (2) restrained Fries's counsel from citing precedents favorable to their client; and (3) prohibited the defense from addressing the jury on the meaning of the law on treason. These acts, according to Article 1, caused Fries, to be deprived of his Sixth Amendment right to a fair trial[16] and to be "condemned to death without having been heard by counsel, in his defense, to the disgrace of the character of the American bench, in manifest violation of law and justice, and in open contempt of the rights of juries, on which, ultimately, rest the liberty and safety of the American people."[17]

The next five articles concerned Chase's conduct in the trial of James Callender, accused of libeling John Adams. Article 2 claimed that, moved by a "spirit of persecution and injustice . . . the said Samuel Chase, with intent to oppress, and procure the conviction of, the said Callender," refused to excuse from the jury John Basset, who was already convinced that a libel had been committed.[18] Article 3 alleged that Chase prohibited a witness for the defense, John Taylor, from testifying because he could provide evidence on part of only one of the charges. Article 4 concerned aspects of Justice Chase's behavior during the trial and claimed that he showed a desire for Callender's conviction. Articles 5 and 6 criticized Chase's lack of compliance with Virginia state laws because he had Callender jailed and because he disregarded the length of time that must elapse between a trial and the presentment of a grand jury.

The two remaining articles alleged misconduct by Justice Chase with respect to two grand juries. Article 7 accused him of refusing to dismiss a Delaware grand jury that had asked to be relieved of further duty; the article claimed that Chase referred to a seditious atmosphere existing in Delaware and demanded that the jury remain in session in order to investigate a certain printer.

Article 8 contained the most serious imputation of misconduct. It pertained to an "intemperate and inflammatory political harangue, with intent to excite the fears and resentment" of the Baltimore grand jury before whom Chase had delivered it in 1803. It accused him of voicing a recognizably Federalist position and attacking the governments of Maryland and of the United States, thus "tending to prostitute the high judicial character with which he was invested, to the low purpose of an electioneering partizan."[19]

The eighth article might well have been put at the head of the list. Had it been presented in first position, in keeping with the importance of the accusation made in it, it might then have received the most attention, and Justice Chase's trial would have centered on his major misconduct rather than on the tedious and endlessly repeated details of the justice's behavior in the Fries and Callender trials. Because, however, six of the eight articles concerned Fries and Callender, a summary of Chase's performance in these two trials must be recounted.

John Fries had originally been tried and convicted in Pennsylvania before Supreme Court Justice James Iredell and District Judge Richard Peters. (At that time Supreme Court justices rode on circuit and heard cases in company with a local federal district judge.) Fries had been found guilty of resisting a law of the United States that required windows in private residences to be measured, counted, and recorded as the basis for setting the tax rate for each house. John Fries and several other persons acted to prevent the assessors from measuring residents' windows. Fries reportedly threatened at one time to shoot an assessor in the legs if he attempted to do any measuring; at another time he said he would lock the assessor in a stable and feed him on rotten corn.

John Fries did not deny these actions, but said, in defense of his conduct, that he doubted the existence of the tax law and certainly had no traitorous intent in opposing it. The court found him guilty, but granted a new trial when a juror was discovered to have said before the trial that Fries should be convicted.

Chase, sitting with Peters, presided in Fries's second trial. Before the trial opened, Chase distributed a paper referring to court decisions establishing, he said, that forcible resistance to a law of the United States constituted an act of war and was therefore treason. Upon learning of Chase's pretrial statement, John Fries's attorneys withdrew from the case. That Fries committed the acts no one doubted. His attorneys felt that if they could not explain and defend these acts because the judge had already defined them as treasonable, their client's cause had been irredeemably compromised. Fries, therefore, had no legal representation in his second trial. The outcome of this trial, like the first, resulted in Fries being found guilty and sentenced to death. The alleged impropriety of Chase's pretrial pronouncement and the restrictions he placed upon the defense lawyers became the foundation for the first article of impeachment.[20]

The next five articles arose from Justice Chase's behavior in the trial of James Thompson Callender, a scandalmonger who employed his pen against holders of political power. According to Fawn M. Brodie, Callender, "Primarily and obsessively a defamer of the great," was "detested by Republican and Federalist alike."[21] At the time of his trial before Justice Chase for a libel of Adams, Callender was detested by the Federalists, whose leaders and policies he viciously attacked. When Thomas Jefferson came to power, Callender turned his unrestrained attention upon the Republicans and was detested by them in turn.

Callender was charged with violating the Sedition Act, the last case involving that act and the only one ever conducted in a southern state. The prosecution accused him of referring to the "reign" of John Adams as "one continued tempest of malignant passions." Callender allegedly said that Adams behaved like a despot, wished to invoke a war with France to favor "the British tyrant," had a corrupt administration, and was a "professed aristocrat." The evidence produced against him concluded with Callender's observation: "Take your choice, then, between Adams, war and beggary, and Jefferson, peace and competency."[22] All of these statements would be repellent to Federalist Samuel Chase, and none more than the last because Chase had campaigned actively for a second term for Adams.

During the Callender trial Justice Chase had frequently interrupted defense counsel to the point that they refused to continue their presentations. Furthermore, Chase excluded a defense witness from testifying and required questions by the defense to be given to him in writing before being put to a witness. Callender was found guilty, sentenced to nine months' imprisonment, and fined $200. James Morton Smith called Chase's behavior in the Callender trial a "most striking instance of judicial prosecution. . . . He personally initiated the sedition proceedings . . . [the] principal object was to demonstrate that the laws of the United States could be enforced in the Old Dominion, one of the two states whose legislature had denounced the Alien and Sedition Laws as unconstitutional."[23]

Chase's deportment in the Fries and the Callender trials consumed the lion's share of attention during the Senate trial to the detriment of the more damaging accusation contained in the final article of impeachment.

The Senate received the eight articles on December 7; and on January 2, 1805, with the Senate sitting as the High Court of Impeachments, the trial opened, Vice-President Aaron Burr, under indictment in two states for killing Alexander Hamilton, presiding.[24] Justice Chase, appearing before the Senate on opening day, asked for a postponement in order to prepare his defense. In his remarks to the High Court of Impeachments, Chase said: "I have committed no crime or misdemeanor whatsoever, for which I am subject to impeachment . . . I deny, with a few exceptions, the acts with which I am charged; . . . all acts admitted to have been done by me, were *legal*; and I deny, in every instance, the *improper* intentions with which the acts charged, are alleged to have been done, and in which their supposed criminality altogether consists."[25]

Referring to the harsh epithets with which his character had been described in the articles of impeachment, Chase observed that his accusers had been " 'puling in their nurse's arms', whilst I was contributing my utmost aid to lay the groundwork of American liberty."[26] Presiding officer Burr admonished Chase for this comment and ruled any such recrimination inadmissible because the justice was asking for a postponement, not replying to the charges. The Senate agreed to Chase's request for postponement and delayed further action for a month.

The trial began on February 4, 1805, with Justice Chase responding to the articles of impeachment in a speech lasting two and a half hours. Five attorneys were associated with Chase in presenting the defense. Luther Martin served as chief counsel and was joined by Robert Goodloe Harper, Joseph Hopkinson, Philip Barton Key, and Charles Lee.[27] Samuel Chase began his rebuttal by claiming that no high crime or misdemeanor had been put forth in any of the articles. Next he analyzed the allegations made against him in each article, explained his own view of the circumstances described, and denied having done anything that made him subject to impeachment.

Respecting his management of John Fries's trial (Article 1), Chase said that he considered the legal definition of treason to have been settled: under the controlling authority of former court decisions, resisting a law of the United States was classified as treason. Therefore, he felt bound to hold that Fries, who had resisted such a law, had committed an act of treason. He announced his ruling before the trial began in order to save time both for the court and for defense counsel. Closing his refutation of the charges contained in the first article, Chase reviewed the constitutional provisions for impeachment and announced his conclusion "that no civil officer of the United States can be impeached, except for some offense for which he may be indicted at law . . . a judge cannot be indicted or punished according to law, for any act whatever, done by him in his judicial capacity . . . through error of judgment merely, without corrupt motives."[28]

Thus, Chase, constructing his own pattern of impeachment, proceeded to show that it did not fit him. The pattern he devised established that impeachment is a criminal proceeding, evidence presented at an impeachment trial must meet the same standards as evidence presented in a court of law, and corrupt motives must be proved in order to convict a judge of misconduct in office. Because none of these self-announced requirements could be applied to his deportment in the Fries trial, Justice Chase asked the Senate to find him not guilty on Article 1.

The next five articles alleged impeachable behavior in the James Callender trial. Chase explained that his decision not to excuse John Basset from the jury (Article 2) proceeded from his belief that Basset was being unreasonably scrupulous. Although Basset had heard about the material classified by the prosecution as a libel of Adams, he had not made a judgment on its accuracy or on whether it had been published with intent to defame. Therefore, Justice Chase refused to exempt him because prospective jurors should be excused only if they had formed an opinion on a defendant's guilt.

Article 3 accused Chase of prejudice for not permitting testimony from a witness able to prove the truth of only part of one of James Callender's allegedly libelous statements. Chase pointed out that the indictment against Callender consisted of twenty distinct charges, proof of any one of which meant conviction. Even if Callender should be found not guilty by reason of the testimony of the excluded witness, the outcome of the trial would not have been affected because the defense did not attempt to refute the other nineteen libels.

"Manifest injustice, partiality, and intemperance" were attributed to Chase in Article 4 because he (1) required James Callender's defense counsel to submit written questions that would be asked of a witness; (2) refused to postpone the trial; (3) used rude and contemptuous language; (4) made vexatious and numerous interruptions of defense counsel, causing them to withdraw from the case; and (5) displayed "indecent solicitude" for conviction of the defendant.

Samuel Chase responded to these charges with assurance. He insisted that it was proper to require submission of written questions so that the judge could determine whether the evidence to be obtained should be admitted. Respecting criticism of his refusal to postpone the trial, Chase said that insufficient ground existed to do so because the defense had no reasonable expectation of securing the witnesses it purportedly wanted to call, no matter how long the postponement; furthermore, the defense had no plans or probability of getting some of the material it wanted. Chase denied allegations of rudeness and vexatious interruptions and stated that he had no desire to convict James Callender. If any part of his behavior seemed offensive, he added, it was unintentional, not caused by improper motives, and clearly not impeachable.

Article 5 concerned Justice Chase's ordering Callender's arrest and confinement. The justice asserted that he had violated neither a law of Virginia nor of the United States in doing so. Article 6 accused Chase of violating a Virginia law by holding James Callender's trial during the same term in which Callender had been indicted by a grand jury. Chase said he knew of no such state law, its existence had not been advanced by Callender's attorneys when they asked for delay, and his co-judge, a district judge in Virginia, had not only never referred to such a law but had also concurred in denying postponement.

Article 7 detailed Justice Chase's refusal to dismiss a grand jury in Delaware, an event occurring five years before his impeachment. It had slight significance, possibly none, absorbed much time during the trial, and presented Chase with no difficulty in deflecting its impact. Believing that "a highly seditious temper had manifested itself in the state of Delaware,"[29] Chase, according to Article 7, had held the grand jury in session to investigate a printer he believed to have published libelous material about the government. Chase pointed out that it was an everyday occurrence for a judge to refuse dismissal of a grand jury if he believed it ought to continue in session. He maintained that his directing the jury's attention to a possible violation of a law and requesting the district attorney to help the jury had been ordinary acts, routinely a part of his official duties.

The eighth and final article described Chase's "intemperate and inflammatory political harangue" to a grand jury in Baltimore in 1803. Chase acknowledged expressing his objections to certain political trends but explained that he had no intention of exciting anyone's resentment against the government of the United States or of the state of Maryland. He introduced to the Senate a copy of the remarks he had made to the Baltimore grand jury, remarks that included his objection to universal suffrage and to a contemplated change in the Maryland judiciary. He also had commented to the jury that "the independence of the national judiciary is already shaken to its foundation."[30] Chase pointed out that no law forbade him to state his opinions. "The expression of political opinions by a judge, in his charge to a jury," Chase acknowledged, might be "improper and dangerous," but he argued that "there are many improper and very dangerous acts, which not being forbidden by law cannot be punished."[31]

This article came closer to capsizing Chase than did any of the others. Particularly damaging was his acknowledgment, had the managers exploited it, that using the bench to proclaim political arguments could indeed be "improper and dangerous." Public officials can be punished in a court of law for illegal conduct just as any other citizen can be, but public officials who act improperly without necessarily violating the law can be reached only by impeachment.

Throughout his step-by-step refutation of the eight articles, Justice Chase insisted that his conduct did not fit the pattern of impeachability that he had described as the correct one. The core of his rebuttal stressed the position that he had not violated any laws and had neither exhibited nor harbored any bad intentions in any of the actions claimed to be improper. These two themes also dominated the arguments of his attorneys during the trial.

Chase's rhetorical style, characteristic of the day, is exemplified in the concluding portions of his defense:

> This respondent now stands not merely before an earthly tribunal, but also before that awful Being whose presence fills all space, and whose all-seeing eye more especially surveys the temples of justice and religion. In a little time, his accusers, his judges, and himself, must appear at the bar of Omnipotence, where the secrets of all hearts shall be disclosed, and every human being shall answer for his deeds done in the body, and shall be compelled to give evidence against himself, in the presence of an assembled universe. To his Omniscient Judge, at that awful hour, he now appeals for the rectitude and purity of his conduct, as to all the matters of which he is this day accused.[32]

On February 9, 1805, the prosecution began its case with a speech by Manager John Randolph. Of Chase's claim that to be impeachable an act must be indictable, Randolph said, "It is not an indictable offense under the laws of the United States for a judge to go on the bench in a state of intoxication. . . . It is indictable no where, for him to omit to do his duty, to refuse to hold a court. And who can doubt that both are impeachable offenses, and ought to subject the offender to removal from office."[33] The argument that an offense need not be criminal to be impeachable ran throughout the Chase trial and, for that matter, formed the central issue in many of the succeeding impeachment trials.

Following Manager Randolph's opening, the examination of prosecution witnesses began, a proceeding that lasted from February 9 until February 15. The parade of witnesses assembled by the managers supported, as one might expect, the allegations against Justice Chase. Several attorneys said they had never heard of a judge announcing the law before trial began as had happened in John Fries's trial for treason. One of the witnesses, William Rawle, had been the prosecuting attorney against Fries. Chase's lawyers, desiring to soften the effect of the justice's act, reminded the Senate that Chase, on the very day after issuing it, revoked his order announcing the controlling law on treason and forbidding defense counsel to argue that law's validity. The prosecution countered that the damage had already been done. Withdrawal of the order did not signify any change in the justice's position on the law of treason nor could it wipe away the impression his original action had made.

George Hay, defense counsel for James Callender in the latter's trial for seditious libel, testified that in sixteen years of practicing law he had never been put down or interrupted as often as he had been by Justice Chase.[34] His humiliation at such treatment had caused him to withdraw from the case. He added that he had never heard of a judge requiring lawyers to submit written questions before putting them to a witness.

The excluded witness of the Callender trial, John Taylor, reported that Chase, in interrupting the defense lawyers, had been playing to the audience but "thought the interruptions were in a very high degree imperative, satirical, and witty" and not delivered in an angry manner. However, Taylor observed, "the audience laughed, but the counsel never laughed at all,"[35] hardly a surprising response by the defense attorneys, who no doubt perceived the sallies as directed against their client and themselves. That Chase's interruptions were intended to be jocular was frequently advanced by his attorneys, later in the trial, to account for his behavior.

John Heath, a lawyer, testified that he called at Chase's lodgings on a matter unrelated to the Callender trial. During Heath's conversation with the justice, David M. Randolph, the federal marshal, came in with the list of members of the jury. According to Heath, Chase asked whether "any of those creatures called democrats" were on the panel; if so, Chase said, "strike them off."[36] Both David Randolph and William Marshall, appearing later in the trial as witnesses for Chase, contested Heath's testimony. Randolph said that the incident had never happened and that at no time had he conferred with Justice Chase about composition of the jury. William Marshall, clerk of the federal court and brother of Chief Justice John Marshall, said Chase had never referred to wanting a jury devoid of Republicans, had indeed said that he wished "Callender might be tried by a jury of his own politics."[37] This stark contradiction remained unexplained; the discrepancy was never resolved because neither side tried to discover which account was true—a serious omission on the managers' part, assuming that their witness, John Heath, had not merely imagined Samuel Chase's comments about the jury.

John Basset, whose acceptance as a juror had created a controversy, testified that he had told Justice Chase he belonged to the Federalist party, had seen extracts from Callender's allegedly libelous book *The Prospect Before Us*, thought them seditious, and believed whoever wrote the book to be guilty of sedition. Although subsequent Chase witnesses strove to show that Basset did not know whether Callender had written the allegedly libelous material, it seems unlikely that he could be unaware of that fact; Callender's authorship had never been questioned or denied.

Another witness told of riding on a stagecoach with Chase and discussing *The Prospect Before Us*. Justice Chase, referring to Callender, said, "Pity you have not hanged the rascal."[38] Chase's attorneys insisted that this prejudicial remark was facetious and not evidence of a determination to convict the defendant.

Respecting the justice's refusal to dismiss the Delaware grand jury, George Read, the district attorney whom Chase had directed to investigate the supposedly seditious printer, testified that he had found nothing of a seditious nature in the publications of the suspect printer. Later in the trial, a defense witness sustained the account by repeating that District Attorney Read had turned up no seditious material, "but there was a paragraph against his honor. Judge Chase said that was not what he alluded to. He was abused from one end of the continent to the other; but his shoulders were broad enough to bear it."[39] These comments presented a new view of Chase—an unvindictive man able to accept personal attacks and not equate them with sedition; Article 7 did not damage his position.

The managers concluded their case with a review of the performance of Samuel Chase before the Baltimore grand jury as detailed in the eighth article. Witnesses testified that Justice Chase referred to weakness in the national government, attacked the repeal of the Judiciary Act of 1801, criticized changes in the judiciary provisions of the Maryland constitution, and opposed universal suffrage. John Montgomery, a Maryland legislator who had drawn the bills changing his state's court system and suffrage requirements, recounted the scene in which Chase, in his address to the Baltimore grand jury, strongly attacked those bills. Montgomery recalled the justice's urging the jury to fight against such evil changes, saying that the people had "been misled by misrepresentation, falsehood, art, and cunning."[40]

Another prosecution witness, John T. Mason, commented that Justice Chase "delivered the charge from a written paper, which he had before him. He wore his spectacles at the time, and though he turned over leaf by leaf, he occasionally threw up his head, and sometimes raised his spectacles on his forehead, and spoke as if he was making what I considered an enlargement of the original charge, by extemporary observations in addition to what he had written."[41]

This seemingly inoffensive description precipitated a concerned response from the defense over whether the written statement of Chase's address to the Baltimore grand jury formed the complete record of all that he had said. Mason's comment worried Chase's attorneys, who repeatedly asked other witnesses, but not Mason himself, whether Chase had made any interpolations as he read his address. The defense attorneys wanted to show that the relatively mild written statement, which they introduced in evidence, comprised the sum total of the justice's utterances. The managers did not pursue the matter, however, despite its potential significance.

The managers' case against Justice Chase was designed to sustain the articles by demonstrating that he had (1) prejudiced the Fries trial, a claim supported by several attorneys; (2) harassed defense lawyers and put unusual burdens upon them, a claim supported by attorneys who had been objects of his actions; (3) made a biased comment on the composition of the jury in the Callender trial for libel, a charge that remained unproved; (4) accepted on the jury a man who had expressed an opinion on the matter to be tried, an allegation acknowledged by the juror himself; (5) stated that James Callender should be hanged, a charge acknowledged by Chase's defenders but asserted to be meant as a joke; (6) refused to dismiss the Delaware grand jury, a charge accepted as a fact by respondent's side but supported on the ground that Chase had valid reasons for retaining the jury; and (7) attacked actions of the national and Maryland governments before the Baltimore grand jury and urged the jurors to fight against them. Justice Chase's address to the Baltimore jury, a printed copy of which had been made part of the evidence, was obviously a fact. The points at issue, inadequately expounded by the managers, were whether he had made additional comments more glaringly partisan than the printed record and whether a judge, in addressing a grand jury, could properly advance his own political preferences and denounce actions taken by the national and state governments.

On February 15, 1805, Robert Goodloe Harper opened the case for Chase.[42] He told the Senate that the charges against Justice Chase as delineated by the managers had been unsupported to such a degree that he would be satisfied to rest his case just on the material presented by the prosecution. Because, however, some errors had been put forth, he intended to correct them. Harper reviewed the articles of impeachment, attempting to explain away everything that looked bad for his client. For example, he acknowledged that Justice Chase had said that James Callender should be convicted but called the comment merely a jest. He denied that Chase had ever referred to a seditious temper existing in Delaware and called such expressions "offensive and improper."[43]

Witnesses for respondent testified regarding Chase's action on the second day of the Fries trial, when he withdrew his restrictions on the defense attorneys' right to argue the law of treason and asked them to continue to represent Fries. According to one witness, Chase told the attorneys that if "they persisted in stating to the jury their sentiments on the law, they must do it at the hazard of their legal reputations."[44] The witnesses did not believe this comment had been made in a menacing fashion, as prosecution witnesses had claimed. A later witness, testifying to the same matter, said that the justice told defense counsel they might proceed as they saw fit, "having a regard to their own characters."[45] This testimony does not seem helpful to Samuel Chase's position; it merely confirmed facts advanced by the prosecution without modifying them in furtherance of the justice's cause.

William Marshall, the chief justice's brother, testified in support of Chase's acceptance of John Basset as a juror. Marshall argued that although Basset had formed a negative opinion of the alleged libelous writing, he purportedly did not know that James Callender had written it. Marshall told of an analogy Chase offered in which he observed that everyone in a community where a murder had been committed would declare that the murderer should be punished. However, a person who had not formed an opinion that the defendant was the murderer could be a proper juror even though he had announced his opposition to murder. This analogy worked out badly for James Callender because his authorship of the alleged libel was never in doubt, Basset being a rare example of ignorance of that fact.

When cross-examined by Manager Randolph on the matter of Chase's interruptions of the attorneys, Marshall said, "I have rarely seen a trial where the interruptions were so frequent."[46] Although proffered in support of respondent's position, Marshall's testimony confirmed two prosecution claims: that a man accepted as a juror had formed an opinion that the writing in question was a libel and that Chase had made an unusual number of interruptions.

Chief Justice John Marshall also appeared as a witness for the respondent. He said that Chase's courtroom behavior seemed unusual, noting particularly the justice's interruptions of James Callender's defense counsel whenever they tried to discuss the constitutionality of the Sedition Act. Of the requirement that questions be written and submitted to Chase before being put to a witness, the chief justice said, "I never knew it requested that a question should be reduced to writing in the first instance in the whole course of my practice." Asked whether it was customary to exclude a witness from testifying if he could prove only a portion, not the whole, of a particular charge, Marshall replied, "I never did hear that objection made by the court except in this particular case."[47]

The chief justice's denials of support for his colleague's actions must have done Chase some harm. Senator Plumer recorded his dissatisfaction with Marshall's performance, noting: "There was in his manner an evident disposition to accommodate the Managers. That dignified frankness which his high office required did not appear. A cunning man ought never to discover the arts of the *trimmer* in his testimony."[48]

A succeeding defense witness, Philip Gooch, a practicing attorney, reported that when James Callender's lawyers tried to advance their arguments against constitutionality of the Sedition Act, Justice Chase chided them in a "pleasant manner," saying, "you show yourselves to be clever young men, and I believe you know that testimony of this kind ought not to be adduced, but perhaps you do it to blind the people and to work up their minds to a state of opposition."[49] Although Gooch testified as a defense witness, his recollection of Chase's reproof would surely fail to further the justice's cause. Even granted its being delivered in a pleasant manner, a statement suggesting that Callender's attorneys desired to inflame the public mind cannot be viewed as an impartial judicial admonishment.

Gooch also made an insignificant comment that would be used later by Luther Martin in his summary argument for Chase. Gooch said that Chase, after telling one of James Callender's attorneys that his previous comment had been a non sequitur, "made him a bow."[50] Luther Martin subsequently made great fun of the terrifying portent of Chase's bow, developing it into one of comic majesty rivaling that of Poo Bah in *The Mikado*.

In connection with Justice Chase's political commentary to the Baltimore grand jury, another defense witness was asked whether, in criticizing persons seeking changes in the laws, the justice had referred to "degenerate sons." The witness said that Chase had done so, and recalled the justice as regretting "to see sons taking part in destroying the fair fabric their fathers had raised."[51] The adjective *degenerate* does not appear in the transcript of the speech as submitted at the trial. The managers failed to seize this opportunity to demonstrate that a harsh term that did not appear in the record had been heard by one of respondent's own witnesses. Had this anomaly not slipped past them, the managers could have argued, and probably proved, that Samuel Chase had said more to the grand jury than was shown in the written record.

With succeeding witnesses, Robert Goodloe Harper continued his efforts to establish that Chase's remarks to the Maryland jury had been in written form. The witnesses did not testify that every word uttered by Chase had been written down, but reported that the justice had read his address from a book. One witness present during the address to the Baltimore grand jury said that he expected the address to be held against Chase because John Montgomery, advocate of the laws Chase was attacking, had been paying close attention and would certainly consider the address "an animadversion upon the measures Mr. Montgomery had been anxious to carry in the legislature of Maryland." The witness testified that he found Chase's presentation "both imprudent and impolitic; and I have always thought political charges ought not to be delivered from the bench."[52] The next witness reported that he met John Montgomery shortly after Chase had finished speaking and heard Montgomery say that the speech was "such an one as Mr. Chase would be impeached for."[53]

Montgomery, a witness earlier in the trial, was recalled to the stand in order to amplify his previous testimony on Samuel Chase's charge to the Baltimore grand jury. He said that the justice had accused the national administration of not promoting the general welfare but of acting only to retain its unfairly acquired power. Chase objected, Montgomery said, to repeal of the law creating additional circuit judges, denounced universal suffrage in Maryland, and opposed contemplated changes in that state's judicial system. "I did not mean to state that he said Mr. Jefferson was weak or feeble, but that the administration or the government was so."[54] Montgomery reported Chase as urging the grand jurors to work against passage of the Maryland judiciary bill. No such statement appears in the written record. Montgomery said he had called this omission to the attention of several people, including Justice Chase's son Thomas, who had prepared the copy. The managers let slip another chance to argue the validity of the transcript. They did not even comment on the discrepancy, much less make it into a significant challenge to the respondent's case.

The next day both sides completed their testimony. Certain differences on the facts and many differences on their interpretation emerged. Factual differences include: (1) the prosecution claimed that Justice Chase had said he wanted no Republicans on the Callender jury, a contention flatly contradicted by witnesses for Chase; (2) the managers quoted Chase as referring to a seditious temper in Delaware, but his attorneys denied that he had made such a statement and said it would be damaging if he had; and (3) the two sides did not agree on whether Chase had attacked the national administration in his address to the Baltimore grand jury or had urged the jurors to oppose adoption by Maryland of changes in the state's judiciary.

The managers and Chase, however, agreed on certain other important facts: (1) Justice Chase had announced the law he would invoke in John Fries's treason trial before the trial opened, (2) he had had James Callender arrested and tried for seditious libel in the same term of court; (3) he had rejected a witness in Callender's trial who could testify to only a part of the charge against the defendant; (4) he had accepted a juror who believed that published material central to Callender's trial was libelous; and (5) he had frequently interrupted and admonished defense attorneys. While not disagreeing on these facts, the prosecution and the defense differed on their significance. The managers sought to establish that the justice's actions were wrong, caused by corrupt intentions, and impeachable; the defense contended that the acts were justifiable, undertaken with proper judicial motives, and not impeachable either as crimes or as official misconduct.

The battle was never really joined, however, on the last, and most crucial, charge. Samuel Chase's attorneys tried to establish that he had read his speech to the grand jury in Baltimore so that anything claimed to be inflammatory or prejudicial would have to be pointed out in the written record, not merely advanced as unsupported recollections of earwitnesses. Although neither side thought political argument from the bench to be proper, Chase's attorneys defended it as at least acceptable, if unwise, under English precedents and not illegal under United States procedure. The managers on their part failed to hit hard on, least of all prove, the charge that Chase had made extemporaneous changes in the written material as he delivered it to the Baltimore jury, nor did they even pursue witnesses' testimony indicating that Justice Chase had made oral interpolations in the text as he delivered his speech.

On February 20 the attorneys began their summaries. Peter Early, for the managers, spoke first. He reviewed Article 1 and insisted that John Fries had not had a fair trial. He reminded the Senate that no one questioned that Fries had done what he was accused of doing. The question turned upon the law of treason and the defense attorneys' right to challenge its validity, a right of which they had been deprived by Justice Chase's order forbidding argument on the law itself. Early found that Chase's countermanding of his own order on the second day of the trial was proof of a tardy recognition of his error, an error that could not be expunged from the jurors' minds. Continuing with Articles 2, 3, and 4, Early reexamined what he saw as the erroneous acceptance of John Basset as a juror in James Callender's trial, the exclusion of John Taylor's testimony on the libel, and the haste with which Chase had scheduled the trial. Respecting the justice's unwillingness to dismiss the Delaware grand jury, Early called Chase "a hunter after accusations" with a "thirst for punishment."[55] On the eighth article, the political speech to the Baltimore grand jury, Early said he would not "trouble the court with many observations ... not because of any opinion that it is unimportant. I believe it equally important with any in the catalogue."[56] It is surprising that Early laboriously reworked the already overemphasized and wearisome technicalities of the Fries and Callender trials and gave the potentially most damaging charge only passing notice.

Next came Manager George W. Campbell. Hoping for "pure and unstained impartiality," he disclaimed "any design or wish, that party considerations, or difference in political sentiments, should, in the remotest degree, enter into the investigation, or affect the decision of this question." He developed the point that impeachment is a civil investigation, an inquest into official conduct, not a criminal prosecution that would be tried in ordinary courts. Samuel Chase's conduct, Campbell said, showed misuse of his official position, a determination to "oppress, under the sanction of legal authority, those who became the objects of his resentment in consequence of differing from him in political sentiments."[57]

Manager Campbell pointed out that when criticized for some of his rulings in James Callender's trial, Chase had reminded his critics that the district judge sitting with him had not objected to his interpretations. Campbell observed that the co-judge in the Callender trial had been wrong in agreeing with the justice in his rulings, but Chase's conduct could not be excused because someone else was also wrong. Manager Campbell, unimpressed by the respondent's explanation that many of the statements for which he had been criticized had been meant to be facetious, found the matters too serious for jest and argued that citizens' rights had been trifled with.

Next, Manager Christopher Clark spoke on Articles 5 and 6 concerning Justice Chase's jailing of James Callender and holding Callender's trial in the same session of court as his indictment. He commented that because ignorance did not serve as an excuse "in an unlettered individual, shall it constitute the apology of him who was expressly appointed to expound the law and administer justice?" Why, Clark wondered, if Chase lacked knowledge of the laws of Virginia, had he felt compelled to act "with such fatal precipitancy. We can only account for this, by supposing that it was the intention of the judge to act in conformity to his previous declaration [to convict Callender], however jocularly it may have seemed to have been made."[58]

Then came the turn of Samuel Chase's lawyers. Joseph Hopkinson spoke first. He summarized the constitutional provisions on impeachment and insisted that an impeachable offense must be indictable. Then he turned to his major assignment, demolishing the criticisms of Chase's management of John Fries's treason trial. The Fries trial, he remarked, had taken place five years before. Why had it taken so long to raise these fraudulent criticisms? If the respondent displayed any difficulties in refuting the charges, it was because of their "unreasonable staleness" not their validity, Hopkinson said.[59] He analyzed Justice Chase's pretrial statement detailing the law of treason. He said that it had been issued before Fries's trial opened in order to save time. Furthermore, the jury had not been aware of the statement; it would not have become known to the public until after the trial, except that Fries's attorney revealed it.

Next came Philip Barton Key, who spoke on Articles 2, 3, and 4. Respecting Chase's acceptance of John Basset as a juror in James Callender's case, Key explained the valid bases of excusing a juror, indicating that they did not apply to Basset, and concluded his rebuttal of Article 2 by asserting that if Chase had committed any kind of error—Key said that he had not—no allegation or even hint of corruption attached to his conduct.

On the justice's refusal to hear John Taylor's testimony (Article 3), Key explained that Chase had been entirely correct, that Taylor could speak only to a small part of the alleged libel, and that his testimony on even that part did not constitute the best evidence available. Key disposed of Article 4 by arguing that Chase's requirement of written questions was not unusual, thereby brushing past the testimony of several witnesses, including that of John Marshall. Key held that Chase's decision against putting off Callender's trial for libel until the next term was within his discretion; Justice Chase had offered a postponement, but the defense attorneys declined to accept the offer because they would still have had Chase as judge. Key either denied or labeled as jokes the charges of rudeness, interruptions, and Chase's alleged desire for Callender's conviction. He stressed that no corrupt motivation for any of the justice's words or deeds had been produced.

Charles Lee, attorney general under Presidents Washington and Adams, spoke next; his assignment was to dispose of Articles 5 and 6. Chase's ordering Callender's arrest, as detailed in Article 5, lacked any characteristics of a crime, showed no evidence of malicious intent, and was an entirely correct and legal order within the discretion of the judge, Lee insisted. Of Article 6, alleging that Justice Chase intended to oppress and convict Callender by holding trial in the term of his indictment, Lee said that no Virginia law prohibited trial of a misdemeanor in the same term. "No such law has been produced, and I must be allowed to deny that any such law of Virginia exists." Commenting on the allegations of misconduct toward Callender's counsel, Lee observed: "To the logical Mr. Wirt he was logical; to the polite Mr. Nicholas, he was polite; to the zealous and pertinacious Mr. Hay, he was warm and determined. If the counsel had conducted themselves with propriety towards the court, there would have been no interruptions."[60] This description of the court as a mirror of the behavior of the attorneys does not seem to fit the ordinary view of the source of courtroom decorum.

Luther Martin, chief counsel for the defense, spoke next. Henry Adams characterized Martin as "rollicking, witty, audacious . . . boon companion of Chase and the whole bar; drunken, generous, slovenly, grand . . . the notorious reprobate genius."[61] Martin opened with a review of the background of the impeachment provisions. He scorned the suggestion that the Constitution empowered the House of Representatives to impeach every citizen or that a person not holding office could be impeached. Why Martin brought up this dead issue or what it had to do with the Chase trial is impossible to say.

Martin next proceeded to another irrelevancy by repudiating the conclusion, advanced, he said, by the managers, that a judge can be removed only for crimes committed in his official capacity: "A judge, then, might break open his neighbor's house and steal his goods;—he might be a common receiver of stolen goods; for these crimes, he might be indicted, convicted and punished, in a court of law; but yet he could not be removed from office, because the offense was not committed by him in his judicial capacity."[62]

What caused Luther Martin to introduce this second extraneous comment is particularly unclear. Respondents' attorneys in impeachment trials work hard at narrowing, certainly not expanding, the grounds on which an officer may be impeached. Furthermore, the charges against Chase related to performances in his judicial capacity. Martin's reason for pulling in a comment that did not concern Justice Chase and that widened the reach of the impeachment clause is mysterious.

Luther Martin completed his introductory remarks with the assertion that only an indictable offense was impeachable—the major thread of the respondent's case. Having established the base for his arguments and having abandoned the inexplicable irrelevancies, Martin examined the charges against Samuel Chase article by article with skill and force; he showed great argumentative ability and sedulous preparation. He employed no palliatives or evasions such as some of his colleagues had delivered when they suggested that in this or that instance Chase had been right but had acted without corrupt motive even if he were wrong. Concluding his defense of Chase's pretrial announcement of the law of treason in the Fries case, Martin declared:

> I deny that the court was guilty on the first day, of any impropriety; I take higher ground . . . and do contend, that the conduct of the court on the first day, was correct and proper, and during the whole trial I find nothing improper in their conduct, except their almost humiliatingly soliciting the counsel of Fries to do their duty, instead of committing them to gaol for the impropriety of their conduct, which the court ought to have done.[63]

Surely a bold stroke by Luther Martin! Not content to support unequivocally Justice Chase's ruling on treason that brought about the resignation of John Fries's attorneys, Martin chided the court for not backing up its ruling by jailing the attorneys. His refutations of Articles 2 and 3 (accepting a possibly prejudiced juror and rejecting testimony in Callender's trial) were more detailed and argumentative than those of his colleagues, but he covered generally the same positions. In refuting Article 4, however, Martin introduced a somewhat different treatment of the judge's dealings with Callender's attorneys. Because of the bitterness toward the Sedition Act in Virginia, Chase, according to Martin, feared some public outburst at the trial. Thus, to forestall trouble, he

appears to have been anxious, as his best security, to keep the by-standers in good humor, and to amuse them at the expense of the very persons, who were endeavoring to excite the irascibility of the audience against him. Hence the mirth, the humor, the facetiousness, by which his conduct was marked during the trial . . . it is admitted that he kept the by-standers in great good humor, and excited peals of laughter at the expense of the counsel.[64]

A most ingenious argument, especially from the man who would have had Justice Chase jail Fries's lawyers for improper courtroom behavior. That the persons at whose expense Chase provided public mirth were lawyers for the defendant did not trouble Luther Martin, at least in this instance.

Martin greatly enjoyed examining the claim that Samuel Chase had been rude to James Callender's counsel, William Wirt, by referring to one of Wirt's conclusions as a non sequitur and then bowing to him. It is difficult, Martin observed,

to determine the merit or demerit of *a bow* without having seen it . . . ; to discover, therefore, whether there was anything *rude* or *improper* in this *bow*, I could have wished that the witness, who complained so much of its effect, had given us a *fac simile* of it. . . . But it seems this *bow*, together with the "non sequitor," entirely discomfited poor Mr. Wirt, and down he sat "and never word spake more!"—If so, it was a saving of time.[65]

Luther Martin presented an exhaustive, commanding, and dextrous summation of most of the defense arguments. William Plumer observed in his diary that Martin "really possesses much legal information and a great fund of good humor—keen satire and poignant wit. He is far from being a graceful speaker. His language is often incorrect—inaccurate, and sometimes is too low." On the same day, February 23, that he recorded his impression of Luther Martin, Plumer made another notation in his diary. A friend told him that Manager Peter Early had said "he was weary of the cause and intimated his regret, that the impeachment was ever brought forward." Plumer thought the majority of House members shared this opinion; "still I think as the work has commenced it will end in the removal of the accused from office."[66]

The final speaker for Samuel Chase was Robert Goodloe Harper, veteran of all three impeachments. He said he would range rapidly over the first six articles and then concentrate on Articles 7 and 8. He opened by expressing regret that the prosecutors had injected political and party considerations into the trial; because they had, however, Harper called the court's attention to the particular necessity that those of different political beliefs from Chase's should be generous to the accused. Because Justice Chase was staunchly Federalist, because he had been accused of displaying political prejudice in the courtroom, and because the Senate membership consisted of twenty-five Republicans and nine Federalists, Harper's argument was urgent and real. He accused the managers of stirring a flame of party hatred against

> an aged patriot and statesman, bearing on his head the frost of seventy winters. . . . His footsteps are hunted from place to place, to find indiscretions, which may be exaggerated into crimes. The jests which, flowing from the gaity and openness of his temper, were uttered in the confidence of private conversation; the expressions of warmth produced by the natural impetuosity of his character, are detailed by companions converted into spies and informers, and are adduced as proofs of criminal intention.[67]

Harper insisted that an offense must be criminal to be impeachable. But in a strangely tangled passage Harper changed course and made the inexplicable announcement that he could suppose "cases where a judge ought to be impeached, for acts which I am not prepared to declare indictable." He suggested failure to hold court or holding court for too short time to transact necessary business as examples of impeachable offenses because they "are a plain and direct violation of the law, which commands him to hold courts a reasonable time for the dispatch of business; and of his oath, which binds him to discharge faithfully and diligently the duties of his office."[68]

Then Harper issued another confusing statement:

Habitual drunkenness in a judge, and profane swearing in any person, are indictable offenses. And if they were not, still they are violations of the law. I do not mean to say that there is a statute against drunkenness and profane swearing. But they are offenses against good morals, and as such are forbidden by the common law. They are offences in the sight of God and man,

80

definite in their nature, capable of precise proof and of a clear defense.[69]

This observation advances the broadest description of impeachment made by anyone concerned with the subject, one far removed from the usual position of Samuel Chase's attorneys that only crimes constitute bases for impeachment. Harper argued that drunkenness and swearing were indictable, and if not, nevertheless violated the law even though no statute prohibited either activity. If these contradictory requirements could not be met, Harper produced a final manifestation of impeachable conduct: acting in a manner offensive to God and man. So sweeping a grant to present and future managers of impeachment trials would have twisted constitutional meanings beyond recognition; furthermore, it was antithetical to the respondent's position in the Chase, and every other, trial. If Harper's commentary defies explanation, even more so does the failure of the managers to seize upon it for support in their own summation.

Then Harper swiftly resumed the defense's major posture by stating, if somewhat illogically in view of his previous remarks, that the "great principle for which we contend . . . [is] that an impeachment is a criminal prosecution, and cannot be maintained without the proof of some offense against the laws."[70]

On the seventh article, refusal to dismiss the Delaware grand jury, Harper reviewed the evidence and defended the correctness of Justice Chase's position in retaining the jury. Respecting the allegation that the justice had uttered a condemnation of Delaware by referring to a seditious spirit infecting the area, Harper pointed out that numerous and reliable witnesses had testified that Chase had not made such a statement. In this direct clash with prosecution testimony, as with the testimony on Chase's alleged insistence that no Republicans serve on the James Callender jury, the defense had the stronger position and argued it more vigorously.

The final article of impeachment has been mentioned as offering the strongest charge against Samuel Chase. Harper evidenced no fear in analyzing this article. He said that Justice Chase had not criticized the character or motives of Thomas Jefferson's administration in his address to the Baltimore grand jury but that if he had, he deserved censure. Samuel Chase's belief that the republic was in danger had caused him "to point out, what he considered as the pernicious tendency of certain measures of the federal government, in order to shew in a stronger light, the danger of adopting similar measures in the state."[71]

Harper noted that John Montgomery, author of the Maryland bills that Chase opposed and the man who had said the justice should be impeached because of his remarks, had been the lone witness to the supposed improper criticism of the national administration. Other witnesses, several of them vigorous adherents of the policies of the Jefferson administration, did not hear any expressions derogatory of its conduct, character, or views. Harper reminded the Senate that a true copy of the justice's remarks formed part of the evidence and that it contained no such criticisms. This comment is correct. The essentially unexamined issue concerned whether Samuel Chase had made additions to the written script when he delivered his address.

Chase's behavior before the Baltimore jury might "perhaps be ill-judged, indiscreet, or ill-timed," Harper acknowledged, because "I am one of those who have always thought that political subjects ought never to be mentioned in courts of justice. But is it contrary to law?" he asked. "Admitting it to be indecorous and improper, which I do not admit, is every breach of decorum and propriety a crime?"[72] Harper concluded by arguing that all the charges against Samuel Chase had been disproved, that the accusation "has dwindled into nothing. It has been scattered by the rays of truth, like the mists of the morning, before the effulgence of the rising sun. Touched by the spear of investigation, it has lost its gigantic and terrifying form, and has shrunk into a toad."[73]

Manager Joseph H. Nicholson followed Harper. He regretted the necessity of the impeachment but asserted that the best interests of the country required it. Otherwise, "if the holy sanctuary of our courts is to be invaded by party feelings; if justice shall suffer her pure garment to be stained by the foul venom of political bigotry," the nation's freedom would be lost.[74] On the key dispute over whether an impeachment could be grounded only on an indictable offense, Nicholson made a blunder as inexplicable as that of Chase's counsel, Robert Goodloe Harper's. He said that defense attorneys had claimed the managers had

resorted to the forlorn hope of contending that an impeachment was not a criminal prosecution, but a mere inquest of office. For myself I am free to declare, that I heard no such position taken. If declarations of this kind have been made, in the name of the managers I here disclaim them. We do contend that this is a criminal prosecution, for offenses committed in the discharge of high official duties.[75]

According to Albert J. Beveridge, this confused and contradictory observation produced a noticeable impact. "The Senate was dumbfounded, the friends of Chase startled with joyful surprise; a gasp of amazement ran through the overcrowded Chamber!"[76] It is true that Nicholson floundered his way back to the original Republican position—grounds for impeachment include more than criminal acts—but he had punctured his position beyond repair.

Next for the managers came Caesar Augustus Rodney. He stated that the trial had been based not on just a single bad performance by the accused but on "a variety of transactions at different periods of his life."[77] Rodney tried to salvage the managers' case, so damaged by Nicholson, by reasserting that impeachable offenses need not be indictable. Citing Judge Pickering's trial as precedent he pointed out that no federal or state law made drunkeness or swearing indictable, yet the Senate had convicted the judge.

Rodney made one significant comment on the otherwise overworked Callender trial:

When a poor miserable object like Callender, without character and without influence censures the measures of our administration, or reprobates an unconstitutional law, the respondent considered him guilty of a crime and deserving of punishment. But a man elevated to the bench may declaim in the strongest language against any measure, or law of the United States, or of an individual state with perfect impunity![78]

John Randolph, leader of the prosecution and the major force behind the move to impeach Samuel Chase, spoke last. Beveridge has described Randolph as "fearless, honest, and impolitic" and said that during the Chase trial he was "nervously exhausted, physically overwrought and troubled, [but had been] the most brilliant and effective Congressional partisan leader of our early history." Dumas Malone also referred to Randolph's dominant role in the impeachment proceedings and noted his excessive self-confidence and "his extraordinary powers of speech and parliamentary skill."[79]

Manager Randolph's introductory remarks contained an argument of importance. If impeachment could be applied only to an indictable offense, "For what, then, (I pray you) was it, that this provision of impeachment found its way into the Constitution? Could it not have said, at once, that any civil officer of the United States, convicted on an indictment should *(ipso facto)* be removed from office?"[80] He believed that the Founding Fathers designed the impeachment provisions to cover actions not indictable. Randolph gave a hypothetical example of a president's vetoing every bill brought for his signature. "This surely would be an abuse of his constitutional power, richly deserving impeachment; and yet no man will pretend to say it is an indictable offense."[81]

Then Randolph began a refutation of the respondent's case from the beginning; he had nothing to display that had not been said many times before. Midway through his speech, he apologized to the court for the desultory style of his address and said that he had misplaced his notes. Beveridge attributes such bumbling to Randolph's having just lost an important vote in the House of Representatives: "Physically exhausted and in despair at his overthrow as dictator of the House, [Randolph] went to his ineffective management of the Chase impeachment trial."[82]

Unsympathetic Federalist chroniclers were greatly offended by Randolph's performance. He spoke, said John Quincy Adams, "with as little relation to the subject-matter as possible—without order, connection or argument; consisting altogether of the most hackneyed commonplaces of popular declamation . . . with much distortion of face and contortion of body, tears, groans, and sobs." William Plumer strongly seconded Randolph's own reference to his argument as desultory "if by argument he meant what he *uttered*. The word *argument* I think inapplicable to his performance—it is too dignified for such a feeble *thing*."[83]

On March 1, 1805 the Senate met to vote on the articles of impeachment. Before meeting as a court, the Senate had debated the form in which to phrase the question of guilt. Robert Wright (Republican, Maryland) urged that the precedent set in Judge Pickering's trial be followed and the question be put, Is the respondent guilty as charged? James A. Bayard (Federalist, Delaware), chairman of the managers in William Blount's trial, moved that the question be, Is the respondent guilty of high crimes and misdemeanors? Bayard's motion won seventeen to sixteen.[84] The ambiguous phrase "guilty as charged," so handy in the Pickering trial, was dropped.

The Senate found Chase innocent on Article 1, his conduct during the Fries trial, by a vote of eighteen to sixteen. A majority of the senators agreed with the justice's refusal, described in Article 2, to excuse an allegedly biased juror in James Callender's trial; the vote was twenty-four not guilty and ten guilty. On Article 3, detailing Chase's refusal to hear a witness who could testify to only part of one of the charges, and on the potpourri Article 4, concerning the justice's general deportment in the Callender trial, a majority found him guilty but by a margin nowhere near the two-thirds necessary for conviction. The vote was eighteen guilty, sixteen not guilty on both articles. Samuel Chase stood completely exonerated of guilt on the fifth article, which charged him with improperly ordering James Callender's arrest and confinement; all thirty-four senators voted not guilty. Advocates of conviction fared little better on the sixth article, describing Chase's refusal to put off Callender's trial until the next term of court; thirty senators voted not guilty, and four voted guilty. The senators found Justice Chase innocent of impeachable conduct under Article 7, his management of the Delaware grand jury, by a vote of twenty-four to ten. On the major article, eight, Chase's address to the Baltimore grand jury, the guilty vote was nineteen, with fifteen senators voting not guilty.

Thus, the High Court of Impeachments found Samuel Chase guilty on three of the eight articles of impeachment—3, 4, and 8—but not by a number even approaching the two-thirds vote needed for conviction. Vice-President Aaron Burr, having announced the totals for each article, said, "It appears that there is not a constitutional majority of votes finding Samuel Chase, Esquire, guilty on any one Article. It, therefore, becomes my duty to declare that Samuel Chase, Esquire, stands acquitted of all the Articles exhibited by the House of Representatives against him."[85]

All nine Federalist senators voted Chase not guilty on each of the articles. The steady ranks of the Federalists were joined by six Republicans—Stephen R. Bradley (Vermont), John Gaillard (South Carolina), Samuel Mitchill (New York), Israel Smith (Vermont), John Smith (Ohio), and John Smith (New York)—who also voted not guilty on every article; hence, the not guilty vote never fell below fifteen. Of these fifteen, all except Senator Gaillard represented northern states. The profile of the senator who voted not guilty reveals him to be a Federalist, with certain Republican features, who resided in the North.

Only four Republicans—John Breckinridge (Kentucky), William Cocke (Tennessee), Benjamin Howland (Rhode Island), and Samuel Maclay (Pennsylvania)—voted Chase guilty on each of the seven articles for which a guilty vote was recorded. Excepting Howland and Maclay, southern and border state Republicans proved to be the most consistent in voting guilty. Their number included both senators from Samuel Chase's home state, Maryland. The profile of the senator voting to convict shows him to be a Republican residing in a southern or border state. Therefore, although party proved dominant in the vote on Justice Samuel Chase, region had some influence on the outcome.

The Republican ranks were in no respect a match for the Federalist ranks in cohesive support of their party's position. John Quincy Adams told of leaving the Senate with William Cocke on the day the trial ended. Cocke spoke harshly of John Randolph's conduct of the impeachment, charging him "with excessive vanity, ambition, insolence, and even dishonesty, which he exemplified by the misrecital of the Virginia law referred to in the fifth article of the impeachment, which [Cocke] said must have been intentional." Adams also reported Cocke's regret that the impeachment had been brought forward; even though he had found Chase to be guilty on all but one article, Cocke was glad the justice had been acquitted, as it "would have a tendency to mitigate the irritation of party spirit."[86]

Although the vote went against them, the managers did not accept Chase's acquittal as the end of the story. Immediately following announcement of the verdict, John Randolph introduced in the House of Representatives an amendment to the Constitution providing for presidential removal of federal judges upon joint address of both houses of Congress. Equally chagrined at losing, his fellow manager Joseph H. Nicholson proposed an amendment authorizing state legislatures to recall senators.[87] Senator Plumer commented that Randolph pronounced "a violent phillippic against Judge Chase and against the Senate," and that both Randolph and Nicholson showed angry passions.[88] Senator Adams noted that "the leading managers vented their spleen against the decision with all their virulence . . . I had some conversation on the subject with Mr. [James] Madison, who appeared much diverted at the petulance of the managers on their disappointment."[89] Nothing came of Randolph's or Nicholson's efforts to rebuke the Senate for its verdict.

Congressional involvement with the Chase impeachment and trial stretched from January 5, 1804, to March 1, 1805. Thus, for nearly fourteen months the House and the Senate were intermittently concerned with investigating, prosecuting, or trying Samuel Chase. Why, after all this time spent on one public figure, did the outcome prove so disappointing to the Jeffersonians? Why did the Republicans fail to mass their membership and vote Chase guilty? How could a jurist whose vehement Federalist views were well known and who had expressed them publicly in political campaigns and from the bench escape conviction by the party against which he had directed his onslaughts? First, the Republicans had been pulling apart over how to settle the Georgia land swindle, and John Randolph had alienated some Republicans by his violent opposition to the Jefferson administration's resolution of the disputed land claims.[90] Second, party identity and organization were not strong in the early nineteenth century. Third, the impeachment articles had been framed in an ambiguous, oratorical, and complicated style to the fatal detriment of the prosecution's case. Fourth, the managers were inadequately prepared, did not advance their arguments coherently, and failed to expose gaps and inconsistencies in the respondent's presentation. Fifth, the development of Article 8, the exhortation to the Baltimore grand jury, might have saved the day for the prosecution, but the managers failed to pursue it vigorously. Sixth, Samuel Chase's attorneys outclassed John Randolph and his colleagues, showing superior preparation, logic, and control.

Samuel Chase's embroilment with the House of Representatives and the Senate is instructive in several respects. Especially notable is the superiority of his attorneys, who deflected most of the managers' arguments and won an acquittal that would seem scarcely in doubt if one looked only at the transcript of the trial rather than at the political milieu in which it took place. That an irascible and partisan official can win in a trial conducted and judged by his political opponents presents evidence that partisanship is not an absolute determinant in an impeachment trial.

Certain issues raised in the William Blount and John Pickering cases recurred in Samuel Chase's trial: (1) must an impeachable act be criminal? (2) must the offense charged be committed in office? and (3) must corrupt motives be demonstrated in order to convict? These questions were raised but not settled. The device, invented for the Pickering trial, of asking whether the respondent stood guilty as charged was resurrected briefly in Chase's trial. This locution is probably and justifiedly dead.

Justice Chase survived the challenge to his continuance in office and remained on the Supreme Court until his death in 1811. Certainly, he personified the harsh, fervently partisan jurist who had brought the judiciary to a low point in public confidence. Chase did not match the image enshrined in long and honored judicial tradition of the calm, impartial, and scrupulous judge. Even so, a majority supporting the justice's conviction was found only on his exclusion of a witness, on his requiring written questions and behaving rudely in James Callender's trial, and on his address to the Baltimore grand jury; none of the guilty votes on these three articles achieved the requisite two-thirds majority.

Their inability to convict Samuel Chase ended the drive of the Jeffersonians to cleanse the bench of their opponents by the impeachment method. Plans, if any existed, to move against John Marshall died with the Chase trial.

James Hawkins Peck. *State Historical Society of Missouri.*

5

James Hawkins Peck

The Judge was to be stung, mortified, degraded, rendered contemptible and ridiculous before the people of Missouri, and, if possible, worked out of his seat, that some one else might be worked into it more propitious towards these hollow and meretricious claims.

—William Wirt

The nation's fourth impeachment took place at the beginning of Andrew Jackson's first administration. The victory of the Democrats in 1828 signalled a new and energetic direction of United States policy.[1] Occasional evidence of the ferment of Jacksonian democracy can be detected in the impeachment and trial of James H. Peck in 1830 and 1831.

But the slender threads connecting Judge Peck to the Jacksonian epoch do not compare in significance with the major reasons for his impeachment: first, he was a judge during a period when courts were detested with as much ferocity as they had been in the early years of President Jefferson's administration, and second, he ruled against powerful political and financial figures in a land title case involving property in the former Louisiana territory. That ruling brought him to near ruin.

James H. Peck had been appointed to the federal bench by Democratic-Republican President James Monroe when Congress established a district court in the newly admitted state of Missouri in 1822. Peck had served as a Tennessee militiaman in the War of 1812. He moved to St. Louis in 1817 and established a law office. Other attorneys practicing in St. Louis at that time and destined to be involved in varying degrees with Peck's subsequent impeachment included David Barton, Thomas Hart Benton, Luke E. Lawless, and John Scott.[2] Barton and Benton became Missouri's first United States senators in 1821. Barton supported Peck's appointment as the first federal district judge for the newly created state, and Benton would later testify for the prosecution in the Peck trial. Lawless, a close legal and social associate of Benton's, directly initiated and pursued Judge Peck's impeachment; Scott, Missouri's first congressman, presented the petition calling for impeachment to the House of Representatives in 1826.

James H. Peck's impeachment arose from differences over land policies in the former Louisiana territory. The old French families, notably the influential Chouteaus, exerted strong pressure for settlement of uncertain land claims in favor of the claimants.[3] They and their supporters wanted the early land grants, however unclear the titles, to be recognized as lawful. They opposed overzealous reliance on technicalities and urged Congress to provide for settlements favorable to those whose claims might not be unassailably legal and might in some cases be unsupported by any documentation. Both Thomas Hart Benton and Luke E. Lawless were allied with the Chouteaus and wanted recognition of the ancient titles to be acknowledged without excessive expectation of proof of validity. Lines were sharply drawn on the issue of land policy. Lawless, Benton, and the Chouteaus would all be hostile to any court decision disallowing a claim for lack of definite legal proof of ownership—a powerful force to be arrayed against anyone.

Judge Peck ran afoul of this powerful force and, thereby, of the impeachment mechanism because of his ruling in one of many land claim cases, the status of which had become an intense political issue in Congress in the decade from 1822 to 1832. Because proof of ownership was often weak or lacking, Congress had assigned the sorting out of clouded titles under French or Spanish land grants to the federal district courts. J. F. Darby, a St. Louis attorney and a contemporary of Peck, observed that "up to the year 1811 there were not three perfect titles to land in the whole territory of Upper Louisiana."[4] The situation had not improved much when Judge Peck became a participant in the land claim cases.

Peck heard the first Spanish land grant case to be tried before a United States judge, *Antoine Soulard v. the United States*, in 1825.[5] An act of Congress in 1824 instructed a judge to determine that land granted under French or Spanish jurisdiction had been made by a proper authority and in addition the act required the judge to refer specifically in his decision to a treaty, law, or ordinance that justified conferring the claim.[6] Judge Peck made a comprehensive study of the Spanish regulations governing grants. The king of Spain had provided for sale or gifts of land by his local governors, some of whom the king empowered to subdelegate this authority to other Spanish agents. The regulations required those possessing land to secure title to it, have it surveyed, and be established on their property within a specified time; otherwise they forfeited the land.

Judge Peck, complying with the act of Congress, requested Antoine Soulard to show the authority of the Spanish official, in this
case the lieutenant governor, to make the grant claimed by Soulard
and to point out the specific law authorizing the grant. Although he
had been the surveyor of Upper Louisiana as an agent of Spain, Soulard could not comply with the request. He said he had lost the document proving that the concession had been made and could not
demonstrate that he had ever occupied or cultivated the land purportedly given to him by the Spanish government.

Peck ruled the Soulard claim invalid for want of authority in the
lieutenant governor to make such a gift, for failure of Soulard to
meet the requirements that the Spanish authorities had laid down
for validating land grants, and for absence of any law that could be
relied upon in support of the claim. Judge Peck stated in this key
ruling that his decision did not affect the mass of such claims, only
those that, like Antoine Soulard's, rested on inadequate evidence.[7]

Luke Edward Lawless, the losing attorney in the Soulard case, set
course immediately to reverse the decision. He was even more determined to insure that Judge Peck would not preside in any of the
other land claim cases en route to his court. Lawless's long struggle
to have Peck removed from the bench began soon after the judge announced his holding in the Soulard case.

Because of widespread interest in the case several attorneys asked
Judge Peck to publish his decision in a St. Louis newspaper, a request with which he complied in March 1826. His ruling was
printed in the *Republican*, a newspaper strongly opposed to Benton.
Several days later, on April 8, a letter criticizing Peck's decision appeared in another newspaper, the *Enquirer*, a paper once edited by
Senator Benton and continuing to support him. The anonymous letter, signed "A Citizen," was subsequently revealed to have been
written by Lawless.[8]

Judge Peck held the letter to be a contempt of court, sentenced
Lawless to twenty-four hours in jail, and suspended him from practice in federal court for eighteen months. As the basis of his contempt ruling, Peck found that Lawless acted "with intent to impair
the public confidence in the upright intentions of said court, and to
bring odium upon the court, and especially with intent to impress
the public mind, and particularly many litigants in this court, that
they are not to expect justice in the cases now pending therein."[9]

Lawless's letter and Peck's reaction to it form the heart of the controversy that led to the judge's impeachment. In the letter, Lawless
listed eighteen alleged errors in the Soulard ruling. Peck viewed the

allegations as deliberate, malicious distortions of his decision. The eighteen criticisms and Judge Peck's refutation of them, endlessly and repetitiously debated in the impeachment trial, were mainly technical. However, to illustrate the nature of the argument, I will discuss three of them.

Lawless claimed that in the Soulard decision Peck had held that "by the [Spanish] ordinance of 1754, a sub-delegate was prohibited from making a grant in consideration of services rendered."[10] The key word is *prohibited*. Peck's opinion had stated that the Spanish ordinance did not *authorize* the specific grant received by Antoine Soulard. Peck noted that the "A Citizen" letter distorted his language and meaning by reporting him as saying that grants for services had been prohibited, when he had said only that a particular grant had not been authorized. Peck said that this misrepresentation would dash the hopes of all claimants whose grants of land were based on services to Spain; he had carefully limited his ruling to the Soulard grant, he pointed out, and only because it lacked the necessary authorization. Lawless waved aside this criticism, calling it a quibble over words and merely a violation of grammatical propriety. The judge had the better of this dispute; it is impossible to accept an assertion that saying a particular act is not authorized is the same thing as saying all such acts are prohibited. Such a shift of terms goes well beyond loose grammar.

A second example from "A Citizen" finds Lawless alleging that Judge Peck said that "a sub-delegate in Louisiana was not a sub-delegate as contemplated" by a particular Spanish ordinance. The judge had actually stated that "the Lieutenant Governor of Upper Louisiana was not a sub-delegate."[11] He pointed out that the "A Citizen" treatment of his ruling not only misrepresented his meaning but also made him sound ridiculous. Peck had said that a particular official, the lieutenant governor, had not been empowered to serve as a subdelegate of the king of Spain in granting title to land. Lawless twisted this statement to have Judge Peck say that a sub-delegate was not a subdelegate—obviously ridiculous, as the judge pointed out.

The last example concerns the eighteenth criticism in the "A Citizen" letter. In it Lawless claimed that Peck had ruled that acts of Congress recognizing rights of claimants with incomplete titles did not protect claimants who had unconfirmed titles. Peck made no such general disavowal of rights under unconfirmed titles, but held only that no act of Congress authorized confirmation of such a claim as Soulard's.[12] Again, Judge Peck protested the twisting of his words and expressed concern over the serious alarm Lawless's misrepresentation would create in other claimants who would assume, thanks to the "A Citizen" distortion, that their titles could not be confirmed under any circumstances. Lawless retorted that the assumption that such acts did not protect unconfirmed titles had been made by Lawless himself, not by Judge Peck.[13]

This statement is one of the strangest aspects of the Peck-Lawless controversy. Several times during the impeachment trial Lawless insisted that he had assumed that relevant acts of Congress did not validate unconfirmed titles, and that Lawless did not intend to impute such a belief to Judge Peck. No clue exists in the "A Citizen" letter that Lawless had suddenly switched to presenting his own instead of the judge's position. Logic is against such a reading, for how could Judge Peck be criticized for an interpretation of the law made by someone else?

Peck described the "A Citizen" letter as a deliberate distortion of his decision, devoid of valid criticisms. Nor, Peck asserted, had Lawless even touched upon the judge's basic assumption that Soulard had abandoned his claim voluntarily by failing to act in accordance with the Spanish regulations calling for grants to be surveyed, possessed within three months, and cultivated within a specified time.

Lawless, for his part, considered himself entirely justified in publishing an analysis of an already printed decision. He invoked freedom of the press in support of his right to criticize a judicial opinion. He also asserted that the "A Citizen" letter contained nothing either false or malicious; even if it had, he said, he could be charged only with a libel, not a contempt. His sentence for contempt "was not only illegal, but unjust, tyrannical and oppressive."[14]

The Soulard case had been appealed to the United States Supreme Court, and Lawless might have been satisfied to wait for its ruling, hoping for a reversal of Judge Peck's decision.[15] But preventing Peck from hearing pending land claim cases could not be achieved even were the Soulard decision to be reversed. So Lawless began a single-minded drive to have the judge impeached.

Peck's behavior could be found wanting only if Lawless demonstrated that it fitted the category "high crimes and misdemeanors"; the judge obviously had done nothing that could be classified as treason or bribery. Lawless, therefore, had to show that Judge Peck's punishment of him for contempt of court did lie within that category. He also had to find a member of the House of Representatives willing to introduce an impeachment resolution—a task in which he succeeded.

Missouri Congressman John Scott brought this seemingly parochial controversy before the House on December 8, 1826, eight months after publication of the "A Citizen" letter and Peck's sentencing its author for contempt. Scott, at this time an ally of Thomas Hart Benton, presented a petition from Lawless accusing Judge Peck of acting in "a manner cruel, vindictive, and unjust."[16] Congressman Scott called for Peck's impeachment. The petition was referred to the Judiciary Committee, of which Daniel Webster (Federalist, later Whig, Massachusetts) was chairman. The committee took no action, and the matter ended. Two years later Congressman George McDuffie (Democrat, South Carolina) reintroduced Lawless's petition. Once more it was disregarded.

Despite the two rejections, Lawless persisted in his effort to get Peck off the bench, and the third try brought success. One year after the second failure, on December 15, 1829, Congressman McDuffie again presented an impeachment petition. This time it came before a more hospitable Judiciary Committee chaired by James Buchanan (Democrat, Pennsylvania).[17] In the following months the Judiciary Committee examined witnesses and also permitted Judge Peck to question them. Congressman Buchanan reported to the House of Representatives on March 23, 1830 the committee's recommendation that James H. Peck be impeached "of high misdemeanors in office."[18]

Peck sent a memorial to the House of Representatives after the Judiciary Committee had recommended his impeachment. He noted that only one charge—finding Lawless's "A Citizen" letter a contempt and sentencing Lawless for publishing it—had been made against him. Grounds for the charge were, he said, without foundation. He asked for, and received, permission to send a statement to the House of Representatives.

Judge Peck's statement was presented to the House on April 14, 1830. It included a review of the history of the land grant litigation and described his careful preparation for appraising claims under titles that were lost or confused. He referred to the many land claim cases comprising the docket and observed that "Mr. Lawless is concerned as attorney and counsel in more than one-third of them."[19] Peck believed that some of the litigants had scant legal basis for their claims and had taken care "to interest in their success many of the gentlemen of the bar, whose compensation, from the evidence

96

reported by the Judiciary Committee, it is presumable was contingent, and who, having, therefore, large interests at stake on the result, felt, very naturally, a degree of solicitude for the event not less keen than that of their clients."[20]

Peck's statement warned the House that his accuser, Luke E. Lawless, had a continuing personal and financial interest in winning the Soulard and other such cases, an interest that could account for the relentless effort to get Judge Peck out of the way after he had ruled Antoine Soulard's claim invalid and even though the precipitating event had occurred four years earlier.

Peck referred to Lawless's "A Citizen" letter as a "tissue of assumptions . . . not one of which is true in point of fact . . . and some of them so glaringly and ridiculously absurd, as to have satisfied any reader, who believed the statement, that the Judge was totally destitute either of common sense or common honesty."[21] He noted that Antoine Soulard's case had already been appealed to the Supreme Court and commented ironically that Lawless "could scarcely have intended to pay Judge Peck so high a compliment, as to imply that the Supreme Court of the United States would follow his track through all these causes, and *establish his errors into law* as fast as he should commit them."[22] The judge reviewed the authorities on contempt and acknowledged an attorney's right to challenge a judge's decision as long as he did it fairly. He concluded with the comment: "Judge Peck is perfectly aware of the purposes to be answered by his removal, and is, therefore, not at all surprised at the pertinacity with which it has been sought for the last four years."[23]

One week after hearing James H. Peck's statement, the House of Representatives began to debate the impeachment resolution. Most of the speeches revealed either forthright attacks on or defenses of his conduct. But Edward Everett (National-Republican, Massachusetts), proposed a compromise. Everett, "though not holding the Judge altogether unworthy of censure, was unwilling to proceed so far as to impeach"; he offered a resolution expressing House disapproval of Peck but stating that "there was not sufficient evidence before it to justify his impeachment for a high misdemeanor in office." Tristam Burges (Federalist, Rhode Island) wanted to soften Everett's proposal. He suggested that the resolution state that even though the House could not entirely support Judge Peck's conduct, "yet, that perceiving no evidence of ill intent on his part, it would not sanction the impeachment."[24] The House did not accept either of these mild censures.

The impeachment vote, taken on April 22, 1830, carried 123 to 49 in a House of Representatives composed of 139 Democrats and 74 National-Republicans and Federalists, a 65 percent majority for the Democrats; only 19 of the majority party members voted against impeaching Judge Peck.[25] In addition to Lawless's persistent pressure, another factor may explain why Congress tied itself up in an impeachment concerned with just one alleged improper act. That factor was a deep and growing hostility to Supreme Court decisions that moved in the direction of consolidating power in the national government. State laws that opponents of the Court viewed as legitimate were being struck down as national authority was asserted at the expense of state authority.

Hostility toward the federal courts peaked in the decade from 1821 to 1831 and resulted in serious discussions in Congress about ways to halt the centralizing tendency of federal court decisions. Congress considered passing laws to make the Senate the final appellate court, to limit terms of federal judges to six years, to permit presidential removal of judges upon request of the legislatures of two-thirds of the states, and to abolish the right to appeal state court decisions to the Supreme Court.[26] Amid this deluge of efforts to restrict the courts, the proceedings against Judge Peck may have appeared as a convenient vehicle by which some congressmen could express their anger at the federal bench in general.

Democrats initiated and conducted the prosecution. Most Jacksonians preferred a relaxed policy of settling land claims in favor of those claimants who could not produce irrefutable proof of ownership. Thus, Judge Peck's Soulard decision would be offensive to many of them, and accounts in part for the partisan bias apparent in the House of Representatives decision to move forward. The House elected a five-member board of managers, four Democrats and one Federalist, to prosecute Peck. James Buchanan served as chairman; the other managers were George McDuffie, Ambrose Spencer (Democrat, New York), Henry R. Storrs (Federalist, New York), and Charles A. Wickliffe (Democrat, Kentucky).

On May 4, 1830 the Senate convened as the High Court of Impeachment, Vice-President John C. Calhoun (Democrat, South Carolina) presiding. This session contained thirty-six Democrats, six Whigs, three Federalists, and three National-Republicans—a 75 percent Democratic party majority composed of senators with varying degrees of commitment to Andrew Jackson's brand of democracy. Three future presidents sat in the Congress that impeached and tried Judge Peck: James K. Polk (Democrat) and James Buchanan in the House of Representatives and John Tyler (Whig) in the Senate. Both Polk and Buchanan voted for Peck's impeachment, and Buchanan served as chairman of the managers. When the Senate voted at the end of the trial, Tyler voted to convict.[27]

The trial opened with Buchanan's reading of the single impeachment article. It detailed Judge Peck's decision against Antoine Soulard, appeal of that decision to the United States Supreme Court, publication in the *Republican* of Peck's ruling, publication in the *Enquirer* of Lawless's letter criticizing that ruling, and Peck's holding of Lawless in contempt therefore. No one disputed the fact that all of these actions had taken place; the only substantial question concerned the legality of Judge Peck's punishment of Lawless.

The article of impeachment described the conduct of Judge Peck as exhibiting unawareness "of the solemn duties of his station, and that he held the same . . . during good behavior only." It charged him "with intention wrongfully and unjustly to oppress, imprison, and otherwise injure the said Luke Edward Lawless" and with acting "arbitrarily, oppressively, and unjustly, and under color and pretence that the said Luke Edward Lawless was answerable to the said court." The article referred to Peck's sentencing Lawless to jail as an act "to the great disparagement of public justice, the abuse of judicial authority, and to the subversion of the liberties of the people of the United States."[28] The question of what constitutes a contempt received extensive discussion during the Peck trial and led to a statute changing the provisions of the federal law on contempts.

James H. Peck and one of his attorneys, William Wirt, appeared before the Senate on May 11, 1830.[29] Peck, noting that the affair from which his impeachment arose had occurred four years before, requested time to organize his defense. The Senate granted him two weeks.

Jonathan Meredith, another of Judge Peck's attorneys, read the judge's answer to the impeachment article when the Senate reconvened as the High Court of Impeachment on May 25. As he had in his earlier statement to the House of Representatives, Peck gave a thorough and temperate response to the impeachment article. He explained why he had published his ruling in Antoine Soulard's case and noted English and United States precedents as justification for doing so. Next he analyzed his reasons for viewing Lawless's "A Citizen" letter as a contempt; he added that if he had erred, he had committed merely an innocent error of judgment, "free from all feelings, designs, and intention on his part, wrongfully, arbitrarily and unjustly, to oppress, imprison, or otherwise to injure the said

Luke E. Lawless, under color of law."[30] He contended that in the absence of proof of bad intent, his impeachment could not be sustained.

Because of the magnitude of Lawless's misrepresentations in the "A Citizen" letter, Judge Peck believed that the senators could understand the matter only if he explained the controversies surrounding the land grant cases. The Soulard claim, he pointed out, had not been substantiated under either Spanish or United States law. Having thoroughly discussed the grounds for his decision, Peck examined the misleading and false statements that Lawless had published about it. He said of Lawless, "That a man of sufficient discrimination to be placed as leading counsel in the management of cases of so much importance, could have accumulated such a mass of misrepresentation, through innocent mistake, was, and still is, in the opinion of this respondent, utterly incredible."[31]

Lawless had written the "A Citizen" letter, Peck told the Senate, with the intention of bringing the judge into disrespect and of inflaming the groups seeking settlements of their land claims. Thereby, Lawless hoped "to array against the Judge, a power which might overawe and control him in the decision of the pending cases, or render him perfectly odious if he should dare to follow up in these cases the principles which he had laid down in Soulard's."[32] Describing Lawless's response to the contempt, the judge stated that not only had he declined to purge himself, but had also read in court a paper reasserting the truth of what he had said in the "A Citizen" letter "in open defiance and contempt of the opinion which had been solemnly pronounced by the court, and to the evil example of the bystanders, and of all others who should have business to do in the court."[33]

The managers did not deliver their reply to Judge Peck's statement until December 13, 1830, in the second session of the Twenty-First Congress and more than six months after the judge had responded to the impeachment article. James Buchanan reported that the House of Representatives had studied Peck's answer, considered him guilty, and stood ready to prove the impeachment article. Witnesses for both sides were announced. Buchanan requested a postponement because one of the prosecution witnesses "had been overset on his way and had his collarbone twice broken, but was likely to recover and to be able to attend the court."[34]

Therefore, the Senate adjourned the trial until December 20, the day George McDuffie opened the case for the managers. He began his argument by claiming that the Lawless "A Citizen" letter, even if false and malicious, could be challenged only by a libel suit. McDuffie next stated that the letter presented a correct analysis of Judge Peck's ruling in Soulard's case; hence, the punishment of Lawless was illegal and autocratic.

No legislative act, McDuffie argued, gave a judge power to punish as a contempt anything not done in the presence of the court and not resulting in an interference with the administration of justice. Lawless's publication did not meet either requirement: it was not done in court and it did not interfere with the judicial process because the Soulard case had already been settled. The only proper course open to Peck, McDuffie insisted, would have been to sue Lawless for libel, a process requiring indictment and trial. Instead, Peck had summarily punished the person who had offended him, a person no longer within the supervision of the court.

Manager McDuffie agreed that judges must be able to punish an act threatening the process of justice. But he reminded the Senate that the Judiciary Act of 1789, which authorized a judge to punish a contempt occurring in any case before him, restricted punishment to fine and imprisonment only. Therefore, Judge Peck had exceeded the law when he suspended Lawless from practice.

Next the manager turned to the "A Citizen" letter and reviewed its eighteen points as sedulously as had Peck but with different conclusions on each point. He opened his analysis by stating that the judge's interpretation of the letter and his punishment of Lawless showed the "extraordinary process of hypercritical cavilling by which he has managed to distort a perfectly innocent publication into a false and defamatory libel." After he had summarized all the points in the letter and had had it read to the Senate, McDuffie commented that the judge's reaction proved him "guilty of a wanton, unprovoked and outrageous act of judicial tyranny, which calls aloud for exemplary punishment."[35]

Manager McDuffie supported the accuracy of Lawless's letter and attacked Peck's review of it as a misrepresentation. McDuffie criticized Peck for violating freedom of the press, hoping that he would "not live to see the day, when the liberty of the press shall be scouted and sneered out of the Senate of the United States by a vain and arrogant pretender to judicial infallibility."[36]

Judge Peck's analysis of the Lawless letter as presented earlier to both the House of Representatives and the Senate does not support Manager McDuffie's comments, certainly not the "uninterrupted stream of denunciation and calumny" that he purported to find.[37] Nor do the language and tone of Peck's various responses support

McDuffie's frequent reference to the judge as tyrannical, high-handed, or vengeful.

The day after McDuffie's introductory statement, the managers called their first witness, Luke E. Lawless, who sought to establish that Judge Peck had exhibited passion and bitterness when he sentenced Lawless for contempt of court. His "A Citizen" letter, Lawless insisted, was not a contempt either factually or intentionally, and Judge Peck could not legally punish his publication of it. No justification at all existed for Peck's suspending him from practicing law, he added.

Jonathan Meredith questioned Lawless when the managers had completed their questioning of the star witness. Again, Lawless asserted with vigor and assurance that he had published his letter criticizing the Soulard decision for the purpose of championing free speech and a free press. He insisted that the "A Citizen" letter was neither a libel nor a contempt. However, if held to be a libel, it could be punished only in the usual way: by indictment and trial by jury. Meredith asked why other land cases had been removed from the court after the Soulard decision; Lawless replied that they had been withdrawn "because the parties felt certain, after hearing Judge Peck's decision in Soulard's case, that their causes would be decided against, and they hoped that if the Supreme Court should reverse his decision, Congress would interfere, and grant them some relief." Lawless said that 146 land cases had been withdrawn from the courts and that he served as attorney in "perhaps some 10 or 15."[38]

Six other prosecution witnesses followed Lawless, all but one of whom had been present at the contempt hearing before Judge Peck. They testified that Peck spoke in a vehement, excited, acrimonious, and abusive manner. Four of them reported being startled by Peck's observation that in China a convicted slanderer's house was painted black "as emblematic of the heart of the inhabitant, and as a warning to all persons to beware of him."[39] These witnesses also enlarged upon the theme of contempt, pointing out, variously, that Peck had no authority to punish Lawless for comments on a settled case, that the opinion of a judge was a proper subject for criticism, and that Judge Peck's treatment of Lawless jeopardized guarantees of fundamental importance—free speech and a free press. They supported the previously advanced argument that had Peck chosen to move against Lawless for libel, indictment and trial by jury would be required; if convicted, Lawless would receive a sentence determined by another judge, not by Peck, the offended party.

Henry S. Geyer appeared as one of the managers' witnesses.[40] He became counsel for Lawless after the contempt had been levied. He had entered the case, he said, because of public and congressional antagonism for judges and because of mounting demands to limit the tenure of the federal judiciary. Geyer feared that Judge Peck's punishment of Lawless would increase hostility against the bench; he hoped to convince Peck to change his ruling and thus remove a further cause of public enmity against judges. Geyer, asked by Peck's lawyer about the desire of local attorneys to have the Soulard decision published, said, "I expressed such a wish, and it was the general wish of the bar. The effect of the decision upon other claims made it a matter of interest to know what was the prospect of their being confirmed."[41]

Another peculiarity of the trial, nearly as fantastic as the reports of the blackening of slanderers' houses in China, concerned frequent references to Judge Peck's eye problems. Geyer noted that Peck "was then in feeble health, and his eyes, I think, were bound up, or covered with goggles."[42] Other witnesses commented about Judge Peck's eyes being bandaged, making it necessary to read recorded testimony to him. J. F. Darby, a contemporary of Peck, reported that the judge

> had conceived a notion that if he exposed his eyes to the light he would become blind. Whenever, therefore, he was about to leave his room to come out in the face of open day, he had a large white handkerchief bound around his eyes, so that he could not see at all; . . . [he would] hear and try causes perfectly blindfolded. . . . It was a most singular and striking case to see a judge on the bench, holding court and dispensing justice, with a large white handkerchief tied around his head.[43]

Thomas Hart Benton made a brief appearance as a witness for the managers at the end of the trial, just before the summary speeches began. As a young lawyer he had specialized in land claim cases, and Manager Wickliffe asked about some extracts Benton had made from a Spanish ordinance on gifts of land. No significance attached to this part of Benton's testimony because it bore no relationship at all to the land grant problems central to the Peck-Lawless conflict. Wickliffe then inquired about Lawless's deportment in court. Benton said it was "respectful; but it is, as I have said, impassioned and warm."[44] Benton's testimony did not affect the course of the trial. However, as a prominent senator appearing for the prosecution before his brother senators, he might be viewed by the managers as a valuable asset. Testimony of the prosecution witnesses tended to demonstrate that Judge Peck had shown intense displeasure and animosity when he sentenced Lawless for contempt of court, and that the sentence itself had been unjustified and illegal.

Jonathan Meredith opened the case for James H. Peck on January 5, 1831, with a concise review of the charges and facts as Peck's defenders saw them. He described the difficulties in determining the land grant claims and noted the suspicious circumstances of the Soulard case:

> the concession was alleged to be lost; the claim had never been presented for confirmation . . . ; no establishment or cultivation of the land was pretended, nor, though [Soulard] was himself the surveyor, had there been any location or survey until the latter end of February, 1804—several months after the Treaty of Session was publicly known, and but a few days before the possession of Upper Louisiana was actually delivered to the authorities of the United States.[45]

Meredith argued that these facts had not been satisfactorily accounted for in the Soulard trial; such inadequate explanations as had been given came from witnesses who were also claimants.

The "A Citizen" letter, said Meredith, presented a gross misrepresentation of the Soulard decision and was intended to arouse public anger. If the public believed that the letter truly represented Judge Peck's conclusions, "no rational mind could account for them on other ground than judicial corruption—for no ignorance this side of idiocy, could have fallen into such egregious error. . . . We will show that these effects were not confined to the land claimants of Missouri, . . . as evinced by memorials to Congress to deprive the District Court of its entire jurisdiction over land causes, and to vest it in another tribunal."[46]

Following Meredith's opening statement, James H. Peck's witnesses were called, and from January 6 to 11, 1831, the Senate heard their testimony. They portrayed the judge as courteous, firm, and amiable. Spencer Pettis, a Democratic congressman from Missouri, praised Judge Peck's private as well as judicial deportment: "in delivering an opinion at great length, [Judge Peck] becomes warm, and gesticulates much. . . . He is very firm but very mild in his disposition."[47]

Peck's witnesses referred to Lawless as the one having a reputation for unruly conduct. More than once he had made harsh and immoderate comments about a jurist who decided a case against him.

One witness, Sheriff John K. Walker of St. Louis County, recalled that Lawless wanted to fight a duel with Peck. Walker reported Lawless as saying that "if Judge Peck would pledge himself to meet him, and give him a chance at him . . . as soon as he recovered his eyesight, he would let him off from going to Washington City" to face impeachment. Walker doubted that the judge would gratify this wish, and Lawless said, "By God, then, I will have him before the Senate."[48] This threat illustrates Lawless's control of the course of action against Peck. It does not, however, support the hypothesis that he mainly wanted to have the judge permanently off the bench so he could not sit in future land claim cases—unless, of course, Lawless intended to slay Peck, a not unusual occurrence in Missouri in that day.

Robert Wash, a defense witness and judge of the supreme court of Missouri, sought to refute the manager's contention that the "A Citizen" letter could be characterized as harmless because the public need only compare it with Peck's published opinion in the Soulard case and form a sound judgment on whether Lawless's criticism was valid. Judge Wash explained Peck's objection to this argument; the letter had been printed in one newspaper and the court decision in another. According to Wash, Peck said that the "A Citizen" letter and his Soulard decision would probably not be readily compared because of the fact "that one would be read by one class of readers, and the other by a different class; . . . that the two might never be seen together; . . . that if the argument was a sound one, there would be no sense in that law or custom of China by which a calumniator was doomed to have his house blackened."[49]

That Wash recounted the reference to the Chinese practice of painting slanderers' houses black shows that this curious and irrelevant piece of information fascinated the respondent's witnesses as much as it had the prosecution's. Although referred to on six separate occasions in the defense testimony, the matter did not seem to have been of any importance except for the numerous recountings of it and for its bizarre connotations.

Summation of the case against Judge Peck began on January 17, 1831 with a speech by Ambrose Spencer, leading off for the managers. He noted the threat to the judiciary if Congress, spurred by the existing hatred of the courts, should propose a constitutional amendment establishing fixed and limited terms for federal judges. By demonstrating that the impeachment procedure stood to protect the country from overbearing jurists, Spencer argued that the Senate could forestall the disastrous blow to judicial independence that the removal of life tenure would cause. By finding Peck guilty, senators might be saving the entire federal judiciary from serious harm.

Manager Spencer described an impeachable judicial offense as an illegal act committed with bad intent by a judge in his official capacity, or as an otherwise legal act not warranted in a given instance. He said that Luke E. Lawless had written a harmless letter; Peck had reacted to it with violence because it exposed the weakness of his opinion in the Soulard case, an opinion that was "launched forth with high expectations that it might procure for its author a niche in the temple of fame, or a judgeship in a superior court."[50] Spencer saw Peck's reaction to the letter as the vindictive response of a man deprived of present and future honors. This explanation for Peck's behavior had not been brought forth in the trial and was never documented or even explained. It should also be remembered that several St. Louis attorneys, including Henry S. Geyer, had asked Peck to publish his Soulard decision. The allegation that the judge had published his decision for his own aggrandizement stood inaccurate and unproved.

The next spokesman for the prosecution, Manager Charles A. Wickliffe, examined the requirements for impeachable offenses and insisted that an indictable act need not be proved because "any official act committed or omitted by the judge, which is a violation of the condition upon which he holds his office, is an impeachable offense under the constitution." Wickliffe, reaching for historical support for his argument, claimed that the central issue in John Pickering's trial had been the judge's failure to require bond in the *Eliza* case. The manager continued: "If precedent is to have any authority in this court, I consider the question settled by the Senate of the United States, in the trial of Judge Pickering."[51] It is impossible to see how Wickliffe could have gotten that impression from the Pickering trial, or even if he had, how it would aid his case against Peck.

Trying to impress the Senate with Peck's alleged vanity and arrogance, Manager Wickliffe alluded to him as the "Lord Chief Justice of Missouri." The blackening of houses in China also appealed to Wickliffe, who said that Peck "dared not adopt his Chinese law . . . he could not cause Lawless' house to be blackened; he, nevertheless, strove to blacken his reputation by consigning him to the walls of a jail."[52] In conclusion, Wickliffe urged the Senate to uphold freedom of the press and convict Judge Peck of violating it by his punishment of Luke E. Lawless.

Summation of James H. Peck's defense began on January 19, 1831 with a speech by Jonathan Meredith. He advanced four propositions held to be the heart of the defense: (1) the federal district court had power to punish for contempt; (2) Lawless's conduct was a contempt; (3) Peck had legal justification for punishing Lawless; and (4) even should a determination be made that the Lawless case was not an appropriate one for exercise of the court's contempt power, Judge Peck could not be impeached for that act because it "did not proceed from the evil and malicious intention with which it is charged, and which it is absolutely necessary should have accompanied it, to constitute the guilt of an impeachable offense."[53] Carefully analyzing the misrepresentations contained in the Lawless letter, Meredith said they were likely to undermine public confidence in Peck's integrity or his intelligence. Meredith also insisted that Luke E. Lawless's thorough familiarity with land claim matters made his distortions of Peck's ruling willful and intentionally designed to affect pending cases, a design fulfilled by the withdrawal of 146 such cases.

William Wirt closed for Peck's side in a speech lasting for three days—an elaborate, closely reasoned performance. Wirt began with a review of the distorted picture the managers had drawn of Judge Peck's character and words. Citing specific instances of statements wrongfully attributed to Peck, Wirt said the statements were often the opposite of the judge's actual and documented position and could not be found in any records cited by the managers.

He insisted that to be impeachable the act complained of must be indictable and done with bad motives; he reminded the Senate that the burden lay on the managers "to make good the charge, both as to the *illegality of the act* and the *guilt of the intention*. It is not enough for them to prove that the act was unlawful (though *this* I apprehend is beyond their power) but they must go farther, and prove that this unlawful act was done with a guilty intention."[54] Relying on his extensive examination of authorities and precedents relating to a court's powers to punish for contempt. Wirt argued that Peck had acted lawfully. He said that no evidence of guilty motives had been presented and no impeachment in England or in the United States had ever been based on a mere error in judgment. He did not concede, however, that Peck had made any such error.

Wirt analyzed the Soulard case and the tangled history of the Spanish land grants, including specific instances of forgeries and frauds. He demonstrated that Judge Peck had studied the land grant claims carefully before giving judgment and that he had sound reasons for being skeptical about the Soulard claim. Vanity, Wirt said, had not induced Peck to publish his Soulard opinion, nor would fair criticism of that opinion have aroused any animosity in Peck or in his supporters. "It is the *foul criticism* and the *dishonest view* to which we object. It is the gross misrepresentation, the lawless spirit, the contemptuous purpose, the scandalizing the court with the wicked intention of destroying its authority—it was this that was the subject of punishment and the proper subject, according to every authority."[55]

Having previously demanded that the managers produce any evidence that courts were entitled to punish for contempt only in pending cases, Wirt noted that they had been unable to do so. He gave numerous examples of contempts levied for actions related to decided cases and reminded the Senate of Lawless's own testimony showing that he intended his "A Citizen" letter to affect cases on their way to Judge Peck's court. Such action by Lawless displayed two characteristics of contempt, Wirt argued, "scandalizing the court . . . [and] prejudging the public mind with regard to pending causes."[56]

Next, Wirt noted that Lawless had expected a large financial return from his handling of Soulard's and other land claim cases, and that his anger at Peck's ruling had inspired the "A Citizen" attack on the judge. "*His* was the situation and *his* the temper for revenge," Wirt said of Lawless.[57]

Wirt then asked why Lawless had not merely informed his clients that the Soulard case had been lost, that he was appealing the decision, and that he expected reversal of Peck's ruling. Why had Lawless not signed the "A Citizen" letter, Wirt wondered. Stating that Lawless was motivated by revenge, Wirt concluded: "The Judge was to be stung, mortified, degraded, rendered contemptible and ridiculous before the people of Missouri, and, if possible, worked out of his seat, that some one else might be worked into it more propitious towards these hollow and meretricious claims."[58]

The trial concluded with speeches by managers Henry R. Storrs and James Buchanan. Storrs began with a review of English and United States cases on contempt. Contempt could occur, Storrs argued, only by virtue of an actual obstruction of judicial proceedings or by insulting references to the judge during the course of a trial. He ended his discussion with a survey of the first nine points in Lawless's "A Citizen" letter; each criticism of Judge Peck's decision, Storrs insisted, was accurate and written in respectful language.

Buchanan opened with a short comment on freedom of the press, a freedom he believed Judge Peck's punishment of Lawless had violated. Next he discussed the nature of an impeachable offense: "I freely admit we are bound to prove that the respondent has violated the constitution, or some known law of the land. This I think was the principle fairly to be deduced from all the arguments on the trial of Judge Chase."[59] Thus, the manager voluntarily added to the burden of the prosecution by stating that it must prove that James H. Peck had violated a law.

Like his fellow manager Wickliffe, Buchanan tortured the meaning of John Pickering's impeachment trial by citing it as a Senate precedent for convicting a judge whose decisions were contrary to law, and then adding that the managers in Pickering's trial had not been required to demonstrate bad intent; Pickering's intoxication on the bench, he said, constituted "gross official behavior. Would the Senate in that case have gravely listened to an argument to prove that the judge might have got drunk without any evil intention? Certainly not . . . the Senate inferred his intention from his conduct, and turned him out of office."[60]

James Buchanan stood on shaky ground. If the Chase trial in 1805 proved serviceable to his argument that the managers must show a violation of the law in order to persuade the Senate to find Judge Peck guilty, Buchanan's reference to John Pickering's trial could only remind informed senators that the decision in that case did not rest upon an illegal act. It rested instead upon the pragmatic necessity of removing a malperforming jurist whose motives in getting drunk had never been mentioned by anyone at his trial.

In his review of the allegations in the "A Citizen" letter, Manager Buchanan claimed that it set forth fair criticism of Judge Peck's opinion, did not misrepresent that opinion, and contained no disrespectful language. Buchanan concluded with a plea for Peck's conviction because impeachment provided the only means for removing a tyrannical judge. If the Senate failed to convict Peck, people "will soon begin to inquire whether the judicial office ought not to be limited. . . . If the people must either be cursed during a long life with an arbitrary and oppressive judge . . . or the constitution must be so amended as to limit the term of office of the inferior judges, I should choose the last alternative, as the least of two great evils."[61] Thus, he urged the Senate to recognize that the case of one federal judge threatened overpowering consequences. A failure to convict might result in putting federal trial judges on fixed terms of office.

The managers' case rested upon several bases. First, they claimed that Peck illegally punished Lawless. They insisted that had Lawless's letter been shown to be inaccurate or malicious, which they argued it had not, the only legal remedy would be an action for libel. Such an action required trial by jury, not summary punishment handed out by the victim of the libel. Their second major claim concerned Judge Peck's purported violation of freedom of the press; any citizen, including a lawyer, they said, could express fair criticisms on public matters without suffering punishment for doing so. Third in their catalogue of Peck's misdeeds, the managers argued that his punishment of Lawless displayed a vindictive spirit prompted by rage at Lawless's criticism of the Soulard ruling. The managers alleged (without substantiation) that Peck had counted on the ruling to bring him fame and higher judicial office. Finally, they contended that contempt of court consisted only of an action (1) committed in the presence of the court, or (2) calculated to impede justice, or (3) addressed to a pending case. Lawless's publication of a critical letter met none of these requirements.

Peck's attorneys in their summation countered the managers' claims point by point. They sought to refute the charge of abuse of the contempt power by citing English and American precedents supporting the authority of courts to punish for contempts like Lawless's. They insisted that Judge Peck respected freedom of the press and had never spoken or acted in any manner to the contrary. Why, Peck's attorneys asked, if the "A Citizen" letter represented a factual treatment of the Soulard decision, had Lawless not signed it? Instead of publishing the letter, why had he not merely informed his clients of the outcome of the case and of his expectation that it would be reversed? As to the managers' third claim, bad motives, Peck's attorneys pointed out that the judge's reputation for fairness had been supported by several witnesses; bad motives, respondent's lawyers argued, could instead be found in Lawless's relentless pursuit of Peck. They commented on Lawless's reputation for hotheaded remarks, and said that he had reacted so vigorously to Peck's decision because of disappointment at losing a case upon which much of his present and probable future revenue depended. This explained Lawless's vendetta against the judge. Peck's attorneys stated that the "A Citizen" letter constituted a contempt because it did not present an accurate treatment of the Antoine Soulard decision. The writer intended the letter to arouse hostility against Judge Peck and thereby affect pending land claim cases; moreover, they pointed out, the Soulard case had been appealed to the Supreme Court and so could not be classified as settled.

Echoes of the earlier impeachment trials were heard. Must an impeachment be grounded on an indictable offense as was claimed in Samuel Chase's trial and, to lesser degrees, in William Blount's and John Pickering's? Must knowing and illegal intention be proved in order to sustain a verdict of guilty? This question had come up many times in Judge Pickering's trial. Is an alleged incorrect ruling by a judge a proper subject for impeachment, a question occurring frequently in Justice Chase's trial? These questions run through many of the succeeding trials also; spokesmen for one side or the other have referred to preceding impeachment trials as having established a precedent favorable to their cause even though these matters were, and remain, debatable.

When James H. Peck's trial ended, the Senate sat once more as the High Court of Impeachment to reach its decision. On January 31, 1831 the vote was taken. Twenty-one senators found Peck guilty, twenty-two not guilty. The guilty votes were cast by eighteen Democrats, two Whigs, and one Federalist. Senators voting not guilty included fifteen Democrats, three Whigs, two National-Republicans, and two Federalists.[62]

A composite portrait of the senator who voted to convict Judge Peck proves less easy to compose than was the portrait of the senator who wanted to try William Blount, or to convict John Pickering or Samuel Chase. A study of the vote does reveal, however, that senators most likely to vote Peck guilty were Democrats and resided in a southern or border state, where the greatest antagonism existed toward the federal judiciary. By voting against Judge Peck, states-righters in the Senate may have been showing their opposition to the nationalizing trend of the federal judiciary. In addition, senators from the border states would usually be disposed toward a generous interpretation of questionable land claims, an interpretation that favored the claimant. They would thus be displeased with Judge Peck's position on land grants.

A composite portrait of the senator who voted Peck not guilty shows him to be a Democrat from the Northeast. The majority of non-Jacksonians (Whigs, Federalists, and National-Republicans) also voted not guilty; these men, with one exception, resided in the Northeast or North. Obviously, region was a factor in the Senate vote.

John Quincy Adams, commenting on partisan connotations of the Peck affair, observed that both senators from Andrew Jackson's home state, Tennessee, voted not guilty, showing, Adams believed, "conclusive proof that no personal influence of the President was exercised against the Judge . . . the will of the President was favorable to the Judge. It is highly probable that Jackson did not wish to see an impeachment of a Judge, commenced by [James] Buchanan, successfully carried through."[63]

Upon announcement of the Senate's verdict, Vice-President John C. Calhoun declared that "James H. Peck, Judge of the United States District Court for the District of Missouri, is ACQUITTED of the Charges contained in the Article of Impeachment exhibited against him by the House of Representatives."[64]

James Buchanan was not to be totally thwarted by his defeat in the Senate. He returned to the House of Representatives, where he introduced a bill restricting contempts in federal courts to (1) misbehavior in the presence of the court or so near thereto as to cause an obstruction of justice, (2) misbehavior in any official transaction, or (3) disobedience to any lawful command of the court. This bill foreclosed any possibility that Senate failure to convict Judge Peck could ever be used to support an argument that the Senate had confirmed his application of the contempt power. Congress swiftly enacted this measure, which became law on March 2, 1831, scarcely a month after Judge Peck's acquittal. James Buchanan had won partial revenge for his failure to convict Judge Peck.[65]

Congress concerned itself with James H. Peck from the end of 1826 until January 1831. The trial took just over a month. After his acquittal Peck returned to his post as federal district judge in Missouri, where he served until his death in 1836. Nearly one hundred years later, in 1932, Judge Charles B. Davis touched upon the impeachment ordeal at the presentation of a portrait of Judge Peck to the United States District Court for the Eastern District of Missouri. Davis observed that the acquittal "ended the great humiliation which had hung over Judge Peck for almost five years. . . . The outcome was a vindication, but the stigma of the indictment was not removed. The impeachment deprived the first judge of this Court of the position in public esteem to which he was justly entitled. . . . There is little reason to believe that the blight of his impeachment will ever be erased from Judge Peck's career."[66]

Because of the relative obscurity of the central figure, Peck's reputation will probably not achieve the rehabilitation conferred posthumously, if briefly, upon Andrew Johnson. Persisting interest in Johnson's trial and its political setting has brought new insights and judgments, so that more than a century after his death scholars continue to examine and reevaluate his place in history. James H. Peck is not likely to become an object of sustained scholarly study; if he were, the results would probably be favorable to him.

Judge Peck's trial is valuable for its lengthy review of contempt and for bringing about an act of Congress that remains in force. His experience is also instructive because it is the only federal impeachment initiated and directed by just one complainant and the only impeachment in which just a single charge of misconduct was levied. In every other trial the managers advanced a general pattern of misconduct, habitual bad performance, to show the unfitness of the officer to continue in his post. Peck's trial indicates that a politically isolated respondent can win an acquittal in the Senate.

Peck can be appraised as a victim of one lone man's determination to see him removed from the bench, a determination abetted by the existing congressional displeasure with the federal judiciary. Judge Peck acted correctly in all respects except one: he should not have suspended Luke E. Lawless from practice; that suspension was not authorized by the law. Otherwise, he acted correctly. His Soulard decision conformed to all Spanish and United States laws regulating land claims; the Supreme Court reversal of his decision came after Congress had changed the law and does not modify the correctness of Peck's ruling at the time he delivered it. Lawless's letter distorted Peck's Soulard holding. Designed to disparage the judge, it also succeeded in interfering with the flow of cases into the district court. Although Judge Peck might well have elected to sue Lawless for libel, his decision to hold him in contempt did not violate existing law on that subject. In my view Peck's acquittal was justified.

West H. Humphreys. *The Tennessee State Library and Archives.*

6

West H. Humphreys

He believed in secession as a right, and he believed in the people of Tennessee exercising that right.
—John U. Smith

After thirty years' absence from the national political arena, the impeachment procedure was used on two occasions within a six-year period. Both of these employments of the process had immediate connections with the Civil War. The first, that of federal district judge West H. Humphreys, occurred in 1862, while war was being waged. The second, that of President Andrew Johnson, took place in the tumultuous aftermath of the war: the Reconstruction period. Judge Humphreys enjoyed no political support at all, at least in the North; he had deserted his post as a federal judge to serve the Confederacy. President Johnson had estranged himself from the controlling forces in Congress by his vetoes, his positions on Reconstruction, and his apparent failure to comply with acts of Congress. Thus, both star performers in the 1860s impeachments and trials were divorced from the mainstream of politics in their era.

Judge West H. Humphreys became the subject of the fifth impeachment and trial in the nation's history. Like Senator William Blount and Judge John Pickering, Humphreys did not appear in his own defense. In the Blount and Pickering trials some explanations or excuses had, however, been presented in aid of the respondent, but no one came forward with explanatory or mitigating statements on Humphreys's behalf. Humphreys, then, was tried in absentia and with no defense at all. His proved to be the shortest and only uncontested trial in the annals of impeachment.

Members of the 1862 Senate lacked any experience in performing as judges in federal impeachments; no holdover senators from the Peck affair served in Humphreys's trial. Moreover, secession had caused twenty-two senators from the Confederate states to leave their seats, voluntarily or by expulsion. The forty-eight remaining members of the 1862 Senate—twenty-seven Republicans, fourteen Democrats, and seven from minor parties—all of them caught up in the perils and tensions of the Civil War, had little interest in studying the records of past impeachment trials, nor did they have much reason to do so. The evidence against Judge Humphreys was too clear-cut to require analysis and debate.

The Senate experienced no substantive and only slight procedural difficulties in conducting the Humphreys trial. It removed him from office unanimously, disqualified him from holding any future federal office unanimously, and gave only one afternoon to the entire proceeding.

West H. Humphreys, a federal district judge in Tennessee, had been appointed to the bench in 1853 by Franklin Pierce, a fellow Democrat. Humphreys had both a political and a judicial career. He served as a member of the Tennessee legislature, as attorney general of the state during the governorship of James K. Polk with whom he established close personal and professional bonds, and as a delegate to the state's constitutional revision convention in 1834. He was personal attorney for Polk and for Andrew Jackson.[1]

Judge Humphreys held pronounced and candid preferences for the Southern cause. He made public speeches favoring the South's position and promoting the legitimacy of secession from the Union. Oliver P. Temple, a Tennessee attorney, records that he saw jurors wearing secession badges in Humphreys's court in Knoxville, while Humphreys was presiding as a United States judge, and heard many derogatory references to the national government from participants and spectators in the courtroom.[2]

In 1862, following Tennessee's adherence to the Confederate states, West H. Humphreys accepted appointment as a district judge from Jefferson Davis and remained in this position until the Confederacy collapsed. His failure to resign from the United States district court created a problem: Abraham Lincoln could not appoint another judge until Humphreys's post became vacant by his death, resignation, or removal from office following conviction under impeachment. No mechanism other than impeachment existed for filling a federal judgeship held by a chronic absentee.

Unlike Justice Samuel Chase, Judge Humphreys had not been accused of making argumentative speeches from the bench nor, except for his failure to prohibit secessionist badges in his courtroom, of acting in partisan fashion while performing his duties as a United States judge. His secessionist views, known before the outbreak of the Civil War, did not directly prejudice his official conduct.

In the atmosphere of the then-raging Civil War, it was to be expected that the Senate would readily convict him of high crimes and misdemeanors. Judge Humphreys's unconcealed commitment to the Confederacy, his desertion from his position under the Union, and his acceptance of an appointment under the Confederate states clearly exemplified neglect and abandonment of his oath of office to the United States.

Congressman Horace Maynard (American party, later a Republican, Tennessee) initiated the proceedings against West H. Humphreys on January 8, 1862, when he informed the House of Representatives that Humphreys had failed to hold court in Tennessee for several months.[3] The House in the 37th Congress was composed of 105 Republicans, 43 Democrats, and 30 members of miscellaneous parties, giving the Republicans a 59 percent majority. However, party loyalty played no role in Judge Humphreys's impeachment nor in his trial. Congressman Maynard asked that the Judiciary Committee be instructed to investigate the judge's alleged neglect of duty. The committee inquired into Humphreys's flight from his federal post and reported to the House of Representatives on March 4. The committee substantiated Maynard's information that the judge had not held court for six months and confirmed that he had not resigned his post; it recommended that Humphreys be impeached.

Two months later, on May 7, 1862, the House of Representatives notified the Senate that it had impeached West H. Humphreys of high crimes and misdemeanors. The vote to impeach is not recorded in the *Congressional Globe* but was probably unanimous.[4] On May 22, the House brought seven articles of impeachment to the Senate.

The articles were presented by five managers appointed by Speaker Galusha A. Grow.[5] The managers included John A. Bingham (Republican, Ohio), who would also serve as a manager in the trial of Andrew Johnson; John Hickman (formerly a Democrat but now a Republican, Pennsylvania); George Hunt Pendleton (Republican, Ohio); Charles Russell Train (Republican, Massachusetts); and George Washington Dunlap of Kentucky, a Unionist. The initiation and prosecution of Judge Humphreys's impeachment do not reflect partisan division; at this time no significant party-based issues divided Congress or required consideration in forming a case against the absconded judge.

The seven articles of impeachment charged Humphreys with (1) inciting rebellion in a public speech at Nashville and asserting that states had a right to secede; (2) openly and unlawfully supporting Tennessee's ordinance of independence from the United States; (3) organizing armed rebellion; (4) opposing the authority of the United

States; (5) refusing, since July 1, 1861, to hold court as a federal district judge; (6) acting as judge of an illegal tribunal, decreeing confiscation of United States property, and unlawfully arresting loyal citizens; and (7) arresting and imprisoning William G. Brownlow.

The trial opened June 9, 1862, Vice-President Hannibal Hamlin (Republican, Maine) presiding.[6] The managers asked for and were granted a postponement until June 26 in order to obtain the attendance of their witnesses against Judge Humphreys. On that day the Senate notified the House that it had convened as a "High Court of Impeachment for the trial of West H. Humphreys."[7] The president pro tempore of the Senate, Solomon Foot (Republican, formerly Whig, Vermont), presided during the trial over a Senate in which the Republicans held a 56 percent majority.

Judge Humphreys had not responded to a summons for his appearance, and the Senate instructed the managers to proceed without him. The prosecution called twenty-three witnesses, of whom all but four attended on the opening day of the trial. One of the absentees, Andrew Johnson, was excused from appearing because of his duties as military governor of Tennessee. It would have been a curious footnote to impeachment history had the man destined to be the subject of the most important political trial in the United States been a prosecution witness in the impeachment trial immediately preceding his own.

Charles R. Train led off for the managers with a review of the facts to be presented against Judge Humphreys and an analysis of the seven articles of impeachment. Only Article 5, failure to hold court, charged Judge Humphreys with malfeasance in office, Train pointed out. The other six articles catalogued Humphreys's behavior as either gross misconduct that violated the "good behavior" clause of the constitution or as high treason for organizing armed rebellion against the United States.

Article 1, detailing Judge Humphreys's inflammatory speech at Nashville, presented no problems. No doubt existed that the judge had made the speech, and no evidence could be found that its contents were other than they had been reported to be: a call upon the citizens of Tennessee to rebel against the United States.

Respecting Article 2, advocacy and support of the secession of Tennessee, Manager Train said of Humphreys that he was "not one of those men who may have yielded to circumstances, to outside pressures, giving a reluctant adhesion to the rebellion; but we shall find him upon the evidence, one of the earliest advocates of the

118

doctrine of the right of the States to secede . . . and one of the leaders in the rebellion from its earliest inception."[8]

Article 3 charged Judge Humphreys with high treason, an indictable as well as an impeachable offense. Had this been a serious trial, aimed at removing a reluctant incumbent, the Senate would necessarily have had to study the facts alleged in Article 3 and determine whether they met the constitutional definition of treason. However, Manager Train made only a brief reference to the fact that Humphreys organized armed rebellion and levied war against the United States. He said that he did not "deem it necessary to call two witnesses to any overt act [as stipulated in the Constitution] because we understand that that rule of law, as applicable to treason, only applies to an indictment for that offense."[9] In any event, the managers directed little attention to the treason article; West H. Humphreys's conviction on whatever charges might be brought against him was inevitable.

Article 4 accused Judge Humphreys of a criminal violation of an act of Congress: opposing the authority of the United States government. Failure to hold court as a United States district judge, as set down in Article 5, proved to be another obvious and incontrovertible fact in the roster of Humphreys's bad conduct. Articles 6 and 7 dealt with specific examples, three in Article 6 and one in Article 7, of unlawful and unjust activities in the course of his tenure as a Confederate judge.

The first two of the managers' witnesses, Jacob McGavock and Issac Litton, had served as clerk and deputy clerk, respectively, in Judge Humphreys's federal district court. McGavock testified that he had taken federal district court records to Murfreesboro, Tennessee at the request of Humphreys, that certain of the records were in Humphreys's handwriting, and that Judge Humphreys had not been seen recently in Nashville. Earlier, when the House of Representatives had been discussing the impeachment and speculating about how to find the judge and notify him of the proceedings, Horace Maynard explained Humphreys's disappearance: "When the Federal troops arrived in the city of Nashville, he hastened away with great speed."[10]

Isaac Litton testified concerning Humphreys's activity as a Confederate judge. He reported Humphreys's sequestering of Northern sympathizers' property and his requiring bonds and loyalty oaths on pain of imprisonment from persons not supporting the Confederacy. In the midst of Litton's tedious and essentially purposeless testimony, Willard Saulsbury (Democrat, Delaware) made a point that must have been very welcome to most of the listening senators and probably to the managers as well. Saulsbury said that he doubted the necessity of grinding through all the proofs of the judge's various misconducts. The senator saw no reason for needlessly prolonging the trial; he observed that "If the managers . . . are satisfied that they have proved the fact that West H. Humphreys . . . has presumed to act as a judge of the Confederate States of America . . . that is a sufficient ground for his conviction. I have no hesitation in saying that if that fact is clearly proved, and I think it has been proved, I would unquestionably vote for his conviction."[11]

Because there was no doubt at all that Judge Humphreys had been a United States district judge, had abandoned his post without resigning, and had subsequently become a Confederate judge, Senator Saulsbury's criticism led to a change in the procedure. Instead of calling the nineteen witnesses who remained to be heard, the prosecution, reminded by Saulsbury's comment that its case had already been made, contented itself with presenting only three additional witnesses.

The first of the three, John U. Smith, a Nashville attorney, gave evidence supporting the facts that (1) West H. Humphreys had abandoned his federal post and (2) had publicly supported the right of the South to secede from the Union. He testified that Humphreys had not sat as a United States judge since the April 1861 term. Smith had been present when Humphreys gave his pro-secession speech in Nashville in December 1860. Reporting a conversation with the judge after the Nashville meeting, Smith said that Humphreys favored "the State of Tennessee seceding from the Union; he believed in secession as a right, and he believed in the people of Tennessee exercising that right, under the circumstances that surrounded them."[12]

H. G. Scovil, who had been arrested for sedition and rebellion against the Confederacy, testified next. He recounted having been brought before Judge Humphreys's Confederate court on the charge of giving aid and comfort to the citizens of the United States and had been required to post bond "inasmuch as I was a dangerous man and sympathized with the United States . . . and had been uttering treasonable and seditious language, hostile to the southern confederacy."[13]

The final witness, William G. Brownlow, subject of the seventh article, had been arrested and charged with treason against the

Confederacy for an editorial he printed in a Knoxville newspaper, the *Whig*, of which he was editor and publisher. Having been denied bail, Brownlow was put in prison; he was released before trial. He described his and other people's disagreeable experiences in Judge Humphreys's Confederate courtroom and the "violent political harangues" delivered there by the judge.[14]

Upon the closing of Brownlow's testimony, the managers recalled Isaac Litton, deputy clerk of Humphreys's federal district court, to give some brief additional testimony. Then John Bingham told the Senate that he had consulted with his brother managers and had found no desire among them to present any further evidence. Bingham said that the case against Judge Humphreys had been made and no reason existed to detain the Senate needlessly with further witnesses, merely to corroborate what had already been established. Therefore, Bingham asked "in the name of all the people of the United States, whose rights have been invaded and outraged by this recusant judge, that there be judgment of conviction against him . . . by this High Court of Impeachment."[15]

Thereupon, a vote was taken on each article, and more than the necessary two-thirds majority of the Senate found Humphreys guilty on each charge with the exception of the second specification of Article 6: that he had confiscated United States property. On this charge the vote was twelve guilty, twenty-four not guilty.[16]

On Article 1, the speech to incite rebellion, and on Article 5, refusal to hold court, the Senate voted unanimously for conviction. On Article 2, advocating secession of Tennessee, the vote was thirty-six to one; the same total was recorded for the charge (part of Article 6) of requiring bond from Northern sympathizers to insure that they would cease opposing the Confederate cause by acts or words. The single no vote on Article 2 was cast by Orville H. Browning (Republican, Illinois); James W. Grimes (Republican, Iowa) cast the lone dissenting vote on the first part of Article 6.

Article 3, organizing armed rebellion, received thirty-three guilty, four not guilty votes. The four who found Humphreys innocent were Henry B. Anthony (Republican, Rhode Island), William P. Fessenden (Whig, Maine), Lafayette S. Foster (Republican, Connecticut), and James Harlan (Republican, Iowa). Humphreys's actions in defiance of the authority of the United States, as detailed in Article 4, received more no votes—ten—than did any of the other articles in which the guilty votes exceeded the requisite two-thirds majority needed to convict. Four Republicans, four Democrats, a Whig, and a Unionist cast the ten not guilty votes.

The Senate supported the third part of Article 6, describing Judge Humphreys's unlawful arrest of loyal citizens, by a vote of thirty-five guilty, one not guilty; John P. Hale (Free-Soil, New Hampshire) stood alone in this vote. Article 7, the arrest and imprisonment of William G. Brownlow, also received just one not guilty vote, cast by James W. Grimes, also the sole dissenter in the vote on part one of Article 6.

The senators, in order to make their determination of guilt, must either have had outside knowledge of Humphreys's conduct or have decided, in advance of hearing any evidence, to vote guilty, because most of the articles had not been substantiated or even discussed during the trial. By 3:15 P.M., having convened as the High Court of Impeachment at noon of the same day, the Senate had heard all testimony and had found Humphreys unequivocally guilty. Thus ended the nation's shortest impeachment trial.

After a brief recess, the Senate reconvened to settle upon a verdict. A strained argument developed over whether the Senate must, or could, vote separately on the two matters in question: removal from office and disqualification from holding further office. Some senators thought the two issues could not be divided. Lyman Trumbull (Republican, Illinois) claimed that "It is one judgment upon one finding. We may . . . declare that he is removed from office and stop there, but I think it would be a singular proceeding."[17]

Senator Trumbull acknowledged that he had not looked into impeachment precedents. But lack of information did not deter him from insisting that the two questions must be combined in a single vote, as if that had been the historic method. In fact, the two-thirds vote to convict on any article of impeachment results in the official's removal from office; the Senate need not even consider voting to disqualify him from a further national post.

Some senators referred to the vote following John Pickering's trial in 1804. They believed that a precedent had been established in that trial to vote first on removal from office and then on barring from subsequent office. This conclusion had no basis in fact, as several senators including the president pro tem Solomon Foot recognized. The second issue, prohibiting further national office, never came up at Judge Pickering's trial. Having removed him from his judgeship, the Senate dissolved itself as a High Court of Impeachments, and no more was heard about the matter of Judge Pickering or his possible eligibility for serving again in a federal post.

A motion was made to vote on whether West H. Humphreys should be removed from his judgeship, to be followed, if the first vote favored such removal, by a second vote to determine whether he should be disqualified from ever again holding a national office. Senator Trumbull, persisting in his effort to lump the two issues together, moved to amend the motion to require a conglomerate vote embracing both propositions, not a separate vote on each. The vote on Trumbull's amendment to put the question of removal and disqualification as one was passed twenty-seven to ten. Appealed to for a ruling on the divisibility of the two parts of the question, Foot said: "From the authority of the Pickering case, the Chair is obliged to say that it is a divisible proposition."[18]

Thus, the presiding officer voided adoption of the Trumbull amendment, and the Senate cast two separate votes on removal of Humphreys and on disqualifying him from again holding national office. On the question of removal, the Senate voted thirty-eight to zero; on the question of disqualification, thirty-six to zero. The verdict was announced that West H. Humphreys "be, and he is hereby, removed from his said office, and that he be, and is, disqualified to hold and enjoy any office of honor, trust, or profit under the United States."[19] So Humphreys went into the history books as the second official convicted under impeachment, the first to be prohibited from ever again holding federal office, the third to be tried in absentia, and the first for whom no defense or excuse of any kind had been made.

Seven senators did not vote at all during the trial. Five of the seven absentees were Democrats, one was a Unionist, and one a Whig. Eleven senators voted Humphreys guilty on all counts: ten Republicans and just one Democrat, Joseph A. Wright of Indiana. This modest clue suggests that the Democrats in the Senate displayed less interest in convicting Humphreys than did the Republicans; yet, as noted, no one spoke a word of explanation or extenuation on his behalf. Unlike any other of the impeached officers, Humphreys had no constituency of any kind and is the archetypal outcast of impeachment history.

West H. Humphreys's property had been confiscated during the Civil War, and he had been disenfranchised under the provisions of the amnesty proclamations of Abraham Lincoln and Andrew Johnson. He did not apply for a pardon.[20] He died in 1882, twenty years after removal from his judgeship and disqualification from further national office.

The fifth impeachment and trial produced no new information about constitutional meanings and intentions. It did, however, underline the continuing problem of establishing a clearer path for getting rid of an absentee, sick, or demented judge. It will be recalled that the managers referred to Humphreys's having violated the "good behavior" clause, but because such violation had never been defined, least of all made impeachable, the reference had no consequence.

Once again Congress had missed a good opportunity, as it had following John Pickering's trial, to clarify the removal process for defective or nonperforming judges. It would have been particularly easy at this time to pass a law stating that "good behavior" included, among other things, faithful attendance to official duties. Congress could have established that judges found to exhibit such defects as chronic failure to hold court or mental or physical incapacity to perform their duties had violated the good behavior clause, under which all life-tenured judges are secured in their posts. Such violation, making a judge unfit for office, would then qualify as a high crime and misdemeanor.

The House of Representatives and the Senate had to give some time and attention to Humphreys's defection from January 8 through June 26, 1862: committees met, investigators were dispatched to find proof of the obvious, articles of impeachment were constructed, and on at least eighteen occasions before the trial either the House or the Senate discussed some aspect of the Humphreys case. It was a waste of congressional time to determine that a vacancy existed in a post voluntarily abandoned by a jurist who had no intention of resuming his office. It is also notable that the 1862 Senate, having voted thirty-nine to zero against Judge Humphreys on the first article, continued to vote on the other articles (even dividing Article 6 into three separate segments) as if a different conclusion on any one of them would have modified or reversed the outcome.

The Senate reached an inevitable decision in the trial of West H. Humphreys; it could not have decided in his favor. No amount of analysis or imagination would produce an argument supporting his innocence of the charges brought against him, nor an argument that the charges were not impeachable. Thus, Humphreys's trial created yet another impeachment "first." It stands as the shortest and the only uncontested trial, and also as the only trial up to that time in which the Senate verdict could not possibly have gone the other way. In the four preceding impeachments a contrary verdict was possible. But Judge Humphreys's guilt shone too conspicuously to have allowed a rational conclusion that he should be found innocent.

Andrew Johnson. *Library of Congress.*

7

Andrew Johnson

> Historians should view the trial of impeachment for
> what it was: . . . one of the great legal cases of history,
> in which American politicians demonstrated the strength
> of the nation's democratic institutions by attempting to
> do what no one could justifiably expect them to do—to
> give a political officer a full and fair trial in a time of
> political crisis.
>
> —Michael Les Benedict

The circumstances of Andrew Johnson's impeachment and trial
have been analyzed more carefully and more often than have any of
the nation's other impeachment experiences. That Johnson is the
only president to have been impeached, that he and Congress engaged in intractable and notorious conflicts, and that jarring dis-
agreements existed throughout the country over the best way to
settle post-Civil War issues make the epoch and Johnson's role in it
an inviting study. Also, more of the participants have written about
the Great Impeachment in reminiscences, diaries, and autobiogra-
phies, or have themselves been the subject of biographies, than has
been the case with the actors in other American state trials. No lack
of information, therefore, exists on Andrew Johnson or on the causes
that brought him to the bar of the Senate.

There do exist, however, as there did in his day, differences of
opinion over the issues that split the president and Congress. Scholars' analyses of the Johnson era (1865–69) reflect nearly opposing
outlooks on those matters. Early appraisals generally viewed
Johnson's radical Republican opponents as harsh avengers and
Johnson as a martyr to the hope for a Lincolnian peace and
Reconstruction.[1] More recent appraisals view the radical Republicans as generally sincere believers in a reconstruction designed to
foster the political and legal goals for which the Civil War had been
fought and see Johnson as a protagonist of many of the positions
of the pre-Civil War South. The question remains open whether
Andrew Johnson's opposition to congressional Reconstruction and
his alleged efforts to frustrate it included impeachable acts.

Although Johnson's trial took place just five years after the trial of West H. Humphreys, only twenty-two of the fifty-four senators who sat in judgment on Johnson had served in that capacity for Humphreys. Twenty-three of the thirty-two senators new to impeachment were Republicans and nine were Democrats, giving the Republicans a majority of nearly 80 percent. In the House of Representatives, Republicans controlled 70 percent of the seats. Even though an antagonistic majority confronted him in both houses of Congress, Andrew Johnson carried a fair share of responsibility for his impeachment; it is apparent that Johnson's personality and demeanor as well as his policies contributed to his difficulties with Congress and with the public.

Like the five principals in the previous impeachments, Johnson, a Democrat, had had wide political experience. He served as a local legislator in Tennessee, was elected five times to the House of Representatives (1843–53), and was a two-term governor of Tennessee (1853–57). Elected to the United States Senate in 1857, he continued in office when the Southern states seceded, the only senator from the South to remain in the Senate. In 1862 Abraham Lincoln appointed him military governor of Tennessee, whereupon he resigned his Senate seat. Johnson's support of Lincoln's policies, his remaining in the Senate, and his able administration as military governor caused him to be chosen as vice president in 1864 on the National Union (essentially Republican) ticket; he became president in 1865, after the assassination of Abraham Lincoln. Despite this wealth of exposure to political life, Johnson had no real party constituency when he succeeded to the presidency. In addition, as a southerner from a state that had seceded, he lacked a local base of power and was, therefore, a political orphan in a geographic as well as in a party sense. These two weaknesses, coupled with his meager capacity for political finesse, contributed markedly to his near downfall.

Andrew Johnson had been a hero to the North when he denounced secession and remained in the Senate; his frequent assaults on leaders of the rebellion kept him favorably known to the public, as did his work as military governor. These deeds appeared to indicate that, upon his unexpected succession to the presidency, he would demand real changes in the political and legal structure in the South and would insist on full compliance with the requirements laid down by the national government as conditions for restoring the former Confederate states to the Union.

Many observers assumed that Johnson would abandon the charitable course for Reconstruction sketched by President Lincoln, a course that the radical Republicans had condemned while Lincoln was alive. For a brief period this assumption seemed correct. Ulysses S. Grant, who met Johnson in 1863 while the latter served as military governor of Tennessee, criticized him for "his ever-ready remark 'Treason is a crime and must be made odious,'" which Grant considered extreme and needlessly frightening to southerners.[2] Johnson himself, only a few days after becoming president, commented to a group of visitors that he had often said "that traitors must be made odious, that treason must be made odious, that traitors must be punished and impoverished. They must not only be punished, but their social power must be destroyed."[3] That was as strong a statement as even the most radical of the Republicans could have uttered. But Johnson's "traitor" talk can be accounted for by his hatred of the planter aristocracy, not by acceptance of plans for Reconstruction that dealt with black rights or with national supervision of political reordering in the South.

Soon after he became president, Andrew Johnson began to view the South as an oppressed region. He disturbed even moderate Republicans by granting pardons to leading rebels, by opposing black suffrage and civil rights, and subsequently by vetoing bills dear to the radical Republicans and supported increasingly by the more moderate members of that party. If the former rebels resumed control in the South, as they were doing, and the blacks remained without rights and were to be kept that way, the Civil War had been fought for nothing; Southern Unionists, not just radical Republicans, believed this to be true. The president's steady movement toward restoring the antebellum South's government structure, his "poor-white" hostility to congressional plans for assuring black rights, and his impeding of congressional efforts to restructure the South to make the losses of the Civil War less unbearable split the executive and legislative departments into implacable opposition.

But Johnson believed himself to be furthering President Lincoln's goals. In a fleeting moment of triumph after Congress had failed to override his veto of the Freedmen's Bureau bill (February 22, 1866), Johnson gave an impolitic speech naming Congressman Thaddeus Stevens and Senator Charles Sumner as examples of opponents to good government and comparing his own policies with those of Lincoln. He asked his audience if they had ever heard his adversaries "at any time quote my predecessor . . . as coming in controversy with anything I advocated? . . . Where is there one principle in reference to this restoration that I have departed from?"[4]

Beneath such specific differences lay a basic struggle for dominance. While Johnson sought to maintain what he saw as rightful presidential authority, Congress sought to restore its traditional primacy, a primacy that some congressional leaders thought had eroded during the period of presidential management of war and Reconstruction. The central question was, Whose policy was to be adopted as the basis for Southern reconstruction and readmission? That of Congress or that of the president?

In addition to clashes in principle, which would have sufficed to bring an impeachment, Andrew Johnson had other liabilities that, standing alone, would not have caused him serious trouble but, combined with his political estrangement from Congress, became handy weapons to use against him. First, he had been drunk at his inaugural as vice president and had given a boisterous and rambling address, embarrassing President Lincoln and other attending dignitaries. This performance fixed his image, at least to the extent that it was easy to call him a drunkard, or hint at it, whenever his public speeches sounded extreme and uncontrolled. That Johnson had been intoxicated at his inaugural is well documented, but no other evidence exists that he had a drinking problem.[5]

The second personal attribute that antagonized Johnson's enemies was his speaking style. Essentially a stump orator—volcanic, repetitious, and unrestrained—he delivered slashing personal attacks on his congressional foes. His opponents and even some of his adherents described his campaign speeches as crude and unpresidential. It is easy to see why Johnson became a ready target for a description of himself as intemperate, vulgar, or both.

Finally, Andrew Johnson lacked talent for conciliation. He self-righteously saw his opponents as willfully wrong, men with whom no compromise could be made. When to these traits of personality are added the far more serious differences that divided president and Congress, Andrew Johnson's impeachment appears fated. It is fair to note that some of Johnson's opponents—Edwin M. Stanton, Benjamin F. Butler, Thaddeus Stevens, Charles Sumner, George S. Boutwell, and Benjamin F. Wade— were not men of cool and temperate language either, nor did they display more capacity for compromise and conciliation than did the president whose removal they sought. Were intransigence and heavy-handedness the concern of this study, it would be difficult to decide to whom to award the prize.

Although the abrasive personalities of many participants in the Johnson-Congress controversy deepened the rift between them and nearly precluded rational debate, both sides held sincere convictions on the subjects that led them to personal and political deadlock. The opposing forces split on fundamental questions of government and civil rights—topics on which compromise is not natural or even possible.

Five major issues brought forth the deadly strife between the two branches. One difference, centered in political theory, had both legal and practical consequences. The question was, Had the South left the Union and so did it stand in relation to the North as conquered territory, or was secession not possible and so the rebellious states had never been legally out of the Union?[6]

The radical Republicans, led by Sumner and Stevens, held that (1) the former Confederate states had seceded; (2) having been defeated in war, they could become part of the United States only by way of the procedure any other territory must follow; and (3) the terms for admission and determination of whether those terms had been met were the province of Congress.

Andrew Johnson, and Lincoln before him, believed that the South had never been out of the Union. However, Johnson did accept the requirements that to resume full participation in government each Southern state must abolish slavery, ratify the Thirteenth Amendment, expunge its ordinance of secession, and repudiate the debts incurred in waging the Civil War. But Johnson did not accept the premise that the national government could control the internal functions of a state or force compliance with national regulations through military governors. He was a states-righter, and one who did not fear the resumption of authority by those former rebels who, eligible to take an oath of allegiance to the United States, had received pardons and restoration of their property rights.[7] He also believed that the president had the power to recognize that a state had met Reconstruction requirements and the power to announce its resumption of full partnership in the Union.

Underneath this basic difference in constitutional theory lay a practical political anxiety. Upon readmission of the Southern states, the Democratic party would supersede, or at least threaten the dominance of, the Republicans, in part because each freedman would be counted at full strength, not as three-fifths of a person as the Constitution had previously provided.[8] This reordering of the electoral base would give the South more congressmen, and the added members would be Democrats and would be white men elected by white men. Former slaves would gain nothing by the new census provision, for they would not be allowed to vote and their enumeration would simply swell the roster of Southern, erstwhile rebel, congressmen. Thus, friction between Johnson and Congress over Reconstruction policy had partisan overtones relating to future control of the national government.

The second major issue—the political, economic, and legal position of former slaves in a reconstituted Union—created another source of disharmony. Republican concern for strict enforcement of the Reconstruction Acts arose from real events in the South: the Black Codes, atrocities committed against former slaves, and restoration of rebel leaders to political power. These events caused even the moderate Republicans to agree that nationally supervised military rule must be continued in order to protect the rights of black people. Johnson's states' rights posture remained undented, and he displayed an ambivalent, at times a hostile, attitude toward insuring freedmen's rights.

On the matter of black suffrage, Johnson frequently pointed out that only five Northern states permitted blacks to vote. He used this fact to buttress his argument that each state could determine eligibility to vote; if Ohio could restrict the franchise to white males, so could Mississippi, each state possessing the same internal powers as every other state. Although unable to counter the truth of this argument, the radicals, and some moderates also, did deplore it and did not intend that Southern states should reenter the Union until they had provided voting rights for blacks.

Black leaders had looked to Johnson's presidency as one that would support their goals; his attacks on the planter aristocracy throughout his earlier political career had suggested his sympathy for their position. But Frederick Douglass, a slave who escaped from the South in 1838 and subsequently edited an abolitionist newspaper, expressed his disappointment with the president's indifference to black rights and his pardoning of former rebels. He told Johnson, "You enfranchise your enemies and disenfranchise your friends."[9]

The third breach between the executive and legislative branches stemmed from Johnson's assertion that Congress was not a legally constituted legislative body because it lacked representatives from the former Confederate states. Andrew Johnson sometimes commented on the alleged illegal composition of the legislative branch at the same time that he was speaking against ratification of the Fourteenth Amendment—a double-barreled irritant to his congressional opponents.

A fourth source of discord arose from Johnson's incendiary performance in the congressional campaign of 1866, in which he tried to secure the election of legislators friendly to his Reconstruction policy. He had spoken in several cities in support of his Reconstruction plan, describing what he saw as congressional encroachments on presidential authority. His efforts to enlist public support proved unsuccessful for at least two reasons. First, he did not make recommendations for specific congressional candidates who would sustain his positions. Thus, his speeches lacked definition because he did not describe any action he desired from his hearers; they were given in a political vacuum. Second, he was garrulous and repetitious. He boasted to a friendly New York audience that he had "never made a prepared speech in my life."[10] This stump-orator spontaneity did not work. The newspapers gave his speeches extensive coverage, and his repetitions became obvious and subject to ridicule; so also did his frequent exchange of comments, some angry, with his audiences. His behavior was usually considered disorderly and too informal, his attacks on his opponents too undignified and graceless to befit the nation's chief executive. The campaign also supplied a scene unique in the annals of politics: a president stumping the country in opposition to the party (Union, Republican) that had elected him while that party campaigned relentlessly against the policies and deportment of the man, now president, whom they had accepted as vice president just two years earlier.

Finally, although by no means exhausting the roster of frictions, the fifth issue splitting President Johnson and Congress concerned his vetoes of several congressional measures; these vetoes drove moderate Republicans toward the radical position. The vetoes of the Freedman's Bureau and Civil Rights bills created deep-seated enmity toward President Johnson because most people recognized that the Southern states had not protected black rights and had no plan to do so. The national government had to guarantee those rights if they were to be enforced. In his veto messages, Johnson not only made no counter-proposals for protecting blacks in the absence of federal guarantees but also showed antipathy for any kind of federal activity designed to guard the welfare or secure the political-legal rights of former slaves.

Among the congressional enactments that aggravated the hostility between the executive and legislative branches, the Tenure of Office Act (1867) ranks first as the precipitating cause of the impeachment.[11] Johnson's entire cabinet, exhibiting a most unusual unanimity, opposed the act as unconstitutional and supported the president's decision to veto it. Ironically, Secretary of War Edwin M. Stanton, destined to be the officer whose dismissal brought the act into force, "contributed the lion's share of the resulting veto message."[12] Johnson's alleged violation of the Tenure of Office Act when he suspended Secretary Stanton formed the central theme of the impeachment trial.

Congress had designed the act to reduce Johnson's opportunities to replace civil officers with men of his own choice. The act protected each civil officer whose appointment required Senate confirmation until his successor had been qualified; that is, Senate approval of a replacement had to be obtained before an officer could be fired. The president, under provisions of the tenure act, could suspend an official during a recess of the Senate, such action to be confirmed or rejected by the Senate when it resumed its session.

Provisions relating specifically to the cabinet stated that members held office during the term (plus one month) of the president by whom they had been appointed and that they could be removed only with consent of the Senate. Much time in the impeachment trial would be spent in arguing about whether the act covered Abraham Lincoln's appointees. Stanton, the obvious example since his removal triggered the impeachment, had not been reappointed by President Lincoln following his reelection in 1864, nor had Stanton ever been appointed to any office by President Johnson. Whether the Tenure of Office Act protected Stanton, whether Johnson had abided by the act (or tried to) when he suspended Stanton, whether any president, harmonious and comfortable relations with his cabinet being a necessity for effective executive government, could be restricted in this way—all these uncertainties will be examined during discussion of the trial.

Thus, five substantive issues—the legal relation of the South to the Union, the establishment and protection of freedmen's rights, the claim by the president that Congress lacked legal status because Southern representatives were not included in it, the president's performance in the 1866 campaign, and Johnson's vetoes and alleged failure to abide by the acts passed over his vetoes— form the heart of the controversy that culminated in impeachment and trial.

The first rumbling of impeachment had been heard on December 17, 1866. Congressman James M. Ashley (Republican, Ohio) introduced a motion to suspend the rules so that he could present a resolution to investigate impeaching Andrew Johnson.[13] The House of Representatives supported Ashley's motion by a vote of ninety to forty-nine, a result that did not meet the two-thirds majority needed to suspend the rules. Therefore, nothing came of the first official mention of impeachment.

Soon afterward, January 7, 1867, Congressman Ashley introduced a direct impeachment resolution.[14] He accused Johnson of high crimes and misdemeanors, usurpation of power, and corrupt usage of presidential appointment, pardoning, and veto powers. This second try at impeachment was referred to the Judiciary Committee. The committee reported on February 28 that shortness of time because the congressional session was nearly over did not allow it to complete the investigation, and it recommended further inquiries into the president's conduct. At this time, although there was much criticism of Johnson, most of his congressional opponents thought that impeachment would not succeed, mainly because the objected-to acts did not appear to fall within the constitutional description of impeachable offenses.

At the opening of the 40th Congress, on March 7, 1867, Congressman Ashley moved that the Judiciary Committee continue its investigation. After lengthy and inconclusive examination of witnesses and documents, the committee failed to recommend impeachment.

Six months after the new Congress convened, but while it was in recess, Johnson suspended Secretary of War Stanton when he refused to resign after the president requested him to do so. Stanton experienced increasing discomfort in working with Andrew Johnson, and many people had expected him to withdraw from the cabinet because of his differences with the president. Stanton's conduct of the War Office commanded respect, but he did not have a particularly strong following in Congress; vigorous congressional support arose later when he became the cause célèbre and convenient hero for a legislative faction passionately determined to cast out Andrew Johnson and now, apparently, presented with the means to do so.

To replace the suspended secretary of war, Johnson appointed Ulysses S. Grant as ad interim secretary pending the return of Congress, when he would inform the Senate of his action and solicit its approval. Stanton's suspension created little immediate outcry because of the popularity of General Grant and because of uncertainty, even among devout Republicans, that the tenure act encompassed cabinet members.

Meanwhile, Congress continued its impeachment investigation; and on December 7, 1867, nearly a year after Congressman Ashley had introduced the resolution to impeach, the Judiciary Committee recommended that the House of Representatives impeach Andrew Johnson. To the despair and rage of the radicals, the House defeated the recommendation by a vote of 108 to 57. All fifty-seven votes in favor of the resolution were cast by Republicans, as were sixty-six of the no votes.[15] The failure to impeach is surprising, considering the antagonism that Johnson had stirred; he had not, however, violated any law, and for that reason even some of his most committed foes backed away from impeaching him. Thus ended the second consideration of impeachment.

It would soon be followed by a third, and successful, impeachment effort. When the Senate, on January 13, 1868, refused to concur in Andrew Johnson's suspension of Secretary Stanton, as few could have imagined it would, General Grant, who had acted as secretary of war for five months, promptly gave the keys to his office to Stanton and abandoned his post.

Andrew Johnson understood that he had Grant's promise to stay in office. As a result, Johnson believed Edwin M. Stanton would be forced to seek a court opinion about the legality of his suspension. Such a proceeding would require the court to determine whether the Tenure of Office Act secured Stanton to his cabinet position, and if the court held that it did, to decide whether the act was constitutional. Johnson believed that Ulysses S. Grant had further agreed that should he become uncomfortable because of the myriad legal and political differences that swirled around his temporary appointment and should he, therefore, decide to resign, he would present his resignation to the president, not just walk away from his job. Thomas and Hyman, in their biography of Stanton, support Johnson's view: "Grant assured the President that he would not . . . give Stanton back the keys to the War Office short of a court order requiring the return, and in any case not without notification to the President."[16] Upon Grant's departure from the War Department, Edwin M. Stanton immediately reassumed the office.

An angry exchange of letters between Johnson and Grant followed.[17] Their differences on this issue arose from what may have been a misunderstanding or may have been a breach of faith by the general. Johnson believed that Grant had betrayed him and had done so knowingly, a belief he directly stated in a letter to the general. Grant replied that his "honor as a soldier and integrity as a man have been so violently assailed . . . that I can but regard this whole matter, from the beginning to the end, as an attempt to involve me in the resistance of law . . . and thus to destroy my character before the country."[18] Congressman James G. Blaine (Republican, Maine) observed of Johnson and Grant that "the wrath of both men was fully aroused, and the controversy closed by leaving them enemies for life—unreconciled, irreconcilable."[19]

Andrew Johnson fired Secretary Stanton on February 21, 1868. Although the Senate had not agreed to the suspension of Stanton and could hardly be expected to endorse his being fired, the president, nevertheless, formally removed him from the war office. He appointed Lorenzo B. Thomas as secretary of war ad interim, but Thomas never actually took possession of the office. Edwin M. Stanton continued to occupy it day and night to thwart Johnson's plans to supplant him. This second attempt to dispose of Stanton was a goad to Congress. That act and Johnson's falling-out with the popular war hero Ulysses S. Grant rekindled the impetus for impeachment.

The third try at impeachment succeeded. The day that Johnson announced his dismissal of Stanton, John Covode of Pennsylvania, "an archradical" according to Hans L. Trefousse,[20] moved an impeachment resolution, which the House of Representatives immediately referred to the Reconstruction Committee.[21] The very next day, February 22, 1868, the committee brought in a recommendation for impeachment that the House, composed of 143 Republicans, 49 Democrats, adopted, after two days of denunciatory speeches, by a vote of 126 to 47.[22] This vote reflected entirely partisan positions, all Republicans voting yes, all Democrats no.[23]

The Republicans prevailed in their third attempt because the president persisted in trying to be rid of Secretary Stanton, a direct and hostile affront to Congress, and a threat to enforcement of the Reconstruction Acts, which Stanton actively supported. Thus, the president's attempt to remove the secretary, added to all the past confrontations and to Johnson's inflexible stances, made impeachment possible.

As soon as the vote to impeach had been recorded, Congressman Thaddeus Stevens moved that the Senate be notified of Andrew Johnson's impeachment and a committee be appointed to prepare the charges; the House agreed to both motions. The committee assigned to prepare the articles required only four days to complete its task, reporting back to the House on February 29.

Next, the House elected seven managers, all Republicans, as would be expected: John A Bingham (Ohio), George S. Boutwell (Massachusetts), Benjamin F. Butler (Massachusetts), John Logan (Illinois), Thaddeus Stevens (Pennsylvania), Thomas Williams (Pennsylvania), and James F. Wilson (Iowa). Michael Les Benedict classifies Bingham as a conservative, Wilson as a centrist, and the other five managers as radicals.[24]

Thaddeus Stevens, whom Boutwell referred to as "able, bold, and unscrupulous," was leader of the House of Representatives, a long-time abolitionist, and an uncompromising exponent of radical reconstruction.[25] He would have been chairman of the managers except that he was in failing health. When it appeared that Stevens might act as pro forma chairman, with Benjamin Butler doing most of the work, the conservative Bingham said he would not serve as a manager under Butler, the most fiery, extreme, and heavy-handed of Johnson's adversaries.[26] The managers, wanting to preserve an impression of purpose and unity, then elected Boutwell as chairman. Congressman Bingham remained dissatisfied, and once more the managers, needing to retain the leading conservative as one of the prosecutors, deferred to his wishes. Boutwell resigned as chairman and nominated Bingham to succeed him; and thus the organizational pattern of the board of managers was finally accomplished.

Opposing the managers as attorneys for Andrew Johnson were Benjamin R. Curtis, a Republican and former Supreme Court justice; William M. Evarts, a conservative Republican who had denounced Johnson's policies;[27] William S. Groesbeck, a Democrat and former congressman from Ohio; Thomas A. R. Nelson, a Unionist (later Democrat) and former congressman from Tennessee; and Henry Stanbery, a Republican who had resigned as attorney general in order to defend Johnson. All of the president's counsel served without pay. Fearing Johnson's temper and readiness to respond impulsively and ferociously to challenges, they insisted that he not attend the trial at any time, a requirement to which Johnson acceded reluctantly. Thus, the sixth impeachment trial, like William Blount's, John Pickering's, and West Humphreys's before it, was conducted in the absence of the central figure.

On March 4 the managers, accompanied by the House of Representatives acting as Committee of the Whole for the occasion, marched over to the Senate chamber and presented eleven articles of impeachment.[28] The next day the trial began.

Before summarizing the 1,600 pages of testimony and supplementary statements that comprise the trial of Andrew Johnson, it seems worthwhile to note the major concerns. Although hairsplitting, tedious repetitions, and belaboring of many side issues characterized the debate on the eleven articles of the Great Impeachment, the trial showed the substantive questions to be:

1. Did Johnson violate the Tenure of Office Act? If so, did he do it willfully?

2. Was the tenure act constitutional? If not, must the president, nevertheless, abide by it until a court determined its validity?
3. Did the president ignore, circumvent, or obstruct enforcement of congressional reconstruction measures?
4. Were any of the actions or inactions of President Johnson high crimes and misdemeanors and thus impeachable?

Two peripheral matters, but ones consuming much time during the trial, were whether the Senate was a "court" when sitting for an impeachment and whether Johnson's intemperate speeches could be classified as impeachable offenses.

The trial opened on March 5, 1868, with the swearing in of Chief Justice Salmon P. Chase as presiding officer; he in turn administered the oath to the senators.[29] The Senate, now qualified to undertake the most notable state trial in United States history, included forty-two Republicans and twelve Democrats, a majority of 78 percent for the dominant party. Michael Les Benedict categorizes twenty-eight of the forty-two Republican senators as follows: ten were radicals, five centrists, and thirteen conservatives.[30] Thus, the partisan bias against Johnson was somewhat balanced by the moderate to conservative bent suggested by the Benedict survey. Only one state that had seceded, Johnson's home state, Tennessee, which had been readmitted in 1866, had representation in the Senate during the trial.[31] The constitutionality of conducting a trial before a Senate in which ten states had no representation was briefly raised and then dismissed near the beginning of the trial.

The only business of the first day, apart from the swearing in ceremony, concerned the legality of having Benjamin F. Wade participate in the trial. Senator Wade, a hard-line radical Republican from Ohio, served as president pro tem of the Senate and would succeed Andrew Johnson as the nation's president should the latter be removed from office. Thomas A. Hendricks (Democrat, Indiana) questioned Wade's fitness to be a judge in a matter so significantly affecting his own future. After a lengthy discussion in which Republicans countered objections to Wade by questioning the propriety of Johnson's son-in-law, David Patterson (Democrat, Tennessee), sitting as a judge, the Senate adjourned until the next day.[32] On March 6 more discussion took place. Finally, the Senate decided that Wade should take the oath and that senators opposing his participation could raise the issue again if, during the trial, Wade cast a vote on a substantive matter.[33]

On March 13 Henry Stanbery, Benjamin R. Curtis, and Thomas A. R. Nelson, representing Andrew Johnson, asked for a postponement of forty days to prepare the reply to the articles of impeachment. Citing the precedents of the Samuel Chase and James H. Peck trials in support of the request for a delay, Stanbery observed that Justice Chase, who had known for a year before the trial what the accusations against him would be, had been given thirty-two days to prepare a reply to eight articles of impeachment, and Judge Peck, who had known the accusation against him for four years, had been granted fifteen days to reply to only one article. President Johnson, Stanbery pointed out, had just learned of the charges brought against him. Not a lawyer as were both Chase and Peck, Johnson had to depend entirely on his recently appointed counsel for his defense. After a two-hour debate, the Senate granted the respondent ten days to prepare the reply to the articles.[34]

When the Senate reconvened on March 23, Garrett Davis (Democrat, Kentucky) moved that the trial be postponed until senators from the South had been restored to their seats. The Senate defeated this motion, supportive of Johnson's belief that Congress was not properly constituted in the absence of representatives from the South, by a vote of forty-nine to two.[35]

Of the eleven articles of impeachment brought against Andrew Johnson, nine concerned some aspect of his dealings with Edwin M. Stanton. [36] Each article on Stanton itemized an act committed by the president that showed him to be "unmindful of the high duties of his office and of his oath of office." Article 1 described the president's suspension of Stanton; Articles 2 and 3 detailed his appointment of Lorenzo Thomas to the War Department; Article 4 claimed that Johnson had conspired with Thomas and others to prevent Stanton from functioning as secretary of war and had become thereby "guilty of a high crime in office"; Articles 5, 6, and 7 charged Johnson with conspiring with Thomas and others to violate the Tenure of Office Act. Article 8 alleged that Johnson had unlawfully sought to control disbursement of funds appropriated for the military service, and Article 11, a cumulative article, added the potentially serious charge that the president had interfered with enforcement of acts of Congress.

Article 1, squarely directed to Stanton's suspension, did not even mention Ulysses S. Grant's five months' tenure as secretary of war nor the fact that Grant had actually supplanted Stanton as secretary, a feat Lorenzo Thomas had proved unable to accomplish. Grant by this time had become the leading candidate for the Republican presidential nomination, and the Republicans may not have wanted to embarrass themselves by naming him in their indictment of Johnson. Or perhaps they feared that if the general, whose political attachments seemed flimsy at best, had been forced to justify at a dramatic trial his acceptance of the secretary of war's post, he might, in protecting his own reputation, be driven to a defense of Johnson. Grant's testimony of the conditions under which he accepted and then abandoned the secretary's post would have made an interesting addition to the trial record.

Although Article 9 also referred to Stanton, it basically addressed President Johnson's alleged instructions to Major General William H. Emory to disregard an act of Congress requiring that all orders of the president or the secretary of war relating to military operations be issued through the general of the army (Ulysses S. Grant).

Article 10 described Johnson's effort to bring Congress "into disgrace, ridicule, hatred, contempt" in various public performances in which he did "make and deliver, with a loud voice, certain intemperate, inflammatory, and scandalous harangues, and did therein utter loud threats and bitter menaces."[38] The article set forth three specific examples of speeches in which Andrew Johnson had put responsibility for failure of Reconstruction upon the head of Congress. Drafted by Manager Benjamin Butler, it exhibited the same wild language it accused the president of using.

The final article claimed that Johnson had said Congress was not properly constituted because of the absence of the Southern states and that he assumed he could disregard the laws of such a body. He had, the article continued, failed to abide by the Tenure of Office Act and the act requiring that orders relating to military matters be given by the general of the army. In addition, he had attempted to prevent execution of the Reconstruction Act of March 2, 1867. Article 11, created by Manager Thaddeus Stevens, although in part repetitious of preceding articles, commanded the most respect. In pointing out that Johnson had disobeyed three laws, it brought a serious question into consideration, Must a president enforce a law that he considers unconstitutional?

Although the Tenure of Office Act was directed at Andrew Johnson, not at a thoughtfully devised revision of the appointment and removal power, it was the law. The only route for a president lies in bringing a questioned law as swiftly as possible into the courts for judicial determination. Several observers believed that President Johnson wished to follow this route and that only General Grant's perfidy prevented him from getting a court test of the issue.

On March 23, 1868, the Senate, composed of forty-two Republicans and twelve Democrats, sat as a Court of Impeachment to hear attorneys Curtis, Stanbery, and Evarts read the respondent's reply to the articles.[39] Respecting the problems surrounding Edwin M. Stanton, the attorneys pointed out that a president is responsible for the acts of his cabinet and that Andrew Johnson could not rely upon Stanton; they said that the president had determined that the Tenure of Office Act did not cover Stanton, wanted a court test of that act, and had never violated it or intended to violate it. They challenged the fairness of quoting excerpts from Johnson's speeches, denied that in them he had abused Congress, and reminded the Senate that the speeches complained of had not been official acts but had been, instead, the same exercises of free speech that all citizens enjoyed. Finally, the attorneys insisted that Andrew Johnson had never denied the validity of any acts of Congress. They did, however, acknowledge his saying that the South should be represented in that body and that it was incomplete without Southern legislators.

In conclusion, William M. Evarts asked that, following the managers' response to Johnson's reply to the articles, there should be a thirty-day interval to enable counsel to prepare the president's case. The Senate voted forty-one to twelve against granting the request; all twelve votes favoring the postponement were cast by Democrats.[40] The next day, March 24, the managers presented a brief response to Johnson's reply to the articles, a response denying any validity to the answers. The Senate then continued the trial until the following Monday, a postponement of five days instead of the thirty days the president's attorneys had requested.

Benjamin Butler opened the case for the managers on March 30, 1868 with a flamboyant speech lasting for three hours.[41] He reviewed English and United States precedents on impeachment with a view to showing first that senators who had expressed their opinions on the respondent's conduct could not, thereby, be barred from sitting in the trial, and, second, that impeachable offenses need not be criminal in nature. Butler desired, as set down in his first point, to blunt criticism that because many of the senators already considered Johnson guilty, his trial lacked an essential element of fairness: an impartial jury. This criticism had been raised even before the trial and had become a significant complaint against the proceedings. But Butler argued that, despite the obvious fact that many senators had formed opinions antagonistic to Johnson, the Senate's constitutional impeachment role required it to judge the president's conduct. A senator represented a constituency that deserved to have its representative participate in this, as in any other, parliamentary concern.

However correct this position, Manager Butler subsequently provided ammunition to those who questioned the possibility of impartiality in Johnson's case when, urging the Senate not to reverse its position, he said:

Senators, you passed this tenure-of-office act. . . . The President then presented it to you for your revision [i.e., vetoed it] and you passed it again notwithstanding his constitutional argument upon it. The President then removed Mr. Stanton, and presented its unconstitutionality again, and presented also the question whether Mr. Stanton was within it, and you, after solemn deliberation and argument, again decided that Mr. Stanton was within [it], and that the law was constitutional. Then he removed Mr. Stanton . . . and again, after solemn argument, you decided that Mr. Stanton was within its provisions and that the law was constitutional.[42]

When William M. Evarts summarized the president's case at the end of the trial, he referred to the problem of Senate impartiality. Evarts insisted that the central issue was political and that the Constitution "never forces honorable men into a position where they are judges in their own cause, or where they have in the course of their previous duties expressed a judgment."[43] Reality, however, forces the conclusion that in such dramatic public events as a presidential impeachment senators would have expressed, or at least have formed, opinions during the months leading up to the trial.

Butler's second general point in his opening statement set forth his contention that impeachment covered more than indictable acts. He argued that impeachment included any act "subversive of some fundamental or essential principle of government, or highly prejudicial to the public interest, and this may consist of a violation of the Constitution, of law, of an official oath, or of duty, by an act committed or omitted, or, without violating a positive law, by the abuse of discretionary powers from improper motives, or for any improper purpose."[44]

Charles Sumner, in an opinion filed after the trial, made much the same observation. He said that the fact that judgment in impeachment was limited to removal from office demonstrated that the process was "political and nothing else. . . . The Senate removes from office; the courts punish. [Impeachment is a political proceeding before a political body, with political purposes; . . . it is founded on political offenses."[45]

When it became Johnson's attorneys' turn to describe impeachable acts, Benjamin Curtis said, "There can be no crime, there can be no misdemeanor without a law, written or unwritten, express or implied. . . . My interpretation . . . is that the language 'high crimes and misdemeanors' means offenses against the laws of the United States."[46] Impeachment history does not sustain Curtis's appraisal, but, rather, supports Butler's and Sumner's descriptions of the nature of acts that come within the impeachment clause, namely, that the acts complained of need not be criminal.

Manager Butler went on to offer supporting arguments for all of the eleven articles. He accused Johnson of treachery, recklessness, madness, and blasphemy; in addition, he claimed that in the fashion of Cromwell or Napoleon, the president harbored designs to overthrow the government. "Denunciatory attacks upon the legislature have always preceded . . . a seizure by a despot of the legislative power of a country." Andrew Johnson failed in his plan only "because of the want of ability and power, not malignity and will." Although Butler spent some time on Johnson's deportment in his campaign speeches, calling him a "ribald, scurrilous blasphemer, bandying epithets with a jeering mob,"[47] this article (10), Butler's own creation, did not occupy an important place until later in the trial, and then more because so much time was given to it than because it advanced an impeachable offense.

Early in the trial the proceedings were interrupted by a lengthy argument over the power of Salmon P. Chase as presiding officer to rule on admissibility of evidence.[48] The Senate concluded that the chief justice could rule on all questions of evidence and on incidental questions but that any such rulings became subject to a Senate vote to decide the matter if requested by a senator. The chief justice was authorized to submit any question of admissibility to a Senate vote if he so chose.[49]

Another matter arose concerning the role of the chief justice in the trial. On a purely procedural issue, the Senate vote resulted in a tie, and Chief Justice Chase cast the deciding vote. No one questioned his right to do so until the next day (April 1) when Charles Sumner, having heard the minutes of the previous day, moved an order that the Constitution did not authorize the chief justice's voting in the trial. The Senate voted twenty-seven to twenty-one against adopting the order.[50] All twenty-one senators supporting Sumner's position were Republicans, while sixteen of their number joined eleven Democrats in voting against it.

After the vote on the role of the chief justice and a long argument over the meaning of conspiracy and the intention of President Johnson to use force to oust Secretary Stanton, there followed an examination of several prosecution witnesses on Lorenzo Thomas's actions relating to his effort to secure possession of the War Office. In the midst of one particularly tedious exchange, Chief Justice Chase said that he found the evidence adduced both irrelevant and protracted. Although the examination continued into the next day, the witnesses stayed closer to a factual report of the conduct of Stanton and Thomas during their mock-serious confrontation. Efforts to demonstrate that Lorenzo Thomas, as Andrew Johnson's agent, planned to obtain his new post by force proved far from conclusive. In fact, Thomas's statements that he would "kick that fellow out" or "break open the door" (as variously reported) seemed vainglorious and reflective of the ad interim secretary's moment in the spotlight rather than a report of serious intentions.[51] Later in the trial, when he appeared as a defense witness, Lorenzo Thomas was asked by Manager Butler if he had not:

Q. meant to call on General Grant for a military force to take possession of the office?

A. Yes.

Q. Did you mean that when you told it, or was it merely rhodomontade?

A. I suppose I did not mean it, for it never entered my head to use force. . . .

Q. It was mere boast, brag?

A. Oh, yes.[52]

After finishing with their testimony on Thomas's conduct, the managers presented witnesses who commented on President Johnson's campaign speeches and verified transcripts of them.[53] The lengthy attention to the speeches, consuming about two days, was designed to show the president's wrangling exchanges with his audiences and his reckless language in assaulting his opponents, especially those in Congress. For example, in his Cleveland speech he said, "But Congress, factious and domineering, had taken to poisoning the minds of the American people. . . . Every friend of theirs who holds an office as assessor, collector, or postmaster wanted to retain his place. . . . This gang of office-holders—these blood-suckers and cormorants—had got fat on the country."[54]

One other matter occupied much time in the managers' case: the scope of the president's removal power throughout the nation's history.[55] Although the authority of a president to dismiss a cabinet officer formed the central issue in the Johnson trial, history did not provide much help to either side, least of all to the prosecution. However the managers produced lists of hundreds of government employees who might be fired by Andrew Johnson were he not restrained by the requirement of obtaining Senate confirmation of a successor before he could dismiss an incumbent officeholder. The managers' support, in this way, of the Tenure of Office Act underlined not only its validity but also the great number of people it protected. On their part, Johnson's lawyers argued that historically the president had possessed, and had exercised, the power of removal of department heads; they too introduced long lists purporting to substantiate their position.[56] All told, the prosecution called twenty-five witnesses and concluded its testimony on April 9, 1868.

The defense began its case the same day with an opening statement by Benjamin Curtis.[57] He analyzed the Tenure of Office Act and argued that it did not apply to Edwin M. Stanton and that Congress in passing it had never intended to compel President Johnson to retain a confidential adviser whom he had not appointed and did not trust. Curtis said that Johnson understood that the law did not cover Stanton and so he could not be charged with any willful intention to violate it. "I suppose everyone will agree that so long as the President of the United States, in good faith, is endeavoring to take care that the laws be faithfully executed, and . . . is preserving, protecting and defending the Constitution of the United States, although he may be making mistakes, he is not committing high crimes or misdemeanors."[58]

He applied the same logic to Article 2, the appointment of Lorenzo Thomas; because President Johnson viewed his suspension of Stanton as constitutional and legal, he was entitled to make an ad interim appointment. Curtis then moved to Article 8, similar to Article 2 except that it added to the alleged illegal appointment of Thomas an assertion that Johnson had unlawfully sought to control disbursements of funds for the military. Noting that the managers had not produced admissible evidence on the latter point, the respondent's attorneys felt no necessity to refute it.[59] Curtis disposed of the "conspiracy" articles (4, 5, 6, and 7) quickly; because the managers had presented nothing fitting a legal description of conspiracy, he said his team had nothing to refute.[60]

Respecting Johnson's speeches, Curtis commented that instead of considering whether the content of the speeches had been true or false, the accusers had elevated themselves into a school of manners. He doubted that the president could be impeached for lack of decorum. He called attention to the constitutional protection of free speech, pointing out that Congress was expressly prohibited from restraining it. When William Evarts summed up the president's case at the end of the trial, he made much the same observation. He pronounced the speeches to be "crimes against rhetoric, against oratory, against taste, and perhaps against logic [but that it was] a novelty in this country to try anybody for making a speech."[61]

On Thaddeus Stevens's potpourri Article 11, Benjamin Curtis said little, asserting that it did not contain any new material, presenting just an amalgam of the other articles. But the final article did present new and potentially damaging charges, and Curtis's cavalier dismissal of it would not have been successful had the managers done an adequate job of exploiting the charges contained in it. Article 11 claimed that Johnson, having described the 39th Congress as one representing only part of the states, had implied that he need not heed its legislation and that it was not competent to propose constitutional amendments; the president had also prevented execution of the Reconstruction Act of March 2, 1867.[62] These two points had not been raised in the other articles and could have had serious impact, particularly the claim that Johnson had interfered with enforcement of a law.

Despite Curtis's easy rejection of Article 11, it proved to be the one in which the managers had the most confidence and the one that would be voted on first at the end of the trial. The anti-Johnson forces believed that if a two-thirds majority could be found on any article, it would be on number 11. But the managers did not develop Johnson's impeding execution of the Reconstruction measures, a strange omission and a detriment to their case, because if failure to execute the laws could be proved, it would have been a strong factor in convicting the president. The impressive arguments on Reconstruction policy did not come up at all in the trial and can be found only in the opinions filed at the conclusion of the proceedings by Senators Henry Wilson, Charles Sumner, and James W. Patterson, all Republicans. As Wilson described Johnson's thwarting of the Freedmen's Bureau bill, "To protect the freedmen he had wickedly abandoned to the control of their enemies and the nation's enemies,

Congress passed a civil-rights bill; the President attempted to arrest it by a veto; and failing in that, he has utterly neglected to enforce it . . . the President has sought to prevent the enforcement of the laws passed over his vetoes."[63]

Senator Sumner observed that Johnson "took to himself legislative powers in the reconstruction of the rebel States, and, in carrying forward this usurpation, nullified an act of Congress, intended as the corner-stone of reconstruction."[64] Senator Patterson noted with dissatisfaction that the Reconstruction portions of Article 11

> do not seem to have received that attention which their importance would justify. The evidence upon the records by which they are supported is very slight. I have been the more surprised at this inasmuch as [the article] sets forth that the President attempted to prevent the execution of the act entitled "An act to provide for the more efficient government of the rebel States." This I have deemed the *primum mobile* which has impelled the entire policy of the Executive.[65]

It was left, then, to the written opinions of various senators to comment on Andrew Johnson's conduct respecting Reconstruction, the trial having supplied little information or argument on the subject. Manager George Boutwell spoke of the difficulty in securing proof that the president had thwarted execution of the Reconstruction Act of 1867. The difficulty came about, he said, because many subservient officeholders in both the North and the South had proved unwilling to reveal any information about the president's performance. Southern officeholders approved of Johnson's actions because through him, Boutwell claimed, they expected to "possess and exercise that power which the slaveholders of the South possessed and exercised previous to the rebellion. [These men] have exerted their power to close up every avenue of information."[66] This explanation and some inconclusive testimony on alleged presidential interference with Reconstruction in Alabama constituted the prosecution's development. Therefore, Benjamin Curtis had been no more cavalier in his treatment of Article 11 than had the managers, and the potentially most damaging charges against President Johnson remained essentially unexamined.

Lorenzo Thomas, the first defense witness, testified to his ad interim appointment and his efforts to take over the War Department. Benjamin Butler referred to Thomas as "a weak, vacillating, vain, old man," a cruel but seemingly accurate description, judging by Thomas's responses during the trial.[67] Thomas's report of his dealings with President Johnson did not reveal a conspiracy or any deliberately illegal deed.

Throughout the trial the defense presentation was frequently interrupted by the managers' objections to admissibility of evidence, objections that the Senate usually sustained. For example, the second witness, war hero William Tecumseh Sherman, who had twice declined appointment as secretary of war ad interim, was called to testify about his conversations with President Johnson concerning Secretary Stanton's removal and whether he, Sherman, knew of any presidential plans to use threats or force to effect the removal.[68] Ten times the Senate supported the managers in their demand that Sherman's testimony be excluded. Later, when Secretary of the Navy Gideon Welles was asked whether the cabinet had ever discussed the use of force to evict Stanton, Welles replied, "Never, on any occasion—" and was stopped in mid-sentence by Manager Butler. The Senate upheld the manager and refused to admit the testimony.[69] These acts diminished any presumption that the Senate had a concern for learning all the facts.

One of the president's counsel, Henry Stanbery, had been sick and unable to attend during much of the trial. Four days before the conclusion of testimony, William Evarts asked for a postponement so that Stanbery could be present. Butler objected vehemently, pointing out that the government had come to a standstill because of the trial and that the South was in turmoil. He declaimed: "While we are waiting for the Attorney General to get well . . . numbers of our fellow-citizens are being murdered day by day. There is not a man here who does not know that the moment justice is done on this great criminal these murders will cease . . . the true Union men of the south are being murdered, and on our hands and on our skirts is this blood if we remain any longer idle."[70]

Evarts reacted to Butler's argument by saying, "I have never heard such a harangue before in a court of justice. . . . All these delays and the ill consequences seem to press upon the honorable managers except at the precise point of time when some of their mouths are open."[71] The Senate took no action resulting from this exchange except to adjourn for that day.

The rest of the testimony for Andrew Johnson concerned his speeches and the role of the cabinet in presidential decision making. The latter consideration was intended to show that President Johnson had consulted his cabinet about his veto of the Tenure of Office Act, that he honestly believed the law to be unconstitutional, and that he had no inclination to violate any laws. Once more the managers objected to the admissibility of evidence on cabinet participation in Johnson's veto of the tenure act; the Senate upheld the objections and thus again thwarted the defense in its desire to demonstrate the president's actions and his purposes. In a letter written during the trial, Chief Justice Chase commented on Senate rejection of the respondent's testimony. "I was greatly disappointed and pained," the chief justice wrote, that the Senate "excluded the evidence of members of the Cabinet as to their consultations and discussions (in one of which Mr. Stanton took a concurring part), and the advise given to the President. . . . I could conceive of no evidence more proper to be received, or more appropriate to enlighten a court as to the intent with which [Johnson had acted]."[72] Sixteen witnesses appeared on President Johnson's behalf; testimony ended on April 20.

Summary for both sides began on April 22 with filing of an argument by Manager John Logan.[73] He emphasized the political nature of impeachment and its coverage of non-indictable acts such as abuse of power. He analyzed the executive's appointment and removal power, stressing the Senate's coordinate role in appointment and insisting that it extended equally to removal. Logan attacked President Johnson's acts and motives with abandon, calling him a traitor, a man of arrogance, untruthful, vapid, and vulgar. Reaching a crescendo of vilification, he wrote:

> Almost from the time when the blood of Lincoln was warm on the floor of Ford's Theatre, Andrew Johnson was contemplating treason to all the fresh fruits of the overthrown and crushed rebellion, and an affiliation with and a practical official and hearty sympathy for those who had cost hecatombs of slain citizens, billions of treasure, and an almost ruined country. His great aim and purpose has been to subvert law, usurp authority, insult and outrage Congress, reconstruct the rebel States in the interests of treason . . . and deliver all snatched from wreck and ruin into the hands of unrepentant, but by him pardoned, traitors.[74]

Next came Manager George Boutwell, who addressed the Senate on the appointment and removal power, the charges against Andrew Johnson, and their substantiation by the prosecution. One portion of Boutwell's presentation has often been quoted: his description of a "hole in the sky" into which he wished that Johnson could be thrown.[75] Later, when summarizing the respondent's case, William Evarts had fun with the "hole in the sky" expression. He referred to the "astronomical punishment" proposed by Boutwell, who had "discovered an untenanted and unappropriated region in the skies, reserved, he would have us think, in the final councils of the Almighty, as the place of punishment for convicted and deposed American Presidents. [Laughter]."[76]

Despite Boutwell's "hole in the sky" and his references to Johnson's "criminal designs" and "mad schemes," his performance was thorough and usually temperate. He reminded the Senate that the consequences of Johnson's policy included limiting the vote to white males without regard to their disloyalty and working to secure swift readmission of the rebellious states for his own political advantage. His summation struck the main points against the president: (1) Johnson had violated the Tenure of Office Act; (2) a president could not determine for himself the constitutionality of a given act but must faithfully enforce all laws; and (3) Johnson had not only failed to execute the Reconstruction Acts but also had forestalled their enforcement by others. These constituted the serious charges, far more potent a threat to Andrew Johnson's tenure than his blustering speeches or presumed conspiratorial intentions, both of which took up great amounts of time and beclouded the real issues.

Following Boutwell came Thomas A. R. Nelson, first spokesman for the respondent. Rebutting the hard designations of Andrew Johnson as tyrant, traitor, and usurper, he sketched the president's steadfast devotion to the Union and to the Constitution. Nelson regretted the breach between the president and Congress. He explained that it sprang from an honest difference of opinion, a difference based on Johnson's continuation of Abraham Lincoln's Reconstruction policy and on the belief held by both presidents that the rebellious states had never been out of the Union.

Nelson considered the question of whether the Senate in an impeachment sat as a court. Manager Butler in his opening speech had argued that the Senate did not sit as a court and was "bound by no law . . . which may limit your constitutional prerogative. . . . You are a law unto yourselves."[77] Nelson contested this argument on historical and constitutional grounds, insisting that the accusers prove their charges by legally established courtroom standards, not by parliamentary rules. He explained Johnson's position on each article, restating that the Tenure of Office Act was unconstitutional and that Johnson had been right in abiding by his cabinet's advice. Furthermore, Nelson continued, no president should be saddled with a confidential adviser for whom he was responsible and whom he did not trust. Nelson pointed out that the Senate debate, when the tenure bill was being considered, proved that Secretary Stanton was not covered by it nor was he intended to be.

Nelson made two curious comments. The first attempted to establish that because Secretary Stanton still held his office, Johnson could not have removed him and so could not be charged with that violation.[78] This tortured construction did not change the fact that the president had certainly intended to be rid of Stanton and had taken all available steps toward that end. The second comment concerned Nelson's belief that the House and the Senate lacked power to bring an impeachment or to try one because ten states remained unrepresented in either body. "I shall not argue the question. . . . I think it would be an idle consumption of time to do so. I only advert to it so that I may place upon record this fact."[79] Why Nelson raised a point so irritating to the Congress without intending to argue its merit is difficult to understand.

William S. Groesbeck gave the next speech for the president's side. He opened by saying that efforts to impeach elective officers reflected a bad policy; only officers with life tenure should be impeachable, he averred. Having made this extraneous and nonconstitutional observation, he proceeded to discuss whether the Senate sat as a court. He used the five preceding impeachment trials to show that in each of them the Senate called itself a court. Once more the respondent sought to remind senators that only the evidence produced before them, not party policy or public rumor, should be the basis of their judgment. The speech centered upon the legality of removing Stanton and appointing Thomas. The ground proved familiar, but Groesbeck showed good command of the subject except for his strange comment about who should be impeached and a statement that Johnson had been abiding by the Tenure of Office Act when he suspended Stanton.

Manager Thaddeus Stevens followed Groesbeck[80] and discussed mainly his own Article 11. He stated that the tenure act protected Stanton because Johnson was completing President Lincoln's term of office and the act extended to appointees during the term for which Lincoln had been elected. President Johnson, he argued, did not have a term of his own. Stevens said that Johnson must have thought the Tenure of Office Act was valid because he had suspended Stanton under its provisions. However, Stevens went on, when the Senate refused to approve the suspension, Johnson violated the tenure law by appointing Lorenzo Thomas in defiance of the Senate's failure to concur in Secretary Stanton's suspension.

Ambiguities and contradictions swirl around President Johnson's intentions respecting conformance with the tenure act. Among the contradictions none proved more remarkable than the statement of William S. Groesbeck in his summing up for the president's side. The managers, he said, had claimed that, in suspending Secretary Stanton, Johnson had "acted under your law. He did. I can adjust that suspension to the terms of your law . . . I tell you it was an overture from the President."[81] Had the managers seized upon this comment, Johnson's case would seem to have been compromised beyond redemption. Their failure to do so, as well as other failures on both sides to exploit unusual or illogical positions advanced by their opponents, leads to the conclusion that the two sides did not consistently listen to each other but instead gave set speeches, often unrelated to opposing arguments. Groesbeck's potentially calamitous statement indicates that he had not paid attention to his own colleagues' case, which they grounded on the correctness of the president's determination not to employ an act deemed illegal by him and his cabinet, an act not yet tested in court, and one in any case not believed to be applicable to Edwin M. Stanton.

Andrew Johnson did not cite the Tenure of Office Act in either his suspension or his removal of Secretary Stanton,[82] however several questions arise concerning both his intention and his procedure. Why did his first action to be rid of Stanton consist of a suspension rather than a dismissal? Why did he send his reasons for the suspension to the Senate, as required by the tenure act whenever the Senate was in recess, rather than simply discharge Stanton as an action within the authority of the executive and not calling for Senate involvement until he nominated a successor?

Documentation that President Johnson relied upon the Tenure of Office Act does not exist, but logic and reflection upon these questions suggest that he did. If he believed that the president had a constitutional and historically utilized power to remove, he would have acted directly to fire Edwin M. Stanton. It appears probable that he hoped to confound his Republican opponents by naming the widely popular General Grant under authority of the Tenure of Office Act, with the expectations that the appointment would not be rejected.

Manager Stevens next turned to the constitutionality of the Tenure of Office Act. He urged the Senate to stand by its former decisions affirming its constitutionality. Stevens asked if the president could "expect a sufficient number of his triers to pronounce that law unconstitutional and void—those same triers having passed upon its validity upon several occasions?"[83] This argument stressed the

153

fact that a majority of senators had already found Andrew Johnson's position wrong and emphasized that the Senate had already determined that the law was constitutional.

Turning to Johnson's role in advancing his own Reconstruction policy and impeding that of Congress, Thaddeus Stevens made a sweeping claim of dominance for Congress, saying

> Neither the President nor the judiciary had any right to interfere . . . in reconstruction further than they were directed by the sovereign power. That sovereign power in this republic is the Congress of the United States. . . . Andrew Johnson did usurp the legislative power of the nation by building new States, and reconstructing, as far as in him lay, this empire. . . . When Congress passed a law declaring all these doings unconstitutional . . . he proclaimed it unconstitutional, and advised the people not to submit to it nor to obey the commands of Congress.[84]

However, just at the point where specifics would have strengthened and illustrated his denunciation, Stevens backed away. He said, "I have not time to enumerate the particular acts which constitute his high-handed usurpation."[85] Once again, the managers let slip a chance to enumerate Andrew Johnson's acts that fell within the classification of impeachable conduct.

Next came Manager Thomas Williams, who referred to the world as straining "its ears to catch from the electric messenger the first tidings of a verdict which is either to send a thrill of joy through an afflicted land, or to rack it anew with the throes of anarchy and the convulsions of despair."[86] He claimed that the president "had in effect reopened the war, inaugurated anarchy, turned loose once more the incarnate devil of baffled treason and unappeasable hate, . . . ordained rapine and murder from the Potomac to the Gulf, and deluged the streets of Memphis as well as of New Orleans, and the green fields of the south, already dotted with so many patriot graves, with the blood of martyred citizens."[87]

Williams then abandoned his sensational style and presented a well-reasoned, lawyerlike summary of the case. He detailed the president's thwarting of the tenure act, said that Johnson planned to force the return of the Southern states on his own terms, and claimed that the president had abused the pardoning power. Williams gave a major part of his time to recounting the deliberate, as he viewed it, illegality of Johnson's efforts to be rid of Secretary Stanton. To diminish the argument that the cabinet supported the president's position on the Tenure of Office Act, he delivered an attack on the entire cabinet system and its alleged nonconstitutional and illegitimate development into an advisory group. Williams called the cabinet "a mere cabal . . . [that] could not have held together so long under an imperious, self-willed man like the present Executive, without a thorough submission to all his views."[88] In this broadside, Williams failed to comment on Edwin M. Stanton's approval of Johnson's tenure act veto, and Williams could hardly have been intending to suggest that Stanton had been a submissive cabinet member.

William M. Evarts spoke first in summation of the case for Andrew Johnson. He used an unrhetorical and often witty style; the senators interrupted his speech many times with laughter, especially when he made fun of Manager Boutwell's proposal to hurl Andrew Johnson into a black hole in the sky, or when he made slighting references to Manager Butler's military record, or when he gave examples of congressional speeches attacking Andrew Johnson in language as violent and discourteous as that of which the president stood accused.

A comment by Evarts on presidential succession did not become a reality of government until more than a hundred years later, when Gerald Ford, never elected to a nationwide office, assumed the presidency in 1974 under authority of the Twenty-fifth Amendment. Evarts observed that, were Johnson removed, "there will be no President of the United States; for that name and title is accorded by the Constitution to no man who has not received the suffrages of the people for the primary or the alternative elevation to that place." Then, without naming Benjamin Wade, president pro-tem of the Senate, Evarts pointed out that the nation "will be without a President, and the office sequestered will be discharged by a member of the body whose judgment has sequestered it."[89]

Evarts analyzed next the attempted removal of Stanton, finding it neither unusual nor alarming. He then reviewed the nature of impeachable acts, asserting that the charges against President Johnson did not conform to constitutional descriptions of impeachable conduct because they did not concern grave public matters, subversive of government. At most, the president has stumbled over a statute, a statute not only unconstitutional but also one that did not include Secretary Stanton within its scope. Evarts also pointed out the unusual imbalance of party strength in Congress, three-fourths of the House and of the Senate being of one party. Then, feigning not to expose so sensitive a topic, he added, "I do not touch upon the particular circumstances that the non-restoration of the Southern States has left your numbers in both houses of Congress [greater] than they might under other circumstances be."[90] He called upon the Senate to put aside partisanship and distinguish between illegality and offensive political stances. The president's counsel had experienced no discomfort in acknowledging, at an earlier time, the disreputable tone of Andrew Johnson's speeches nor in acknowledging the possibility that his political positions could be considered abominable. But they held steadily to their course that distasteful conduct or unpopular policies did not fit the constitutional model of impeachable acts. Evarts dismissed the conspiracy articles and Article 11 as trivial and unproved. He gave no significant attention to President Johnson's alleged violation of the Reconstruction Acts, but neither had the prosecution.

Henry Stanbery came next for the president's side. He reviewed the articles and analyzed the managers' efforts to sustain them, efforts that in his view had not been successful. He presented no new arguments, but he made a strong statement concerning the president's steadfast support of the Constitution and the laws, support he had personally observed closely in his two years' service as Andrew Johnson's attorney general.

Now came the prosecution's final turn. The valedictory speech, delivered by the chairman of the managers John A. Bingham, began on May 4, 1868 and continued for two full days and most of a third. Bingham spent a major part of his time stressing the necessity of presidential obedience to all laws. He argued that the executive could not decide for himself which laws were unconstitutional and therefore need not be enforced, as had "his highness, Andrew Johnson, first king of the United States, in imitation of George III."[91] Later he said, "If I am right in the position that the acts of Congress are law, binding upon the President and to be executed by him until repealed by Congress or actually reversed by the courts, it results that the willful violation of such acts of Congress by the President, and the persistent refusal to execute them is a high crime or misdemeanor."[92]

In the course of his presentation Bingham reviewed all the articles but gave only slight attention to the president's alleged interference with enforcement of the Reconstruction Acts. When he finished, "there were manifestations of applause in different portions of the galleries, with cheers," a breach of propriety that caused the chief justice to order the galleries cleared for a brief period.[93]

On May 16 the Senate reconvened as a court and agreed to accept the motion of George Williams (Union Republican, Oregon) to vote first on Article 11. The result revealed thirty-five voting guilty and nineteen not guilty, just one vote short of conviction.[94] Seven Republicans, often called the "recusants," joined the unbreakable ranks of the twelve Democrats in acquitting Andrew Johnson: William P. Fessenden (Maine), Joseph S. Fowler (Tennessee), James W. Grimes (Iowa), John B. Henderson (Missouri), Edmund G. Ross (Kansas), Lyman Trumbull (Illinois), and Peter Van Winkle (West Virginia).

Perhaps, hoping that a delay in the proceedings might produce a different result by giving time to persuade even one of the renegade Republicans to change his vote, Zachariah Chandler (Republican, Michigan) moved for a ten-day postponement, a motion that passed thirty-two to twenty-one.[95] All twelve Democrats, joined by nine Republicans, voted against it; two of the apostate Republicans in the vote on the eleventh article, Senators Ross and Van Winkle, returned to the Republican fold and voted for postponement, acts that may have given false hope to the impeachers that the two men might be wavering.

When the Senate reassembled on May 26, it voted first on Article 2, which charged Johnson with violating the tenure act when he made Lorenzo Thomas secretary of war ad interim. The results were identical with the vote on Article 11: thirty-five favoring, nineteen opposing. Next, the Senate voted on Article 3, producing precisely the same outcome.

When these three votes demonstrated the impossibility of securing conviction, the Senate passed a motion to adjourn sine die. The greatest state trial in United States history, its preeminence threatened briefly in 1974 when Richard Nixon stood at the threshold of impeachment, ended with the announcement of Chief Justice Salmon P. Chase: "So the Senate, sitting as a court of impeachment for the trial of Andrew Johnson, upon articles of impeachment presented by the House of Representatives, stands adjourned without day."[96] He did not make the customary announcement that the respondent stood acquitted of the charges laid against him.

Thirty senators filed their opinions after the trial: twenty-four Republicans and six Democrats. Among the twenty-four Republicans were six of the seven who had voted Johnson not guilty. The six recusants who filed for posterity the reasons for deserting their party did not make a strong case supporting Andrew Johnson. Instead, all reported they believed as a matter of judgment and conscience that offenses they considered impeachable had either not been charged or had not been proved. They also, variously, expressed special concern that convicting a president must be for misconduct of the greatest magnitude, seen to be so by all reasonable men, and without taint of partisanship.

Senator John Sherman (Republican, Ohio), who found Johnson guilty on the three articles presented for a vote, stated in his filed report that he would have voted the president not guilty on Articles 1, 4, 5, 6, 9, and 10 had they come before the Senate for decision, mainly because he believed that the tenure act did not protect Edwin M. Stanton. Sherman had publicly advanced that view when the Senate debated the tenure bill.

On the day the trial ended, Stanton resigned. His letter to President Johnson stated, "having this day failed to be supported by two-thirds of the Senators, ... I have relinquished charge of the War Department." Three days later, the Senate approved John M. Schofield, a Union general in the Civil War, to be the next secretary of war.[97] Johnson, in a fence-mending concession to the Republicans, had nominated Schofield on April 23, while the trial was still in progress.

As occurred in the Samuel Chase and James Peck trials, the losing side did not accept the verdict and proceed to other business. The House of Representatives instructed the managers to investigate rumors of bribery in connection with securing votes of not guilty. Nothing was discovered.

In July 1868 Thaddeus Stevens made another try at impeachment by presenting five new articles; he stated that lack of specific charges against Andrew Johnson had caused the failure of the managers to secure a guilty verdict.[98] Congressman Stevens received support in this effort from Thomas Williams and from Republican Charles Hamilton of Florida, whose state had just been restored to the Union that month. One hundred three representatives agreed to consider the new impeachment resolution, but it was subsequently tabled on the motion of George S. Boutwell, who was more realistic than his brother Republicans about the chance of securing another impeachment vote or convicting Johnson in another Senate trial.[99] Then Congress finally laid the matter aside for good.

The impeachment and trial of Andrew Johnson spread over a period of one year and five months, from December 17, 1866, to the end of the trial on May 26, 1868. It heavily involved all three branches of government. The president, obviously absorbed in the matter for the three months of the trial, had been sporadically attentive to it during the preceding year. Salmon P. Chase presided over the Senate for the trial period (March 5 to May 26), to the presumed detriment of his Supreme Court duties. Managers and other members of the House of Representatives were immersed in the trial and in the year-long efforts to accomplish the impeachment.

Why, given the long and serious struggle to be rid of Andrew Johnson, with many newspapers and much of the public aroused to demand conviction, with the widespread recognition that he had failed to fulfill congressional plans for restructuring the South, and with the preponderance of Republicans in the Senate, did the effort fail? Among possible answers to this question, the following seem to be the strongest: (1) genuine doubts, even among some who voted guilty, that impeachable acts had been charged or proved; (2) uncertainty that the Tenure of Office Act protected Secretary Stanton; (3) failure by the managers to produce convincing evidence that President Johnson had neglected to execute the laws; (4) excesses of language and argument by the managers and more persuasive presentations by the president's attorneys; (5) indications that Johnson had quieted down and would be relatively cooperative for the remainder of his term; (6) and finally, Republicans' fear of Benjamin F. Wade, the super-radical who would become president upon Johnson's conviction.[100]

Despite such reasons, it remains hard to understand how a president who had not carried out the acts of Congress, who had claimed authority in an area that was arguably congressional, and who was tried for his conduct by a Senate made up of nearly 80 percent of the opposing party escaped conviction. It is even harder to understand why the managers did not state Andrew Johnson's violations plainly and argue them convincingly. Instead, the managers spent days on the Tenure of Office Act, when many participants already knew that key senators doubted that the act protected Secretary Stanton; and they gave long hours to discussing Johnson's lurid campaign speeches, which, however discreditable, few could believe constituted impeachable acts.

In comparison with efforts to draw profiles of the voting blocs in the five earlier impeachments, sketching the characteristics of the opposing sides in the Johnson trial becomes an easy task, in part because no geographic biases appeared in Johnson's impeachment and the core of the division occurred on party lines. All senators who voted guilty were Republicans. Every Democrat voted not guilty. Obviously, the seven Republicans who joined the Democrats determined the outcome of the trial, but their defection does not destroy the image of the Johnson impeachment as an intensely partisan occurrence. The Democrats proved as monolithic in supporting Andrew Johnson as did the majority of the Republicans in opposing him.

Johnson's remaining months as president were undramatic. He failed to receive the Democratic presidential nomination in 1868, and saw his enemy, Ulysses S. Grant, elected to succeed him. Johnson did not attend the swearing-in ceremony because Grant refused to ride to his inaugural in the same carriage with him.[101]

Andrew Johnson returned to a warm welcome in Tennessee, a notable contrast to the bitter shouts of traitor that had been his lot when he left the state to become vice president. Although scarred by his near-conviction, disappointed at his failure to be the Democratic nominee for president in 1868, and thwarted in his attempt to weld a new national political coalition, Johnson, nevertheless, had no intention of staying out of politics. In 1869, the same year of his leaving the presidency, he became an unsuccessful candidate for the United States Senate. After other fruitless tries for public office, he was finally elected to the Senate in 1875.[102] A special session in March permitted Johnson to return to Washington six years after his departure. He received a generous reception in the Senate chamber, in which he had so recently been on trial. Johnson made only one speech in his brief tenure there—an attack on President Grant's policy toward the South. He died soon afterward, in July 1875, a kind of hero in Tennessee and no longer an archvillain in the North.

The persistent themes of past impeachments echoed through the Johnson trial, and the value of his experience to the history of impeachment will always be great because of the office he held. Did it verify the rather tenuously established doctrine of earlier United States impeachments that holds an officer liable to impeachment, and possible removal, for nonindictable acts? Did it clarify the issue of whether corrupt motives must be demonstrated? Must the acts, in order to be impeachable, have been performed as part of official duties? Did Johnson's impeachment sustain recusant Republican Edmund G. Ross's claim that, destructive as it seemed to him to have been, it could be significant in some future day if a bad president menaced the political system, at which time the remedy "may be as patriotically, as fearlessly, and as unselfishly applied as it was on this occasion rejected"?[103]

Unfortunately, with respect to the comfort that certitude brings, these questions can be answered either way; no plainly definitive precedent emerged from Andrew Johnson's experience. However, his trial did produce strong support for the position that impeachment extends to misconduct not necessarily criminal in nature and that willful malperformance need not be proved.

On the problem of the fairness of the Senate sitting as a judicial body in a cause on which it had already taken a position, it is unarguable that the Senate bears the constitutional duty to be the deciding body in an impeachment; it is equally unarguable that a fair trial presupposes an impartial hearing agency. The strange situation surrounding William Blount's impeachment trial in 1799 will come to mind in this connection. How could senators who had already deprived Blount of his Senate seat for high crimes and misdemeanors subsequently sit as judges in a trial in which they would decide whether he had, indeed, committed the acts for which they had just expelled him? Arguments of unfairness brought forth by Andrew Johnson's attorneys, who could easily demonstrate the hostility of many senators to Johnson, prove persuasive but do not change the reality: the Senate is required to be the court in an impeachment trial.

What if the verdict had gone the other way? What would have been the consequences to the nation and to the literature of impeachment? It seems probable that the effects of Andrew Johnson's conviction would have been bad, in part because the charges against him were not strongly substantiated, in part because the accession of Benjamin Wade to the presidency might have resulted in more political, social, and economic upheaval than characterized Johnson's remaining months in the White House. This last point does not suggest that Johnson should have escaped conviction because his successor might have been a worse disaster, only that several senators had expressed fear and antagonism at the thought of Benjamin Wade as president, a view that influenced their vote.

The crucial bad effect of a guilty verdict would stem from the fact that a firm case had not been made that the unpopular Johnson had breached his oath of office. His conviction could then be recorded in the annals of impeachment as a precedent for turning out a politically repudiated president. The Johnson case might be cited as proof that attacks upon Congress furnished examples of high crimes and misdemeanors and that political intransigence and intemperate speechmaking are impeachable. What then of the doughty Harry Truman and his robust criticism of the "do nothing 80th Congress" in 1948? Thus, the verdict must be supported as correct considering the evidence presented in the trial: an impeachment trial has to produce proof of abuse of office or inability to perform official duties, not political intransigence or unwary speechmaking.

No one has ever believed that Andrew Johnson's escape provided an impeachment precedent establishing selective enforcement of the laws as a course open to a president. And not until Richard Nixon advanced his extraordinary notion that any presidential act became legal by the mere fact of the president's doing it had any such grandiose view of the executive power been put forth.[104] Certainly, Johnson made no such assumption, nor has anyone else used the outcome of Johnson's trial as a basis for claiming that a president has the right to disregard laws he does not consider constitutional.

The only president to be impeached, Andrew Johnson, and the trial in which he starred will continue to be interesting subjects for study and debate. His experience demonstrates the extra turmoil and disruption characterizing a presidential impeachment and trial and the resultant halting or slowing of government business. Impeachment remains the only way to reach a president whose continuance in office would put the Constitution and the laws in peril. The enormous power of the presidency when used for evil looms as a far greater threat to the country than does the transitory upheaval caused by an impeachment. This lesson the nation learned again, by indirection, in 1974, when Richard Nixon's conduct brought him to the edge of impeachment and trial, processes abandoned only because he resigned.

William W. Belknap. *Library of Congress.*

8

William W. Belknap

If I swear, I shall tell the truth, and that will ruin
Secretary Belknap.
—Caleb P. Marsh

Like the two officers whose trials immediately preceded his own,
Judge West H. Humphreys and President Andrew Johnson, Secretary
of War William W. Belknap was a participant in the Civil War and in
the reconstruction period that followed it. A general in the war,
Belknap was appointed to public office by Johnson and later by Ulysses S. Grant and knew several of the principal actors in both the
Humphreys and Johnson trials. His troubles, however, were not directly tied to Civil War issues, but to the besetting problems of the
scandal-ridden Grant administration: improper financial dealings.
Belknap resigned only a few hours before the House of Representatives unanimously impeached him for high crimes and misdemeanors connected with his management of post traderships.

One characteristic of William Belknap's impeachment is unique:
he is the only national official whose trial took place after he had
resigned. William Blount, although not in office when he was tried
in 1799, had not resigned but had been expelled by the Senate. An
unusual characteristic of Belknap's experience is the unanimous
vote in the House of Representatives to impeach him; this characteristic was not duplicated until 1986, when the House impeached
Judge Harry E. Claiborne unanimously.[1]

Although the trial of William Belknap occurred only eight years
after that of Andrew Johnson, just twelve senators, eleven Republicans and one Democrat, sat in both trials. During the period separating the Johnson and Belknap impeachments, the South had
regained its congressional representation and Colorado had been admitted to the Union, creating twenty-two additional new senators
since President Johnson's trial.

William Worth Belknap, an attorney, had been a member of
the Iowa legislature, having been elected to that body as a Douglas Democrat. After the Civil War, Andrew Johnson appointed him

collector of internal revenue in Iowa,[2] the position he held at the time Ulysses S. Grant appointed him secretary of war in 1869.

Secretary Belknap was identified with the radical Republican positions on Reconstruction, but it was not the struggle between radical Republicans and moderates that brought William Belknap to grief. His downfall came from the same source that caused most of the scandals of President Grant's flawed administration— unmitigated greed. Belknap's casual management of War Department finances and appointments extended to more than just one episode, but the first Mrs. Belknap presumably generated the most conspicuous crime, a crime, however, that could not have occurred without Secretary Belknap's active participation.[3]

The first Mrs. Belknap died in 1870, and Belknap later married her sister. Both women, as well as Belknap himself, participated in the social life of the capital. Benjamin Perley Poore recorded details of the Belknaps' reputation for giving lavish parties; unless, he observed, the Belknaps acquired additional sources of income (cabinet members earned $8,000 a year), they would be unable to maintain the social position they enjoyed. As Poore phrased it: "the Belknaps were either obliged to retire from society or . . . replenish the family coffers."[4]

The first Mrs. Belknap, knowing how lucrative military post traderships had proved, encouraged a friend, Caleb P. Marsh, to apply for one. Assignments to post traderships were made by the secretary of war, and Mrs. Belknap told Marsh that she would ask her husband to appoint him to one of such positions. Subsequently, in late 1870, Caleb P. Marsh requested Secretary Belknap to appoint him post trader at Fort Sill, in Oklahoma, a position then held by John S. Evans. Belknap appointed Marsh but asked him to see Evans and make an arrangement that would protect Evans's property rights in the buildings and stock at Fort Sill.[5] The two men conferred about the tradership; their conference resulted in an offer by John S. Evans to pay Marsh $12,000 a year if the latter would withdraw so that Evans could retain his post. Marsh agreed to give up the appointment and to accept the bribe. He shared the money equally with Mrs. Belknap. Thus, for doing nothing at all, Caleb P. Marsh received a sum exceeding Secretary Belknap's annual salary and passed half of it on to his benefactors. The Belknap family received more than $20,000 from this unlawful transaction.

When Caleb P. Marsh testified at the Belknap impeachment trial, he stated that he had never had any financial understanding with

the secretary that induced the latter to appoint him to the post tradership. Asked why he gave money to the Belknaps, Marsh explained
his reason as being "simply because I felt like doing it. It gave me
pleasure to do it."[6] His first payment had been made to the now deceased Mrs. Belknap, Caleb P. Marsh said, and subsequent payments
were made to the second Mrs. Belknap or to the secretary himself.
At no time, according to Marsh, did Secretary Belknap exhibit any
curiosity about the financial contributions; he asked no questions
about the source of the payments or why Marsh was sending him
any money at all.

These curious transactions began to unfold to public view when
the House of Representatives Committee on Expenditures in the
War Department, having learned of the Evans-Marsh-Belknap arrangements in February 1876, summoned Caleb P. Marsh to testify
about them. Prior to appearing before the committee, Marsh conferred with Secretary and Mrs. Belknap. The latter revealed that
she had been aware of the financial arrangements between Marsh
and her sister, the first Mrs. Belknap. Marsh told the Belknaps that
when he appeared before the committee he would not lie, but he
would be willing to leave the country in order to avoid testifying.[7]
Belknap told Marsh not to flee the country, because the House committee would look upon such an act as confirming the secretary's
involvement.

When he testified before the expenditures committee, Caleb P.
Marsh told its members that "if I swear, I shall tell the truth, and
that will ruin Secretary Belknap." He described the first Mrs.
Belknap's urging him to apply for a tradership and "if I wanted one
she would ask the Secretary for one for me . . . I do not remember
saying that if I had a valuable post of that kind that I would remember her."[8] Marsh's uncertain comment that he did not remember
promising to divide his unearned money with her must have appeared to the members of the expenditures committee, and later to
the senators listening during the trial, as a clear, if unspoken, understanding that he would do just that.

Secretary Belknap discovered that the House of Representatives,
having learned of the post tradership trickery, was about to impeach
him. He hurried to the White House to resign. President Grant accepted the resignation at once, apparently believing that William
Belknap wanted to resign because his wife had engaged in illegal activities. The president found out that he had made a mistake. He
learned on the same day on which he accepted the resignation that
Belknap was involved directly in a crime, had misled the president

about his reasons for wanting to leave the cabinet, and faced immediate impeachment by the House of Representatives.

Ulysses S. Grant's trusting and credulous nature has been well documented. Even so, his apparent readiness to accept the story that William Belknap's resignation sprang from the desire to protect his wife's reputation stretches trust and credulity all out of shape. A *New York Tribune* account four years earlier (1872) had described Belknap's methods of awarding post traderships and the benefits accruing thereby to members or friends of the administration.[9] And in February 1876, less than a month before Belknap's resignation, the *New York Herald* had demanded an investigation of corruption in the War Department and had included Orvil Grant, the president's brother, as among the beneficiaries of the department's patronage.[10]

William Belknap's performance in office could hardly be unknown to President Grant. Perhaps Grant's ignorance of the political and economic environment surrounding and destroying his administration led him to be foolishly trusting of a loyal, to him, cabinet member. As explained by radical Republican George S. Boutwell, Ulysses S. Grant lacked "any element of suspicion, and his confidence in his friends was free and full. Hence it happened that he had many occasions for regret."[11]

As early as 1872 Belknap had been accused of violating the neutrality laws by selling government arms to French agents and manufacturing cartridges for them. An investigating committee substantiated the facts but exonerated Belknap of violating any laws. William B. Hesseltine notes that although the committee found no evidence of illegality, "there was . . . ample evidence of carelessness if not corruption in the War Department."[12] That episode and newspaper exposés of problems surrounding management of the post traderships should have warned the president to be suspicious of his secretary of war.

The House of Representatives that impeached Belknap in 1876 was composed of 169 Democrats, 109 Republicans, and 14 miscellaneous—a 58 percent majority for the Democrats. Republicans had suffered a big loss in the 1874 election because facts of the sordid dealings of members of President Grant's administration had become known. By unanimously supporting Secretary Belknap's impeachment, Republicans in the House showed their desire to divorce themselves from the taint of corruption hanging over their party and to demonstrate their willingness to forward the cause of cleansing the government.

The Senate that tried William Belknap had a total of seventy-six members: twenty-nine Democrats, forty-five Republicans, one Anti-Monopolist, and one Conservative—giving the Republicans a 59 percent majority, about the same percentage by which the Democrats controlled the House.

On March 2, 1876, the day of Secretary Belknap's resignation, Hiester Clymer (Democrat, Pennsylvania) reported to the House of Representatives for the Committee on Expenditures in the War Department. The committee, said its chairman, had "found at the very threshold of their investigation such unquestioned evidence of the malfeasance in office of General William W. Belknap" that the matter must be brought at once to the attention of the House.[13] Congressmen Clymer moved that Belknap be impeached of high crimes and misdemeanors, that the Judiciary Committee prepare articles of impeachment, and that a committee be appointed to inform the Senate of the impeachment. All three resolutions passed unanimously.

One month later, on April 3, the House of Representatives reported to the Senate that it had elected seven managers to conduct the trial and that it stood ready to present five articles of impeachment. All five of the articles detailed aspects of the Fort Sill tradership deal and the unlawful financial benefits accruing from it to Caleb Marsh and, through him, to William Belknap. Scott Lord (Democrat, New York) was elected chairmen of the managers; the other members were George F. Hoar (Republican, Massachusetts), George A. Jenks (Democrat, Pennsylvania), J. Proctor Knott (Democrat, Kentucky), Elbridge G. Lapham (Republican, New York), William P. Lynde (Democrat, Wisconsin), and John A. McMahon (Democrat, Ohio). Although the zeal of the Democrats for convicting William Belknap might be expected to exceed that of the Republicans, two Republicans accepted service as managers, indicating the party's concern about widespread corruption and the need to be a part of exposing and stopping it. In all the preceding impeachments the managers had been from the same party or at least of the same political outlook. The Belknap impeachment became the first in which the major parties joined forces to conduct a prosecution.

Before considering the trial, the following facts of the Belknap case should be reviewed: (1) Caleb P. Marsh applied for an army post tradership at the instigation of the first Mrs. Belknap; (2) Secretary of War William W. Belknap appointed Marsh to the tradership at Fort Sill; (3) Belknap asked Marsh to work out an arrangement with the incumbent trader, John S. Evans, to protect the latter's investment at the Fort; (4) Marsh agreed to accept $12,000 a year (later reduced to $6,000) from Evans as a condition for the latter's retaining his post; and (5) Marsh split the money he received from Evans with the Belknaps. William Belknap's knowledge clearly extended to all five items. However, the fifth item forms the key element in the trial. Whereas Belknap acknowledged accepting money in person and by mail from Caleb P. Marsh, he maintained that he understood it to belong to his wife and had no reason to inquire about its source; on this crucial issue the secretary tried to exempt himself from any guilty involvement.

On April 4, 1876 Scott Lord presented the five articles of impeachment to the Senate. The articles described Belknap's appointment of Marsh to the post tradership, the kickback arrangements between Evans and Marsh permitting the former to continue as trader, and the transferring of part of Marsh's bribe money to Secretary Belknap—$24,450 over a six-year period. Belknap was categorized as "criminally disregarding his duty as Secretary of War, and basely prostituting his high office to his lust for private gain. . . . [He acted] against public policy, and to the great disgrace and detriment of the public service."[14]

All the articles accused the secretary of high crimes and misdemeanors. Bribery, specifically listed in the Constitution as an impeachable offense, did not appear explicitly among the managers' charges although several people mentioned it during the trial, and George A. Jenks, when summing up for the prosecution, directly referred to Belknap's offense as bribery.[15] It is difficult to determine why the managers employed the phrase "high crimes and misdemeanors" to describe unlawful taking of money instead of using the plain, constitutionally prescribed word *bribery.* One explanation may be that the managers could not prove that Secretary Belknap appointed Caleb P. Marsh because Marsh had promised him money to secure the appointment.

The day following the managers' presentation of the impeachment articles, April 5, Chief Justice Morrison R. Waite administered the oath to the senators, who, now duly sworn as a court of impeachment, agreed to the managers' request that the Senate summon William Belknap to appear on April 17. On that day Belknap came before the Senate, accompanied by three attorneys: Matthew H. Carpenter, a prominent lawyer and former United States senator; Jeremiah S. Black, briefly one of Andrew Johnson's attorneys and a chief justice of Pennsylvania's supreme court; and Montgomery

Blair, postmaster general in Abraham Lincoln's first administration and scion of a powerful Maryland political family. Carpenter presented Belknap's response to the articles, a response not refuting or even alluding to the substance of the charges but merely stating that William Belknap held no office and as a private citizen prayed "judgment whether this court can or will take further cognizance of the said articles of impeachment."[16]

Chairman of the managers Scott Lord gave the House of Representatives' reply to Belknap's response on April 19. Lord pointed out that William Belknap had been an officer of the United States when he performed the acts charged against him. He resigned with full knowledge that the House would impeach him, and by resigning he clearly intended to evade being tried. Therefore, the Senate should reject the respondent's plea that because he had become a private citizen by the time of the trial he could not be impeached and tried.

William Belknap's rejoinder to the managers, presented on April 27, stressed that (1) he had resigned before the House of Representatives brought charges against him, (2) he could be tried only in a court of law, and (3) he had resigned because Hiester Clymer had promised to drop the impeachment if he withdrew from office. This offer, Belknap claimed, persuaded him to resign because he knew Caleb P. Marsh had given information to the committee that, although not harmful to Belknap himself, reflected on a member of his family. Therefore, he gave up the office because the matter under study by the Committee on Expenditures, "though it involved no criminality on his part, was deeply painful to his feelings."[17]

Whether Clymer made any such offer or whether he said anything at all that Belknap could reasonably understand as an agreement to halt impeachment upon the latter's resignation did not emerge clearly during the trial. Scott Lord rejected Belknap's assertion and said that Clymer had no authority to promise to drop the charges.

When Congressman Clymer testified during the trial as a prosecution witness, neither side asked him about the purported promise.[18] On the last day of the trial Scott Lord adverted to it again in his concluding speech for the prosecution. He pointed out that the respondent's attorneys had made no effort to prove the existence of an understanding between Clymer and Belknap and had not even asked the former about it when he was on the stand. Lord claimed that had Belknap "resigned because of a contract with Mr. Clymer . . . counsel should have proved the fact for what it is worth; and I say again, if it were true, he would have proved it."[19] It seems equally arguable that the managers could have shown the allegation to be a phantom by questioning Clymer themselves, but they failed to do so. Thus, this intriguing bit of possible information hung untested in midair.

Before arguments began on the substantive charges, Matthew Carpenter, speaking for Belknap, asked that the trial be postponed until December, a delay of eight months, and that the time allotted to debate the request for postponement be extended from the usual one hour for each side to two hours. The Senate approved the additional time for debate on the proposal by a vote of forty-eight to thirteen,[20] and Montgomery Blair opened the argument for delaying the trial.

Blair felt that more time would be needed to present the respondent's position opposing Senate jurisdiction over a private citizen. He also noted that the House of Representatives appeared ready to offer more articles against William Belknap, asking: "Are we to have impeachment in broken doses?"[21] Finally, Montgomery Blair argued, because the nation was in the midst of a fervent presidential election contest, the excitement of the campaign precluded calm and fair consideration by the Senate of the issues prompting the impeachment.[22] Belknap no longer held office; hence, no reason existed for hurrying the trial, and good reasons existed for postponing it.

Matthew Carpenter, appearing in Belknap's behalf, also spoke in favor of postponing the trial. He referred to the inflamed state of public opinion against William Belknap, to his honored service in the Civil War, and to the lack of urgency in moving promptly to the trial because the subject was no longer in office. Carpenter also sought to establish that Belknap acted as he did in order to protect a lady, presumably Mrs. Belknap. The defense made many oblique references during the trial to Belknap's unwillingness to discuss his situation because of his chivalrous impulses.

Carpenter noted that many Republicans actively opposed William Belknap, a fact that left him with no firm political adherents. Entreating the Senate to put off the trial until after the presidential election, he observed: "The democrats can only exhibit their virtue by finding corruption in the republican party to be rebuked, and republicans can exhibit their virtue only by out-Heroding Herod in punishment of whatever corruption democrats may pretend to find. Both parties are therefore interested in making the most of the alleged misconduct of the respondent."[23] The Senate did not accept the defense arguments and unanimously declined to postpone the trial.

The Senate reassembled as a court on May 1. The day was given to a lengthy exchange over whether the managers or Belknap's attorneys should have the first and last word when they debated the subject of Senate jurisdiction. Each side tried to use past impeachments to substantiate its claim to be both first and last. The managers' assertion that they had the right to open and close the debate was correct, based on former impeachment experiences. But Belknap's attorneys presented a technical legal point: because their reply to the articles was a demurrer, they were entitled to speak first and last, as provided in any court of law. The Senate sustained Belknap's attorneys by a vote of thirty-four to twenty.[24] The votes supporting the managers' position were cast by nineteen Democrats and by one Republican, Henry L. Dawes (Massachusetts).

Because of the vote, Montgomery Blair began the argument when the Senate resumed the hearing on May 4.[25] Blair referred to Senator William Blount's case in 1799 as having settled for all time that a private citizen could not be impeached. Next Blair pointed out that William Belknap exercised no powers of government; he insisted that Belknap's resignation arrested the impeachment proceedings and that no assumption of illegality could be drawn from a resignation inspired by the desire to avoid a pending prosecution. Urging the Senate to recognize that it had no jurisdiction, Blair observed: "If this court is to be opened to the persecution and prosecution of private men, and party passion and personal hate are to be invited to set themselves here upon private men because they may have been obnoxious officers, we have not yet passed by the days of tyranny."[26]

Scott Lord, replying to Blair, agreed that impeachment did not extend to any private citizens, but William Belknap, he pointed out, had been secretary of war on March 2, 1876, when the House of Representatives voted to impeach him. Also, because the Senate could issue a verdict of disqualification from ever again holding national office, Belknap remained answerable to impeachment and should be tried. A man could not exempt his public performance from scrutiny by resigning at the moment his misconduct was about to be revealed and examined. Lord also relied upon the Blount precedent but with conclusions different from Montgomery Blair's. He noted the belief of A. J. Dallas, one of Blount's attorneys, that an officer who resigned to escape prosecution was subject to impeachment. Then Lord quoted Jared Ingersoll, William Blount's other attorney, who had said, "I certainly shall never contend that an officer may first commit an offense, and afterward avoid punishment by resigning his office."[27] Although the Blount case is frequently cited as establishing that a former officeholder is not subject to impeachment, the observations of Blount's two attorneys respecting a *resigned* official dent such a conclusion.

On May 5, Matthew Carpenter continued the defense argument against the Senate's accepting jurisdiction. He reviewed at length the constitutional debates establishing the impeachment provisions; they had been designed, he said, to remove an unworthy public official and could not be stretched to reach a private citizen. Sidestepping the fact that an official could not only be removed from his post but also barred from again holding a national office, Carpenter claimed that "the sole object for which the power of impeachment was given is removal from office. . . . Must this court go on and sentence a man after he is dead,—either physically or officially dead? It is equally absurd to talk of removing a man from an office which he no longer fills. . . . The suit abates because there is no further object to be attained by its prosecution."[28]

The next day, George A. Jenks took up the argument for the managers. He examined the historical and constitutional bases for impeachment, emphasizing the fact that William Belknap held office when he performed the acts with which the House had charged him. If resignation could be interpreted as excusing an officer from trial, then, Jenks stated, "It is equivalent to saying that official crime can go unpunished at the option of the criminal. It was an infamy for [Belknap] to go and withhold material facts to get his patron, the Chief Executive, who had trusted him, to accept his resignation."[29]

Manager George F. Hoar followed Jenks. Hoar, one of two Republicans serving on the board of managers, disputed the claim of Belknap's attorneys that intense political passions and party divisions made a fair trial impossible. He reminded the senators that the House of Representatives had voted unanimously to impeach, and he expressed confidence in the Senate's ability to pronounce an honorable decision. The Senate must accept jurisdiction, he argued, because the strongest weapon it had against official malperformance consisted not in its capacity to remove but in its capacity to give a judgment of perpetual disqualification from holding further office. "Impeachment is not likely to be a favorite process with the Senate or the House," he added. "There is no likelihood that we shall ever unlimber this clumsy and bulky monster piece of ordnance to take aim at an object from which all danger has gone by."[30]

Hoar reviewed the political scandals of the Grant administration and the public's reliance on Congress to insure that corruption be exposed and punished. Such a reminder from a well-respected Republican congressman was no doubt expected to have special force with his fellow Republicans in the Senate, whose vote to accept jurisdiction over Belknap he sought to enlist. The fact that Hoar served as spokesman for this particular argument indicates the managers' design to refute any notion that the desire to try the former secretary represented mainly a Democratic party effort.

On May 8, 1876 Jeremiah Black, concluding speaker on the subject of Senate jurisdiction, reasserted the position held by him and his brother attorneys: William Belknap became a private citizen the moment President Grant accepted his resignation. Thereby he became exempt from the impeachment mechanism. It was entirely legal for Belknap to relinquish his office, Black said, and no inquiry into his motives for doing so could be instituted nor any blame attached to him for resigning. Scoffing at the managers' argument that the opportunity to disqualify Belknap from further office constituted a sound reason for the Senate's accepting jurisdiction, Black, like Matthew Carpenter before him, claimed removal to be the sole object of impeachment. "You cannot pronounce a judgment of removal without disqualifying; and you cannot pronounce a judgment of disqualification without removal, because the judgment which the Constitution requires you to pronounce is a judgment of removal *and* disqualification—not removal *or* disqualification."[31]

Black and Carpenter either did not know about, or did not care to call attention to, Judge John Pickering's trial in 1804, in which the Senate removed the judge but never considered disqualification, or the West Humphreys trial in 1862, in which the Senate decided that Judge Humphreys should be both removed and disqualified but held that the two issues were distinct and must be voted on separately. Their colleague, Montgomery Blair, when summing up for the defense at the end of the trial, demonstrated his knowledge of the true relationship between removal and disqualification. Without purporting to correct the Black-Carpenter inaccurate analysis, Blair replied to an inquiry on the subject by saying: "Can there be conviction without judgment of disqualification to hold office? The disqualification to hold office has not been considered as at all necessary. They may give it or they may not. It has never been maintained, I believe, by any commentator upon the Constitution, that it was necessary on conviction to add to the judgment disqualification as a part of the sentence."[32]

Jeremiah Black, concluding speaker for the respondent, reworked the theme of nonimpeachability of a private citizen. He alluded to an earlier reference by Manager George F. Hoar quoting John Quincy Adams's conviction that an officer's liability to impeachment for acts committed while a public official did not end when he left office but stayed with him throughout his life.[33] Black delighted in demolishing the argument and Adams along with it. He observed:

> the public history of Mr. Adams shows that he of all men that ever lived was the least reliable upon a question of law. He was too fond of personal controversy to care which side he took. It appears from the citation itself [the quote given by Manager Hoar] that the general opinion of the House . . . was that the power of impeachment applied only to persons actually in office. Mr. Adams of course opposed what everybody else believed to be true. Nothing indeed would have given him greater pleasure then to be impeached. It would have given him an opportunity to come over here and lay about him right and left. His organ of combativeness was always in a state of chronic inflammation. He enjoyed nothing so much as . . . the rapture of the strife. . . . He tried to provoke a motion for his own expulsion from the House, and that failing, he presented a petition from some outside enemy to expel himself.[34]

So much for John Quincy Adams, son of a president, a president himself, senator, congressman, minister to the Netherlands, Portugal, Russia, and England, secretary of state, and indefatigable diarist.

Upon the conclusion of Jeremiah Black's speech, the Senate adjourned for a week. Reconvening on May 15, senators debated the question of jurisdiction behind closed doors until May 29, when they accepted jurisdiction over Belknap by a vote of thirty-seven favoring, twenty-nine opposing, less than the two-thirds that would be needed for conviction at the end of the trial.

The thirty-seven senators who supported Senate jurisdiction over Belknap included twenty-four Democrats and thirteen Republicans. The twenty-nine who voted against accepting jurisdiction included twenty-six Republicans, two Democrats, and one Anti-Monopolist, Newton Booth.[35] Of the Democrats who voted, 92 percent supported accepting jurisdiction, while 89 percent of the Republicans who voted rejected Senate jurisdiction. This vote revealed strong partisan commitments; it also paved the way for most Republicans to avoid convicting Belknap at the end of the trial on the ground that he was not subject to the impeachment process.

The trial opened June 1 with an observation by Matthew Carpenter that the Senate had not approved accepting jurisdiction by a two-thirds vote; Carpenter insisted that such a majority must be part of every element of an impeachment trial. He doubted that any senator who believed the Senate lacked jurisdiction could subsequently vote William Belknap guilty. Thus, the proceeding should cease.[36] He then asked for time to confer with his absent colleagues, Montgomery Blair and Jeremiah Black, to see if they preferred to continue or to view the Senate's acceptance of jurisdiction as void because not attained by a two-thirds vote. The Senate adjourned until June 6, when, after much procedural discussion and amending of amendments, the Senate ordered Belknap's answer to the articles of impeachment to be delivered on June 16 and trial on the evidence to begin July 6.

Jeremiah Black appeared before the Senate on June 16, stating that the defense would not make a plea because William Belknap was a private citizen. He acknowledged, however, the Senate's authority to order the trial to proceed as if the respondent had pleaded not guilty. Because twenty-nine senators had disavowed Senate jurisdiction, Black was confident that the respondent's case had already been won. The Senate agreed to file Belknap's non-response to the articles, and after weeks of procedural delays, oceans of repetitive speeches, and many efforts to shift the date, the trial on the issues finally opened on July 6.

The managers summoned twenty-six witnesses, eight of whom were present at the time testimony began. Manager William P. Lynde gave the opening speech, stating that Senate jurisdiction over William Belknap had been settled by a majority vote, as required for all such decisions. He then described the history of the post traderships and the various regulations governing their management. Traders were required to supply soldiers, Indians, and emigrants with good products at fair prices. He quoted the recommendation of the officers at Fort Sill that John S. Evans be continued as post trader.

Lynde next recounted the Marsh-Evans arrangement allowing Evans to retain his tradership by paying Marsh and demonstrated that Mr. and Mrs. Belknap knew of the scheme. He also pointed out that Secretary Belknap had been aware of the *New York Tribune* story of 1872 describing abuses on the posts and in appointment procedures. Belknap responded to that story, Lynde said, by requiring traders to reside on their posts and requiring supervision of prices charged by them, but the secretary did not act on the matter of John

S. Evans's payments to Caleb Marsh. Lynde documented Belknap's receipt of half of such payments.

Next Manager John A. McMahon examined six prosecution witnesses who verified the Evans-Marsh contract, the delivery of money from Caleb Marsh to Belknap, and the secretary's knowledge of conditions at Fort Sill. Belknap's attorneys did not cross-examine the witnesses. Matthew Carpenter, before any witnesses had been called, had stated the respondent's position: "there can be no legal conviction, the Senate having already determined the material and necessary fact that the defendant is not, and was not when impeached, a civil officer of the United States."[37] Therefore, the Belknap counsel felt no obligation to counter the facts as presented by the prosecutors.

They changed their tune the next day, however, when Carpenter reported that the reason for their original decision to take no part in the trial had been based on the fear that by doing so they might jeopardize their position that the Senate lacked jurisdiction. However, as they listened to the questioning of the previous day, the respondent's attorneys realized that they would have to cross-examine or run the risk of a one-sided trial record. Therefore, they would henceforth participate in examining the managers' witnesses.

Major General Irvin McDowell was recalled in order to be examined by Belknap's attorneys. Replying to a question by Matthew Carpenter about whether sales at Fort Sill at exorbitant prices did not constitute the main abuse relating to the Marsh-Evans arrangement, McDowell said, "No, it was a man holding a place and exacting or receiving a large sum of money for it, having no capital, and doing no service for the money he received."[38]

Carpenter must have been disappointed by General McDowell's answer. He had hoped to demonstrate that John S. Evans had not levied excessive charges at Fort Sill because of having to pay Caleb Marsh. Despite McDowell's reply, Carpenter continued to insist that allegations of price-gouging formed the major element of the Fort Sill scandal, and that he could prove that Evans had not overcharged his customers. Carpenter later observed:

> I do not understand that the Government of the United States is interested in or has any right to inquire whether a particular sum remained in the pocket of Marsh or went to the pocket of Belknap, so long as the exchange involves no dishonesty. If no injury has been done to the Government nor sustained by the soldier, then the theory on which they ask you to presume that this respondent was guilty falls to the ground.[39]

Thus, even if the prosecutors should prove that William Belknap received payments, as Carpenter indicated that he had, they would still need to prove that the government or someone had been injured thereby, according to Carpenter's reasoning. By trying to divert attention from abuse of office to an argument that no harm had come to anyone from the Belknap-Marsh-Evans arrangements, Carpenter may have hoped to screen the transaction from close scrutiny.

Another prosecution witness, however, Adjutant General E. D. Townsend, did refer to dissatisfication with prices at Fort Sill, a dissatisfication that had been reported to Secretary Belknap along with the belief that the high prices resulted from the payments John S. Evans had to make to Caleb Marsh. A letter from the commanding officer at Fort Sill in February 1872, addressed to Townsend and forwarded by him to Secretary Belknap, complained vigorously about the prices and stated bluntly that"it is very evident that the officers and men of this garrison have to pay most of the $12,000 yearly."[40] The adjutant general testified that despite this unequivocal accusation Belknap took no action relating to the subsidy.

Caleb P. Marsh, the managers' eighteenth witness, testified on July 10 and 11. A reluctant witness, Marsh described his social relations with the Belknaps and his procedure for forwarding to them their share of the money received from Fort Sill. He said that "one or more times" he had "paid the Secretary of War money personally."[41] He explained how he had received the appointment, and described his contract with John S. Evans allowing the latter to retain the post by paying Marsh to withdraw his application for it.

Testifying for the prosecution, General William B. Hazen, a Civil War hero and boyhood friend of James A. Garfield, told the senators of informing Congressman Garfield (Republican, Ohio) on February 4, 1872 of the Evans-Marsh arrangements and the consequent higher costs to the soldiers at Fort Sill.[42] Congressman Garfield gave the information on the post tradership deal to the *New York Tribune,* which published it on February 16, 1872. Belknap read the newspaper article, but made no inquiries about the problems described by the *Tribune* or by General Hazen and took no action to correct them.[43] As Marvin E. Kroeker observes, "it is clear that the basic evidence on which Belknap was impeached in 1876 was readily accessible to high government officials in 1872."[44]

Hiester Clymer also testified and described the evidence Caleb Marsh had presented to the House Committee on Expenditures in the War Department, the committee's subsequent reading to Secretary Belknap of Marsh's testimony, and the secretary's failure to take advantage of the committee's offer that he appear before it to refute Marsh. Neither side, as noted above, asked Clymer about his reported promise to drop the impeachment if Belknap resigned from the cabinet. All told, the managers called twenty-two witnesses. They closed their case on July 12.

The respondent presented seventeen witnesses, all of whom appeared on the same day the prosecution completed its case. They reported that William Belknap had a reputation for honesty and integrity. The defense made no effort to secure from its witnesses refutation of any of the damaging charges concerning Belknap's appointment procedures or of his receiving money from Caleb Marsh; the testimony referred only to his high standing before the events that precipitated the trial.

John S. Evans had been subpoenaed by the managers and was also considered the main witness for the defense. His arrival in Washington had been delayed by floods, causing a one-week postponement of the trial. On July 19 Evans detailed the arrangements with Caleb Marsh that permitted him to continue his tradership. His payments to Marsh, he said, did not force him to raise prices at Fort Sill. Lower transportation costs and the enlargement of Fort Sill had increased his profits. That John Evans could have lowered his prices if he had not had to pay Marsh is self-evident; so is the fact that his customers were, in truth, paying the subsidy. Asked whether Secretary Belknap knew about the Evans-Marsh contract, Evans said that to the best of his knowledge the secretary was not aware of it. However, Evans did acknowledge that when Belknap informed him that Caleb Marsh had been appointed to the Fort Sill post, the secretary had suggested that Evans might make some arrangement with the new appointee because Belknap "did not know whether [Marsh] wanted to go there particularly or not."[45]

The rest of the day was given to a brief statement by Major General Winfield Scott Hancock, who attested to Belknap's good reputation.[46] Hancock's testimony was followed by discussion of procedures for the summaries that would conclude the trial. The Senate ruled that each side could have three spokesmen, the order of the speeches to be determined between the managers and Belknap's lawyers. In a digression from the normal impeachment practice, the opposing attorneys decided that the defense should speak first; in earlier trials the managers both opened and closed the summation.

Montgomery Blair, opening for the respondent on July 20, 1876, justified every aspect of William Belknap's conduct and even boldly questioned why he had not been accused of bribery. He noted that the House Judiciary Committee "did not see their way clear to make that charge. The evidence did not, in their judgment, warrant them in charging General Belknap with having received a bribe; yet by circumlocution they have made a charge which no sensible man can distinguish from that charge. If it is not a charge of bribery, it is not a charge of anything."[47]

Then Blair analyzed the constitutional requirement of a two-thirds vote for conviction and repeated the defense contention that the vote accepting jurisdiction, lacking such a majority, acknowledged the Senate's incompetence to try, let alone to convict, William Belknap. He reminded the Senate of Belknap's concern that John Evans should not lose his investments at Fort Sill because Caleb Marsh had been appointed to succeed him as post trader. Belknap, Blair asserted, demonstrated his concern for justice in arranging to preserve Evans's assets.

That Marsh received money from Evans would appear entirely ordinary to Belknap, who assumed, Blair said, that the two men had formed a business partnership. The remittances received by Secretary Belknap could be explained easily: the present Mrs. Belknap, a woman of property, had directed her income to be sent to her husband, and he had no concern or interest in its source. And Blair asked:

> Was it a circumstance to put the Secretary on his guard that she [Mrs. Belknap] received money from Marsh and that Marsh remits it to Belknap by her direction? ... Consider too, the present relations of these parties. They are now man and wife, and this disables us from giving you a full explanation and a complete showing of what took place between them and to whom all this money was recognized to belong.[48]

In other words, the first Mrs. Belknap had made a bargain with Caleb Marsh that he continued to honor after her death by sending money to the current Mrs. Belknap. William Belknap knew nothing of this corrupt deal and took care of the money, thinking it belonged to his wife. The defense could clarify the entire situation and absolve Belknap of any suspicion of involvement were it not for legal inhibitions respecting testimony of spouses.

Montgomery Blair referred in conclusion to the miserable heat of Washington in July "and the staleness of the subject itself, which leaves me to talk to so many empty seats. Can that be called a trial when we have the spectacle of more than half these seats empty?"[49]

Senators' indifference to attending impeachment trials has been noted in several impeachment proceedings.

When Blair had finished, his colleague, Jeremiah Black, asked for a recess because of the illness of Belknap's other co-counsel, Matthew Carpenter. Scott Lord reported that the managers' opening speaker, Elbridge Lapham, was also sick. The Senate, displaying impatience with the many delays, ordered the trial continued, and a reluctant Manager William P. Lynde, who had been scheduled for the following day, opened the case for the prosecution. Lynde addressed only the question of jurisdiction, a presentation originally planned to follow Manager Lapham's review and appraisal of the evidence in the case. Lynde restated the managers' belief that the two-thirds rule applied only to the vote on conviction; an ordinary majority vote sufficed for accepting jurisdiction as it did for any vote taken during the trial. Manager Lynde wanted the senators to respond directly to the question of William Belknap's guilt, not to focus on the jurisdiction issue.

A physician's affidavit attested to Lapham's continuing illness, and the Senate agreed that his argument could be printed rather than delivered in person. In his report Lapham reviewed the facts as presented by the managers, noting that respondent had neither answered nor denied them. William Belknap's witnesses, Lapham observed, supported his previous good character, but none of them affirmed or even commented on his being innocent of the activities that had caused his impeachment. Lapham referred to the defense theory that the money sent

> by Marsh was the income of a fund in Marsh's hands belonging to the defendant's second wife. The fatal difficulty with that theory was that after the Tribune article the income was diminished by one-half, and no investigation or inquiry was ever made why it was so reduced. Had her property been lost or her income been depreciated, or what was the cause of so sudden and great falling off of income?[50]

Because testimony during the trial proved that Secretary Belknap had read the damaging *Tribune* account of high costs at Fort Sill, Manager Lapham reminded the senators that Secretary Belknap obviously knew about the payments by John Evans to Caleb Marsh and undoubtedly knew the source of the funds Marsh sent on to him. If truly serving only as a receiver of income belonging to his wife, Belknap had not acted as an attentive guardian when he failed to ask Marsh why Mrs. Belknap's income had decreased so abruptly.

Next, Manager George A. Jenks, continuing Lapham's argument, analyzed the legal definition of bribery and fitted Belknap's receipt of money from Marsh as squarely meeting that definition. To refute the claim, advanced by the defense, that gratitude for the Marsh family's care of Mrs. Belknap accounted for the secretary's giving Caleb Marsh a financially rewarding appointment, Jenks cited unchallenged testimony that William Belknap had indicated one month before Mrs. Belknap had even become sick that he would give Marsh a tradership. Jenks observed: "They must have been gifted with prescience to ascertain this kindness in advance, to arrange for the appointment on the basis of what did not exist . . . , the allegation that the appointment was in consequence of the kindly feeling induced by the attention of Mr. Marsh to the Secretary's wife during sickness is simply a manufactured statement, and not true."[51] Jenks pointed out that Marsh had applied for a post before he took care of Mrs. Belknap and understood that he would receive a tradership at a time preceding any act of his that would inspire gratitude. If collusion existed, Manager Jenks suggested, it had involved Caleb Marsh and William Belknap. This hypothesis belies Caleb Marsh's testimony that the first Mrs. Belknap had instigated his applying for a tradership and hints at a more extensive connivance on the secretary's part than had been developed in the trial.

Had Caleb Marsh invented his conversations with Mrs. Belknap? If so, what purpose would such fabrication serve? Were Belknap and Marsh cooking up a tale in hope of minimizing the secretary's role in the arrangements? If they were conspiring to suppress the secretary's involvement, why did Marsh warn the Belknaps that he would tell the truth when he testified and then proceed to testify that Mrs. Belknap had started the whole thing? Whoever initiated the bargain and whatever efforts were made to obscure its origin, the facts stand clear that the Belknap family received substantial funds from the transaction, and it could not have taken place without Secretary Belknap using his official position to accomplish it.

Following Manager Jenks, Jeremiah Black spoke for the respondent's side. Again he argued the defense contention concerning the need for a two-thirds vote by the Senate to accept jurisdiction over Belknap. He repeated, with not even a nod at Jenks's immediately preceding showing to the contrary, that Belknap appointed Marsh in appreciation of his kindness to Mrs. Belknap.[52] He acknowledged that the secretary received money from Caleb Marsh but did not know why it was being given to him. Black explained away this unlikely behavior by asserting that "this money was received by him in consequence of some explanation furnished to him by his family which made all his acts consistent with his own sense of official propriety."[53]

Once again the defense relied upon its assumption that the deceased Mrs. Belknap had lined up a payment arrangement with Caleb Marsh about which Secretary Belknap knew nothing. Fearing that the assumption might be difficult for some of the senators to accept, Jeremiah Black switched his ground completely and, with no showing of embarrassment at reversing his position one hundred and eighty degrees, acknowledged that Marsh had given money to Belknap as a donation to and for the secretary. He insisted that it was entirely proper and customary for public officers to accept presents and noted particularly those "large gifts" received by President Grant, whose "wealthy friends in New York gave him money not with any evil design upon his integrity, but because it was a pleasure to themselves; and the President appointed them to office afterward not because they had bought his favor, but because he thought the public good required it."[54]

Black's effort to associate Belknap and Ulysses S. Grant as equally free in accepting presents must have made many Republican senators uncomfortable. The Republican party, far from applauding Grant's gift and appointment policy, had become increasingly embarrassed by it and eager to revive the image of Republican competence and integrity.

Black summarized the defense position as follows: (1) "no more than a bare suspicion" existed that Secretary Belknap knew why Caleb Marsh sent money to him; (2) the evidence supported only that the money received came "as a gracious gift which Marsh sent him solely because it gave him pleasure to do so"; (3) "a naked present like this is not criminal in him that gives or in him that receives it"; and (4) accepting such presents was not unlawful and "therefore not impeachable."[55]

The last speaker for the respondent, Matthew Carpenter, focused on Belknap's past record for honesty, his service in the Civil War, his not being guilty of accepting a bribe because bribery required that the recipient behave corruptly as a consequence of being bribed, the Senate's lack of jurisdiction, and the delicate familial problems that robbed the defense of its best arguments.

Carpenter developed the last point at length, saying that only William Belknap, his two wives, Caleb Marsh, and John Evans had actual knowledge of the transaction that precipitated the impeachment. He pointed out that the only competent witnesses to the arrangements, the secretary and his wife not fitting that category, were Caleb Marsh and John Evans. These two men, Matthew Carpenter argued, had exonerated Belknap of any involvement in or knowledge of a criminal act. Striking the usual defense theme about William Belknap's sense of honor, Carpenter reported that Belknap had forbidden his attorneys to develop the case fully. The secretary had "facts and testimony which would exonerate himself by subjecting others to criticism, and perhaps censure; and no matter whether influenced by the dictates of chivalric manhood or the impulses of tender affection, he has a right to say to his counsel, 'let that alone; make the defense without that; and, if I must be convicted, the consequences must fall upon me, and not upon you.' "[56]

William Belknap, the defense contended, would not disclose the truth because his chivalrous impulses forbade him to do so. This strategy revealed Belknap as innocent and plainly identified his wife as the culprit. It is difficult to image how anything could have tarnished Mrs. Belknap's reputation more thoroughly than this valorous protection of her.

Matthew Carpenter made a comment of continuing significance in the literature of impeachment when he referred to the necessity of showing that the respondent had exhibited a pattern of misconduct. He asked the Senate if it could "for the blot of a single day, in a long and otherwise spotless life, full of gallant action, and upright administration in high offices and public trusts, brand this man as infamous before the world?"[57] This argument is flawed by the fact that Secretary Belknap's transactions extended over a six-year period and could not be honestly termed "the blot of a single day."

Last speaker in the trial, Scott Lord, summed up for the managers. His presentation touched all the prosecution's major contentions: (1) the Senate had, and had accepted, jurisdiction; (2) William Belknap had been proved guilty of accepting money for making official appointments and knew of and profited from the arrangements between Caleb P. Marsh and John S. Evans; and (3) the respondent had presented no defense to the charges. Lord scoffed at Matthew Carpenter's allegation that only Belknap's delicacy prevented the defense from proving that the secretary believed the Fort Sill money belonged to his wife. Manager Lord pointed out that Belknap had aided Carpenter several times during the latter's summation by "handing him fragments of evidence which he though would sustain this strange plea." Thus, Belknap's purported order to his attorneys to stay away from any evidence implicating

Mrs. Belknap was, Lord said, "hollow nonsense."[58] Lord concluded with a reference to the improved state of political morality that viewed receipt of gifts by public officials and use of office for personal advantage as unacceptable conduct.

The Senate agreed to decide Belknap's guilt or innocence on August 1, 1876, with each senator authorized to state the reasons for his vote and to file a written opinion that would be printed as part of the trial proceedings. Sixty-two senators responded to the roll call. The Senate found William Belknap guilty by a vote of thirty-seven to twenty-five on Article 5, accepting money from Caleb Marsh, a vote not attaining the two-thirds needed for conviction. On the other four articles twenty-five senators always voted not guilty; thirty-five voted guilty on Article 1, and thirty-six on Articles 2, 3, and 4.[59] The thirty-seven senators voting guilty on the "bribery" article, number 5, included twenty-two Democrats, one Anti-Monopolist, and fourteen Republicans. Those voting not guilty included twenty-four Republicans and one Democrat; but only three of the Republican senators who voted against conviction gave Belknap the straight-out endorsement: innocent of the charges.[60] The other twenty-one Republicans, joined by one Democrat, voted not guilty on the technical ground that Belknap's resignation had moved him out of reach of the impeachment mechanism.

Like their brothers in the House, Senate Republicans were embarrassed by William Belknap and the other malefactors of their party. By the device of finding him outside the jurisdiction of the Senate, they spared themselves from convicting a prominent member of the administration without at the same time compromising the principles for which they wanted the Republican party to be known. It should be emphasized, however, that fourteen Republicans did not resort to avoiding judgment on the basis of lack of jurisdiction, but, instead, found Belknap guilty as charged.

Party connotations of the vote are conspicuous. Of the twenty-three Democrats voting, twenty-two found Belknap guilty; only William W. Eaton (Democrat, Connecticut) voted not guilty, and his vote was based not on Secretary Belknap's innocence but on his belief that a private citizen is not liable to impeachment. Of the thirty-eight Republicans voting, twenty-one found Belknap not guilty for want of jurisdiction; just three found him not guilty of the charges, and fourteen found him guilty. The Democrats' zeal for conviction exceeded that of the Republicans, the majority of whom took refuge in the "no jurisdiction" device and so avoided the painful decision the evidence would probably have forced them to make. The composite portrait of the senator voting guilty reveals him to be a Democrat, but one with certain Republican features; the composite portrait of the senator voting not guilty shows him to be a Republican. No significant geographic pattern emerges from the Belknap vote; a comparison of the regions from which the guilty and not guilty votes came shows both sides to be scattered throughout the country.

The Senate had provided that senators could file written opinions at the end of the trial. Only four senators took advantage of this opportunity: Thomas M. Norwood (Democrat, Georgia), John Stevenson (Democrat, Kentucky), Bainbridge Wadleigh (Republican, New Hampshire), and George Wright (Republican, Iowa).[61] The two Democrats and Wadleigh all voted guilty; Wright voted not guilty. The three senators who had voted guilty stated, variously, that resignation did not affect eligibility for impeachment, that the evidence presented sustained the charges, that the respondent's case did not include denial of the allegations, and that William Belknap had committed the acts forming the base of the impeachment while he still held public office. Senator Norwood, commenting on the belief of some senators that resignation barred impeachment, said that such a belief made the Senate "the only court in Christendom whose jurisdiction, in a criminal case, depends on the volition of the accused." Senator Wadleigh held that if an official could escape impeachment by resigning, then the process "becomes an empty threat. The punishment of disqualification can never been inflicted, and thus one of the chief safeguards of popular governments is shorn of its strength and becomes a mere farce."[62]

George Wright, one of the only three Republicans who had found Belknap innocent, believed that the Senate had jurisdiction over a resigned officer but did not believe that Belknap had been proved guilty of bribery. He found no evidence that Caleb Marsh paid the secretary to influence the latter's official conduct or that William Belknap accepted the money with intent to be influenced in his official duties. Senator Wright observed that "It may have been ever so immoral and reprehensible for one in the position of the respondent to take this money, but that is not the question. . . . Was it legal bribery?"[63] He believed that it was not and found Belknap innocent, even as he suggested that a public official had acted immorally and reprehensibly.

187

Despite the unfavorable outcome from his point of view, Scott Lord believed that "great good will accrue from the impeachment. . . . It has been settled thereby that persons who have held civil office under the United States are impeachable, and that the Senate has jurisdiction to try them. . . . The trial and its discussions have presented also to the public mind clearer views of official accountability."[64] Lord might have been right about the trial presenting "clearer views of official accountability," but his claim that Secretary Belknap's experience established a precedent of Senate jurisdiction over a resigned officer cannot be viewed as "settled." Contrarily, examples following the Belknap trial indicate that resignation will halt impeachment proceedings.

The question of jurisdiction dominated the Belknap trial. Only three senators, it will be recalled, doubted his guilt. The other senators voting not guilty did so solely on the basis of lack of jurisdiction; they did not consider the question of culpability.

The result of the Belknap trial provides a strong argument that resignation becomes a quick and available escape hatch for an official on the brink of impeachment. Such a result thwarts the second stage of the impeachment provisions: the opportunity of prohibiting a convicted officer from holding another national office. The device of resigning permits the resigned official to evade the penalty of disqualification and leaves the public unprotected from his future reappointment or reelection. Even so, distaste for impeaching a private citizen has proved stronger than fear that a resigned official might resume a public post.

Past impeachment trials provided support for both sides in William Belknap's trial. The experiences of Andrew Johnson, James H. Peck, Samuel Chase, and William Blount were used by both the managers and the respondent, with Blount's trial being cited more often than all the others combined. Reliance on Blount is not surprising. Both he and Belknap were already out of office at the time of their trials, and in each case the Senate concerned itself more with whether it had jurisdiction than with whether the accused had violated his oath of office.

William W. Belknap's impeachment and trial covered about five months, from early February when Hiester Clymer's House committee on expenditures began its inquiry into corruption in the War Department until August 1 when the trial ended. The House of Representatives impeached Belknap unanimously on the same day, March 2, 1876, that his alleged crime was disclosed to it; it exhibited articles of impeachment to the Senate on April 4; and formal proceedings began on April 17. The relative rapidity with which Belknap's trial moved along can probably be accounted for by the political setting in which his questionable conduct occurred. Republicans, severely shaken by revelations of malperformance by some of Ulysses S. Grant's associates, had no desire to protract the trial, particularly after the respondent's counsel failed in their efforts for a postponement until after the impending presidential election. Having lost that attempt, the sooner the trial could be concluded and perhaps forgotten, the better the electoral chances for Republicans might be. Thus, although some repetitions occurred, the florid and lengthy speeches characterizing earlier trials did not appear in Belknap's; once the defense realized that postponement would not be granted, both sides displayed an intention to proceed directly and swiftly to conclusion.

After his acquittal, William W. Belknap lived for awhile in Philadelphia and then returned to Washington, D.C., where he practiced law until his death in 1890. Ulysses S. Grant 3d commented that "evidently there were many, fully conversant with the facts, who still trusted him to handle their affairs and legal business."[65] Elliott Coues noted that "General Belknap only pretended to hold up his head after [his impeachment and trial], to the day of his death. I knew him well, and never believed him guilty, but this is no place to reopen the case—nor even to gallantly give *place aux dames*."[66] Thus, another contemporary of Belknap's thought that his wives engineered the illegal post tradership activities.

The nation's seventh experience with an impeachment trial must be recorded as a success of sorts for William Belknap, but a tainted one. Although the Senate did not cast the requisite two-thirds vote against him on any of the five articles, a majority found him guilty on all of them. Only three of his brother Republicans voted a clear-cut not guilty. Twenty-one Republicans, joined by one Democrat, felt compelled to explain that their not guilty vote was based on the belief that Belknap's resignation removed him from Senate jurisdiction; these men could easily have said "not guilty" and stopped, but they proved unwilling to find William Belknap innocent, and they wished to be explicitly recorded as avoiding judgment on him. If not found guilty, Belknap was certainly not found innocent. He goes into the history books as a flawed public official.

Charles Swayne. *Library of Congress.*

9

Charles Swayne

[Judge Swayne] cannot be justified by saying "I did not
think I was doing wrong." The defense, if made by a common criminal, would be adjudged ridiculous; when made
by a judge . . . it is contemptible.
—Henry W. Palmer

On December 14, 1904, nearly twenty-nine years after the trial of
William W. Belknap, the House of Representatives notified the Senate that articles of impeachment would be presented to it accusing
Charles Swayne, federal district judge of the northern district of
Florida, of high crimes and misdemeanors. Four of the trials preceding Swayne's had been of jurists, and the four that were to follow his
would also be of federal judges; thus, nine of the twelve impeachment trials in the period from 1799 to 1986 concerned members of
the judiciary.

Judge Swayne's impeachment originated in a joint resolution
passed by the Florida legislature on September 7, 1903, its second
request to Congress to oust him from his federal post. The resolution called upon the Florida congressional delegation to recommend
an investigation of Charles Swayne "to the end that he may be impeached and removed" from office.[1] The resolution claimed that
Judge Swayne (1) was corrupt; (2) lived in Delaware in defiance of
the federal law requiring judges to reside in their districts;[2] (3) injured the interests of Florida by his corruption and by his frequent
absences; (4) was ignorant and incompetent; and (5) administered
the federal bankruptcy act in a manner leading to waste of assets
"until such administration is in effect legalized robbery and a
stench in the nostrils of all good people."[3]

Charles Swayne, born in Guyencourt, Delaware, in 1842, received
a law degree from the University of Pennsylvania and practiced in
Philadelphia for ten years. He moved to Florida in 1885 and was an
unsuccessful Republican candidate in 1888 for the Florida supreme
court.[4] Benjamin Harrison, a Republican, appointed Swayne to the
federal bench in 1890. According to Don A. Pardee, judge of the Fifth
United States Circuit Court and a friend of Swayne's, President

Harrison selected Charles Swayne for the district court post to ensure swift and firm hearing of cases stemming from election frauds in Florida, frauds allegedly committed by the Democratic party. Swayne complied with the president's wishes by acting vigorously in scheduling and hearing cases. Judge Pardee said that Swayne's decisions in the fraud cases made him "persona non grata with the Democrats in Florida."[5]

Another evidence of partisan hostility, according to Pardee and other friends of Swayne, occurred when Congress reduced the size of the northern district of Florida in 1894. His supporters viewed the alteration as a vindictive act perpetrated by the Democrats. When Congress changed the boundaries, Judge Swayne did not comply with the law requiring judges to live in their districts; several years elapsed before he established permanent residence within the borders of his district as redrafted by Congress.

Circuit Judge Pardee directly injected a partisan tinge into the impeachment proceedings when he wrote to a Republican congressman urging that Swayne's impeachment not go forward. He said, "being satisfied as I am that the original prosecution is based on political grounds, and that [Swayne's] district limits were changed to his prejudice, I do not think that a Republican House should vote impeachment against him."[6]

Pardee's plea did not challenge the substantive charges against Charles Swayne; Pardee contented himself with raising doubts about the motives of Swayne's accusers rather than striking at the complaints themselves. Congressman David A. De Armond (Democrat, Missouri) protested the introduction of Pardee's letter. He called it judicial interference in the legislative process and repudiated any validity to the suggestion that the investigation of Judge Swayne sprang from political antagonism.[7]

Congressman Henry D. Clayton (Democrat, Alabama) also wanted to dispel any thoughts that party loyalty would influence the inquiry into Charles Swayne's conduct. He observed that the people of Florida had confidence that Congress would not allow partisan feelings to dominate its deliberations.[8]

The House of Representatives in the 58th Congress contained 207 Republicans and 178 Democrats, a nearly 54 percent margin for the Republicans. Justifying Congressman Clayton's confidence in its impartiality, the House referred the Florida legislature's request for an investigation to the Judiciary Committee. The committee spent more than a year investigating the accusations, found them substantiated, and presented articles of impeachment against Judge

Charles Swayne on December 13, 1904.[9] The articles fell into four groups: (1) filing false expense account claims, (2) accepting use of a private railroad car, (3) failing to reside in his district, and (4) imposing unlawful sentences for contempt of court.

Following debate on the committee report, the House voted 198 to 61 to impeach Swayne, a 76 percent majority favoring impeachment. Speaker Joseph Cannon (Republican, Illinois) then appointed a committee to prepare the articles for presentation to the Senate. The committee reported back to the House on January 10, 1905, setting forth twelve articles; three committee members, all Republicans, supported only the articles that detailed Judge Swayne's padded expense accounts and dissented from the other charges laid against him.[10]

A furious and lengthy debate ensued, with congressmen arguing the validity of the accusations against Charles Swayne as if they were conducting the trial itself and as if they had forgotten that the House of Representatives had already impeached the judge and had notified the Senate of its action. During this mini-impeachment trial, the House examined all the issues and most of the arguments that would come before the Senate in the actual trial.

Following this unusual spectacle, the House of Representatives displayed a change of heart. A month earlier it had impeached Charles Swayne by a vote of 198 to 61. This time it voted 165 yes and 160 no on the charge of filing false expense accounts; yes 162, no 138 for improperly using a private railroad car; yes 159, no 136 for not living in his district; and agreed, without voting, to impeach Swayne for imposing unlawful sentences for contempt of court.[11]

Party affiliation emerged as the dominant factor in this "second" impeachment of Judge Swayne. Of the 165 congressmen finding him impeachable on the false expense account claims, 143 were Democrats and 22 were Republicans. The 160 congressmen voting against impeachment on those charges included 157 Republicans joined by just 3 Democrats. The Democrats' commitment to impeaching Swayne, although shared by a few Republicans, became nearly extinguished by strong, if recently activated, Republican opposition.

On January 21, 1905 the House informed the Senate that the speaker had appointed seven managers to conduct the prosecution: Henry D. Clayton, David A. De Armond, Marlin E. Olmsted (Republican, Pennsylvania), Henry W. Palmer (Republican, Pennsylvania), James B. Perkins (Republican, New York), Samuel L. Powers (Republican, Massachusetts), and David H. Smith (Democrat,

Kentucky). Although Charles Swayne was a Republican, four members of that party, joined by three Democrats, became managers in his trial; this was the first board of managers to be composed of a majority of the accused's own political party.

Henry W. Palmer presented the twelve impeachment articles to the Senate on January 24, 1905. The articles embraced the four basic charges as mentioned: that Judge Swayne had (1) made unlawful claims for expenses, (2) improperly accepted free transportation from a railroad company, (3) disregarded the residency requirement, and (4) imposed three unwarranted sentences for contempt of court. The first three articles set forth specific instances in which Swayne had allegedly made false claims for living and travel expenses incurred when he held court outside his district. Articles 4 and 5 described the judge's use of a private railroad car belonging to the Jackson, Tampa, and Key West Railroad, a company in receivership; Swayne used the car, which was under the control of a receiver appointed by Circuit Judge Pardee and Swayne, without compensation to the bankrupt company. The next two articles dealt with Swayne's failure to reside in his district as required by federal law. Articles 8 through 12 gave details of Swayne's punishment of three men for contempt of court, an unlawful punishment according to the prosecution.

Following presentation of the articles, the Senate president pro tem, William P. Frye (Republican, Maine), asked to be excused from presiding at the trial because of the press of legislative business and his incomplete recovery from a recent illness.[12] The Senate agreed to his request and chose Orville H. Platt (Republican, Connecticut) to serve as presiding officer. The Senate that tried Judge Swayne was composed of fifty-eight Republicans and thirty-two Democrats, a margin of just over 64 percent for the majority party.

The same day on which the articles of impeachment were presented, Chief Justice Melville W. Fuller administered the oath to the senators, and on January 27 "the Senate, sitting as a court" met to debate the time to be allowed Charles Swayne's attorneys, Anthony Higgins and John M. Thurston, for replying to the articles.[13] The Senate settled on February 3, and on that day Thurston gave Swayne's refutation.

The respondent's reply centered on one major contention: none of the articles levied an impeachable charge. Respecting the judge's allegedly padded expense accounts, John M. Thurston claimed that the judge acted entirely in good faith and in conformity with established practice. Thurston presented exhibits showing that many federal jurists received the maximum allowable reimbursement, $10 a day, when serving away from their districts, and did not itemize their expenditures. Swayne, Thurston insisted, in submitting a flat $10 expense account for each day he spent on official business outside of his district, had violated neither law nor custom. His use of the railroad car did not diminish the funds of the railroad company, Thurston argued, because the company maintained the car at all times for its officials and lent it to patrons and friends when it was not needed for company purposes. Judge Swayne had not asked to use the private car; his two trips on it had no connection at all with his judicial duties. Swayne denied the charges in Articles 6 and 7 that he did not reside in his district, saying that "notwithstanding the dismemberment, out of undeserved hostility to him, of the northern judicial district," he had moved into his new district.[14] His family remained elsewhere until he could find suitable housing for them in Pensacola.

Swayne sought to refute the remaining five articles, concerning claims of unlawful sentences for contempt, by showing that the sentences he imposed were correct and had been affirmed when appealed to the circuit court. He acknowledged one error, committed without malice, in both fining and imprisoning attorneys E. T. Davis and Simeon Belden for contempt.[15] Thus, on the four groups of accusations—false expense claims, unauthorized use of a railroad car, failure to live in his district, and illegal sentencing for contempt—Charles Swayne denied that he had acted improperly or outside the law. Manager Henry W. Palmer gave the House of Representatives replication to Swayne's reply to the articles on February 6, a short statement denying any validity to the respondent's effort to refute the charges.

The trial began on February 10, with Charles Swayne attending. Palmer opened with a summary of the accusations against the judge and the evidence supporting them. He pointed out that Swayne had knowingly overcharged the government for his expenses when he held court outside his district. The government allowed reimbursement not to exceed $10 a day, and Judge Swayne's documented expenses fell conspicuously below the authorized maximum he had in each instance received.[16] His false claims could not be excused as an innocent mistake. Palmer observed:

The respondent must be judged in this case the same as every other man is judged . . . he cannot be justified by saying, "I did not think I was doing wrong."

The defense, if made by a common criminal, would be adjudged ridiculous; when made by a judge, supposed to be learned in the law, it is contemptible.[17]

Concerning use of the private railroad car, Palmer argued that Swayne had depleted the assets of the bankrupt company because his use of the car deprived the company of revenue it would have received from ordinary rental of the car. Furthermore, because other railroads transported the private car over their lines, the company had to reciprocate and provide an equivalent amount of free transportation to those railroads for their private cars. Palmer noted that Swayne should not have accepted favors from people having business before his court. "It was the kind of misbehavior in office . . . indictable at common law . . . and it is clearly impeachable."[18]

Manager Palmer next turned to the residence question, documenting the brief periods that Judge Swayne spent in his district—"an average of about sixty-one days in each year."[19] He stated that the judge had not established a permanent home in his new district and actually resided in Delaware. Earlier, during the hearings of the House Judiciary Committee to determine whether Swayne should be impeached, the committee found that the judge had not even pretended to reside in his new district until May 1903, nearly ten years after the boundaries had been changed, and that his testimony consisted of excuses for his nonresidency rather than denials. The Judiciary Committee had also found that Swayne had been advised not to bother to move because the next Congress would be Republican and would restore his district to its original dimensions.[20] Manager Palmer pointed out that the problem concerning Swayne's residency did not stem from failure to hold court; no one claimed that. Instead, it arose from the fact that Swayne was not within reach between court sessions to conduct judicial business.

Finally, Palmer analyzed the remaining five articles detailing Judge Swayne's punishment of attorneys Simeon Belden and E. T. Davis and a bank president, W. C. O'Neal, for contempt of court. Belden and Davis incurred the judge's wrath by bringing suit against him to secure possession of a block of land they understood him to own. The ownership of the tract in which it was located was the subject of a case due to be tried before Judge Swayne. The case, contested in the courts for several years, had come to be known as the Florida McGuire case. Belden and Davis served as attorneys for the plaintiff, Florida McGuire, who claimed to own the tract including block 91, allegedly purchased by Swayne. Judge Swayne found Belden and Davis in contempt for bringing suit against him and punished them with disbarment for two years (a punishment he subsequently withdrew), a fine of $100 each, and a jail sentence of ten days. Manager Palmer argued that the attorneys had not committed a contempt of court; even if they had, the sentence was unlawful, he insisted.

The last article, 12, described the case of O'Neal, upon whom Judge Swayne imposed a sixty-day jail sentence because of a fistfight between O'Neal and a receiver in bankruptcy, Adolph Greenhut. The latter, disabled by the fight, could not perform his receivership duties, a fact that Swayne considered an interference with the court. O'Neal denied any connection between his fight with Greenhut and any matter identified with Judge Swayne or his court and added that Greenhut was the aggressor. Manager Palmer argued that Swayne lacked authority to punish O'Neal; the 1831 federal law (issuing from Judge James Peck's impeachment trial) required that a contempt must occur in the presence of the court or so near to it as to be an obstruction of justice. O'Neal's act did not fit this requirement. Furthermore, he did not hold an appointment as an officer of the court and did not resist any order of the court.

Following Palmer's opening statement, Manager Marlin E. Olmsted began examining prosecution witnesses respecting Judge Swayne's expense accounts. Two witnesses testified on February 10, 1905; on the following day, too nervous to appear in person, a female witness reported Swayne's expenses by deposition. All three witnesses—a hotel clerk and two boarding house managers—showed that the judge's room and board when he was serving outside his district fell well below the $10 a day he had claimed. Charles Swayne's attorneys did not challenge any of the expense account testimony.

On February 13 three prosecution witnesses testified about the railroad fares that Judge Swayne paid as he traveled to various cities outside his district. One of the witnesses, a railroad conductor, reported that the judge had an annual pass from the railroad. Swayne's right to such a pass was not in question, Manager Olmsted commented. The objection arose from his using the pass and then charging the government for his transportation. Three more witnesses, all railroad conductors, reported that Judge Swayne habitually used a pass while traveling on their trains. One of the conductors said the judge had only once presented a ticket for his fare, and that had been when he was riding with the House committee investigating his conduct. Thus, the only evidence of Charles Swayne's paying for his transportation occurred after he had become a target for impeachment.

On the first three articles, concerning claims for reimbursement for expenses, Swayne's attorneys never challenged the facts set forth by the managers. Any refutation available to them would lie outside the reality presented by examining his claims and comparing them with his actual expenditures. Such a comparison did not provide Charles Swayne with an arguable position, for he had plainly requested refunds for money he had not spent.

Next, Manager James B. Perkins conducted questioning on the group of articles detailing Judge Swayne's failure to reside in his district. Perkins called twelve witnesses: a tax collector, postmaster, hotel manager, real estate man, and several lawyers. These witnesses testified that (1) Charles Swayne's name did not appear on the tax roll in the northern district of Florida until 1902; (2) his mail, including official court documents, had been regularly forwarded to Guyencourt, Delaware; (3) Swayne remained in Pensacola only during the two terms of court, an average of about sixty days a year between 1894 and 1900, according to one witness;[21] (4) lawyers repeatedly complained about his absences (Swayne's attorneys objected to this allegation as hearsay, and the Senate sustained their objection);[22] (5) Charles Swayne did not legally or actually reside in his district; and (6) his long absences caused serious delays and additional expenses in cases pending before his court.

Swayne's attorneys, nearly silent during the testimony on the expense account articles, came to life when the prosecution examined the residency articles. They questioned the witnesses vigorously, Anthony Higgins doing most of the interrogating. He showed that not one prosecution witness knew Judge Swayne's whereabouts when he was not in Pensacola and had no information about whether he might be away from his district because he had been assigned to hold court elsewhere. The defense stayed away from the data supplied by some of the attorney witnesses who had testified to the necessity of sending material to Delaware for Swayne's judgment or signature. Although raising questions about some of the witnesses' ability to pinpoint Swayne's whereabouts during a given period of absence from his district, the respondent did not convincingly refute the charges levied in the nonresidency articles.

Consideration of Judge Swayne's use of the private railroad car came next. Henry D. Clayton conducted the managers' examination. Two witnesses, one a former conductor for the railroad and the other the court-appointed receiver for the railroad, testified that the car had been provisioned and staffed at the expense of the railroad company when used by Judge Swayne and his party. In cross-examination, John M. Thurston elicited from the receiver the fact that the railroad never made the private car available for rental and that no quid pro quo arrangements existed among the railroads respecting transporting each other's private cars. Thus, Thurston argued that Swayne's use of the car had not substantially diminished Jackson, Tampa, and Key West assets.

When examined by the House Judiciary Committee, Charles Swayne had asserted that he had a right to use the private car.[23] Manager Palmer sought to introduce this testimony, but Thurston objected on the ground that evidence given elsewhere could not be presented during the impeachment trial. After a debate on the question of admissibility, the Senate, for the second time, sided with Swayne's attorneys by voting forty-five to twenty-eight to exclude testimony given before the House Judiciary Committee.[24] The forty-five senators voting in favor of the respondent's position included thirty-nine Republicans; the twenty-eight senators who voted in support of the managers' position included twenty-one Democrats. Several days later, following closed-door debate, the Senate again considered whether to admit statements the judge had made to the House Judiciary Committee. This vote, forty-seven to twenty-nine, displayed approximately the same partisan division among the senators as had the earlier vote; only six Democrats joined forty-one Republicans in voting to exclude the testimony, and only seven Republicans joined twenty-two Democrats in voting to accept it.[25] These two votes, reflecting partisanship, presaged almost exactly the outcome of Charles Swayne's trial.

Next the managers took up the charges concerning improper sentencing for contempt of court; David A. De Armond conducted the inquiry into the cases of Simeon Belden and E. T. Davis. Both men described Judge Swayne as issuing a peremptory order for them to proceed to trial when they felt unable to do so because their witnesses in the Florida McGuire land dispute could not appear on such short notice. They told of their withdrawal of the case from trial, their belief that Swayne owned property in the tract of land involved, their unsuccessful attempt to have him remove himself as judge, and their suit against him for possession of the block of land they believed he owned. This last act caused Judge Swayne to find them in contempt and sentence each to serve ten days in jail, pay a fine of $100, and suffer disbarment for two years; Swayne subsequently withdrew the disbarment portion of the sentence. Simeon Belden described Judge Swayne's manner during the contempt hearing as "abusive." He said that the judge "denounced us as ignorant; that we had disgraced the profession of the law, and that our conduct was a stench in the nostrils of the people there, and especially of the bar."[26]

John M. Thurston, in cross-examining Belden and Davis, designed his questions to suggest that the two attorneys had found time to file suit against Charles Swayne but had not found time to locate their witnesses and proceed with trial of the Florida McGuire case. He also tried to establish that they knew Judge Swayne did not have any financial interest in the tract concerned, and knew it when they filed the suit against him.

The prosecution, having called twenty-nine witnesses, closed its case on February 20, 1905. The managers had proved, with very little effort on the respondent's part to challenge them, (1) that Charles Swayne had regularly requested and received reimbursement for money he had not spent; (2) that the judge had not resided in his district, a point that the defense sought in part to deny, in part to explain on the basis that he was holding court elsewhere; (3) that Swayne had accepted trips in a private railroad car owned by a company in receivership, a fact his attorneys acknowledged but defended because the judge's use of the car had not been a financial burden to the defunct railroad; and (4) that Judge Swayne's sentences for contempt had been unjustified, a position not clearly developed by the prosecutors nor clearly refuted by the defense. The most serious claims against the judge—false expense accounts and failure to establish a legal or actual residence in his district—seemed solidly substantiated by the managers.

On the day the managers concluded, Anthony Higgins began the presentation for the defense, starting off with the last articles: Judge Swayne's sentencing of Simeon Belden, E. T. Davis, and W. C. O'Neal for contempt of court. Higgins argued that the sentences were lawful and levied without malice. Concerning Belden's and Davis's belief that Charles Swayne owned land in the tract involved in the Florida McGuire suit, Higgins insisted that the judge had never owned any property in the tract and "The learned managers have closed their case without offering a scintilla of evidence of any title in him to that land."[27]

Then Higgins turned to the question of Charles Swayne's residence. He stated that the defense would prove that the judge held court for extended periods of time outside his district, in part because the curtailment of the northern district gave Swayne time to accept service elsewhere. His inability to find a suitable house in Pensacola, the fact that his children attended school in Philadelphia, and his family's spending a year in Europe all contributed to Swayne's failure to establish his family in Pensacola in the first years after Congress changed the boundaries of his district. But, Anthony Higgins argued "that a man resides where his family resides is not a . . . conclusive presumption either of fact or of law,"[28] and the defense would show that Judge Swayne did live in his district.

Respecting the expense account charges, Higgins noted that Swayne's expenses had been allowed by the federal marshal; also, he added, a majority of judges viewed the $10 compensation as a fixed allowance. Higgins further alleged that the managers had failed to prove that Judge Swayne had not actually spent $10 a day when traveling on official business. This bold assertion seems groundless; the prosecution had given much time to documenting Swayne's actual expenses, showing them to have been well below the established $10 maximum.

Anthony Higgins dismissed charges connected with use of the private railroad car briefly on the basis that Charles Swayne did not control the receivership when he used the car and that no one had asserted or implied that the judge had accepted a bribe.

The next day John M. Thurston filed a lengthy statement examining English precedents and the seven preceding United States impeachment trials. The statement, "prepared not by counsel for respondent, whose names are attached to it, but by a gentleman who is renowned as a scholar along constitutional lines,"[29] set forth the proposition that, even if true, the first seven articles of impeachment concerning expense accounts, use of the private railroad car, and nonresidence did not constitute impeachable offenses. If Swayne had falsified his expenses and improperly accepted reimbursement from the government, his guilt could only be tested by indictment followed by trial by jury. To find his use of the railroad car unacceptable, bad intent must be, and had not been, demonstrated. And failure of a judge to establish residence in his district, even if proved, could not be found in the Constitution among the list of impeachable acts. Therefore, the respondent demurred to all of the first seven articles as failing to set forth any misdeeds meeting historical or constitutional descriptions of impeachable conduct.

The renowned scholar's statement included certain arguments raised but not settled in previous impeachment trials. One example concerns the belief, brought up by attorneys for William Blount and William Belknap as well as by Charles Swayne, that an alleged criminal act must be tried in court and could not be included as part of an impeachment proceeding prior to trial by jury. The Constitution does not contain such a requirement; far from prohibiting an impeachment trial in advance of a court trial, it provides only that the former does not prelude the latter.[30] The Constitution supports the view of an impeachment trial as a political inquiry quite distinct from a criminal trial.

A second example, the claim that bad intent must be proved, also arose in earlier impeachment trials, notably Samuel Chase's and James H. Peck's. Respondents have insisted that improper motives for their conduct must be demonstrated in order to convict them. It cannot be supposed that the framers of the Constitution intended to make poor judgment, or perhaps even ignorance, impeachable. Contrarily, they cannot have intended that such a deed as falsification of expense accounts could be punished only if the prosecutors could prove willful and malicious determination on the part of the accused official to commit an illegal act. Motive is always difficult to ascertain. This problem remains unsolved; it arose again in 1986 in the trial of Judge Harry E. Claiborne, whose attorneys sought, unsuccessfully, to demonstrate that the judge's underpayment of his income taxes was not willful, therefore not a cause for a finding of guilt.

The last example from the statement filed by Charles Swayne's attorneys—the contention that nonresidence could not be classified as impeachable because it is not specifically listed in the Constitution—is not accurate. Congress had made a judge's failure to live in his district a high misdemeanor, one of the categories qualifying for impeachment. Congress is capable of requiring a federal judge to live in his district and also is able to designate failure to abide by the law as a high misdemeanor.

The first witness for the defense, W. A. Blount, was examined by John M. Thurston respecting Swayne's sentencing of Belden and Davis. Blount reported urging Judge Swayne to charge the two attorneys with contempt for filing suit against the judge and for their failure to proceed with the long-delayed land case. He fully supported Swayne's sentencing except for his disbarring the two men. Blount testified that he informed Swayne that disbarment exceeded his authority to punish for contempt, and the judge immediately withdrew that part of the sentence.

The next seven witnesses also were questioned on the contempt charges. Thurston elicited information contradicting prosecution testimony that Judge Swayne had used abusive language when sentencing the two attorneys for contempt. In addition, the defense produced evidence showing that the Florida McGuire case need not have been postponed. The federal marshal reported that he could have subpoenaed the witnesses needed in the case within two hours of being asked to do so. This point damaged the contention of E. T. Davis and Simeon Belden that they were unable to proceed to trial because they could not assemble their witnesses within the allotted two days. Once again, W. C. O'Neal's fight with Adolph Greenhut was only briefly mentioned and not investigated at all; Davis and Belden continued to be the stars of the contempt portion of the trial.

The next witnesses testified on the residency matter and verified the respondent's contention that he spent only summers in Guyencourt, Delaware.[31] The postmaster at Guyencourt reported that Charles Swayne did not receive mail at Guyencourt during the winter; if any mail did come there, it was forwarded to Pensacola, as requested by the judge. Neither the managers nor Swayne's attorneys made any effort to reconcile the postmaster's statement with earlier prosecution testimony asserting delays and confusion caused by the necessity of forwarding court documents from Pensacola to Guyencourt.

The judge's son, Henry J. Swayne, supported his father's claim that he lived in his district but was often absent because of being called to hold court elsewhere. The defense introduced certificates showing the dates on which Judge Swayne had been assigned to sit outside his district.[32]

Next John M. Thurston, turning to the problem of Charles Swayne's expense accounts, introduced various acts of Congress concerning payments of jurists holding court outside their regular districts. He stated that during debate on judges' expense allowances both the Senate and the House of Representatives had specifically rejected amendments restricting allowances to actual outlays, "thereby showing, as we contend," Thurston argued, "the clear intention of Congress to allow the judges to certify and receive necessary or reasonable traveling expenses whether they paid the money out or not."[33]

The managers objected to admission of this material, insisting that long-established legal principles required statutes to be interpreted as written and passed; reference to congressional debates or other historical information leading to enactment of a law could not be employed to clarify its intent. A record vote was taken on the issue of admissibility.[34] Once again the Senate backed the respondent's position. It voted thirty-four to thirty-three to accept evidence showing Congress to have rejected a requirement that judges' requests for reimbursement must be for money they had in truth expended. The thirty-four member majority consisted of thirty Republicans and four Democrats. The thirty-three senators supporting the managers' position included twenty-three Democrats and eleven Republicans. This vote suggests the partisan tone prevailing in the Senate and augurs, as did the preceding record votes, the result of Judge Swayne's trial.

Then Anthony Higgins addressed the Senate on the touchy expense account problem. He tried to introduce evidence detailing requests for reimbursement filed by other judges, most of whom, he said, construed the statute as Charles Swayne had, namely, as allowing a flat $10 a day. Higgins pointed out that not only had Swayne followed the general practice, but also that none of the certifying officials had ever questioned his accounts. Manager Olmsted protested introduction of other judges' expense accounts: "There is no insinuation, except by counsel [for Swayne], that any one of these honorable judges charged or certified to any amount in excess of his actual expenses. There is nothing upon which to base the insinuation that a judge, having expended two or three or five dollars a day, certified that the expenses were $10 and collected the money from the government."[35]

The Senate voted thirty-four to ten against admitting the accounts of other jurists.[36] It was the managers' first victory in a record vote, and substantial evidence that senators would not accept any implication that other judges had made false claims in the absence of proof that they had done so. The thirty-four voting no were evenly divided: seventeen Democrats, seventeen Republicans; the ten yes votes were cast by nine Republicans and one Democrat.

An effort by the defense to introduce letters from several federal judges indicating their interpretation of the expense account law to be like Charles Swayne's and thus entitling them to $10 without connecting that sum with actual expenditures was denied by Presiding Officer Platt without objection from any senator. Whereupon the respondent's case closed; sixteen witnesses had appeared on Judge Swayne's behalf.

The main points that Swayne's attorneys sought to establish were that (1) bad motives on the part of the judge had to be, and had not been, proved; (2) Swayne's use of the private railroad car resulted in no appreciable loss to the company and had not proceeded from any intention of that company to bribe him; (3) his sentences for contempt had been upheld on appeal; (4) his frequent absences from his district occurred because he had been assigned to official duties elsewhere; and (5) Judge Swayne's claims for reimbursement for expenses had been based on the maximum allowed by Congress, a maximum requested by other jurists when they traveled on official business—in any event, Swayne could be indicted only in a court of law if it were established that he had overcharged the government.

Upon conclusion of the presentation on Judge Swayne's behalf, February 23, 1905, John M. Thurston, no doubt feeling confident of the outcome, offered, in the interest of saving the Senate's time, to forego summary arguments if the prosecutors would do the same. The managers declined, and Marlin E. Olmsted began summation of the case for the prosecution.

Olmsted first discussed the nature of impeachable offenses, arguing that they need not be indictable. English precedents and earlier United States experiences, notably those of John Pickering and West H. Humphreys, furnished verification for that position. He next addressed the respondent's contention that the expense account, residence, and use of the railroad car charges were not official acts and so could not make the judge a subject of impeachment. Olmsted noted, however, that none of these instances of misconduct, as the managers claimed them to be, could have been committed by Charles Swayne as a private citizen. Swayne had been proved guilty, Olmsted insisted, of "high crimes and misdemeanors in matters relating strictly to his judicial office, and in which it would have been beyond his power to offend had he not been a judge."[37]

The rest of Manager Olmsted's presentation focused mainly on Judge Swayne's expense accounts. He stated that the judge had filed false claims; only an extreme torturing of logic would support a request for $10 a day without any reference to true costs incurred by the claimant. Olmsted detailed the actual costs of Swayne's trips. For an official trip to Waco, Texas, Swayne had claimed $230. Relying on the testimony of prosecution witnesses, the manager showed that a very generous allowance for costs and extras brought the Waco trip to "a grand total of $114.80, which undoubtedly exceeds his actual expenses."[38] Olmsted demonstrated, referring again to earlier testimony, that Swayne's expenses for holding court in Tyler, Texas, would be, by a most liberal estimate, $130.15. The judge had certified to expenditures on the Tyler trip of $310. Another expense claim, Olmsted continued, "covers a still more conspicuous in-stance. . . . He certified that his expenses were $410, and upon that certificate drew the money from the Treasury."[39] At the most, Swayne spent $125.35, as based on testimony of hotel and boarding house personnel.

Turning to the defense argument that other judges believed that the maximum allowable charge could be made whether a jurist's ex-penses reached that figure or not, Olmsted insisted that (1) the re-spondent had no proof of such an opinion by other jurists, (2) none of the other judges had ever been accused of certifying falsely, and (3) attempting to explain away an illegal act on the basis that other people did the same thing hardly justified a judge in his wrongful conduct. On this last point Olmsted wondered: "Suppose that in [Swayne's] court a clerk had been arraigned for tapping his employ-er's till, would this respondent have charged the jury that it was an ample defense to show that since the commission of the offense the clerk had learned that others were helping themselves whenever they got a chance?"[40]

James B. Perkins delivered the next speech for the managers when the trial resumed on the following day, February 24. He addressed the question of residence, beginning with a refutation of the argu-ment that even should Judge Swayne's nonresidency be proved, he could not be impeached for it because it did not represent a failure connected with his official duties. Perkins pointed out that Charles Swayne as judge, not as private citizen, was legally obliged to live in the northern district of Florida. He also reminded the Senate that Congress, in passing the residence law, had made its violation a high misdemeanor, and so impeachable.

Perkins cited official records of Swayne's court days in his district and the testimony of witnesses that from 1894 to 1900 he remained in his district only during those court days. The managers sought to prove that Swayne's brief stays in northern Florida, the fact that his family did not live in Pensacola, and his failure to establish a home in his district all demonstrated the judge's disregard of the residency law. Perkins added, "he rented no house, he bought no house, he made no purchase." But when the Florida legislature called for Swayne's impeachment in 1903, Perkins continued, "he bought a house and made himself a legal resident of the district. . . . If the man who for seven long years neglected to obey the law because he thinks he can do it safely, conforms to the law within one short month when danger is coming, does that show good faith?"[41] Per-kins indicated that the impeachment resolution drove Judge Swayne to an obedience he had not formerly displayed. The facts produced in Perkins's speech had all been verified by witnesses and by official documents; they stood essentially unchallenged by the respondent.

Henry D. Clayton spoke next; he analyzed only the contempt articles concerning Simeon Belden and E. T. Davis. Relying on the James H. Peck trial and its aftermath, which produced existing federal laws on contempt, Clayton argued that Judge Swayne's punishment of the two attorneys did not conform to the law. His ruling against Belden and Davis failed to assert that their suit against him "was conduct constituting misbehavior in the presence of the court. There is no allegation that it was misbehavior so near the court as to interfere with the proper administration of justice. There is no allegation in the rule anywhere that it did obstruct or interfere with the administration of justice in Judge Swayne's court."[42] Therefore, Clayton argued, Swayne had exceeded his authority and had punished the two attorneys only because they had sued him. Both Belden and Davis believed Charles Swayne had an interest in the land involved in the Florida McGuire controversy, knew that he had declined to withdraw from serving as judge in the case, and did not know that he had disclaimed any interest in the land in question. They had a right to sue him under the circumstances as they understood them. Judge Swayne's irritation at being sued caused him to find the two men in contempt.

Manager Samuel L. Powers followed Clayton. He also focused on Judge Swayne's alleged abuse of the contempt power, developing specifically the sentencing of W. C. O'Neal. He described the fight between O'Neal and Adolph Greenhut, an affray, Powers pointed out, having no connection with Charles Swayne and no relationship to any matter before Swayne's court. Not accepting O'Neal's effort to explain the facts and thus purge himself of contempt, Judge Swayne sentenced O'Neal to sixty days' imprisonment. Powers argued that the law did not authorize such punishment.

Anthony Higgins, first spokesman for Judge Swayne, challenged Simeon Belden's and E. T. Davis's assertion that they did not know of Swayne's disclaiming any interest in the property involved in the Florida McGuire case and also doubted their statement that they would not have brought suit against Swayne had they known of the judge's disavowal of ownership. Higgins reviewed O'Neal's reputation for rash conduct and supported his being found guilty of contempt of court for his fight with Adolph Greenhut.

Next Higgins took up the charge of nonresidency. This portion of his summation emerged as an explanation of Charles Swayne's failure to reside in his district rather than as an insistence that he had. Higgins pointed out that Judge Swayne had repeatedly been drafted to hold court elsewhere. Because of the judge's frequent absences, his family did not settle themselves in Pensacola but visited him there or at various other places to which he was assigned. But Higgins at no time stated or even implied that Swayne maintained a residence in the northern district of Florida, or even that he had a regular, established base such as a permanently rented room in a boarding house. Thus, the defense accounted for Swayne's failure to comply with the residency law on the basis of his frequently being obliged to hold court elsewhere; it did not, at this time, claim that he had a domicile in his district.

Higgins finished his presentation with a comment on the origin of Swayne's impeachment, its commanding feature being, he argued, legislative interference with the judiciary, caused in this instance by Swayne's sentencing of the three men for contempt of court. This explanation of the motive behind the impeachment had not been mentioned during the trial; it was here raised for the first time and without amplification.

John M. Thurston concluded the case for Judge Swayne the following day, February 25. He restated the defense position that to be impeachable the acts complained of must be crimes and must have been committed in the accused's official capacity. Thurston also referred to the staleness of the charges in the earlier articles: the year 1897 in Article 1, 1900 in Article 2, 1893 in Articles 4 and 5, 1894 to 1900 in Article 6, and 1894 to 1903 in Article 7. Although not insisting that the law required an impeachment to be brought within a prescribed period of time, Thurston stated that courts of equity would not consider a claim "that has laid so long without any attempt to enforce it" and argued that government policy precluded an impeachment trial of an officer "unless the impeachment . . . be brought against him within the limitations fixed for the prosecution of crimes by the statutes of the United States."[43]

Then Thurston moved to the matter of Judge Swayne's expense accounts. He said Swayne had not deliberately misrepresented his actual costs and reminded the Senate that Congress had specifically refused to restrict judges to expenses actually incurred when they served outside their districts, providing they did not exceed $10 a day. Thurston advanced a further explanation for Swayne's procedure: the marshal who paid the $10 and officers of the Justice and Treasury departments would recognize that in such towns as Tyler and Waco a judge would not actually spend $10 a day. Yet all these officers allowed Charles Swayne his requests for reimbursement even though all of them knew "that a certificate for $10 a day meant something more than the mere recovery of moneys paid out."[44] Swayne made his requests for payment openly and obviously did not think he was defrauding the government. Here, again, the judge's response failed to challenge the prosecution's contention that he had not in truth expended the sums for which he claimed repayment. Swayne relied on his interpretation of the authorizing statute as permitting him to charge the maximum. On the expense account articles, the respondent contented himself with acknowledgement and explanation, not contradiction.

Next, Thurston took up Swayne's use of the railroad car, observing that the railroad hired no additional workers for the judge's trips and that the connecting lines that carried the car made no charge to the financially ailing Jackson, Tampa, and Key West Railroad. Respecting food consumed by Charles Swayne and his party, Thurston wondered if "the honorable managers would impeach this man because at the end of every meal on that car he did not walk up, as he would have done at the eatinghouse at the station, and plank down 50 cents per head."[45]

Although believing that current sentiment would be against public officials accepting favors from railroad companies, Thurston said that when Swayne had used the private car, such action was commonplace. No one alleged that Charles Swayne had been impeded or influenced in his judicial capacity by accepting use of the proffered car. This statement stood unchallenged by the managers. The question not dealt with directly concerned the propriety of a jurist's accepting free trips from a railroad in the hands of a receiver appointed by that same jurist, with the bankrupt line provisioning the car and providing the staff. On these articles also, the defense explained but did not refute the prosecution's accusation.

The same situation occurred in John M. Thurston's treatment of the residency articles: he acknowledged that Charles Swayne did not, for several years, live in the northern district, but he produced reasons accounting for the judge's inability to comply with the residency requirement. The malicious dismemberment of his district, Thurston said, caused Swayne's established household to be disrupted and his family to disperse to Guyencourt or Philadelphia because he could not readily find a suitable home in his new district.

Thurston did not, however, refer to any actual domicile occupied by Charles Swayne in Pensacola; he explained once again the necessity forcing the judge to spend large amounts of time away because of frequent assignments outside his own district. Respecting the managers' testimony proving Swayne's failure to vote or to pay a poll tax in his district, Thurston asked, "What Republican would care to register and vote in Florida? Or what Democrat would care to do the same in Vermont?"[46] Thurston also reminded the Senate that Swayne did not have to pay a poll tax because he was fifty-five years old in 1897, the age after which the requirement no longer applied.

The final segment of Thurston's speech concerned the contempt articles. He stated that Belden and Davis knew that neither the judge nor Mrs. Swayne had any interest in the property involved in the Florida McGuire case, a fact announced by Judge Swayne in open court. The attorneys' suit against Swayne "was a fabrication," Thurston claimed, because "they knew he had no interest in that land. As lawyers they knew it was a violation of their oaths to bring him or any other man into court on a false suit."[47]

Thurston described W. C. O'Neal as the prime mover behind Charles Swayne's impeachment, but he did not document or explain O'Neal's starring role in the affair.[48] Respecting his being sentenced for contempt, O'Neal, Thurston claimed, had assaulted Greenhut because the latter, as a receiver in bankruptcy, had brought suit against O'Neal's bank. Thus, Swayne's punishment was justified, appropriate to the offense, and according to law.

Manager David De Armond gave the concluding speech in the trial. He began with a brief comment on Judge Swayne's allegedly unjust contempt sentences. Then he moved to use of the private railroad car, saying, "it is not just the thing for a judge to accept 'courtesies' from those who would be asking courtesies of him."[49] But De Armond did not even suggest that Swayne had been influenced by the railroad's special treatment of him.

Next De Armond discussed the residency matter. Congress had established nonresidency as a high misdemeanor, which the Constitution specifically lists as an impeachable offense, he pointed out. De Armond called for conviction of a judge violating this law and stated that defense arguments designed to restrict conviction to acts committed on the bench or as part of some judicial transaction lacked both historical and legal validity.

Then De Armond commented on the expense account articles. He recounted the managers' unquestioned demonstration of the falsity of Charles Swayne's expense claims. Pointing to an inconsistency in Swayne's position, De Armond observed, "He argues at one point that we have not proven that he did not spend $10 a day, and at another point he insists not only that he did not, but that everybody must have known it."[50] Judge Swayne was guilty of larceny, and the prosecution had revealed his guilt, De Armond said; for this conduct he merited conviction. Reverting to the residency consideration, the manager contended that Swayne himself had acknowledged that from 1894 to 1900 he had no residence in his district. "According to his own statement according to his testimony,—overwhelming, undenied, and undeniable, he had no residence in the northern district of Florida for more than six years."[51]

De Armond concluded with a review of the contempt articles, pointing out that the Florida McGuire case was pending in Swayne's court at the time (1901) the judge had negotiated to purchase a block of the land in litigation. He reviewed Swayne's declining to recuse himself, his subsequent disclaimer of any interest in the land, Simeon Belden's and E. T. Davis's suit against him, and the finding of contempt against the two attorneys. De Armond argued that Swayne should have withdrawn from the McGuire case because his original intention of purchasing a block in the disputed tract from the persons contesting Florida McGuire's ownership indicated his belief that she did not have title to the property. Thus, his capacity for dispassionate judgment when the suit would be tried before him came into serious doubt. Belden and Davis had a right to sue, and Swayne had no justification under the contempt statute of 1831 for punishing them. De Armond referred only briefly to W. C. O'Neal, commenting that he also had been improperly sentenced.

Manager De Armond urged the Senate to convict Judge Charles Swayne. Displaying the rhetorical style he employed during his presentation, he said: "If you remove him from office, what wrong could you do? None. If you leave him in office, what wrongs do you inflict upon the people who must suffer from his maladministration of office? You can not tell. I can not tell. The God of omniscience only can know. A weak, vain, vicious judge; a cruel, vengeful, unrelenting judge; . . . a judge not intending to do justice!"[52]

David De Armond delivered a poor valedictory for the managers' position. He did not present a coherent attack on the respondent's case nor an orderly summation of the prosecution's. Instead, he wandered about among the articles in a disorderly fashion and rarely exposed the evasive quality of many of respondent's attempts to refute the charges levied against him, especially the responses to the expense account and residency articles. This comment does not suggest that De Armond lost the case; it became evident during the trial that the Senate was disinclined to convict.

At the end of the trial, the Senate passed a resolution providing for a vote to be taken on the articles without debate on February 27, 1905. Presiding Officer Platt, before the roll call vote, cautioned the audience not to display any reaction to the voting. He said that applause from the floor or galleries would not be permitted; anyone violating this rule would be ejected. Following Platt's admonition, the Senate voted swiftly and without comment on the twelve articles of impeachment.[53]

The first basic charge, filing false claims for expenses, attained a maximum guilty vote of thirty-three; forty-nine senators voted not guilty. The second basic charge, improper acceptance of transportation from a railroad company in the hands of a receiver, did not impress the senators. Only thirteen voted Charles Swayne guilty; sixty-nine found him innocent. The third group of charges, failure to comply with the law requiring him to reside in his district, secured a maximum guilty vote of thirty-one and a not guilty vote of fifty-one. The last five articles, comprising the fourth general grouping of charges, concerned Judge Swayne's sentencing of three people for contempt of court. Article 12, the W. C. O'Neal matter, received the largest number of guilty votes cast in the trial, thirty-five, with forty-seven senators finding Swayne innocent. Votes on the four contempt articles concerning the two attorneys Simeon Belden and E. T. Davis were identical: thirty-one guilty, fifty-one not guilty. The managers came nowhere near proving their case against Charles Swayne, at least not to the satisfaction of the United States Senate.

Eighty-two senators voted at the end of the trial: fifty-one Republicans and thirty-one Democrats. The thirty-five guilty votes on the O'Neal contempt article were cast by twenty-nine Democrats and six Republicans; only two Democrats found Judge Swayne innocent of this charge. Articles 4 and 5, use of the railroad car, received the smallest number of guilty votes: thirteen, all cast by Democrats. The senators voting guilty, except Francis G. Newlands of Nevada, all represented Southern states. Florida's two senators, Stephen R. Mallory and James P. Taliaferro, both Democrats, voted Judge Swayne guilty on all the other articles but found him innocent on the two dealing with his accepting free transportation from the railroad.

Except for the railroad car articles on which only thirteen senators supported conviction, a steady band of twenty-nine Democrats consistently voted Charles Swayne guilty. An equally steady band of forty-five Republicans consistently voted not guilty. Thus, the

Senate's decision on Charles Swayne clearly reflects partisanship. The majority of Republicans voted not guilty on all the articles, and the majority of Democrats voted guilty on all the articles except the two concerning the judge's use of the private railroad car.

The House of Representatives thanked the managers "for the able and efficient manner in which they discharged the onerous and responsible duties imposed upon them,"[54] but the trial must have severely disappointed the prosecutors. The managers had clearly demonstrated that Charles Swayne misrepresented his expenses and violated the law requiring him to reside in his district. But the Senate vote was not even close on any of the five specific instances set forth in the articles on reimbursement and domicile. Possibly the "staleness," as the defense put it, of most of the charges persuaded senators to vote not guilty.

Charles Swayne's trial exemplified decision making rooted in party. Whatever the motivation of the Florida legislature in requesting the impeachment and the House of Representatives in voting it, the outcome in the Senate proved party to be decisive. The composite portrait of the senator voting not guilty shows him to be a Republican; the composite portrait of the senator voting guilty shows him to be a Democrat.

Region must also be noted in both portraits: the typical senator voting not guilty came from a state outside the South, whereas the overwhelming majority of guilty votes were cast by senators representing former Confederate states. The "solid South" existed in 1905 as a distinct political entity and a stronghold of the Democratic party. Only five Democrats in the 58th Congress, all of them from the West, came from non-Southern states, and no Republican represented any state formerly belonging to the Confederacy.[55] Thus, Southern senators voted guilty and senators from other areas voted not guilty. Party and region in the Swayne trial proved to be, if not identical, closely intertwined; designating the typical senator who voted guilty as a Democrat from the South becomes, in this case, redundant.

Congress gave some part of one and one-half years to investigating, impeaching, and trying Charles Swayne; the trial proper spanned a period of thirty-four days. Both sides referred frequently to earlier impeachment trials, with James H. Peck's and Andrew Johnson's experiences receiving the greatest attention. Relying just on the trial record, it appears that Swayne should have been convicted. His case met the test for impeachability by exhibiting a pattern of misconduct extending over several years. The acts detailed

in the articles brought against him fitted the constitutional prescription for impeachable conduct. In addition, if one accepted the
respondent's proposition that to be impeachable an act must have
been committed by the accused in his official capacity, Charles
Swayne's activities fitted even that proposition. The articles
described acts that could have been performed only by a judge. Pad-
ding an expense account allowed to jurists, neglecting to conform to
a law prescribing judges' residence requirements, and sentencing
people for contempt of court relate squarely to a judge in his line of
duty. Use of the private railroad car, if no more serious than displaying Swayne's poor judgment, would probably not have been open to
an ordinary citizen or to anyone whose good will was a matter of
indifference to the railroad.

Manager David De Armond, urging the Senate to convict Charles
Swayne and not imagine that, thereby, a flood of impeachments
would follow, noted: "Impeachments are not things of everyday occurrence. They do not come up lightly. They come only once perhaps in a generation."[56] De Armond, although essentially correct in
his appraisal, proved to be a poor forecaster. Within the next thirty
years, three impeachments would be voted, one of them within
eight years of Swayne's trial. All three concerned federal judges, yet
another proof of the potential value of the 1980 Judicial Conduct
and Disability Act or of the need to activate the "good behavior"
clause.

Robert W. Archbald. *Library of Congress.*

10

Robert W. Archbald

He has sacrificed his judicial integrity and official rectitude on the altar of greed; he has sorely violated the common rules of judicial ethics and propriety.
—Edwin Y. Webb

The House of Representatives impeached Circuit Judge Robert W.
Archbald in July 1912, and the Senate convicted him in January
1913, just short of eight years after it had declared Charles Swayne
innocent. Judge Archbald became the ninth national officer to be
tried by the Senate, the third to be found guilty, and the second to be
disqualified from ever again holding any position with the federal
government.

Archbald's impeachment took place during a tense presidential
election campaign in which Republicans were split between incumbent William Howard Taft and Progressive (Bull Moose) candidate
Theodore Roosevelt. The rupture between the Republican factions
was not directly reflected in Archbald's trial, but the Senate, several
of whose members faced reelection in a period of public dissatisfaction with government and business practices, postponed the impeachment trial until after the election to give the incumbents
more time to campaign. Some of the issues dividing the Republicans, however, and involving the Democrats as well, did surface in
Judge Archbald's case: regulating business, curbing combinations in
restraint of trade, and controlling rapacious instincts in government
officials. Archbald was a small fish in a sea of big-name profiteers,
but his conduct had become notorious at a time when attention was
turning to unethical financial and governmental practices.

Robert W. Archbald, born in Pennsylvania in 1848, received his
bachelor's degree from Yale and practiced law in Scranton.[1] He was
elected a Pennsylvania state judge in 1884 and won reelection to
that post in 1894.[2] Archbald did not complete his second term on
the Pennsylvania bench because his fellow Republican, William
McKinley, gave him an interim appointment in 1901 as a federal
district judge in Pennsylvania; Theodore Roosevelt, McKinley's
successor, made the appointment permanent. Ten years later, in

January 1911, William Howard Taft elevated him to a circuit judgeship with assignment to the United States Commerce Court, a court established in 1910 to hear appeals from rulings of the Interstate Commerce Commission.[3] Thus, three Republican presidents—McKinley, Roosevelt, and Taft—displayed confidence in Robert W. Archbald's judicial competence and integrity, a confidence that proved misplaced as subsequent information revealed his questionable business transactions. The judge's alleged use of his official position to improve his personal finances brought about his impeachment; his suspect activities spanned the period of his tenure as both a district and a circuit judge.

Public awareness of Robert W. Archbald's probable misuse of office began with a complaint to the Interstate Commerce Commission, made on January 5, 1912 by William P. Boland, who, with his brother Christopher, owned the Marian Coal Company. The Bolands had a case before the ICC protesting the rate charged by a railroad for transporting the company's coal. W. P. Boland recounted to the commission certain misdeeds committed by Judge Archbald: (1) a friend of Archbald's had approached Boland and asked him to discount the judge's note for $500 on the ground that for doing so he would "be saved all the costs" of a suit then pending in Judge Archbald's court, a suit in which Boland was a litigant; (2) Archbald arranged the purchase, through his influence with the Erie Railroad, of a coal dump soon sold for a net gain of $35,000, of which sum the judge would receive one-third;[4] and (3) Archbald induced the Delaware, Lackawanna, and Western Railroad to sell him a coal dump. The Interstate Commerce Commission sent this information and the documents supporting it to William Howard Taft, who directed the Justice Department to study W. P. Boland's accusations against the judge.

On April 23, 1912 the House of Representatives requested President Taft to send it a copy of the complaints filed against Judge Archbald and a report of the Justice Department investigation of them. The president complied with the request and indicated that Boland's charges deserved serious attention, whereupon the House authorized its Judiciary Committee to investigate Archbald's conduct and determine whether he had committed impeachable acts.

Two months later Henry D. Clayton (Democrat, Alabama), chairman of the Judiciary Committee, reported that the committee's investigation had resulted in the unanimous conclusion that Archbald should be impeached because

He has prostituted his high office for personal profit. He has attempted by various transactions to commercialize his potentiality as a judge [and] shown an overweening desire to make gainful bargains with parties having cases before him. . . . He has degraded his high office and has destroyed the confidence of the public in his judicial integrity. He has forfeited the condition upon which he holds his commission and should be removed from office by impeachment.[5]

Congressman Clayton told the House of Representatives that Robert W. Archbald and his counsel had attended all meetings of the Judiciary Committee. After four days of discussion of the charges, the House impeached Archbald on July 11, 1912 by a vote of 223 favoring impeachment to just one opposed.[6] The House at that time contained 228 Democrats and 161 Republicans, a majority of 59 percent for the Democrats. Obviously, the vote did not reflect a determination by Democrats to oust a Republican jurist. Rather, it revealed a strong belief on both sides of the aisle that the complaints against Judge Archbald had been verified and should be adjudicated.

On July 13 the House of Representatives notified the Senate that it had impeached Robert W. Archbald and that the managers were ready to present articles of impeachment. Three Republicans and four Democrats were appointed to conduct the prosecution: Henry D. Clayton, John W. Davis (Democrat, West Virginia), John C. Floyd (Democrat, Arkansas), Leonard Paul Howland (Republican, Ohio), George W. Norris (Republican, Nebraska), John A. Sterling (Republican, Illinois), and Edwin Y. Webb (Democrat, North Carolina).

Clayton presented thirteen articles to the Senate.[7] Six of these alleged misdeeds were performed while Archbald was district judge; six, in his present office of circuit judge assigned to the Commerce Court. The thirteenth article, mainly a summary of the twelve preceding articles, seemed designed to underline the judge's pattern of malperformance and the long period of time during which he exhibited such behavior.

Doubts existed concerning trying Archbald for misconduct that occurred while he was a district judge. Senator William E. Borah (Republican, Idaho) asked at the beginning of the trial whether an officer could be impeached for alleged misconduct committed before he held the office he currently occupied. Henry D. Clayton replied that the managers believed Archbald to be susceptible to impeachment as a district as well as a circuit judge. This matter took up a great deal of time during the trial without being decided.

The following day, July 16, President Pro Tem Jacob H. Gallinger (Republican, New Hampshire) took the prescribed oath and then administered it to the other senators. The Senate before which Judge Archbald would be tried included fifty-one Republicans and forty-five Democrats, giving the Republicans a majority of 53 percent in the upper house.

The next sessions of the Court of Impeachment dealt with Archbald's reply to the articles and the managers' response to his reply. Archbald, represented by the prominent Washington attorney Augustus S. Worthington and by Robert W. Archbald, Jr., claimed that none of the articles set down impeachable offenses. The managers' brief replication simply stated that all thirteen articles described high crimes and misdemeanors of which Robert W. Archbald would be proved guilty.[8]

The respondent's attorneys then turned to the problem of the opening date of the trial proper, insisting that the number of charges and the illness of two of the attorneys who had represented Judge Archbald during the Judiciary Committee inquiry required that the trial begin no sooner than mid-October, a date protested by Manager Clayton as unnecessarily protracting the proceedings. But the Senate gave the respondent more than he had requested. It set the beginning of the trail for December 3, nearly four months later than the opening date desired by the managers but after the national election—probably the real reason for the deferral. The Senate vote putting off the trial was forty-four to nineteen.[9] Thirty-three Republicans joined by eleven Democrats comprised the majority supporting delay of the trial; five Republicans and fourteen Democrats voted against the postponement. Republicans, then, exhibited stronger support for delay than did Democrats.

On December 3, 1912, the Senate convened as the Court of Impeachment with all seven managers, Robert W. Archbald, his son, and A. S. Worthington attending. Worthington announced the association of Alexander Simpson, Jr., with the respondent's counsel.[10] About to unfold before the senators was a tale revealing interlocking directorates among various coal and railroad companies, the grip the railroads held over other enterprises, the cozy relationships among the executives of many large companies, and the participation by Judge Robert W. Archbald in certain speculative ventures. It would prove to be a complex and difficult case for the Senate to hear because of the number of witnesses, 118; the excessive detail with which the various transactions were described; and the tangled threads seeming to catch Judge Archbald in a net of influence-peddling and involvement in schemes to enrich himself.

Although the entire trial will be surveyed to indicate its general course and tenor, emphasis will be given to the major but not necessarily the most time-consuming issues, the five articles on which the Senate adjudged Robert W. Archbald to be guilty. These articles depicted four substantive acts—set down in Articles 1, 3, 4, and 5—all committed while Archbald served as a circuit judge, plus catch-all Article 13 describing his pattern of conduct throughout his entire federal judicial career.

Article 1, which commanded the most guilty votes at the end of the trial, detailed Archbald's entering into a partnership with Edward J. Williams to purchase the Katydid culm dump owned by the Erie Railroad.[11] The Erie Railroad had cases pending before the Commerce Court on which Judge Archbald sat, and he, according to the article, "willfully, unlawfully, and corruptly took advantage of his official position" to secure the dump for himself and his partner.[12]

Article 3 described a similar act. Archbald and associates leased the "Packer No. 3" culm dump from a coal company owned by the Lehigh Valley Railroad Company. Again, the railroad was a litigant before the Commerce Court and, again, Archbald had allegedly used his influence to secure the agreement.

Article 4 set down Judge Archbald's correspondence with an attorney representing the Louisville and Nashville Railroad concerning a suit between the railroad and the Interstate Commerce Commission; the suit had been brought to the Commerce Court but had not yet been decided. The judge requested the railroad's attorney to supply certain information, a request with which the latter complied. Judge Archbald informed neither his colleagues on the Commerce Court nor the ICC lawyers of his exchange of letters with the attorney who represented one of the litigants in a case currently under submission to the court.

The fifth article, once again intermingling deals for a culm dump with railroad interests, told of Judge Archbald's intercession with a coal company to try to secure a lease for a friend. The coal company, whose president also served as president of the Philadelphia and Reading Railroad, had refused to lease the property because it was not company policy to lease any of its culm dumps. Although unsuccessful in his attempt to have the decision reversed, Archbald, according to Article 5, received $500 from his friend for his effort to secure the dump.

These four articles—the Katydid culm dump, the Packer No. 3 dump, the secret letters, and the acceptance of money for trying to influence lease of a dump to a friend—comprise, with the potpourri Article 13, the five charges on which Robert W. Archbald was destined to be convicted.

Except for Article 2, the articles on which the Senate found Archbald not guilty detailed his performance as a district judge. They concerned (1) his offer to assist an attorney to settle a case pending before the ICC; (2) his attempt to induce the Lehigh Valley Coal and the Lehigh Valley Railway companies to purchase some coal land; (3) improper transactions relating to promissory notes; (4) appointment of a Lehigh Valley railroad attorney as jury commissioner; and (5) financial improprieties concerning a vacation trip to Europe.

Peripheral issues such as Judge Archbald's use of official Commerce Court stationery while negotiating his private business ventures took some time in the trial. So did endless disputes over the financial values of the various properties in which Archbald interested himself. Value, or the judge's actual or potential profit, never constituted the central problem as described by the managers. The fact that Archbald involved himself in such transactions at all created the difficulty, not the amount of money he made from them.

In addition to the specifics of the Archbald trial, two well-worn impeachment themes and one unique to the Archbald experience arose in this trial. The basic impeachment question unique to the Archbald trial concerned whether a person could be impeached for deeds performed at a time when he held a different federal office. Impeachment literature discloses no previous consideration of this question except very remotely in the trials of William Blount and William Belknap, where the issue had not been malperformance in a previously held office but whether expulsion or resignation from office precluded further impeachment proceedings. The managers in Archbald's trial argued that he had held a federal judgeship continuously from 1901 until his trial and that promotion to the circuit court did not free him from responsibility for his conduct while a district judge. This argument can be sustained by analogy to the impeachment provisions in various states.[13] Even so, the Senate did not convict Judge Archbald on any of the articles detailing his alleged malperformance as a district judge except for Article 13, which summarized in a general way all the accusations laid against him.

The two recurrent themes of impeachment that surfaced again concerned whether the acts complained of must be indictable in a court of law and must be performed as a part of official duties. The Archbald trial did not answer these questions, but the logic derived from it and from earlier impeachments leads to the conclusion that the charges need not be indictable nor need they be directly a product of the office held in order for the suspect official to be impeached.

Henry D. Clayton gave the opening statement for the managers when the trial began on December 3, 1912. Clayton referred to Archbald's becoming, upon achieving judicial office, "seized with an abnormal and unjudgelike desire to make money by trading directly and through others with railroads and their subsidiary corporations [having or likely to have] litigation in his court." But Clayton did not explicitly accuse Judge Archbald of high crimes and misdemeanors. In his introductory statement for respondent, A. S. Worthington pointed out that the judge had been accused only of violating the good behavior clause. Manager Clayton, Worthington argued, had ignored the constitutional prescription of treason, bribery, or other high crimes and misdemeanors—"the only provision authorizing this proceeding"—because, Worthington believed, should Clayton "rely on that [provision] he will find that he can not expect a conviction."[14] For whatever reason, Clayton's failure to designate Archbald's alleged misdeeds as high crimes and misdemeanors stands as a curiosity.

Examination of prosecution witnesses began the next day. The managers' list of witnesses included ninety-one names; of this number, forty-seven were actually called. During the questioning of many of the prosecution's witnesses, the managers referred to testimony the witnesses had given before the House Judiciary Committee. Robert W. Archbald's attorneys did not protest introduction of statements taken elsewhere as had Judge Charles Swayne's attorneys in the 1905 impeachment trial. Archbald, like Swayne, might have successfully opposed use of testimony taken in another forum; failure even to attempt to exclude it, except in brief and inconclusive references by A. S. Worthington, is surprising because several times the managers refreshed a failing memory or pointed out an inconsistency between statements made to the Judiciary Committee and statements made to the Senate—always to the detriment of Judge Archbald's case.

The first witness, Edward J. Williams, who had collaborated with Archbald in the coal dump transactions, displayed a faltering recollection of the events involving the judge. Manager Edwin Y. Webb conducted the questioning of Williams and eventually elicited from a balky and hair-splitting witness the facts concerning Archbald's and Williams's activities aimed at securing an option on the Katydid culm dump (Article 1). The judge's writing of a letter, on official Commerce Court stationery, to the owners of the dump resulted in a change of heart by the company, which had originally refused to lease the Katydid dump to Williams. Following the judge's intervention, the company issued an option at a favorable price. For using his influence in this transaction Archbald was originally granted half the profits from the dump (later modified to one-third). Manager Webb asked Williams, "What was the judge to do and what did he do to entitle him to one-half of the profits in this culm dump?" Williams, who had already demonstrated his antagonism to appearing as a witness, replied, "It was none of anybody's business, if I wished to give it to him." Pressed further by Webb, Williams finally acknowledged his reason for paying Archbald. "It was partly through his influence I got [the option]."[15]

Another aspect of the Katydid transaction concerned whether Judge Archbald was the "silent party" referred to in a contract in which Edward J. Williams assigned one-third of the profits from the Katydid culm dump property to William P. Boland, a man involved in a case in Judge Archbald's court and, subsequently, prime mover in exposing the judge's conduct. A. S. Worthington insisted that the judge had no knowledge of any contract between Williams and Boland, and no testimony concerning that contract should be heard because the judge had neither involvement in nor knowledge of the Williams-Boland arrangements relating to the Katydid culm dump. The Senate voted on whether to admit evidence concerning Judge Archbald's being the person referred to as the "silent party." This first expression of Senate opinion on admissibility of contested evidence proved to be a triumph for the managers. The vote revealed fifty-five favoring admission, six opposed; all six no votes came from Republicans. After a sparring match with Manager Webb, Williams acknowledged not only that Archbald was the silent party but also that the judge knew that he was a partner; the judge's name did not appear on the contract because, Williams said, "I thought maybe that it was not lawful."[16] Concerning acquisition of a second dump, Packer No. 3, for which Judge Archbald wrote a letter on Edward J. Williams's behalf (Article 3), Manager Webb elicited from the witness the information that he had promised to give Archbald a half-interest in the property.

A. S. Worthington's cross-examination of Williams brought forth no significant assault upon the facts set down by the managers. So

Williams's testimony, however grudgingly given, verified Robert W. Archbald's key role in securing the Katydid dump; showed that the judge profited financially from this and a second culm dump transaction, Packer No. 3; gave support to the presumption that Archbald's judicial position accounted for the success of Williams's ventures; and showed the judge to be the silent partner on a contract. The testimony of Edward J. Williams was seriously damaging to Judge Archbald.

The following day, December 6, William A. May, an executive of the Hillside Coal and Iron Company (a wholly owned subsidiary of the Erie Railroad), reported his company's decision not to sell the Katydid dump and the reversal of that decision because of Archbald's activities in the matter. He stated unequivocally that only the judge's influence caused the company to sell the coal dump; the company would not have dealt with Edward J. Williams in the absence of Archbald's intervention because it considered him to be unreliable. A. S. Worthington's cross-examination of May centered on establishing three major points: (1) the coal company had determined the price of the dump; (2) no one attempted to conceal Judge Archbald's involvement in the sale; and (3) no litigation concerning the Hillside Coal and Iron Company had ever been before the Commerce Court.[17]

Following William A. May's testimony, an attorney for the Erie Railroad who had represented the Erie in two cases before the Commerce Court took the stand. He described introducing Archbald to the vice president of the Hillside Coal and Iron Company after the judge had mentioned an interest in property owned by the company.[18] Next came an accountant for the Boland brothers' Marian Coal Company. He had been a witness to the signatures on the contract in which Edward J. Williams gave a share of the Katydid culm dump profits to W. P. Boland. He reported Williams as saying that Judge Archbald had an interest "in the transaction, and was to be known as the silent party."[19] A. S. Worthington protested admitting the evidence. President Pro Tem Bacon said that "As to whether or not a partnership has been proven and whether the respondent should be bound by statements made by one who is alleged to be his partner, is a question to be determined by the Senate sitting as a court."[20] He then admitted the testimony concerning Archbald being the silent party, a decision to which no senator took exception.

Other witnesses testifying on the Katydid culm dump during the next four days reported various aspects of the negotiations by which

Judge Archbald secured the dump and by which he subsequently sought to dispose of it. One witness, an executive of both Hillside Coal and the Erie Railroad, acknowledged that, until the Archbald incident, Erie had never sold any of its culm dump properties. Manager John A. Sterling tried to establish a connection between the Erie's willingness to sell to Archbald and the fact that suits were before the Commerce Court in which the Erie Railroad was a litigant, but the witness declined to admit such a connection.[21]

The material adduced during these sessions was not disputed by the respondent's side, but implications that Judge Archbald received a great bargain because the Erie Railroad had cases pending in his court and that he had, thereby, effectively solicited a bribe remained just that—implications. However, that Archbald's expression of his interest had induced the company to deal with his associates stood as an established fact. The Katydid witnesses as a whole substantiated the heart of the managers' charges against Judge Archbald: he used his official position to secure a profitable business deal from companies having, or that at some time could have, litigation in his court.

Next the managers turned to Judge Archbald's involvement with the Boland brothers, principal owners of the Marian Coal Company, who were embroiled before the Interstate Commerce Commission with various railroads over shipping rates (Articles 2 and 8). Asked about reporting Robert W. Archbald's conduct to the Interstate Commerce Commission, William P. Boland said he had not wanted to do harm to the judge, "but I was wiped out through the influence of the railroads with him . . . I did not have anything against Judge Archbald. He never done a thing to me in his life until the railroads began to use him . . . Judge Archbald was being used by the railroads to crush us out of existence."[22]

The other matter involving Archbald and the Bolands concerned the judge's offer to help the brothers' attorney sell the Marian Coal Company and settle the rate disputes with the railroads. The managers considered the offer illegal, and the possibility that the judge would receive compensation for helping the attorney compounded the illegality, they believed.

Judge Archbald's attorneys objected to admission of testimony of the judge's arrangements with the Bolands' attorney, insisting that no wrongful act had been demonstrated. Once again the Senate sustained the managers and agreed to admission of the material. Twenty-nine senators recorded themselves as favoring, twenty-five as opposing admission: twenty-one Democrats and eight Republicans supported the managers and two Democrats and twenty-three Republicans supported Archbald.[23] This record vote reveals a partisan division. Only two Democrats sided with the respondent and voted to exclude the evidence. Only eight Republicans voted with the prosecution in favor of admitting testimony showing that Archbald had offered to help the Bolands' lawyer and that the latter had intended to compensate the judge for his assistance.

Next came witnesses on the secret letters charge (Article 4) consisting of correspondence between Judge Archbald and Helm Bruce, attorney for the Louisville and Nashville Railroad. Bruce had appeared for the railroad in a case against the Interstate Commerce Commission, a case then on appeal to the Commerce Court. Archbald had asked Bruce's opinion on the substance of the case in which Bruce had represented the plaintiff and which Archbald and his colleagues on the Commerce Court were in the process of deciding. Bruce proved willing to comply with the judge's request, subsequently won the appeal, and learned from Archbald that "Frankly, the case was won on your argument and brief. . . . You can not fail to note how closely the opinion follows and reflects what is there said."[24] Judge Archbald's clandestine exchange with a lawyer in a case in which he sat in judgment, an exchange confirmed by the judge when he testified later in the trial, demonstrated a violation of acceptable judicial conduct.

After the secret letters interlude, the managers returned on December 12 to the much-explored coal dump matters, concentrating mainly on Article 3, Robert W. Archbald's activities in securing a culm dump lease on Packer No. 3. The accusation against the judge concerned his offer to help the coal company make a purchase in which it had long been interested at the same time that he mentioned a friend's desire to lease the Packer No. 3 culm dump. Having first refused to lease the dump, the company finally agreed to do so. Manager Edwin Y. Webb claimed that this change of mind occurred because Lehigh Valley Railroad had a suit pending before the Interstate Commerce Commission.

Next the managers turned to Archbald's transactions respecting promissory notes. Six witnesses disclosed that the judge had asked people who had business before his court for financial assistance. Several witnesses recounted details of Archbald's receiving money for a trip to Europe. An attorney who practiced in Archbald's court told of being asked to contribute $50 for the European trip and of refusing for fear of embarrassing the judge. Archbald's clerk testified that the money he collected for the judge's European trip, a fund of

$500 or $525, was raised in lieu of a banquet.[25] The promissory note matters and the collection of funds for a European trip were sedulously detailed but did not secure a Senate vote of guilty at the conclusion of the trial, perhaps because they occurred during Archbald's service as a district judge, perhaps because they were not considered significant.

The prosecution closed its case on December 14, having called forty-six witnesses.[26] The respondent's attorneys, in cross-examining prosecution witnesses, gave only occasional challenge to the facts brought forth by the managers. Their questions concentrated on trying to show first that in certain instances (the silent party contract between Edward J. Williams and W. P. Boland, for example) Judge Archbald had no knowledge of the proceedings, and, second, in the matters presumed to be improper (the Katydid culm dump transaction, for example), Archbald had made no effort to conceal his involvement and, thereby, could not have believed he was engaged in any illegal arrangements.

Archbald's attorneys expressed contempt for William P. Boland, who had triggered the impeachment when he reported Archbald's questionable acts to the Interstate Commerce Commission. A. S. Worthington characterized Boland's views of Archbald as "absolutely unfounded and originated in a disordered brain . . . Boland has a deadly bias and prejudice, an unreasonable prejudice . . . against Judge Archbald." Manager George W. Norris commented that the prosecution "had never denied that Mr. Boland was a prejudiced witness and had a bias against Judge Archbald."[27] Boland's objectivity stood undefended by either side although the facts he brought forth remained essentially unrefuted, prejudiced or not.

The defense of Robert W. Archbald began on December 16, 1912, when twelve witnesses appeared. Most testified on various aspects of the judge's activities in trying to acquire the culm dump leases. The first day for the respondent revealed nothing concerning the coal dump transactions that had not already been assiduously covered during the managers' presentation and nothing that improved Archbald's position.

The respondent presented twenty-six witnesses on the next trial day, fifteen of whom gave very brief statements supporting Archbald's reputation for exemplary character.[28] Other testimony dealt with the fact that no effort had been made to conceal the judge's connection with the various transactions alleged by the articles to be illegal.

One of the defense witnesses, George Gray, a United States circuit judge, responded to questions introduced by Manager Henry D. Clayton concerning a suit brought against Archbald twenty-four years before his impeachment, when he was one of three organizers of the Amity Coal Company.[29] Clayton read from the trial transcript showing that the stock subscriptions of the three partners in the long-ago suit had not been paid, a failure termed by the jurist hearing the case "an evasion of the law and a fraud upon the public. In saying this we do not impute an intention to defraud or reflect upon the motives of the gentlemen by whom the Amity Coal Co. was organized."[30] Despite this disclaimer, the connection of Judge Archbald with yet another dubious venture raised further questions about his business ethics.

One of the respondent's witnesses, Mary F. Boland, niece of the Boland brothers and also their secretary, became the first woman to testify in person at an impeachment trial.[31] She gave a brief report on notes she took when Edward J. Williams visited the Boland office. One notation, scarcely helpful to Judge Archbald's cause and making Miss Boland's appearance for the defense surprising, revealed that Williams had told the Boland brothers that Archbald "showed [Williams] a brief he was preparing for the Erie Railroad Co. [Williams] said the judge would tell him most anything."[32]

One new piece of information concerning the Boland brothers surfaced when A. S. Worthington asked a Scranton attorney whether Christopher Boland had requested him to call on Robert W. Archbald and inform the judge that if the Bolands' suit "against the Delaware, Lackawanna & Western Railroad Co. was settled he, Christopher, would withdraw from all impeachment proceedings against Judge Archbald."[33] The managers objected to the question as immaterial. Worthington pointed out that when Christopher Boland had testified on behalf of the managers, the Senate had voted to admit his testimony over Archbald's objection. Therefore, he argued, the defense had a right to adduce testimony indicating that Boland had attempted to affect the outcome of the impeachment proceedings.

After some skirmishing between the managers and the respondent, Worthington was allowed to proceed and did establish that Christopher Boland, motivated by a desire for personal satisfaction, had offered to terminate any further action directed toward impeaching Judge Archbald if his suit against the railroad were settled.

Boland showed more interest in attaining a private goal than in seeing justice done to a presumably flawed public servant.

The testimony of succeeding witnesses concerned the Katydid and the Packer No. 3 culm dumps (Articles 1 and 3). A. S. Worthington brought out the fact that transactions in which some participants advanced the cash and other participants shared in the profits because they had helped to acquire the necessary property, as Archbald had done in the culm dump cases, were commonplace. Thus, the judge's engaging in such an arrangement and receiving income from it could not be viewed as either wrong or unusual. But Manager John A. Sterling denied that such an argument could be applied to Archbald, saying that private citizens had a right to "persuade the railroad company to sell them this property, and it would not constitute an offense. . . . But for Judge Archbald to do it, being a judge and using his influence to persuade railroad companies to do this, is the offense charged in this count."[34]

At the end of the hearing on December 19 the trial was put over until January. Resuming their case on January 4, 1913, the respondent's attorneys presented fourteen witnesses who testified variously that no effort had been made to conceal Archbald's involvement in the culm dump arrangements. In general, the information they produced proved repetitious. Minute details over the location of the various culm dumps involved in the case and the grades and probable profits from the coal retrievable from them were brought forth, matters of no dispute between the two sides and of slight value to strengthening Archbald's cause.

On January 6 the performance picked up with the appearance of Elizabeth Archbald, the judge's wife, who reported on the European trip financed by her cousin and not dependent on any contributions made by associates of Archbald's—contributions not even known to the Archbalds until they were en route to Europe.[35] Following her, Robert W. Archbald took the stand. Alexander Simpson conducted the questioning, leading the judge through all the accusations.

Respecting the Katydid culm dump transaction, Archbald explained that he had tried only to expedite completion of the arrangement, not to influence it. He denied charges that he had used his prestige and authority as a judge to secure the dump. Later, Senator Charles Culberson (Democrat, Texas) asked Archbald if it occurred to him that he put himself under obligations "in asking favors of railroad corporations as to culm dumps" when those corporations could have cases before the Commerce Court. The judge responded,

"I never consciously asked any favor of a railroad . . . I was simply presenting a matter to them as a business proposition."[36]

Archbald termed accusations that he tried to prevent disclosure of his role in the Katydid and other negotiations as entirely false. He had no reason at all to conceal his activities, he said, and had made no effort to do so. As to his being the silent party on the Katydid contract between Edward J. Williams and W. P. Boland, Archbald stated that he had had no knowledge of the contract "until it was produced before the Judiciary Committee. I would not have submitted to any such paper being drawn if I had had any notice of it."[37]

Alexander Simpson asked Judge Archbald why he had used official Commerce Court stationery for various letters he wrote concerning the deals described in the articles of impeachment. He replied that he had done so because he did not have any other paper available. During cross-examination Manager John A. Sterling questioned the judge's use of official stationery:

> Sterling: Did it occur to you that it would look better and be in better taste to write these railroad companies on other paper in reference to these business transactions?
> Archbald: It might have been better taste.
> Sterling: Have you noticed, Judge, . . . that in every instance where you addressed railroad companies or the officials of railroad companies concerning their coal properties . . . you used paper with letterheads "Commerce Court" on it, and that in all cases where you used blank paper it was correspondence not with railroad companies . . . ?
> Archbald: I have not.
> Sterling: Did it occur to you at any time, Judge, that it would help to impress the railroad companies with the idea that you had jurisdiction over them in the Commerce Court?
> Archbald: It did not, Mr. Sterling.[38]

Concerning the secret letters, Judge Archbald explained that he had written to the railroad's attorney only to obtain clarification of certain points raised in the case already submitted for judgment to the Commerce Court. He did not send copies to opposing attorneys or discuss his correspondence with his colleagues on the Commerce Court because he needed the information just for his own use. Senators proved greatly interested in this matter and asked a number of questions. Senator James A. Reed (Democrat, Missouri) asked, "Did you consider it proper, in passing upon a doubtful point in evidence, to hear only from that lawyer who would certainly desire to concur in your view?" Judge Archbald replied, "I certainly should not have written the letter if I had supposed it was improper."[39] Buffeted with sharp questions from several senators, as well as from Manager John A. Sterling during cross-examination, Archbald tried to justify his actions but with little success. The judge had asked an attorney for information and had told neither his brother jurists on the Commerce Court nor the attorneys on the other side that he had done so; this fact stood unchallenged.

The case for Judge Robert W. Archbald concluded with his testimony, a performance aimed at explaining some of the charges made against him and of denying others—particularly those accusing him of using his position to profit from the business arrangements in which he had engaged. The respondent's witnesses, including the judge, numbered seventy-one.

On January 8, 1913 the Senate assembled to hear the beginning of the summaries. Each side had been allotted seven and one-half hours for its presentation. John A. Sterling gave the opening speech for the prosecution.[40] He expressed the managers' confidence that their case had been proved. He sought to refute the respondent's contention that only indictable acts constituted impeachable offenses and reviewed British and United States precedents to the contrary. Sterling also cited precedents supporting the managers' argument that a person could be impeached for performances relating to an earlier office. He added that because of the Senate's power to disqualify a convicted official from further national office, resignation should not preclude impeachment or interrupt a trial; some comments had been made that Archbald might resign.

Then Sterling examined Judge Archbald's conduct in the culm dump matters and the secret letters to an attorney appearing in a case before him. He closed with a reminder that Archbald had displayed a pattern of misconduct. One relatively minor act would not justify removal from office, Sterling observed, but in Archbald's case such a minor act was simply part of a series of bad performances. Sterling pointed out a characteristic that comes as close to being an established precedent as anything that emerges from the chronicles of impeachment: the official must exhibit habitual malperformance, conduct that Judge Archbald had manifested over a long period of time.

Manager Edwin Y. Webb hit hard at Robert W. Archbald's "culm-dump mongering from the time he became a Commerce Court judge until the time he was overtaken"; he noted that Archbald had no knowledge of the coal business and nothing to contribute to his various transactions except his influence as a judge. Webb concluded with a call for Archbald's conviction because he "has prostituted the office which you gave him in his worship of Mammon; he has sacrificed his judicial integrity and official rectitude on the altar of greed; he has sorely violated the common rules of judicial ethics and propriety."[41]

Discussing the relationship of indictability to impeachment, Manager Leonard P. Howland said he had found no evidence in state or federal impeachment history that "indictability is a condition precedent to impeachability . . . the power to impeach is properly invoked . . . whenever by reason of misbehavior, misconduct, . . . or maladministration the judge has demonstrated his unfitness to continue in office."[42]

Manager John W. Davis reviewed the charges in the first six articles, those occurring during Archbald's tenure on the Commerce Court; he pointed out that the judge's dealings with the coal and railroad companies had secured business advantages for him that could have been achieved only because of his position on the Commerce Court, in which "is concentrated all the litigation of all the railroads of the United States."[43] The prosecution surveyed all the charges and insisted that Judge Archbald's abuse of office had been proved.

Alexander Simpson spoke first for the respondent. He opened with an assertion that an impeached official must be accused of violating a law and that no such accusation had been made against Judge Archbald. He agreed with the managers' contention that most of the facts had been admitted to by the respondent's side, but insisted that none of them dealt with criminality. Archbald had done nothing wrong in the various culm dump transactions, there being no law forbidding a judge to engage in any private business except the practice of law.

Respecting Archbald's giving assistance to the attorney for the Bolands in the effort to settle the Marian Coal Company's troubles (Article 2), Simpson said that Archbald acted solely out of friendship; he received no compensation for his help and expected none. Simpson made no effort to deflect the managers' argument that such activity would be regarded as acceptable only if done by someone not on the bench.

Next came consideration of the secret letters (Article 4), which, Simpson observed stimulated more questions from senators than did any of the other articles. Simpson recognized that the exchange of letters with an attorney representing a client in a case Archbald was deciding could be considered a blunder, but it could not, he insisted, be considered a high crime or misdemeanor. Clearly, he continued, Judge Archbald did not have an evil motive in writing to the railroad's attorney, because the judge had posted the reply "into the record in that case and [it] remains in that record unto this day. . . . " Therefore, Simpson contended, the judge's act could be viewed "at most as a breach of the law of ethics [not a] breach of any known law of the land."[44]

Article 5 detailed Judge Archbald's acceptance of money for interceding with the Reading Railroad to extend its lease of certain coal lands. Simpson agreed that the judge had received a fee from the friend on whose behalf he had spoken to the railroad company, but the fee had not been received for—and had no connection with—Archbald's unsuccessful effort to secure the railroad's property. It was, instead, a commission for the sale of property on which the judge had an option—an entirely legal transaction having no connection with the effort to negotiate an extension of the lease from the railroad.

Simpson then moved to a review of Articles 7 through 12, dealing with Robert W. Archbald's performance as a district judge. Simpson noted that these articles contained no significant allegations. He had little difficulty in illustrating that fact. He argued briefly that an official could not be impeached on charges of misconduct in a former office, but focused mainly on the triviality or the inaccuracy of the charges against Archbald during his tenure on the district court bench.

Alexander Simpson concluded his summary with a comment that the case had arisen only because of "the political unrest of the times," an unrest, he suggested, that "does not necessitate the carrying back of this court to the days of the Roman arena, when, because the populace cried out for a victim, the thumbs were turned down."[45] The unrest to which he referred concerned public dissatisfaction with corporate and political corruption, the election of Democrat Woodrow Wilson as president in 1912, and the loss of seven Senate and thirty-four House seats by the Republicans. But Archbald's impeachment arose from his misconduct and had no direct connection with partisan politics. An attempt to account for the efforts to convict Judge Archbald on the basis of recent political shifts disregarded the strong Republican support for his impeachment and conviction.

Augustus S. Worthington gave the last speech for the respondent. Having delivered the apparently compulsory review of constitutional provisions for impeachment and past English and United States experiences with the procedure, Worthington stated that the impeachment articles levied no claim of criminal conduct against Archbald. He also insisted, as had respondents' attorneys in earlier trials, that an impeachable act must be a product of official duties, and he said that none of the charges "relates to anything that has been done in the performance of the duties of the office which Judge Archbald holds. He is not charged with committing any crime. That is admitted. He is not charged even with doing anything wrong in connection with the duties of the office, crime or no crime."[46]

Worthington admitted most of the facts set down in the articles but denied that Archbald used his influence as a judge in any of his business arrangements. While agreeing, then, that the activities ascribed to Judge Archbald had taken place, the defense found no fault in his having engaged in the transactions that the managers had tried to turn into acts of impeachable misconduct. What the respondent emphatically rejected as untrue and unproved were allegations that Archbald had ever taken advantage of his position as a judge to attain a favorable outcome in any of his business dealings.

Then Worthington reviewed the articles concerning the culm dumps (Articles 1 and 3), the attempt to promote purchase by the Lehigh Coal and the Lehigh Railroad companies of a tract of coal land (Article 6), and the general and summarizing final article (13).

Worthington added his own exhaustive review to the already laboriously analyzed culm dump matters. He depicted Judge Archbald as at all times acting legally and at no time hiding or trying to hide his interest in securing the properties involved. Worthington said, "it has not yet been made criminal . . . for a judge to engage in business transactions, if a man is to go into any business whatever it is almost impossible for him to keep from going into a business that relates to coal properties, because [the Scranton area] is built up from the coal mines and the operations that grow out of them."[47]

Worthington gave short shrift to Article 13, terming it merely a summary of the preceding articles. He concluded by expressing his conviction that the Senate would not bring in a guilty verdict now that the respondent's evidence had been presented and the senators could see "how pitifully poor are the real facts against Judge Archbald," a man who had done nothing punishable and had been charged only with inconsequential acts that "any man in his condition . . . might have innocently done."[48]

The proceedings next reverted to the managers' side, with Henry D. Clayton delivering the last speech in the trial. Clayton felt obligated to review constitutional history and impeachment precedents, probably a wearying experience for the Senate, which had

heard these same recountings many times. He also discussed the attributes of judicial good behavior—not really a germane subject because the managers had to prove treason, bribery, or other high
crimes and misdemeanors. They could not rely on the good behavior clause of the Constitution as the device to remove an unworthy
jurist because that clause had never been defined by Congress, least
of all had its violation been made impeachable.

Manager Clayton insisted that the offenses with which Judge
Archbald had been charged need not have been committed in office.
He produced an analogy, made familiar in various forms in earlier
impeachment trials: "Suppose a judge were to commit highway robbery and be put in the penitentiary, would you hold that he could
not be impeached upon the ground that it was not done in his official capacity?"[49]

Next Clayton discussed whether motive must be a factor in deciding the guilt of an accused, arguing that willful misconduct need
not be proved to secure a conviction. He said that "the necessary
effect of this judge's conduct, regardless of his intent, was repeated
misbehaviors . . . we are to pronounce judgment according to . . . the
consequences, and the effect of his conduct."[50]

Manager Clayton countered the defense argument that Robert W.
Archbald had not concealed his connection with the culm dump negotiations, pointing out that the judge had drafted two of the op-
tions for purchase, and his name appeared on neither. Archbald did
reveal his name, however, Clayton said, when that disclosure could
be expected to have an effect upon the railroads. The judge's contribution to the various transactions could only have been his influence as a jurist, Clayton insisted, because in none of them had he
expended any money at all. In the Katydid culm dump arrangement,
Clayton noted, the railroad officials had not responded favorably until Judge Archbald called upon them, thereby proving that his position had been the determining factor.

Manager Clayton finished by thanking the Senate for its courtesy
and reminding his audience that the impeachment mechanism provided the nation with "a remedy to expel from office a faithless
judge. We confidently submit the case to the deliberation and high
judgment of this Senate."[51]

A comment concerning Senate attendance during the trial was
made at a later time by Alexander Simpson, who observed that at
the impeachment sessions "rarely over twenty members were
present";[52] he accounted for this poor record on the ground that regular business of the Senate continued despite the trial. Simpson's

comment brings to mind the problem of judgment being made by senators who did not hear all the evidence.

On January 13, 1913 the Senate met to vote on the articles. Six senators, three Republicans and three Democrats, asked to be excused from voting, mainly on the ground that illness or business elsewhere had kept them from attending the trial. Augustus O. Bacon, who had presided during most of the trial, asked to be excused because of his position. Various other senators during the course of the voting asked to be excused from being recorded on particular articles. The greatest number of requests for exemption concerned Articles 7 through 12 accusing Robert W. Archbald of misconduct during his tenure as district judge and the final Article, 13, containing the miscellany of charges.

Requests to be excused from voting on Article 13 posed a different problem from that raised by the articles covering Archbald's time as a district judge. George Sutherland (Republican, Utah) discussed the dilemma created by voting on an article so general that it touched upon most of the charges levied against Archbald. Sutherland noted that Article 13 included the various articles that preceded it, on some of which he had voted guilty and on some not guilty. "It occurs to me," he said, "I can not consistently vote upon this one article one way or the other."[53] Eight other senators, four Republicans and four Democrats, asked to be excused on the same grounds. Their position is sensible. It seems illogical that a person could vote not guilty on one or more specific complaints and then vote guilty on a composite article that included any one of those complaints.[54]

Article 1 affords the best example of the essentially nonpartisan nature of the Senate's decision making and of the managers' success in demonstrating Archbald's misconduct. That article accused the judge of inducing a company that had a case pending in the Commerce Court to sell him property, the Katydid culm dump, to his financial advantage. The Senate convicted Archbald on Article 1 by an enormous 93 percent: sixty-eight guilty, five not guilty, The five consisted of four Republicans and one Democrat; the sixty-eight guilty votes came from thirty-eight Republicans and thirty Democrats.[55] So in this ninth instance of impeachment and trial the Senate convicted the accused by a convincing and bipartisan majority.

Following the vote on the first article, with its overwhelming guilty verdict, Hoke Smith (Democrat, Georgia) suggested that the Senate go into secret session to consider "whether it is worth while to go on with the vote on these other charges . . . we having disposed of the matter by a vote on one article."[56] Smith withdrew this time-saving proposal after various senators expressed dissatisfaction with it, and the roll call continued.

The vote on the other four articles on which the Senate found Judge Archbald guilty reveals the following totals: the Packer No. 3 culm dump leasing arrangements (Article 3), sixty to eleven, an 85 percent majority for the managers' position;[57] the secret letter exchanges with an attorney representing a client in a case being heard before Archbald's court (Article 4) secured a 72 percent guilty vote, fifty-two to twenty;[58] the acceptance of a fee for trying to help a friend get a culm dump lease (Article 5), sixty-six to six, a 91 percent guilty vote;[59] and the catch-all Article 13, forty-two to twenty, barely meeting the required two-thirds majority to convict.[60] Thus, the managers attained easy convictions on Articles 1, 3, 4, and 5 and a less pronounced victory on 13. They achieved a majority win on Article 2 (the judge's offer to assist an attorney to settle the Marian Coal Company's problems) by 64 percent, not by the requisite two-thirds.[61]

On none of the six articles detailing Archbald's performance as a district judge could the managers come even close to a majority vote of guilty. On Article 7, for example, first of the articles relating to his tenure on the district court, the vote was thirty-six not guilty, twenty-nine guilty. Nine senators who had found Archbald guilty on some of the preceding articles were among those voting not guilty on Article 7. They explained that they either doubted the authority to impeach for misconduct relating to a former office or found no reason to examine the problem because Archbald's behavior in the office he currently held sufficed to convict him. Some senators among the thirty-six voting not guilty had previously stated that officials could be impeached for malperformance in a formerly held office; these latter, then, obviously found the charges unproved rather than inappropriate.

Senators who filed written opinions following the trial were divided on the question of whether an official could be impeached for misconduct in an office he no longer held.[62] In their statements, thirteen senators directly addressed this matter. Six Republicans and one Democrat argued that the impeachment mechanism could properly be used to challenge acts performed in a previously held office, and four Republicans and two Democrats insisted that it could not. This problem, if such it be, had no real bearing on Judge Archbald's case; the articles accusing him of malperformance in the office he held at the time of his trial proved more than adequate to convict him. No good reason except illustrating Archbald's long-indulged habit of misconduct existed for challenging his performance on the district court bench.

When the votes on all the articles had been cast, the Senate, by voice vote, removed Judge Robert W. Archbald from office. On the motion that Archbald "be forever disqualified from holding and enjoying any office of honor, trust, or profit under the United States," a motion that requires only an ordinary majority to succeed, the vote revealed thirty-nine in favor, thirty-five opposed.[63] Those voting for disqualification included twenty-six Democrats and thirteen Republicans; voting against disqualification were six Democrats and twenty-nine Republicans. The Senate's determination to prohibit Judge Archbald from ever again holding a national office displayed a party-centered decision. The Democrats' appetite for excluding the judge from further office proved much stronger than the Republicans'. Following the vote, President Pro Tem Bacon formally pronounced the Senate's judgment that Robert W. Archbald "is hereby, removed from office, and that he be and is hereby forever disqualified to hold and enjoy any office of honor, trust, or profit under the United States."[64]

A steady band of five senators found Archbald innocent of every charge: Republicans George T. Oliver and Boies Penrose, the two senators from Archbald's home state, Pennsylvania, Henry E. Burnham (Republican, New Hampshire), Thomas B. Catron (Republican, New Mexico), and one Democrat, Thomas H. Paynter of Kentucky. Only one senator, Henry F. Ashhurst (Democrat, Arizona), voted Archbald guilty on every article.

Four of the five senators who consistently voted Archbald innocent—Catron, Oliver, Paynter, and Penrose—filed statements at the end of the trial.[65] Each man explained that he had always voted not guilty because he believed that no crime or misdemeanor had been proved against the judge. Senator Oliver additionally believed that corrupt motives had to be, and had not been, demonstrated. Senator Paynter added his supposition that misconduct as a product of office had to be proved and argued that Archbald had not been shown to have misbehaved in his judicial capacity.

A composite portrait of the senator voting guilty proves difficult to assemble. A few party-centered aspects of the vote have been noted, but the dominant theme is the large majority from both parties mobilized against Archbald on Articles 1, 3, 4, and 5 and the less strong majority against him on Article 13. Results disclose neither a clear preference of Democrats nor a clear reluctance of

Republicans to find Judge Archbald guilty; nor can any regional slant to the voting be discerned.

The House and the Senate were involved with the affairs of Robert W. Archbald for just short of nine months, from April 1912 to January 1913. The trial proceedings began July 16, 1912 and ended January 13, 1913, with an intermission of four months (August 3 to December 3) and of two weeks (December 20 to January 4). Both the managers and Archbald's lawyers frequently referred to earlier impeachments. All the preceding trials were cited, with Andrew Johnson's, James Peck's, and Charles Swayne's receiving the most attention. Occasionally, both sides employed the same presumed precedent to reach opposite conclusions—a hallmark of impeachment trials.

Four central questions characterize Robert W. Archbald's impeachment and trial. First, must the acts of the accused be punishable in a court of law? Second, must such acts have been committed in the accused's official capacity? Third, must evil intent be demonstrated? Fourth, can an officer be impeached for malperformance in a previously held post? Precise responses cannot be given to these questions. None of the written statements filed at the end of the trial yielded opinions any more conclusive than those delivered in the eight earlier impeachment trials. Respecting the need for charging an indictable act, some senators in the Archbald trial thought it was essential, some did not. But the outcome of the Archbald trial supports the theory that has the stronger logical and historical basis: the articles need not allege criminal misconduct.

On this point Andrew J. Montague (Democrat, Virginia) stated during the debate on whether George W. English should be impeached in 1926 that Judge Archbald had been impeached and convicted "for a sort of semi-graft in receiving for himself and friends profits out of a coal dump in which he was in some way interested. It was not an indictable offense. It might not be even a wrong act on the part of an individual; but what you and I as private individuals can do a judge cannot do upon the bench of this nation. [Applause]"[66]

The senators who filed statements following Archbald's trial also exposed different viewpoints on the question of whether impeachment articles must demonstrate that the accused's misconduct occurred as a product of his office. Here, too, the thrust of the trial sustains the argument that it is not essential in an impeachment procedure to demonstrate official, as distinct from general, bad performance. An additional point on this subject must be noted. Like

Charles Swayne, Robert W. Archbald could have committed the deeds with which the House of Representatives charged him only because he held a judgeship. Although Archbald had not been accused of slanting his opinions to benefit the railroads or any other litigants, he did conduct business negotiations in his office, he did use official Commerce Court stationery, and he had no contribution to make to the various transactions in which he engaged except the title and prestige accruing from his post on the federal bench. If the managers had been obliged to refute an argument that misconduct as a product of office needed to be proved, it seems they would have had no difficulty in doing so.

Not much was said about the need to demonstrate bad intent. One senator, George T. Oliver (Republican, Pennsylvania), who had voted Judge Archbald innocent on all charges, explained that because "the evidence utterly failed to disclose any corrupt intent . . . I could not see how I could vote to visit upon [Archbald] the extreme penalties involved in impeachment."[67] Porter J. McCumber (Republican, North Dakota), who had voted guilty on the five charges on which Archbald had been convicted, took an opposing position. He reported his guilty vote as based on the belief "that criminal or corrupt intent on the part of Judge Archbald is unnecessary to establish an impeachable offense."[68] The question of intent was central in the trial of Judge Harry E. Claiborne in 1986. As it had in Archbald's case, the Senate appraised what Claiborne had actually done, not whether he had formed a plan to do wrong.

The last issue, whether charges can be levied for conduct in a former office, seems insignificant, at least as related to Robert W. Archbald. Enough material existed to convict Archbald for malperformance in his present office; no need arose to delve into his previous official activities. The only future occasion in which this problem might be crucial could occur if a resigned and unimpeached official with a flawed record should be subsequently appointed or elected to office. Could the impeachment mechanism then be employed to unseat him from the new position on the basis of how he behaved in the old one? The possibility seems too remote to require serious attention.

One additional aspect of Archbald's experience needs mention: the frequent references to "good behavior"—a phrase rarely used in earlier impeachments. The managers, and even several senators, often alluded to Archbald as violating the good behavior requirement under which he held office. Because so many persons involved in this impeachment proceeding commented on judicial good behavior and noted that Archbald did not stand as its exemplar, it is regrettable that one of the participating senators did not introduce a bill defining good behavior in a judge and making bad behavior an explicit high crime and misdemeanor. James Buchanan's remedy following James Peck's trial consisted in having a law passed to prevent a recurrence of the problems encountered with Judge Peck, a law that established the conditions under which a judge may sentence for contempt. Had the managers or interested congressmen followed Buchanan's example and, in Archbald's case, struggled to activate the good behavior clause, much mischief could have been avoided in the impeachment trials of judges following Archbald.

William Howard Taft, who, as president, had appointed Robert W. Archbald to the Commerce Court, referred to his appointee's impeachment in a speech to the American Bar Association in 1913, the year of the judge's conviction. Taft said that Archbald had been convicted

> on the ground that he sought sales of property from railroad companies . . . which were likely to be litigants in his court, and indicated . . . his hope and purpose that such companies would be moved to comply with his requests because of his official position. . . . [The outcome demonstrated to judges] that they must be careful in their conduct outside the court as well as in the court itself and that they must not use the prestige of their judicial position, directly or indirectly, to secure personal benefit.[69]

The trial of Judge Archbald vindicates the impeachment process and shows that partisan bias does not inevitably prove stronger than the evidence presented against a respondent—in this case flagrant influence peddling. This trial is particularly notable because it is the only one from 1799 to 1986 in which the Senate convicted a respondent who belonged to the party constituting a majority in that body.[70]

The nation's next exposure to impeachment occurred in 1926, when the House of Representatives impeached George W. English, yet another federal judge. English's resignation on the eve of his trial terminated proceedings against him. The next Senate impeachment trial, that of Judge Harold Louderback, took place in 1933, twenty years after Judge Archbald's conviction.

Harold Louderback. *Nevada Historical Society.*

11

Harold Louderback

The witnesses here were the victims of [Louderback's] just conduct. . . . Judges ought not to be drawn into an impeachment by such witnesses. . . . The Senate, sitting as a Court of Impeachment, is not a tribunal for the review of the exercise of judicial discretion.
— Joseph W. Bailey

An interlude of twenty years separated the trial of Judge Robert W. Archbald and the trial of Judge Harold Louderback. Congress had been involved in the impeachment of Judge George W. English in 1926, but proceedings against him stopped when he resigned shortly before his trial. Judge Louderback came to trial in the Senate in May 1933 amid the turmoil of the deep depression signaled by the stock market crash of 1929. Massive unemployment and multiple business failures characterized the period in which Louderback was impeached and tried, a period at the dawn of the New Deal ushered in under the leadership of Franklin D. Roosevelt. Some part of Judge Louderback's problems arose from the era in which he lived: he was a Republican when that party had been disavowed, and he was accused of favoritism in awarding receiverships—a central issue in an era of collapsing businesses.

Three aspects of Judge Louderback's experience occurred for the first time in the chronicle of those officers who were subsequently impeached and tried: (1) the House Judiciary Committee, by the convincing majority of seventeen to five, recommended against Louderback's impeachment, and the House of Representatives overrode the recommendation and voted to impeach him; (2) the seventeen-member majority report of the Judiciary Committee proposed to censure him; and (3) the House revised the articles of impeachment after they had been presented to the Senate and at the behest of the judge's attorneys.

Harold Louderback, born in San Francisco in 1881, received his bachelor's degree from the University of Nevada in 1905 and his law degree from Harvard in 1908. He served as a superior court judge in the city and county of San Francisco (1921–28), first elected for a six-year term in 1920 and reelected in 1926—a term he did not complete because in 1928 Calvin Coolidge, a fellow Republican, appointed him a United States district judge for the northern district of California.[1]

Doubts about Louderback's fitness to be a judge became public at the national level on May 24, 1932, when the Bar Association of San Francisco asked the House of Representatives to investigate his conduct.[2] Congressman Hatton W. Sumners (Democrat, Texas) presented the bar's letter to the House, along with a motion directing the Judiciary Committee to investigate Judge Harold Louderback's performance.[3] The House of Representatives adopted the motion and authorized a committee comprised of Sumners, Gordon Browning (Democrat, Texas), and Fiorello La Guardia (Republican-Progressive, New York) to conduct the investigation. They held hearings in San Francisco and in Washington, D.C., and subsequently recommended to the Judiciary Committee that Louderback be impeached. The committee went against the recommendation and voted seventeen to five against impeachment but agreed to have the minority report favoring impeachment given to the House of Representatives along with the majority report opposing such action.[4]

The Judiciary Committee presented its resolution to the House on February 24, 1933. The committee's resolution stated that the evidence against Judge Louderback did not warrant impeachment.[5] In the majority report, but not part of the resolution, appeared the following appraisal: "The committee censures the judge for conduct prejudicial to the dignity of the judiciary in appointing incompetent receivers, for the method of selecting receivers, for allowing fees that seem excessive, and for a high degree of indifference to the interests of litigants in receivership."[6] The majority's unwillingness to advocate impeachment of a jurist in whom it found a "high degree of indifference" to certain litigants plus evidence that he made poor appointments and permitted unwarranted fees is inexplicable.

A substitute motion introduced by Congressman La Guardia for the minority of the Judiciary Committee recommended impeachment and presented five articles detailing the judge's purported misconduct. The House debate on La Guardia's motion included three spokesmen favoring impeachment and three against.[7] Opponents of impeachment accused the three-man investigating subcommittee of prosecutorial bias and found none of the charges levied against Judge Louderback impeachable.

Those advocating impeachment detailed objectionable acts of the judge, emphasizing his appointments of favored people to receiverships. Commenting on the Bar Association of San Francisco's instigation of the inquiry, Congressman Sumners said: "you can hardly get a lawyer to raise his voice against a Federal judge, on account of the power they have got, and whenever you find a bar association going on record . . . you may know as a matter of horse sense that that judge's conduct has been such as to bring reasonable, substantial doubt of his integrity."[8]

Sumners and his pro-impeachment colleagues proved persuasive. The House of Representatives, composed of 220 Democrats and 215 Republicans, disregarded the Judiciary Committee and chose to impeach Louderback. The vote was 183 favoring impeachment and 142 opposing, a 56 percent majority for the pro-impeachment forces.[9] The 142 congressmen who opposed impeachment included 38 Democrats and 104 Republicans—a vote reflecting greater desire on the part of Republicans than of Democrats to desist from further action against Harold Louderback.

The charges levied against Judge Louderback dealt almost exclusively with his appointments of receivers and their attorneys. Receivers, assigned by a court to be custodians and supervisors of an ailing company, often earned handsome compensation, the amount being determined by the court. During a depression, particularly one that proved so long-lasting as the one beginning in 1929, receiverships become not only more plentiful because of the number of failing businesses but also more sought after. Harold Louderback referred to them as "plums."[10] Sometimes judges making such appointments awarded them to friends or allies who were not always qualified. As Joseph Borkin observes, "The handling of receiverships seems to lend itself particularly to abuse by judges and to criticism by the public."[11]

Three days after adopting the impeachment resolution, the House of Representatives notified the Senate that it had impeached Harold Louderback and had appointed four Democrats and two Republicans as managers to conduct the trial: Hatton W. Sumners, Gordon Browning (Democrat, Tennessee), U. S. Guyer (Republican, Kansas), Lawrence Lewis (Democrat, Colorado), J. Earl Major (Democrat, Illinois), and Randolph Perkins (Republican, New Jersey).[12]

On the last day of the 72nd Congress (March 3, 1933), Manager Gordon Browning presented five articles of impeachment to the Senate.[13] The first described Judge Louderback's dismissal of a receiver, Addison G. Strong, whom he had appointed at the request of both the creditors and the management of a failing brokerage house. Strong was discharged, according to Article 1, because he would not designate as the receiver's attorney a man whom Louderback allegedly preferred. Judge Louderback was accused of promising high fees to the receiver if he would choose the attorney the judge wanted; Strong refused, and the judge fired him and appointed another receiver. Subsequently, according to Article 1, Louderback named as attorney for the newly appointed receiver a man recommended by W. S. (Sam) Leake, to whom the judge was, the article asserted, under obligation.

A further charge in Article 1 asserted that Leake and Louderback conspired to conceal the judge's real residence. The room that Leake rented at the Fairmont Hotel in San Francisco under his own name was actually and regularly occupied by Louderback. The latter had established a legal residence at his brother's home in Contra Costa County, across the bay from San Francisco, and had become a registered voter there.[14] The article termed the Contra Costa residency "fictitious" and a felony because Louderback, in truth, lived at the Fairmont Hotel. The judge, whose marriage was dissolving, had pretended to move, according to Article 1, only to force his wife to bring her pending divorce action in Contra Costa County. Thus, the first impeachment article contained two major accusations: improper conduct concerning a receivership and establishment of a fictitious residence.

Article 2 charged Louderback with allowing excessive fees to a receiver and the latter's attorney in a case in which Louderback's jurisdiction in the matter had been terminated by order of the Court of Appeals for the Ninth Circuit.[15] The appellate court ordered Judge Louderback to have the receiver turn over all assets of the company concerned to the California commissioner of insurance. Louderback complied, but with a proviso that the commissioner not contest the fees he had allowed to the receiver and his attorney. This performance, according to the managers, revealed the judge as "improperly using his said office . . . to favor and enrich his personal and political friends . . . to the detriment and loss of litigants."[16]

Harold Louderback, in an instance detailed in Article 3, assertedly appointed an incompetent receiver and refused to grant a hearing to the company involved to protest that appointment. The managers viewed this action as judicial misbehavior and a misdemeanor in office.

Article 4 claimed that Louderback had unlawfully appointed a receiver without notifying the troubled company and had refused to revoke the appointment after the company objected. This "oppressive, deliberate, and willful" act deprived the owners of the business concerned "of a fair, impartial, and judicial consideration of their rights and the protection of their property, to which they were entitled."[17]

The final article consisted of an amalgam of the four preceding articles, following the pattern of the Robert W. Archbald case in 1913. The complaints contained in it were stated in so vague a fashion as to be essentially unanswerable, a point successfully made by Judge Louderback's attorneys and leading to amendment and enlargement of Article 5 by the prosecutors before the trial began. Except for the allegation that Harold Louderback had established a bogus residence because of domestic difficulties, the accusations in all five articles of impeachment concerned his handling of receiverships.

Following Manager Browning's presentation, the Senate discussed the choice of a date on which the trial should begin. Huey Long (Democrat, Louisiana) suggested postponement of the trial

because if the Congress shall be called into session for remedial legislation, for which the people all over this country are crying, we do not want to sit here and waste the whole time of the special session over the impeachment of some judge in California . . . if we come back here with the Senate fiddling its time away over a little impeachment fiasco . . . messing around here as to whether we are going to impeach somebody with the people starving to death in this country, the Congress of the United States will have the odium it ought to have.[18]

George Norris (Republican, Nebraska) moved that the impeachment be taken up on the first day of the first session of the 73rd Congress; his motion was agreed upon. The Senate that would sit in judgment of Harold Louderback was composed of sixty Democrats, thirty-five Republicans, and one Republican-Progressive—a gain of twelve seats for the Democrats in the Roosevelt landslide election of 1932 that gave the majority party 62 percent of the seats. The Senate also included the first woman to sit as a member of a Court of Impeachment, Hattie W. Caraway (Democrat, Arkansas).

On March 9, 1933 the Senate took the oath prescribed for such proceedings. William E. Borah (Republican, Idaho) and Hiram Johnson (Republican, California) asked to be excused from serving in the trial because of undisclosed reasons that could affect their impartiality.[19] John H. Overton (Democrat, Louisiana) and

Augustine Lonergan (Democrat, Connecticut) asked to be excused because each had voted against impeaching Louderback when they had been members of the House of Representatives in the preceding session.[20] Vice-President John Nance Garner (Democrat, Texas) informed the Senate that he had served as speaker of the House during the impeachment of Judge Louderback by the 72nd Congress and wanted to be sure that his presiding in the trial would be acceptable. The Senate excused the four senators and took no notice of Vice-President Garner's offer to have his qualifications challenged.[21]

The Senate fixed April 11, 1933 for the respondent's reply to the articles; and on that day Louderback and his attorneys, James M. Hanley and Walter H. Linforth, presented his answer.[22] None of the articles, even if true, set forth an impeachable offense as defined in the Constitution, they stated.

Louderback accepted the facts contained in Article 1 but rejected the interpretations put upon them. He had appointed Addison G. Strong, auditor for the San Francisco Stock Exchange, as receiver for the failing brokerage house and had revoked the appointment two days later because Strong desired to select his attorney from a law firm that represented the stock exchange. The judge did not wish any lawyer connected with the stock exchange to serve as Strong's attorney. He had suggested several other lawyers from whom Strong could make his selection. But Strong, "in a defiant and arbitrary manner, declined and refused to have or employ any counsel to represent him as such receiver other than the said firm so representing the said stock exchange."[23] Whereupon, Louderback removed him from the receivership.

Judge Louderback then appointed another receiver, who chose John Douglas Short as his attorney, the latter appointment, according to Article 1, coming about at the insistence of W. S. Leake. The judge said Leake had nothing to do with Short's appointment, denied that Short had received exorbitant fees as attorney for the receiver, and denied knowing that Leake had obtained any money from John Douglas Short.

With respect to the false residency charge included in Article 1, Harold Louderback explained that in September 1929 W. S. Leake had rented a room for him at the Fairmont Hotel in the latter's name, a room for which the judge paid his friend. The reason for this concealment arose from the separation between Louderback and his wife; the judge wanted to avoid the notoriety that would be caused if his marital problems became public knowledge. Several months later, in April 1930, Louderback moved to his brother's home in Contra Costa County, leaving some of his possessions in the Fairmont Hotel to accommodate him for stays in San Francisco. He became a registered voter in Contra Costa County, and any suggestion that he intended "to establish himself a resident of said county in anticipation of any divorce action expected . . . to be brought against him" was false, an assertion later contradicted in the judge's own testimony.[24]

Louderback described as proper his appointment of a receiver and his attorney and his approval of their fees, facts detailed in Article 2. He acknowledged making an error in his order directing the receiver to turn over the assets of the company concerned to the California insurance commissioner. The error consisted of a proviso that such assets should not be delivered to the commissioner if the latter contested the fees the judge had granted. Louderback's proviso, subsequently revoked, did not hamper the commissioner, he claimed. Nothing the judge did enriched any friend or proceeded from partiality toward any of the people involved.

Article 3 also dealt with a receivership problem. Judge Louderback had appointed Guy H. Gilbert friend of both the judge and Leake, as receiver for a motor company, an appointment that had drawn no objections from either the faltering company or its creditors. The judge did not consider Gilbert "to be incompetent, unfit, and/or inexperienced for his duties" as charged in Article 3.[25] Louderback said that no litigant in the case had been deprived of an opportunity to protest Gilbert's appointment nor been put to additional expense or disadvantage because of his serving as receiver. Gilbert also became the receiver in another case, detailed in Article 4. Judge Louderback reported that both the failing company and its creditors requested him to appoint a receiver. He denied disregarding a request for cancellation of the receivership or for discharge of Gilbert as receiver.

Louderback observed that the last article was so indefinite that he could not respond to it without specific charges being made. One of his attorneys presented a motion asking the House of Representatives to make Article 5 more precise; if the House did not comply in a reasonable time, he asked that the article be dismissed.[26]

The Senate next considered the time to be allowed for the House replication, the respondent's answer to the replication, and the date for opening the trial. May 1, 1933 was decided upon for the reply of the House of Representatives to Louderback's answer to the articles, with all pleadings to be closed by May 15, when the trial would begin.

On April 18 Manager Hatton W. Sumners gave the requested amendment to Article 5. In its revised and much longer form the article detailed Judge Louderback's alleged appointment of incompetent receivers, his transactions with W. S. Leake, and his permitting large fees to receivers and their attorneys.[27] Guy H. Gilbert's unfitness as receiver was described: he worked for a telegraph company, continued in that job while acting as receiver, and had no qualifications for the position to which Judge Louderback appointed him. Still a potpourri article, the amended version set forth certain new charges and repeated and amplified material contained in the first four articles; it concluded, however, with a more specific claim than did the preceding articles: "Wherefore, the said Harold Louderback has been and is guilty of high crimes and misdemeanors in office and has not conducted himself with good behavior."[28]

Judge Louderback's response to the amended article consisted of a denial of most of the charges and an explanation of a few of them. He objected to inclusion in the new version of any references to his conduct as a superior court judge in San Francisco and requested further explicit information about some of his purported misdeeds. He concluded with the statement that he had not been guilty of any high crimes or misdemeanors nor had he ever failed to conduct himself in harmony with standards of good behavior.[29]

The trial began on May 15, 1933 as scheduled. Hatton W. Sumners opened the case for the managers. He commented on the importance of the Senate's removal power as the only means of protecting the public from the malperformance of a jurist holding life appointment. Anticipating that Harold Louderback's defenders would raise the customary respondent's argument that to be impeachable he must be accused of a crime, Sumners claimed "that impeachment under the American Constitution is not a criminal action, . . . it is an ouster suit, because the Senate has no power to punish."[30] He touched briefly upon the major charges contained in the articles, affirming that they would be sustained as the managers' case unfolded.

James M. Hanley gave the opening statement on the judge's behalf. He began with a reference to the achievements and solid reputation of the Louderback family. He then reviewed all the charges against the judge and asserted that the defense would be able to prove the falsity of each. In the course of his review Hanley said, with reference to the allegation that Louderback had acted unlawfully in dismissing Addison G. Strong, that Strong's dismissal had divorced "administration of this estate from the hands of the stock exchange of San Francisco," the influence of which "was such that [Louderback] is now being here tried upon articles of impeachment."[31]

At no time did Hanley explain away or try to justify Louderback's behavior; he declared that the judge would be proved absolutely innocent of any wrongdoing. This sturdy assertion of a respondent's innocence stands in vivid contrast with most of the preceding impeachments in which the defense often acknowledged error on the respondent's part but excused it as harmless or inadvertent.

Following the opening statements, Francis C. Brown, first witness for the managers, took the stand. An attorney for the failing brokerage house, Brown testified to his opposition to Judge Louderback's dismissal of Addison G. Strong as receiver and said that the fees subsequently allowed to Strong's replacement and his attorney had been extravagant. Brown reported discussing with the judge certain San Francisco newspaper articles speculating on the latter's possible impeachment. Louderback, Brown said, thought that the impeachment talk might have been generated by Max Thelen, an attorney who had urged Strong's appointment. Louderback felt that Thelen could be instrumental in promoting impeachment because his associate "was president of the Barristers' Club in San Francisco."[32] The idea that dissatisfied attorneys in the stock brokerage case had originated and promoted Louderback's impeachment received further mention only at the end of the trial, when the judge's attorney stated directly that Louderback had been the victim of "disgruntled" lawyers.[33]

Brown's testimony attempted to establish that Judge Louderback had improperly discharged a receiver acceptable to both the creditors and the foundering company and had subsequently appointed another receiver, allowing fees to him and his attorney not justified by the difficulty of their job nor the time spent on it.

Cross-examination of Francis C. Brown by Walter H. Linforth blunted Brown's criticisms of Louderback's conduct. Linforth demonstrated that Brown, as attorney for the failing brokerage house, had accepted the second receiver appointed by Louderback after he had fired Strong, and that Brown had not objected to the fees allowed by the judge and settled upon in open court.[34]

The next witness, Paul S. Marrin, another attorney concerned in the brokerage company receivership, had recommended the appointment of Addison G. Strong as receiver because of his thorough familiarity with both the stock exchange and the company about to go into receivership. Marrin, recounting Judge Louderback's subsequent removal of Strong, said it was caused by the judge's belief that Strong had been disrespectful in not keeping an appointment with Louderback and in his insistence upon selecting his own attorney.

James M. Hanley's cross-examination of Marrin dwelt upon minute details of the case and repeatedly challenged the witness's recollection on minor points. Presiding officer William H. King (Democrat, Utah), probably tiring of all the minutia, asked Hanley why he persisted in asking Marrin the same questions over and over again and admonished Hanley not to argue with the witness. King added, "we are spending rather too much time on matters that may be relevant, but do not require so much time in their elucidation."[35]

Addison G. Strong, central figure in the first charge contained in Article 1, was the managers' third witness. A certified public accountant, Strong had as clients both the San Francisco Stock Exchange and the suspended brokerage house. He recounted his reluctant acceptance of the receivership after being urged to do so by both the creditors and the brokerage firm involved. He insisted that he had not shown disrespect for Judge Louderback by not conferring with him about appointment of an attorney; he had not understood that the judge wanted to see him the very day of his being named receiver. Strong said he could not accept as his attorney the man allegedly urged upon him by Louderback because he did not consider that attorney to be qualified. Strong had also reminded the judge that he, Strong, would be legally and financially responsible for the conduct of his attorney, and, therefore, wanted someone he knew to serve in that capacity. Judge Louderback, apparently urging him to reconsider his refusal to accept an attorney agreeable to the judge, said, according to Strong; " 'I do not know whether you realize what a plum you have picked; do you realize that your fees will be somewhere between $10,000 and $80,000' . . . He then asked me if I knew that he appointed receivers at frequent intervals. I told him that I understood that he did. He then said, 'If you do this work properly, and something of a similar nature comes up, your name will undoubtedly be considered.' "[36]

Walter H. Linforth's cross-examination elicited that Strong had no previous experience as a receiver and that Judge Louderback objected to the attorney Strong wanted to appoint only because he was connected with the San Francisco Stock Exchange. Strong acknowledged that Louderback expressed his objection by saying, "The whole matter is too much of the same family. It is too close a proposition." Linforth underlined this point by adding, "And he gave you that as the reason why he did not want you to employ the regular attorneys of the stock exchange . . . ?"[37] Strong said that was correct. Linforth secured acknowledgment from Strong that because the attorney Strong wanted to appoint served as attorney for the stock exchange and because the exchange was a client of Strong's accounting firm, some possibility existed of embarrassing complications should the stock exchange prove to be improperly involved in the affairs of the failing company.

The first three of the managers' witnesses, testifying on Louderback's removal of Strong, did not produce material indicating, or even hinting at, unlawful conduct by the judge. During the next two trial days, the managers presented nineteen witnesses and closed the prosecution's case.[38] The various receivership matters took up most of the time, with just one brief reference to the question of Judge Louderback's supposedly fictitious residency at his brother's home—a statement by a chambermaid at the Fairmont Hotel that the judge had resided there for most of the preceding two years.[39]

All the managers' witnesses confirmed that Strong had been acceptable to both parties in the brokerage case, and all believed that Strong's failure to call on Judge Louderback following his appointment as receiver had been due to a misunderstanding. Louderback, the witnesses claimed, misinterpreted Strong's failure to appear and looked upon it as intentional disobedience. The judge also resented, several witnesses recounted, Strong's refusal to choose his attorney from among candidates the judge proposed. According to one prosecution witness, Louderback insisted on picking the receiver's lawyer on all occasions when the interested parties had chosen the receiver, and he regarded Strong's insistence upon his own preferred lawyer as insubordinate and therefore dismissed him.[40]

One witness commented on Judge Louderback's practice of selecting either the receiver or his attorney. In this example, the Golden State Asparagus receivership (Article 5), both parties had agreed on a receiver and on an attorney; but according to witness Erwin E. Richter, who represented the asparagus company, Louderback stated that "he would not permit the parties to designate both the receiver and his counsel, but that the parties might nominate either the receiver or his counsel, and that the court would appoint the other party."[41] None of these observations on Judge Louderback's customary handling of receiverships seems extraordinary; a judge had the authority to select both a receiver and his attorney.

Richter also testified on the allegedly exorbitant fees that Louderback allowed in the asparagus company receivership; and when asked by James M. Hanley why he had not protested such fees, Richter observed that Harold Louderback was widely known for granting excessive sums to receivers and their attorneys and that he, Richter, had agreed to the amount "solely for the reason that no better relief could be obtained under the circumstances."[42]

In the matter of the Fageol Motor Company case (Articles 3 and 5), witnesses reported that the creditors and the failing company had agreed on a receiver but Judge Louderback again selected Guy H. Gilbert, beneficiary of several receivership appointments from Louderback and a man with no experience in the automotive business. Fageol's attorney explained that both the creditors and Fageol wanted a receiver with knowledge of the automotive industry because they believed that the company could be revived and an experienced receiver could be expected to contribute to that goal. Another witness, whose bank was the largest claimant against Fageol, said that Gilbert "gave us the utmost cooperation, but he possessed no ability to carry on the work."[43] When cross-examined, the banker acknowledged that the creditors had not protested the fees Gilbert and his attorney allowed and that he, the banker, had written letters to both men praising their work in handling the Fageol receivership.

The potpourri Article 5 had been variously referred to throughout the prosecution's case. It did set forth a few charges not contained in the preceding four articles, but basically produced only more examples of purportedly excessive fees and questionable selection of receivers. A survey of the managers' presentation reveals that it rested on efforts to show that Judge Louderback favored certain people for receiverships who were not always competent and that he allowed improperly large fees to those receivers and their attorneys.

Only one vote concerning admissibility of evidence occurred during the managers' presentation. Desiring to document Judge Louderback's favoritism toward certain persons as manifested by his frequent selections of them to serve as receivers, the managers offered exhibits that included some such appointments made while Louderback served as a California judge. Louderback protested introduction of any data that referred to his tenure as a California jurist, and also argued that a judge's appointment of a person could not be construed as showing an intimate relationship. But by a massive sixty-seven to four vote the Senate agreed to admit the exhibits.[44] Thus, the only vote taken during the prosecution's presentation supported the managers' position.

The case on behalf of Judge Harold Louderback opened on the afternoon of May 18, the day on which the managers had completed their presentation. The judge's attorneys, confident of their position, had considered moving for dismissal of the articles of impeachment when the prosecution finished its case, but reported that Judge Louderback had instructed them to proceed.

In the four days and part of a fifth consumed by the respondent, thirty witnesses were called. All the charges against Harold Louderback received thorough examination and careful refutation. At no time did the judge's attorneys employ the customary respondent's device of demanding proof of criminal behavior. They seemed sure of their ability to prove that Louderback had done nothing wrong and proceeded to their task of demonstrating this fact to the Senate.

The defense met the problems connected with Judge Louderback's appointments of receivers and their attorneys and the fees granted to them (all five articles, variously) through the testimony of several witnesses who detailed the length of time spent in managing the receiverships involved, the acknowledged high quality of the work done, and the appropriateness of the fees the judge had awarded. For example, Armand B. Kreft, formerly referee in bankruptcy for the Northern District of California, testified that he had examined the report of services by the receiver and his attorney in the failing brokerage firm matter (Article 1) and had found the fees allowed to be reasonable. Asked if he, while serving as a referee in bankruptcy, would have allowed the same fees, Kreft replied that he would. During cross-examination, Manager Lawrence Lewis, who sought to show the rarity of such large fees as those allowed in the brokerage house receivership, asked Kreft, "How many fees of $50,000 or more have you known to be allowed to attorneys in receivership cases in San Francisco?" Kreft replied, "I do not recall more than two or three approximating that amount, and I will say, in explanation, that there are not more than two or three that involve a volume of assets comparable with the [failing brokerage house] case."[45]

Questions about the competence of Guy H. Gilbert, whom Louderback appointed a receiver four times, came up frequently, however, the consensus appeared to be that he served diligently. In the Fageol Motors case (Articles 3 and 5) Gilbert's lack of experience in the automotive industry required hiring a manager to conduct business during the receivership. But the prosecution did not demonstrate, or even assert, that Gilbert's tenure had cost the troubled automotive company additional money. Slight, if any, damage to Louderback's position accrued from this example of his assigning an inexperienced receiver.

The only accusation against Harold Louderback that he admitted to be true concerned the proviso attached to his order turning over assets of an ailing company from federal control to the California insurance commissioner as he had been directed to do by the circuit court (Article 2). The proviso stipulated that the company's assets be delivered to state control only upon the California commissioner's agreement not to contest the fees Judge Louderback had awarded to the federal receiver and to his attorney. The judge acknowledged that he had made a mistake and pointed out that he had promptly withdrawn the proviso.

Among the defense witnesses was George D. Louderback, the respondent's brother, who testified concerning the judge's becoming a resident in his home. Beginning in April 1930 Harold Louderback had a room in his brother's house and voted from that residence on five occasions. The judge had slept in the George Louderback residence only four times during the three-year period because he had severe asthma attacks brought on by house plants or the family cat. It is clear from his brother's report that Harold Louderback did not actually dwell in Contra Costa County even though he considered it his home and had established a voting residence there. What significance such evidence might have remained uncertain, and the judge's living at the Fairmont Hotel had not formed a major part of the managers' case nor been made by them to seem sinister or deceitful.

Thirtieth and final witness in the trial was Louderback himself. His attorney, Walter H. Linforth, led him through all the accusations.[46] His living at the Fairmont Hotel in a room registered to W. S. Leake came about, Judge Louderback said, because of domestic difficulties that he did not wish to become public. When he realized, about six months after moving to the Fairmont, that his separation from his wife seemed likely to be permanent, he established his legal residence with his brother and became a registered voter in Contra Costa County in April 1930. Cross-examined by Manager Randolph Perkins, Louderback admitted that were he sued for divorce he preferred to be sued in Contra Costa County because "the publicity in Martinez, a little town of that county, would not be commensurate with the publicity which you would get in a city like San Francisco for one occupying my position. [But I have not] made this change and established my home primarily and solely with this in view."[49]

Removal of Addison G. Strong as receiver (Article 1) was based, Judge Louderback recounted, on his unwillingness to have Strong pick his own lawyer. The judge had informed Strong that he must consult with Louderback before considering attorneys, a requirement Strong did not meet. Instead, he asked an attorney whose firm represented the San Francisco Stock Exchange to serve with him in the failing stock brokerage receivership. Louderback feared a conflict of interest and "was not prepared to have the stock exchange substitute its judgment for mine in the selection of the officials of the court."[48]

When cross-examined about his receivership appointments, Louderback said, "Nobody has ever made a complaint of any receiver, that I have ever been given notice of, either in chambers or by petition in court, not one instance." Asked whether he did not know that in the stock brokerage case, and others, his appointments "became the subject of general controversy and general criticism," the judge replied that if they had "it has been unjust, because if there was any criticism in those cases, the parties or interested persons should have brought the matter to my attention, either in chambers or in court . . . I had not been criticized by any legal proceeding."[49]

Judge Louderback's attorneys asked each of their witnesses who had been involved as receivers or receivers' attorneys whether they had shared any part of their fees with Harold Louderback. All answered no; the managers had made no inquiries along that line, nor had they ever proposed that the judge had accepted any kickbacks.

Several times senators or participants indicated impatience at repetitious or hair-splitting questions. Near the end of the trial Judge Louderback's attorneys asked for a recess; Henry F. Ashurst (Democrat, Arizona), chairman of the Senate Judiciary Committee, commented: "I am about to say something that doubtless I should not say, but I am going to say it at the risk of impropriety. The honorable attorneys are weary, but there are others who are weary from hearing questions that have no relation to the subject repeated over and over and over again. Other men grow weary as well as the honorable attorneys."[50] Senator Ashurst felt that weariness was not a sound excuse for a delay, but even so, he moved for a recess from Friday noon until the following Monday; the Senate agreed to the motion.

On the following Monday came three prosecution rebuttal witnesses whose testimony completed the trial, a completion that brought satisfaction, at least to Senator Ashurst, who exclaimed, "I wonder if I have heard aright or am I correct in understanding that both the honorable managers on the part of the House and the counsel for the respondent have rested?" Senator Hugo Black (Democrat, Alabama), serving as presiding officer, reassured Ashurst by saying, "The Senator is correct."[51]

Upon conclusion of the trial, the Senate considered the amount of time to be allowed for summation. Senator Ashurst proposed three hours, the time to be divided equally between the two sides. Hatton W. Sumners, noting that many senators had been unable to attend the trial regularly, said he thought the managers would, therefore, need more time because they would have to go over the evidence rather that just summarize it. Walter H. Linforth displayed confidence in the respondent's position by saying that his side would not require even the proposed one and one-half hours, and "if the learned gentlemen representing the prosecution in this matter are willing to submit the case to the Senate without argument, so is the respondent."[52] The managers did not accept this offer, and the Senate agreed to permit each side two hours.

The next day, May 24, 1933, the final arguments were delivered. Manager Gordon Browning spoke first. He sought to portray Harold Louderback's friend W. S. Leake as controlling the judge. He reviewed Leake's finances and made an effort to connect some of his bank deposits with the dates on which various attorneys and receivers appointed by Louderback had been paid. Browning said, "When fees were paid in respondent's court Leake's account bulged like the coming in of the tide."[53] The effort to tie the dates of Leake's deposits to the dates when various receivers and attorneys received their pay was farfetched. Unless W. S. Leake and the receivers and attorneys who testified were all lying, none of them had paid Leake anything in connection with their service under Judge Louderback. This last-ditch attempt proved unconvincing, had not been confirmed by any witness, and had not been featured during the trial.

On the matters of appointments and excessive fees, Browning recited all the evidence the managers adduced to show that Judge Louderback appointed favorites, often incompetent, and allowed them exorbitant fees as receivers or as attorneys. Such fees came from the creditors of the failing businesses; Browning referred to "the respondent and Leake and those who are bloodsuckers on these estates" as benefiting at the expense of the creditors.[54] Browning's colorful language also extended to his description of Judge Louderback's original refusal to release records to the California insurance commissioner unless the latter agreed not to contest the fees allowed. He termed this act (promptly rescinded, as noted) "an effort on the part of the respondent to hold his leeches onto a wounded institution and let them suck its blood—his pets and his coadjutors."[55]

Browning's occasionally bombastic language may have been caused by his desire to display passionate revulsion at Louderback's alleged malperformances and to stir his audience into believing that the case against the judge revealed outrageous misconduct. Certainly, the facts he reviewed lacked dramatic appeal and had been gone over so frequently by both sides that they could hardly be relied on to arouse the Senate and rivet its attention on Louderback's wrong and impeachable performances.

Walter H. Linforth, the only spokesman for Harold Louderback in summation, followed Manager Browning. He referred briefly to criminal proceedings (not heretofore mentioned), arguing that this case, "while not criminal, is in the nature and partakes of the character of a criminal proceeding." Consequently, Linforth told the Senate, "the proof must satisfy you beyond a reasonable doubt."[56]

Next he asked the Senate to consider "Who is at the bottom of these charges?" and supplied the answer: "disgruntled attorneys, who, in my humble judgment, have misled the managers. . . . I say to the gentlemen who represent the other side, with great respect for all of them, that they have been misled by this firm of disgruntled attorneys."[57] Linforth was referring to the failing stock brokerage case (Article 1) and the presumed antagonism Judge Louderback engendered by refusing to accept as receiver's attorney the lawyer desired by the stock exchange and by subsequently dismissing the receiver who had been approved by both parties. As a wise and cautious judge, Linforth said, Louderback, having appointed the receiver the stock exchange wanted, needed to have as the latter's attorney someone not connected with the exchange because, as Louderback phrased it, "I do not want too much of the same family in the matter."[58]

Of the men Judge Louderback assigned to act in the receiverships at issue, Linforth insisted, "Every receiver appointed was a decent man. Every lawyer appointed was a competent lawyer. Every receivership was ably managed and conducted."[59] His summation covered all the points concerning receiverships and fees that had been raised by the managers. Quoting frequently from the trial record, including the testimony of prosecution witnesses, Linforth carefully refuted each argument advanced against Louderback's conduct relative to the various failing companies for which he appointed receivers and their attorneys. He commented only briefly on the question of the judge's actual residence, a matter Linforth did not find difficult to explain because the judge voted in Contra Costa County and considered it his domicile.

The final speaker in the trial, Manager Hatton W. Sumners, reminded the Senate of its duty to protect the public and the judiciary from judges who acted improperly. It was not necessary, Sumners claimed, that a malperforming judge "be convicted of a crime and brought before the Senate as a felon in chains." Such a judge need only have behaved in a fashion that aroused "a substantial doubt in the minds of the people over whom [he] exercises authority, that he is not brave, candid, honest, and true," in which case the Senate must remove him from the bench.[60] Sumners strayed a long way from high crimes and misdemeanors in this far-reaching description of the nature of impeachable conduct; it seems possible that he felt the weight of a lost venture and sought to resuscitate the managers' position by advancing "substantial doubt" as a reason for conviction.

Sumners spent some time on the residence matter, a subject heretofore little discussed and of apparent inconsequence. He appeared to find both humor and disgrace in the situation, however.

I could tell you some things about how difficult it was to find where this judge lived; and when we finally found where he lived, he was living under the cover of Sam Leake. . . . Think of any decent self-respecting man living for 3 years in an American hotel registered under the name of another man! . . . [Louderback couldn't live in Contra Costa County because] they had a cat in his brother's house, and he and the cat could not live at the same place, so evidently it was decided that the cat should stay and the judge should go. [Laughter] . . . Do brave, courageous, open and aboveboard men live [in a hotel without registering]? I ask each Senator here, did you ever know since the day of your birth, a brave, courageous, self-respecting man to live in that way? Did you ever know any man to live that way who was not slick, slipping in, sliding about?[61]

Despite such innuendos, Sumners failed to point out any explicit conduct by Louderback concerning his domicile that would pull him within the scope of constitutional prescriptions for impeachment.

His appraisal of the receiverships and fees were also hyperbolic. The payments Judge Louderback allowed to receivers were referred to as taking money "out of the pockets of the widows and the orphans and the impoverished people. . . ."[62]

Following Hatton W. Sumner's summary, the Senate retired behind closed doors, resuming its public session after not quite two hours of private deliberation. The Senate then voted on the articles of impeachment. On Article 1, charging the judge with wrongfully dismissing a receiver and of establishing a false residence, thirty-four senators voted guilty, forty-two not guilty.[63]

Article 2 claimed that Louderback exhibited favoritism in receivership appointments, permitted excessive fees, and improperly attached a proviso before turning over records, as he had been ordered to do by the appellate court. This article fared even less well from the managers' viewpoint, attaining twenty-three guilty and forty-seven not guilty votes.[64] On Article 3, Judge Louderback's appointment of an allegedly incompetent receiver, sixty-three senators voted not guilty with only eleven, seven Democrats and four Republicans, voting guilty.[65] Article 4 claimed that Louderback appointed an incompetent receiver in an instance in which no receiver at all should have been appointed, thereby causing serious damage to the company involved; this article brought forth thirty guilty and forty-seven not guilty votes.[66]

Thus, if the managers still retained any expectation of securing a conviction, it rested entirely on the miscellany of charges in the final article. The vote on Article 5 revealed forty-five senators finding Louderback guilty, thirty-four not guilty.[67] The final article proved to be the only one on which the managers secured a majority for their position, but it was not close to meeting the two-thirds required for conviction. The vote on Article 5 revealed partisanship. Democrats cast thirty-eight of the forty-five guilty votes, a total of 84 percent of those senators who favored conviction. Of the seven Republicans voting guilty on Article 5, four had voted Judge Louderback guilty on all the other articles. The thirty-four senators voting not guilty included twenty-two Republicans and twelve Democrats, a Republican party total of 64 percent of those who favored a verdict of innocent. Upon completion of the vote, Vice-President Garner instructed the clerk to read the judgment "That the said Harold Louderback be, and he is, acquitted of all the charges in said articles made and set forth."[68]

Only two senators filed written opinions following the trial: Josiah W. Bailey (Democrat, North Carolina), who voted not guilty on all the articles, and Elbert D. Thomas (Democrat, Utah), who voted guilty on four articles. Both of them discussed judicial good behavior, with Senator Thomas explaining his guilty votes as "based upon the spirit of the constitutional provision, 'good behavior,' rather than the spirit of 'high crimes and misdemeanors.' "[69]

Senator Bailey had voted Judge Louderback innocent because he found the evidence unconvincing and the main witnesses biased. Of the latter he observed: "Courts must control their receivers and their attorneys. . . . The witnesses here were the victims of respondent's just conduct, of which they should not have complained. . . . Judges ought not to be drawn into an impeachment by such witnesses. . . . The Senate, sitting as a Court of Impeachment, is not a tribunal for the review of the exercise of judicial discretion at the will of disappointed receivers."[70] The trial record sustains the senator's commentary on the foregoing point and also supports his position on the "patience and the wastefulness of a court that took the time to hear [the evidence] and put the public to the expense to pay for the printing of it." Senator Bailey claimed that testimony deserving any serious consideration "might readily have been produced in 2 days, and with more effect."[71]

One wishes that Senator Bailey's recognition of the waste of the Senate's time could have been combined with Senator Thomas's concern for good behavior to produce a sound procedure for handling charges of misconduct leveled against lower-court judges. Thomas believed that a judge must be "a paragon of official virtue" and that the good behavior clause singled out jurists, requiring them to perform "above the average actions of members of the legislative and executive branches. . . . "[72] Whether such a higher moral requirement be true or not, life appointment does set a federal jurist in a different category from legislators and members of the executive branch and makes legal definition of good behavior highly desirable.

The key to appraising the trial of Harold Louderback lies in the weakness of the managers' charges and the ineffective testimony brought forth in support of them. Because the accusations against Judge Louderback proved incapable of persuading even a majority of senators to find him guilty except on the omnibus final article, and then not by the requisite two-thirds vote, and because the

House of Representatives had not displayed vigorous interest in bringing an impeachment, why did Louderback become a target of the procedure?

The only imaginable answer is that he had trod upon some very powerful persons' toes, persons influential enough to instigate his impeachment. The major charge levied against Louderback, judging by the amount of time it consumed in the trial, concerned his dismissal of Addison G. Strong, whom Louderback had told explicitly not to appoint anyone as his attorney who represented the stock exchange but who proceeded to do so anyway, in defiance of the judge's instruction. When Judge Louderback fired Strong, he deprived him and the legal firm he proposed to employ of the large fees they would have earned had they been permitted to act in the matter.

F. M. McAuliffe, a partner in the rejected law office, was vice president of the Bar Association of San Francisco at the time it initiated the proceedings against Harold Louderback. Although circumstantial, this evidence supports a conclusion that a powerful law firm and the San Francisco Stock Exchange had been offended by the judge's unwillingness to follow their lead and had taken steps designed to remove him from his post.

The time consumed by the investigation and trial of Harold Louderback extended from June 1932 until his acquittal at the end of May 1933. Probably because of the inadequacy of the charges brought against him compared with charges levied in most of the preceding impeachments, neither the managers nor the respondent relied on material available from foregoing impeachment experiences. Andrew Johnson's trial received one mention; Charles Swayne's, two; and Robert W. Archbald's, four—making a contrast with most other impeachments, in which references to the earlier trials were frequent.

Judge Louderback returned to his duties following his acquittal and continued to serve on the federal bench for eight years until his death on December 11, 1941 at age sixty-one. His obituary in the *San Francisco Chronicle* referred to Louderback as "one of the most noted jurists in the Western States."[73]

Louderback proved to be a poor target for the impeachment process; the trial record shows that he deserved to be exonerated. Of Judge Louderback's trial Manager Hatton W. Sumners said it was "the greatest farce ever presented. At one time only three senators were present and for ten days we presented evidence to what was practically an empty chamber."[74]

Despite the outcome of the Louderback trial and the Senate's conspicuous disinterest in hearing the case, as described by Congressman Sumners, the House of Representatives did not show any evidence of souring on the impeachment process. Just five days after the Senate adjudged Louderback not guilty, the House undertook investigation, with a view to impeachment, of yet another federal district judge, Halsted L. Ritter, in whose subsequent trial the disillusioned Hatton W. Sumners would once again serve as manager.

Halsted L. Ritter. *Florida State University, Tallahassee.*

12

Halsted L. Ritter

An attempt to convict upon a combination of circumstances of which the respondent has been found innocent would be monstrous. . . . The sum of six acquittals cannot be a conviction.

—Warren Austin

The economic circumstances of the nation remained in nearly the same perilous condition when the Senate tried Judge Halsted L. Ritter in April 1936 as they had been in when his immediately impeached predecessor, Judge Harold Louderback, had been tried in 1933. The Democrats had strengthened their control of both houses by gaining ten Senate and nine House seats in the 1934 election. The Democrats' electoral success could be interpreted as public ratification of New Deal measures promoted by Franklin D. Roosevelt to help restore the economy. The Supreme Court had voided some of these measures as unconstitutional by the time of Judge Ritter's trial. He came before the Senate not only with the burden of refuting the specific charges against him but also with two additional handicaps: being a Republican in a strongly Democratic period and serving as a judge when the judiciary was increasingly under attack for thwarting the popular will as embodied in the executive and legislative branches. Thus, Judge Ritter's impeachment experience occurred in a period of severe economic distress, a period when Republicans were frequently blamed for aspects of that distress, and a period when the judiciary was viewed in some quarters as spoilers of national recovery.

Halsted L. Ritter, federal district judge for the southern district of Florida, was born in Indianapolis in 1868. He received his undergraduate and law degrees from DePauw University and practiced law in Denver from 1895 to 1925, serving, among other public duties, as city attorney, prosecuting attorney of Arapahoe County, and professor at Denver Law School.[1] He left his well-established and profitable practice in Colorado and moved to Florida in 1925 because during brief vacations there the Ritters discovered that the climate had proved beneficial to Mrs. Ritter's health.[2]

On February 15, 1929, four years after Ritter had established a practice in his new residence, his fellow Republican Calvin Coolidge appointed him as a federal district judge for the Southern District of Florida. This appointment, according to Robert Sherrod, who covered Ritter's impeachment trial for *Time* magazine, could be attributed to "no discernible reason except the shortage of Republicans down South."[3] Further evidence that Coolidge's selection lacked broad support was supplied in an article written by Jacobus Ten Broek, who noted that both the Republican and the Democratic state party organizations in Florida had opposed elevation of Ritter to the federal bench because he was considered deficient in training and experience.[4] However, the Senate confirmed the appointment, and Ritter sat as a federal jurist for seven years, until April 1936, when the Senate convicted him on impeachment charges and removed him from office.

The House of Representatives began an investigation of Judge Ritter on May 29, 1933, only five days after the Senate had acquitted Judge Harold Louderback. A request by James Mark Wilcox (Democrat, Florida) to examine Ritter's conduct was accepted by the House and referred to the Judiciary Committee.

A five-member subcommittee composed of Joseph L. Hooper (Republican, Ohio), John E. Miller (Democrat, Arkansas), Hatton W. Sumners (Democrat, Texas), Malcolm C. Tarver (Democrat, Georgia), and Zebulon Weaver (Democrat, North Carolina) investigated the charges: improper conduct in a bankruptcy and receivership matter concerning a failing resort hotel, inaccurate reporting of Ritter's federal income taxes, and practicing law after he had become a judge. Only three of the members were active; Congressman Hooper and Congressman Weaver did not participate in the inquiry. The three members who conducted the hearings, which Judge Ritter and his attorneys attended, spent many months investigating the allegations and finally brought in a two to one recommendation favoring impeachment, with Congressman Miller opposed. The full Judiciary Committee did not accept the subcommittee's inconclusive recommendation to impeach, and Judge Ritter very nearly escaped being charged with the offenses that had brought him to the attention of the House of Representatives.

But Robert Alexis Green (Democrat, Florida) succeeded in getting the Judiciary Committee to reverse its decision,[5] and by the narrow vote of ten to eight it approved a recommendation to impeach Halsted L. Ritter. Nearly three years had elapsed between the beginning of the investigation and the decision to impeach.

The indecisive vote of both the subcommittee and the full Judiciary Committee suggests the feeble quality of the complaints against Judge Ritter and the lack of enthusiasm for pursuing his impeachment. Another matter should be noted: each example of the judge's purported misconduct had occurred six or more years before his trial. The examples were stale and included no references at all to misbehavior during the six years immediately prior to his impeachment. No wonder, then, that the House showed so little enthusiasm for continuing a proceeding grounded on ancient charges against a man whose recent record revealed no evidence of misconduct despite the most sedulous efforts by those eager to find it.

House debate on the impeachment resolution on March 2, 1936 was conducted by five pro-impeachment congressmen, all Democrats, and by seven anti-impeachment congressmen, four Democrats and three Republicans. The major accusation centered on the judge's conduct in the resort hotel case. He stood accused of refusing to dismiss a suit involving the hotel after he had been asked to do so by the plaintiffs. More seriously, he was charged with allowing excessive fees to the attorneys in the case, one of whom was his former law partner, A. L. Rankin. Rankin gave money to Judge Ritter immediately after receiving his purportedly exorbitant fee for participation in the ailing hotel proceeding, a fact not denied by either of the principals. Consideration of these events far overshadowed the other two charges against the judge: income tax evasion and continuing to practice law, charges touched on only briefly by the prosecution during the trial.

Congressmen speaking in opposition to impeachment insisted that no evidence against Judge Ritter had been produced showing corruption or commission of any impeachable acts. He might have made mistakes in judgment, they allowed, but arguments that the judge had behaved in an improper or corrupt fashion were based only on presumption and innuendo. Louis Ludlow (Democrat, Indiana) referred to the high esteem the family enjoyed. Ritter, he said, "springs from a long and honored Hoosier ancestry . . . there are no better people than those who comprised his ancestral train."[6] Another spokesman against impeachment, whose presentation could hardly be viewed as a wholehearted endorsement, acknowledged Judge Ritter's incompetence as evidenced by the high number of reversals of his decisions and mentioned that Ritter often displayed a dictatorial and impatient manner. Thus, he imparted a derogatory image of the judge even as he insisted that the latter had not been guilty of any offenses meriting impeachment.

The pro-impeachment forces, on the other hand, insisted that the judge's participation in conspiracy and bribery in connection with the bankrupt hotel matter had been convincingly demonstrated by evidence obtained during the Judiciary Committee's investigation. Robert A. Green said the judge had accepted bribes and gratuities and had behaved in a manner "flagrant, unconscionable, and deaf to justice. . . . To permit Ritter to continue his pernicious practices on the Federal bench will diminish the faith of our people in our courts."[7] Hatton W. Sumners dismissed references to the judge's fine family and his one-time reputation for upright conduct by observing that presidents did not appoint judges of known bad character. "It is a rare thing," he said, "that we have a case where a judge on the bench, under charges, has not had a good reputation before the thing arose with regard to which he is being charged."[8] Congressman Sumners and his colleagues touched upon all the charges and gave portions of the evidence that supported them.

Several references arose suggesting partisan connotations as underlying reasons for the attacks on Ritter. Sam Hobbs (Democrat, Alabama) resented an insinuation by Louis Ludlow that Ritter's impeachment came about because the judge was a northerner and a Republican. Hobbs said: "I have not seen a solitary human being from first to last in this case who gives a tinker's damn whether Judge Ritter lives on the North Pole or whether he has voted the Republican ticket ever since Noah was a baby! . . . I resent the charge on my account and on behalf of the Members of this House who are just as disinterested in this matter and who are just as honest as [Ludlow] is!"[9] It is apparent from Hobbs's passionate response, and from similar comments by other speakers, that most congressmen wanted party affiliation left outside consideration in forming a judgment. This admirable wish came no nearer to fulfillment in Judge Ritter's case than it had in many of the preceding impeachments.

Following a four-and-a-half-hour debate, the House of Representatives voted on the resolution to impeach. The House in the 74th Congress contained 319 Democrats, 103 Republicans, and 10 members of miscellaneous parties—a majority of 73 percent for the Democratic party. The vote revealed 181 congressmen favoring impeachment and 146 opposing.[10] Those supporting the resolution included 172 Democrats, 7 Republicans, and 2 from miscellaneous parties; those opposing impeachment included 63 Democrats, 81 Republicans, and 2 from miscellaneous parties. The House vote reflected partisan allegiance. Democrats favored impeaching Ritter by 73 percent; Republicans opposed impeachment by 92 percent.

The House of Representatives informed the Senate that it had impeached Halsted L. Ritter and had appointed Sam Hobbs, Randolph Perkins (Republican, New Jersey), and Hatton W. Sumners as managers.[11] Perkins and Sumners had acted in the same capacity in the immediately foregoing trial of Harold Louderback. This three-man bipartisan group is the smallest number of managers who ever conducted an impeachment trial.

Manager Hobbs presented seven articles of impeachment to the Senate on March 10, 1936. The first alleged that Judge Ritter allowed an excessive fee to A. L. Rankin for serving as plaintiffs' attorney in the foreclosure and receivership case of a resort hotel, and accepted "corruptly and unlawfully. . . for his own use and benefit from the said A. L. Rankin [a sum] of money amounting to $4,500."[12]

Article 2 described again the fee Rankin collected in the case referred to in Article 1. In addition, the second article claimed that (1) Judge Ritter had conspired to obtain and share Rankin's fee; (2) the judge had refused the plaintiff's request to withdraw their suit for foreclosure of the first mortgage on the failing resort hotel; and (3) the hotel concerned supplied Ritter, his family, and his secretary with free rooms, meals, and valet service, "all of which expenses were borne by the said receivership to the loss and damage of the creditors."[13]

In the next article, Halsted L. Ritter was accused of practicing law after he had become a federal judge, conduct that violated the law prohibiting any federal judge to do so. The fourth article set down a second example of Ritter's illegally practicing law after he had become a judge, in this instance accepting money for giving legal advice to a friend.[14] Article 5 accused Judge Ritter of evading income tax on $12,000 in 1929, and Article 6 alleged failure to pay federal tax on $5,300 in 1930.

The seventh and final article typifies what had become a habit in the two trials immediately preceding Ritter's—a catchall article in which the prosecutors essentially restated all the charges against the respondent as set down in the specific articles.[15] In the Ritter case this device proved to be indispensable from the managers' point of view; the potpourri article became the only one on which they secured the necessary two-thirds vote of guilty.

Having heard the articles, the Senate was sworn as a court of impeachment and fixed March 12, 1936 for Halsted L. Ritter and his attorneys Frank P. Walsh of New York and Carl T. Hoffman of Miami to appear. Following discussion among the managers, the respondent's counsel, and various senators, the Senate decided that the trial would begin on April 6.

On March 31 Hoffman spoke for the respondent. He moved to strike Article 1 or choose between Articles 1 and 2, both of which dealt with Rankin's activities and payments to the judge. Hoffman pointed out that the articles contained the same charges. He next moved to strike Article 7 because it embraced all the preceding articles. Hoffman noted that combining the charges in the final article "can be but to cumulate adverse votes, if any, upon prior articles, with the hope that the cumulative or collective arrangement may be sufficient to sustain those articles in the vote upon the final article, which prior articles were not sustained when separately voted upon prior to the vote on article VII."[16] His fear proved entirely justified.

But Manager Sumners insisted that Article 7 be retained. "It is not whether he did this thing, that thing, or the other thing, but whether or not the sum total of the things he has done has made the people doubt his integrity as a judicial officer."[17] Carl T. Hoffman's position seems stronger. If the Senate could not convict the judge on the exact charges as set down in the first six articles, it would be unfair and illogical to convict him of an amalgam of those charges.

The Senate settled the differences on Articles 1, 2, and 7 on April 3, when the presiding officer, Nathan L. Bachman (Democrat, Tennessee), ruled that the first two articles were not redundant but presented different bases for impeachment. Article 1 alleged illegal receipt of money by Judge Ritter from Rankin, and Article 2 claimed that a conspiracy involving Ritter, Rankin, and certain other people existed by which the judge obtained the money referred to in the first article. The Senate approved the chair's ruling without a vote.

Bachman noted that the motion to delete Article 7 "on account of duplicity has not, so far as the Chair is advised, been presented in any impeachment proceeding heretofore."[18] For that reason he submitted the question to the Senate, which by voice vote denied the motion. Thus, the managers' position prevailed in the first contested issues of the trial.

Following Senate acceptance of the three articles, Halsted L. Ritter's answer to the charges was entered in the record.[19] The judge insisted that none of the articles set down an impeachable act. To Articles 1 and 2, he stated that the money received from Rankin was payment due him under prior arrangements for dissolution of their law partnership and that he had formed no conspiracy with Rankin or with anyone else. Ritter acknowledged staying at the hotel in receivership without paying (Article 2), but reported that he had neither asked for such an accommodation nor known that his family or associates had received free services. He denied practicing law after becoming a judge (Articles 3 and 4) and said that money acquired from former clients had been earned by legal work he had done before ascending the bench. Respecting Articles 5 and 6, Ritter stated that he had not willfully evaded reporting any income taxes. He denied the allegations in the final article, pointing out that he had responded to most of them in his refutation of the preceding articles.

The next trial day, April 6, a brief replication from the managers reasserted the impeachable quality of the conduct of Halsted L. Ritter as described in the articles and characterized his answer as insufficient, irrelevant, and impertinent. Whereupon, the details having been attended to, the prosecution and the defense delivered their opening statements. Randolph Perkins began the case for the prosecution by reviewing all the charges. Frank P. Walsh gave the opening speech for the respondent. He too analyzed all the accusations against Judge Ritter, denying some and refuting others.

A. L. Rankin, the first prosecution witness, proved to be forgetful or noncooperative; perhaps his performance displayed limited mentality. Walsh had earlier supplied some evidence of this supposition. He commented that Rankin had not been very successful in securing business for the partnership, was not efficient, and kept no accounts of his professional transactions.[20] For whatever reasons, Rankin's testimony contained numerous responses of "I do not recall" or "I don't know."

Rankin's evidence concerned the first two articles, particularly his financial arrangements with the judge. Sam Hobbs tried to discover why Rankin had on two occasions paid Judge Ritter in cash when all his other payments in the matters involved in Articles 1 and 2 had been by check. Hobbs also tried to learn why Rankin had not obtained a receipt from the judge for the money delivered to him.

In response to an inquiry from Joseph T. Robinson (Democrat, Arkansas) concerning his paying in cash rather than by check, Rankin said two reasons prompted this procedure: he was apprehensive about a bank failure, and he feared that "it might subject [Judge Ritter] or me, or both of us, to criticism if I would on the same day that I deposited $30,000 there write him a check for $2,500, I being his former law partner."[21] He made the same explanation for his second payment of $2,000 in cash.

Manager Hobbs extracted an acknowledgment that the bank concerned was a "tower of financial strength" in which Rankin had deposited thousands of dollars.[22] Thus, his inept effort to explain making payments in cash because he feared that the bank would fail was disproved by the witness himself, leaving as the only authentic explanation A. L. Rankin's uneasiness about any public record existing of his payments to the judge.

Frank P. Walsh conducted the cross-examination of Rankin. He introduced several documents and letters dealing with arrangements between the witness and various participants in the affairs detailed in Articles 1 and 2, showing the amount of work done and the amount of time involved; this material was presented with the goal of establishing that the fees Judge Ritter allowed had not been exorbitant or disproportionate to the task. Several senators objected to the testimony, considering it unduly protracted.[23]

The managers then presented their next witness, Bert E. Holland, one of the plaintiffs in the failing hotel suit. Holland and eight succeeding witnesses testified concerning the first two articles. The bulk of the questions focused on Judge Ritter's refusal to dismiss the suit concerning the bankrupt hotel and on his appointment of a receiver over the objections of Holland and other plaintiffs. The managers' questioning was aimed at establishing that the judge had acted arbitrarily in denying the plaintiffs' request to terminate the suit. Additionally, the managers sought to demonstrate that Ritter had conspired with the receiver he appointed and with others to secure financial benefits for them and also for himself.

One of the prosecution witnesses, Martin Sweeny, served as manager of the bankrupt hotel. He reported that the receiver Ritter appointed did very little work and that which he did do was not significant to the operation of the hotel. Sweeny also verified that Ritter had stayed at the hotel without paying. Frank P. Walsh, cross-examining, elicited the information that the hotel provided complimentary services for selected persons; the judge did not enjoy a unique status in this regard.

The length of time devoted to the first two articles, the repetitions in testimony, and the dogged attention to minute details plainly wearied many of the senators. Inquiries were raised several times about the relevance of some of the questions, and a few senators spoke of the need to speed the proceedings along. Both the managers and the respondent's attorneys showed sensitivity to this position and a desire not to offend the Senate by pursuing every minuscule aspect of the case and thereby run the risk of irritating, or losing, their audience. Both sides subsequently showed some effort to restrict their presentations to germane evidence.

Next the managers called two witnesses in support of the claims that Halsted Ritter had practiced law after he had become a federal judge (Articles 3 and 4). The evidence showed that the judge had conferred with A. L. Rankin on cases handled by their firm when the two had been partners. He had, in this connection, written letters on federal district court letterhead. The prosecution did not present any witnesses on the evasion of income tax charges (Articles 5 and 6). The managers' case did not appear to disclose a defective public servant—perhaps an unwise one on occasion, but not one conducting his office in a corrupt or careless fashion.

Eleven witnesses appeared for Ritter on April 10 and 11 to support his contention that he had performed no legal work after becoming a judge and that the fees he had allowed in the failing resort hotel case had been reasonable and in conformity with fees granted by other jurists. They also reported that he had a good professional reputation. Again, the testimony proved tedious and often only remotely connected with the heart of the case; at one point the presiding officer observed "that mere collateral matters should not be permitted to take up the time of the Senate."[24]

Judge Ritter, the twelfth and final witness for the defense, opened with a prepared statement explaining his position on the issues raised in the articles of impeachment.[25] His efforts to disprove the allegations made against him were assured and unflustered, consisting mainly of direct and precise refutations of the accusations.

Respecting the failing hotel, Ritter reported knowing nothing about the case until it came into his court in October 1929. When Judge Ritter was considering appointing a receiver for the hotel, the defense attorney interrupted the hearing to announce that plaintiff Bert E. Holland desired to make a statement. Holland thereupon declared that he wanted the proceeding to be halted. Ritter told the Senate that he had found this to be "a most astonishing situation. I had never had that experience in any case before; and at once it occurred to me that there might be something wrong about the case. Otherwise, why should the defendant's counsel introduce the plaintiff?"[26]

Fearing that Holland's desire to have the suit dismissed would prove detrimental to other plaintiffs, "who were insisting that something be done," Judge Ritter declined to dismiss the case.

Furthermore, he observed, "all parties before the court, were, on the record, asking for the appointment of a receiver," and the "only way in the world to settle this controversy was to appoint a receiver."[27]

He appointed as receiver, at the request of the hotel's creditors, the man who had served as trustee in bankruptcy for two years. Judge Ritter explained his appointment as based on the fact that no complaints had been made of the trustee's service. Of his refusal to dismiss the suit, the judge reported that no motion to dismiss had ever been filed.

Next Judge Ritter detailed the situation respecting A. L. Rankin's fee in the failing resort hotel matter. He pointed out that the lawyers concerned had settled on the amount each would have, that four reputable Florida attorneys had submitted affidavits stating that the $75,000 for all lawyers in the hotel case was a proper amount, appropriate to the work done and the large sum ($3.5 million) involved. The judge concluded this portion of his presentation by noting that the hotel case was one of "7,000 cases which I have attended to. And that is 6 years or more ago." His accusers, he said, "have gone back to my first year—7 years ago—to bring these charges against me in one case out of 7,000."[28]

Judge Ritter gave a rational explanation of his unwillingness to dismiss the bankrupt resort hotel suit, his decision to appoint a receiver, and his approval of attorney's fees. It is easy to sympathize with his complaint about the six-year period that separated his performance in the failing hotel case from allegations that he had behaved improperly in the matter; no new aspects of the hotel affair had risen in the intervening years to bring his conduct under scrutiny, and he had indeed heard many cases in the meantime.

He next turned to his receipt of money from A. L. Rankin. The sums concerned, he said, had been Rankin's payments for settlement of dissolution of the partnership when Ritter became a federal judge. He stated, "It was a perfectly honest transaction . . . the payment of an honest debt which was arranged at the time I left the firm . . . the payments made to me by Judge Rankin were payments on that debt, honestly created, for a consideration, which was the business that I left him."[29]

Ritter flatly rejected claims that he had practiced law after he became a judge (Articles 3 and 4); his denials seemed less firm than his denials of the preceding allegations. His account of accepting $7,500 as a gift from a close friend to whom he had given legal advice was ambiguous. He said he never presented a bill to his friend, nor kept any account of "anything I did for him. He may have been motivated in a way, because he thought he owed me something, to give me that $7,500."[30] This explanation seems damaging to Ritter's cause; he appeared to be acknowledging that he had indeed accepted money for practicing law.

The prosecution had not developed Articles 5 and 6, accusing Ritter of evading full payment of his income taxes, so he had no serious difficulty with those charges. He explained that he had reported his 1929 tax accurately and no criticism could be made of that filing. He had, however, failed to report part of his income in 1930, but that sum had been offset by a loss. "I appreciate the fact that it would have been better," he said, to have included the omitted income, "but there would not have been one dollar payable to the Government . . . there was not one dollar due."[31] Therefore, although the judge had been careless with his 1930 return, no evidence had been adduced that he had defrauded, or intended to defraud, the government.

After his address, and following several questions from senators, Frank P. Walsh asked Judge Ritter about his complimentary stay at the bankrupt hotel, an episode he had not reviewed in his prepared statement. The judge reported that he had indeed gone to the hotel twice but only at the management's request—the first time to inspect hurricane damage, the second to attend a celebration. Walsh, who considered the matter insignificant, only mentioned it, he said, because it had been introduced in the articles; but, as he noted, "the managers abandoned [that charge] apparently. They did not ask any questions about it. I take it that it is abandoned."[32] Thus, the free lodging and services at the hotel joined the alleged income tax evasions as topics that the prosecution failed to develop.

Manager Sumners, in cross-examination, raised an issue not mentioned in the articles of impeachment: Ritter's recommendation in 1930, six years before the trial, of A. L. Rankin for a federal district judgeship in Alabama.[33] Ritter argued that his letters of recommendation should not be admitted because they were not material and had been interjected only in the waning moments of the trial. But Sumners insisted that the letters would help the Senate determine "some of the most fundamental questions that arise in the case, namely, the integrity of the respondent, the credibility of the respondent, and the length to which the respondent was willing to go in order to render service to Mr. Rankin, with whom it is contended in this case he has been mixed up from the beginning . . . not only seeking to serve Mr. Rankin by appointments in his court, but, we claim, seeking to put him upon the bench."[34]

The presiding officer, Vice-President John Nance Garner, granted the managers' request to introduce the letters. The only problem for Judge Ritter lay in the fact that his letters stressed Rankin's close identification with Alabama; in fact, Rankin had registered to vote in Florida in 1926 and had resided there since that time. In his first letter, urging consideration of Rankin, Ritter referred to "A. L. Rankin, of Andalusia, Alabama."[35] In a subsequent letter the judge said, "Rankin never abandoned his Alabama residence."[36] Later, when Rankin responded to an inquiry on the subject, he acknowledged that he had registered to vote in Florida but had "decided, on account of all my property interests in Alabama, that I would maintain my voting place in Alabama."[37] He was allowed to let this lame account of being a registered voter in two states stand without further challenge.

Judge Ritter's attempt to emphasize A. L. Rankin's continued close connection with Alabama is less easy to accept than is Rankin's inept explanation. The latter had displayed confusion in several instances during his trial testimony and might conceivably have a muddled recollection of his dual registration activities. Halsted L. Ritter, however, would unquestionably know that his former partner had to be a Florida resident in order to practice law there. His effort to portray Rankin as an Alabama resident stretched the truth, but even if the matter had been raised in the articles instead of being thrown in at the end of the trial, it is difficult to view the writing of somewhat inflated letters of recommendation as an impeachable act.

Judge Ritter and his witnesses put forth generally convincing explanations for his conduct. The correctness of his activities concerning the bankrupt hotel and the fees allowed to A. L. Rankin seemed adequately supported by the testimony. The charges that he practiced law were less convincingly refuted, as were the allegations concerning his failure to pay his income taxes in full. But the case the respondent presented basically deflected the managers' charges.

Upon conclusion of the trial, the Senate decided to allow four hours for closing arguments, two hours for each side. The first spokesman for the managers, Sam Hobbs, began the summation. He opened with a reminder to the Senate that impeachment charges need not be criminal and quoted the comment of George W. Norris (Republican, Nebraska) when he served as a manager in Robert W. Archbald's trial in 1913: "If good behavior is an essential of holding [a federal judgeship], then misbehavior is sufficient reason for removal from office."[38] Manager Hobbs thus called attention to a prominent, if somewhat unorthodox, Republican senator sitting now as a member of the court, at the same time buttressing his own argument that the managers did not need to prove that Ritter had committed a crime. He reviewed all the articles, underlining the prosecution's main points, and concluded with a reference to the general accusation that the conduct of Halsted L. Ritter had brought the judiciary into disrepute. Hobbs said: "This is not the case of a stupid fool ignorantly erring. It is the case of a judge on the bench, . . . that man cannot be excused as ignorant. His ability is proven by the fact that he has adroitly and plausibly explained and tried to cover up his guilt . . . [we ask the Senate] to purge the bench of this man whom the evidence in this case . . . shows has disgraced it!"[39]

Next came Frank P. Walsh, who had assumed the major role in Ritter's defense. He referred to the diligent and protracted effort of the House of Representatives to find something to the judge's discredit and stated that "after a most rigid inquiry extending over 3 years, nothing could be found against his honor, nothing could be found against the way in which he carried on his judicial duties on the bench."[40]

The only suspicious circumstance in the entire affair, Walsh said, had been Judge Ritter's accepting the money Rankin owed him in cash; all the other charges were inaccurate and unproved. Had Ritter something to hide respecting the money he received from Rankin, Walsh argued, he could have concealed the transaction completely. Or, contrarily, if the judge and his former partner had been fabricating something, they could easily have created a backdated receipt from Ritter to cover the payments.

Walsh insisted that the managers had brought forth nothing detrimental to Judge Ritter. Referring to the catchall final article, Walsh said that if the Senate found the judge innocent, as the evidence demonstrated that it should, on the specific charges, "it would be an outrageous thing to find him guilty under that seventh article."[41] Perhaps Walsh had some prescience about his client's impending fate, or even some clues that the Senate would prove unable to find him guilty on the specifics but would dismiss him from office anyway on the overarching general article.

The final spokesman, Hatton W. Sumners, employed a rhetorical technique in his summation. Of Judge Ritter's taking a cash payment from A. L. Rankin, Sumners said that the respondent's counsel wanted the Senate "to say that is OK." Then he demanded of the senators, "Are you going to do it? Are you going to do it?" On the same subject, he asked, "What cannot a judge do if a judge can take money under these circumstances?"[42] Referring to Ritter's general deportment, he asked, "Is there a person constituting this Court who will say if a judge does not possess integrity that there is anything else upon which a free people can base confidence?"[43] Sumners touched all the key charges, but in a disorganized and emotional fashion.

Following Manager Sumners's valedictory, delivered on April 14, 1936, the Senate met in secret session during the next two days. It deliberated for more than ten hours, emerging in the late afternoon of April 16 to announce that the vote to determine Halsted L. Ritter's destiny would take place the next day.

The Senate in the 74th Congress contained seventy Democrats and twenty-six Republicans, a 73 percent majority for the dominant party. The vote on April 17, 1936 revealed a peculiar verdict: none of the six specific articles attained a two-thirds guilty vote, but, by just one vote, the Senate convicted Judge Ritter on the omnibus Article 7.

Article 1, relating the judge's financial arrangements with A. L. Rankin in the matter of the bankrupt hotel, came the closest of the substantive articles to receiving a guilty vote from two-thirds of the senators. The Senate voted fifty-five to twenty-nine to convict on this article, just one vote shy of the requisite two-thirds. Ritter and his attorneys must have been heartened by the Senate's vote on Article 1 despite the narrow victory for their cause; such modest optimism could only have been increased as the remaining votes on the explicit articles were recorded.

The guilty vote on Article 2, detailing more on the hotel problem and adding conspiracy charges, declined to fifty-two, while the not guilty rose to thirty-two. Article 3, practicing law, showed forty-four guilty, thirty-nine not guilty; Article 4, also a charge of practicing law by giving advice to a friend, brought Ritter his first clear-cut victory: thirty-six guilty, forty-eight not guilty. The same total was recorded for the fifth article, failure to declare his full income in 1929. On the last of the substantive articles, inaccurate reporting of income tax in 1930, the Senate voted forty-six guilty, thirty-seven not guilty. Thus, it would appear that Judge Ritter, if not endorsed by the Senate, had at least escaped conviction.

But the final article proved his undoing by one vote. Fifty-six senators found him guilty, twenty-eight not guilty—an outcome inconsistent with the preceding votes. The fifty-six guilty votes on Article 7 were cast by forty-nine Democrats and seven Republicans;

voting against conviction were ten Democrats and eighteen Republicans. The omnibus article displayed the partisan aspects of the decision on Judge Ritter: 74 percent of the Democrats voted guilty, and 72 percent of the Republicans voted not guilty. A steady band of twenty-six senators—seventeen Republicans and nine Democrats—found Ritter innocent of all charges.

The most extraordinary voting pattern came from Sherman Minton (Democrat, Indiana), whom Franklin D. Roosevelt subsequently named to the appellate court in 1940 upon his defeat for reelection to the Senate, and whom Harry Truman elevated to the Supreme Court in 1949. Minton voted not guilty on all six explicit articles but guilty on the summarizing article. Such a performance cannot be accounted for.

Following the vote to convict on Article 7, Senator Warren Austin (Republican, Vermont), who had voted not guilty on every article, made a point of order asserting that Judge Ritter had not been convicted by a two-thirds vote. He protested the announced verdict on the ground that "an attempt to convict upon a combination of circumstances of which the respondent has been found innocent would be monstrous."[44]

The presiding officer overruled Senator Austin's point of order, whereupon the Senate, having removed Halsted L. Ritter from office, voted on whether to disqualify him from ever again holding a position in the national government. Seventy-six senators voted against permanent disqualification and none voted for it. The *New York Times* commented, "By pre-arrangement the Senate then proceeded to vote down, 76-0, [the] proposed order which would have disqualified the removed judge."[45] The *Times* did not reveal how it learned that the Senate had a "pre-arrangement" not to disqualify Judge Ritter; presumably this agreement was reached during its lengthy deliberations behind closed doors. Probably its inability to achieve a two-thirds vote on any of the substantive charges caused the Senate to shy away from voting in favor of disqualification.

Senators who voted guilty and who elected to file their opinions after the trial did not account clearly for their support of a guilty vote on the omnibus Article 7. Key Pittman (Democrat, Nevada), who presided during most of the trial, had acquitted Judge Ritter on three of the explicit articles and voted him guilty on Article 7. He tried to make his position coherent by explaining that the final article contained charges of which he had found Ritter innocent; so "my vote for article 7 is not to be deemed an approval of such matters in article 7."[46] There being no arrangement by which a senator could vote yes on only segments of an article, Senator Pittman's explanation lacks a logical foundation.

Republican Senators William Borah (Idaho), Robert LaFollette (Wisconsin), Lynn Frazier (North Dakota), and Henrik Shipstead (Minnesota) in a joint opinion argued that evidence against Halsted L. Ritter demonstrated his want of "good behavior," a demonstration sufficient to cause them to vote guilty.[47] William Gibbs McAdoo (Democrat, California) presented a review of the entire case and observed that the evidence had convinced him that Ritter's lack of ethics and judicial character constituted "misbehavior in its most serious aspects, and [rendered] him unfit to hold a judicial office."[48]

These opinions, supplying the grounds for their authors' guilty votes, were centered on good behavior, the absence of which quality in Judge Ritter caused the votes against him on the part of the authors. Because bad behavior does not appear in the Constitution as a cause for impeachment, nor had it ever been defined, such opinions lack constitutional justification.

Three Republican senators, Warren Austin (Vermont), Elmer Benson (Minnesota), and Hiram Johnson (California), all of whom had acquitted Ritter on every article, wrote searing criticisms of the Senate's decision.

Senator Austin reviewed constitutional requirements for impeachment and commented that "The sum of six acquittals cannot be a conviction."[49] Senator Benson, fearing among other things that the result of the Ritter trial reflected political antagonism, observed: "The respondent is of a political faith that constitutes a minority in this Court and a minority in his district where opposing political domination is decisive and powerful. Every inch of his pathway in public life has been critically and minutely examined. . . . I can condemn him for folly, but I cannot convict him of this crime and punish him in the manner prescribed."[50]

Hiram Johnson also attacked the outcome of the trial. He criticized the practice of allowing senators who had been absent from the trial to be recorded on the final vote—poor attendance by senators had often been noted and complained of in earlier trials. Senator Johnson also objected to a conviction based on a "loose" generality, "when solemnly the Court has acquitted upon all the specific charges and then those same specific charges are used to justify conviction."[51]

Congress concerned itself with the activities of Judge Ritter from May 1933 until mid-April of 1936. The House Judiciary Committee spent nearly three years investigating the case and very nearly failed to recommend impeachment. The trial proper extended over a period of eleven days.

Very few references to former impeachment trials appeared during the Ritter trial. The only effort to use an earlier trial as a precedent occurred in Manager Hobbs's summation, when he referred to Robert W. Archbald's trial in 1913 as establishing that misbehavior should be considered a sufficient reason to justify the Senate's removing a judge from his post. The other references, fewer than ten, dealt generally only with procedural issues. Perhaps because the charges made against Halsted L. Ritter were flimsy and poorly developed, the managers could not expect to locate arguments supporting their position in the records of past trials. Obviously, they would not be likely to employ the recent trial of Judge Harold Louderback; the claims against him were also flimsy and they would not wish to remind the Senate of the outcome of that trial. For whatever motive, neither side relied on past impeachment trials to fortify its position in the Ritter case.

All the allegations of misconduct leveled against Ritter occurred in 1929 or 1930. Thus, by the time of the trial, six or seven years had elapsed with no intervening fresh or continuing evidence of Judge Ritter's engaging in treason, bribery, or other high crimes and misdemeanors. His was not a pattern of ongoing bad or unwise behavior. Why did the House of Representatives choose him as its target? Did the House view him as the worst federal jurist in the nation even after it had failed to locate any complaints about his conduct in the six-year period immediately preceding the trial? Why, since the charges against him were not only stale but were also inadequate to satisfy two-thirds of the Senate to find him guilty on a single one, did Ritter emerge as so defective a judge that the House and the Senate should no longer tolerate his continuance in office? Why did the House of Representatives, after its long investigation of Judge Ritter that produced such ambiguous results, resurrect the impeachment after it had essentially been shelved? Was Judge Ritter's fate mere happenstance brought about by a conflict concerning other people, a conflict in which he, by chance, became the victim?

That he may not have been a distinguished jurist and that he belonged to the Republican party in a strongly Democratic era do not supply adequate answers to the foregoing questions. Obviously, however, he lacked strong backing and was clearly a political orphan. But none of these evidences of his isolation account for his elevation to notoriety, and none of the charges against him detailed the substantial or sustained misconduct appropriate to an impeachment.

Arthur Krock, in a *New York Times* article written only a few days after the Ritter verdict, reported that some people believed the Senate's decision had been designed to intimidate the Supreme Court. Krock merely mentioned this theory; he did not endorse it.[52] However, in the absence of firmer clues to support reasons for Judge Ritter's impeachment and conviction, it deserves some notice.

The Court had found unconstitutional several New Deal measures advanced by Franklin D. Roosevelt and passed by large majorities in Congress, an apparent thwarting of the popular will and of the elected executive and legislative branches that aroused antagonism for the Court. Because the House of Representatives had already investigated him in 1933, perhaps Judge Ritter's impeachment emerged as a ready-made and quick route for showing the judicial branch that Congress possessed, and would use, power to chasten it. If so, Ritter became a victim of the politically dramatic moment, a handy target only because proceedings, if inconclusive, had been instituted against him before the deadlock between the Court and the executive and legislative departments reached lethal proportions.

This hypothesis at least makes some sense as one tries to explain why the essentially innocuous Judge Ritter became the subject of an impeachment. Certainly, the examples of bad conduct set down in the articles seem insufficient to account for a belief that Ritter had performed in so malign a fashion as to require a very busy Congress, immersed in legislation designed to ameliorate the ravages of the depression, to tie itself up in an impeachment and trial. Furthermore, the managers' inability to persuade a strongly Democratic Senate to convict him on any specifics underlines the confusion characterizing this trial.

Halsted L. Ritter's experience produced two results new to impeachment history. The first concerns the vote by which the Senate declared him innocent, at least technically, of all the precise charges laid against him and then found him guilty on an omnibus article that included all the allegations of which it had just proclaimed him not guilty. Senators voting guilty on the cumulative article must have decided that multiple accusations, even if not accepted as separately proved by the requisite majority, somehow created a pattern of misconduct meriting conviction.

The second unusual aspect of the proceedings concerned Judge Ritter's response to being found guilty on a potpourri article and then removed from office. He sued in the Court of Claims for his salary, basing his argument on the grounds that the charges levied against him did not fit constitutional standards for impeachable acts and the Senate had no right to find him not guilty on allegations presented in six specific articles and guilty on the seventh, "which charged only matters which were contained in the prior articles."[53] The five-member Court of Claims, noting that a challenge to an impeachment decision had never before been presented to a federal court, held that no tribunal except the Senate had jurisdiction in an impeachment; courts did not have authority, the judges said, to review or set aside a Senate verdict.

Thus, Halsted L. Ritter entered the history books as the fourth national officer to be convicted, the first to be convicted solely on an omnibus article, and the first to attempt to secure a court ruling overturning the Senate's decision.

Harry E. Claiborne. *AP/World Wide Photo.*

13

Harry E. Claiborne

*The American Constitution protects judicial indepen-
dence by providing for the lifetime appointment of federal
judges, with removal only by impeachment. It was never
intended to protect convicted felons.*

—L. Stanley Chauvin, Jr.

In 1986 federal district judge Harry E. Claiborne of Nevada became
the fourteenth federal official whom the House of Representatives
impeached since 1799, the twelfth to be tried by the Senate, and the
fifth to be convicted. He was impeached in July 1986 and convicted
on October 9. Judge Claiborne's misconduct resuscitated the impeachment procedure, nearly dormant for the fifty years separating
his experience and the trial and conviction of Halsted L. Ritter in
1936. The procedure had a brief revival in 1974, when Richard Nixon's malperformances brought him to the brink of impeachment
and trial; he resigned following the House Judiciary Committee's
adoption of three articles of impeachment, and Congress took no
further action against him.

The federal district court in Reno had found Judge Claiborne
guilty in August 1984 on two counts of willfully underreporting
his federal income taxes in two successive years; he was sentenced
to two years in prison and fined $10,000. He spent the twenty-one
months between his court conviction and his incarceration employing every available legal appeal of his sentence. When none
of the appeals succeeded, he was led off in May 1986 to the Maxwell
Air Force Base prison in Alabama, an involuntary residence with
minimum restrictions. Although he had not heard a case or served
in any judicial capacity for more than two years, Judge Claiborne
did not resign from the bench. He continued to receive his annual
salary of $78,700, a fact causing several one-time adherents to turn
away from him, some urging him to resign, others urging him at
least to give up his salary while in prison. He followed neither of
those suggestions and was, of course, under no obligation to do so.
Claiborne remained entitled to his office and compensation until

death, resignation, or conviction under the impeachment provisions intervened to remove him from his post.

Born in Arkansas in 1917, Harry E. Claiborne received his law degree from Cumberland University in Tennessee in 1941. He served in the Air Force, in the Clark County (Las Vegas) district attorney's office, and in the Nevada State Assembly; subsequently, he established himself in private practice, in which he became a successful and colorful criminal lawyer.

Claiborne, a Democrat, was appointed to the federal bench in 1978 by Jimmy Carter upon the recommendation of Nevada Senators Howard Cannon, a Democrat, and Paul Laxalt, a Republican. Claiborne's acceptance of the appointment reduced his income from the $375,000 he had earned the preceding year to the $54,500 salary then paid to federal district judges—a dramatic reduction that Claiborne's accusers would cite as a partial explanation of his underreporting his taxes.

Judge Claiborne's troubles began soon after his elevation to the federal bench. The Justice Department started a probe into his alleged failure to pay sufficient income taxes; purported acceptance of a bribe from Joseph Conforte, who operated a Nevada brothel; and filing of an inaccurate judicial ethics report. Claiborne attributed the Justice Department's "hounding" to his outspoken criticism of the department's "rough-shod" investigations of political corruption in Nevada. Skilled as an advocate, Claiborne appeared to lack the temperament and bearing generally believed to befit a jurist, at least in public deportment. He lambasted the federal agents in pungent and unjudgelike language. "Those bastards," he announced, "are out to destroy Nevada and I'm not going to let them do it."[1]

A federal grand jury indicted Judge Claiborne December 8, 1983 on income tax evasion, receiving a bribe, and filing a false ethics report. He made vigorous efforts first to avoid trial, next to avoid being convicted when tried, and finally to avoid prison following conviction, all to no avail.

Claiborne based his initial effort, to escape being tried, on the claim that he could not be brought before a court of law unless he had been impeached. Such a claim of immunity had not been made by Vice-President Aaron Burr, indicted in 1804 for killing Alexander Hamilton. But it had been made by Vice-President Spiro T. Agnew in 1973, when he faced criminal charges for bribery, extortion, and income tax evasion. Agnew asked the House of Representatives to begin an impeachment inquiry, a request that

Richard Nixon supported.[2] The House declined to honor the request, and the vice president resigned in disgrace.

In the Claiborne instance the Ninth Circuit Court of Appeals rejected the argument that impeachment must precede trial in court; Claiborne's appeal of this ruling to the Supreme Court was also rejected.[3] Thus, both Claiborne and Agnew found no legal support for their construction of the Constitution, which permits a trial following impeachment and conviction but does not prohibit a trial before the official has been impeached. However, as will be discussed in the Epilogue, incarceration consequent to a court trial but prior to impeachment would seem to deprive a jurist of office by a method the Framers did not contemplate. A position contrary to the one Judge Claiborne put forward was advanced in the trials of Senator Blount (1799), Secretary Belknap (1876), and Judge Swayne (1905). In the impeachment proceedings against these three officers, their attorneys argued, unsuccessfully, that a court trial must come before an impeachment trial.

Having failed to forestall going to court, Harry E. Claiborne was tried in March 1984. The trial ended in a hung jury, probably because Joseph Conforte proved to be a confused, unconvincing witness. In a second trial, held in July, the government dropped the claim that Claiborne had received a bribe from Conforte. This trial resulted in the jury finding the judge innocent of filing a false ethics report but guilty on two counts of failing to report $106,000 of taxable income on his 1979 and 1980 returns, a failure the judge attributed to inaccurate work by his accountants. He was subsequently fined $10,000 and sentenced to two years in prison.

Now that they had lost their attempts to have Judge Claiborne declared ineligible for trial until he had been impeached and had lost their battle in court, his attorneys appealed his conviction in all possible legal directions, none of them successful.[4] They also advanced a claim that material relating to income tax evasion had been obtained by burglarizing Claiborne's home. The burglary had been conducted, they alleged, by the FBI and the Las Vegas Police Department; both agencies denied participating in such unlawful entry. The Clark County district attorney's office investigated the break-in, but could unearth no proof that it had taken place.

However, Claiborne might not have salvaged his case even had such proof been discovered. Robert W. Kastenmeier (Democrat, Wisconsin), a member of the House Judiciary Committee, commented during House investigation of the judge's conduct that if an unauthorized seizure of Claiborne's tax records had occurred, such an illegal act would not wipe out the fact that he had submitted false income tax returns.[5] And Barney Frank (Democrat, Massachusetts) noted that proof of unlawfully obtained evidence would, by the exclusionary rule, keep someone out of prison, but "there is a somewhat higher standard between staying out of prison and staying on the federal bench."[6]

Finally, Judge Claiborne struggled to avoid being sent to prison. He claimed that he, or any other judge, would have solid reasons to fear being locked up with criminals, seeming to forget that Maxwell Air Force Base housed only nonviolent white-collar prisoners. His fellow inmates, although not of so elevated a status as he, would be gentlemen crooks, given to obstruction of justice, income tax evasion, or perjury, but not to knifings or throttlings.

Judge Claiborne did not show any notable awe of public opinion. He disregarded calls for his resignation made by Nevada political figures, congressmen from several states, newspapers, columnists, and the American Judicature Society, whose president, L. Stanley Chauvin, Jr., said that Claiborne "violated the public trust and should be removed [because lifetime appointment of federal judges] was never intended to protect convicted felons."[7] As well as disdaining suggestions that he resign, Claiborne showed similar indifference to suggestions that he give up his salary while in prison, a salary he had obviously done nothing to earn since the end of 1983.

But he did show continued interest in being subjected to an impeachment inquiry, insisting that it would provide his first real opportunity to demonstrate that federal agents had pursued him mercilessly and unjustly. Impeachment, he declared, would at last give him a chance to tell his side of the story, an opportunity not available at his trial. He added that he had been treated unfairly because "I'm a judge. Had I been the average citizen and not a member of the judiciary, I wouldn't be facing what I'm facing today."[8]

Claiborne's chief attorney, Oscar Goodman, also looked forward to impeachment and a Senate trial. He said of his client, "If we go to the Senate, it's no holds barred. He's going to let everything hang out."[9] Goodman insinuated that facts and arguments supportive of the judge's position had not been disclosed previously because of unduly restrictive rulings on admission of evidence in his court trial, and that their disclosure would reveal the strength of Claiborne's contentions. He had noted previously that Claiborne had been "hounded, prosecuted, and convicted" because he was "a judge unpopular with federal agents and prosecutors."[10] The vendetta theme appeared throughout Judge Claiborne's court trials and various appeals and recurred peripherally in the course of the impeachment proceedings. It might have raised the substantial question of interference with judicial independence had Claiborne's attorneys been able to demonstrate that the "vendetta" arose because some of the judge's rulings antagonized federal agents. But the revenge motif did not prove adequate to overshadow the unarguable fact that Claiborne had been found guilty of deliberate income tax evasion, a specific crime unrelated to any judicial decisions he rendered, whatever their possible unpopularity.

The spectacle of a federal judge sitting in prison, refusing to resign, drawing his full salary, and possibly remounting the bench after being released stimulated introduction in the House of Representatives of an impeachment resolution on June 3, 1986.[11] The House in the 99th Congress was composed of 253 Democrats and 182 Republicans, a 58 percent majority of the judge's fellow Democrats but a factor of no significance in this instance. Congress, a substantial segment of the judiciary, and portions of the public were offended by Claiborne's stubborn continuance in office after he had been convicted of a crime. Therefore, because Claiborne was alive and well and had no intention of resigning, impeachment remained the only procedure by which his removal from office could be secured.

On June 24, a mere three weeks after the resolution to impeach Harry E. Claiborne had been introduced in the House, a fifteen-member subcommittee of the Judiciary Committee voted unanimously to recommend impeachment to the full committee. Just two days later, the judge's professed desire to be impeached moved closer to fulfillment. The Judiciary Committee, composed of twenty-one Democrats and fourteen Republicans, eight of whom, including Chairman Peter W. Rodino (Democrat, New Jersey), had served on the committee during its investigation of Richard Nixon's conduct in 1974, adopted three articles of impeachment by a unanimous vote: thirty-five to zero. The three articles accused the judge of willfully and knowingly filing incorrect income tax returns in 1979 and in 1980 and of being convicted for those violations. A fourth article stating that Claiborne had brought the federal judiciary into disrepute was adopted following some changes in wording. The four articles were then incorporated into a single resolution that the committee adopted without dissent. Not a word of support for Claiborne was offered by any member of the committee.[12]

In the midst of House appraisal of his deportment, Claiborne received another dent in such judicial reputation as may have remained to him. Chief Justice Warren Burger reported to the House on July 2 that the Judicial Conference had found that Claiborne's behavior might constitute grounds for impeachment.[13] Thus, another institution of government indicated serious doubt of Harry E. Claiborne's fitness to remain in office. A day or two later, the judge's lawyer Oscar Goodman, exhibiting no dismay over actions that had already been taken against his client, stated that Claiborne "was a credit to the judiciary"; the attempted ouster showed "a lack of sensitivity to the entire judicial process" on the part of his detractors, Goodman asserted.[14] This intrepid comment was made after the Judiciary Committee, lawyers all, had voted unanimously for impeachment and after the Judicial Conference and the American Judicature Society had recorded their lack of confidence in Judge Claiborne.

On July 22, a month after the Judiciary Committee's unanimous recommendation, the House of Representatives voted 406 to zero to adopt the impeachment resolution.[15] The magnitude of House repudiation of the judge boded ill for his chance of exoneration in a Senate trial. Lacking partisan, professional, or geographic support, Claiborne joins Judge West H. Humphreys (1862) as the second outcast of impeachment history.

During House consideration of Claiborne's impeachment, no congressman spoke in explanation or support of the judge's conduct; several members referred to his behavior as a mockery of justice. Hamilton Fish (Republican, New York), who had also served during the Judiciary Committee's inquiry into President Nixon's performance, viewed Judge Claiborne as "more than a mere embarrassment. He is a disgrace—an affront—to the judicial office." William J. Hughes (Democrat, New Jersey), referring to Judge Claiborne's conviction for income tax evasion, noted that he "did not cheat just once. He cheated 2 years in a row." Romano Mazzoli (Democrat, Kentucky) called Claiborne's failure to resign "evidence of arrogant behavior," showing "brazenness" and a "contemptuous attitude toward the country, toward the bench, toward the public service." And of the same subject, declining to resign, F. J. Sensenbrenner (Republican, Wisconsin) observed that greater criminals than Claiborne might have been federal judges "but they all had the sense of decency and sense of decorum to step down."[16] In the hour allotted to impeaching Claiborne, seven Democrats and seven Republicans spoke in a similar spirit and tone, and four congressmen, including both of Nevada's representatives, received permission to publish their opposition to Claiborne in the printed record.

Having secured an unambiguous decision to impeach Judge Claiborne, the House selected nine managers, five Democrats and four Republicans, to prosecute the case before the Senate. The prosecution reflected no evidence of partisan bias; only once before, in the trial of Judge Charles Swayne in 1905, had the majority of managers been members of the respondent's political party.

The House of Representatives notified the Senate of its action and reported that the managers were ready to present the articles of impeachment. Then followed a bizarre episode: the Senate declined to receive the message, an entirely unheard-of event in impeachment history and one called "institutionally outrageous" by an anonymous congressman, who added, "You just don't insult the House this way."[17] By existing rules, the Senate must announce a schedule for a trial within one day of receiving articles of impeachment.[18]

Two weeks later, on August 6, the Senate's peculiar stalling tactic ended, and it accepted the articles from the House managers. It then broke with impeachment tradition once more by naming a twelve-member panel of six Republicans and six Democrats, all lawyers, to sift through the evidence and submit its findings to the Senate. A rule permitting this procedure was adopted in 1935, just before the trial of Judge Halsted L. Ritter, last subject of an impeachment trial, but was not used in his case. Claiborne argued that the Senate panel was unconstitutional and that he deserved to present his entire case before all the senators. Every previous trial had taken place before the full Senate or before those members who chose to appear, poor attendance being a hallmark of many impeachment trials.

In addition to the already advanced claims that Judge Claiborne had been damaged by careless tax preparers, victimized by an inexorable band of federal prosecutors bent on his destruction, and convicted on evidence improperly obtained by a break-in at his home, his defenders raised one other argument: his appeals both before and after conviction had been incorrectly or inadequately weighed by the appellate courts. When this argument was presented in Claiborne's impeachment trial, the Senate declined to consider matters connected solely with actions taken within the court system and concerned with admission of evidence or denials of appeals, nor did it accept arguments concerning illegal seizure of material from his residence.

The next flurry of pre-trial activity on Judge Claiborne's behalf centered on an effort to have him released from prison so he could help his attorneys prepare for the coming trial in the Senate. "The defendant has suffered the ignominy of being the only sitting federal judge to be incarcerated," the motion for release stated.[19] Here, again, the judge was not successful.

As the trial date neared, Oscar Goodman made another effort to derail the proceedings even though he had appeared to welcome them. He asserted that Judge Claiborne had not been accused of anything relating to discharge of his office. The accusations against the judge, Goodman reported to the Senate Rules Committee, were based on alleged misconduct, private in nature, not on official misconduct. Hence, the case against Claiborne did not involve impeachable behavior.

Later, before the Senate Impeachment Trial Committee, Goodman made the same argument, insisting that Claiborne's purported misbehavior had to be part of "his official function as a judge."[20] Paul Sarbanes (Democrat, Maryland), a member of the House Judiciary Committee during the Nixon impeachment inquiry, asked whether Goodman meant that, had the judge "committed murder or rape, and not in doing his official duties, that that is not an impeachable offense?" "That is my position," Goodman replied.[21] Clearly, he assumed a most illogical position in light of his earlier argument that a judge must be impeached before being tried in court. Thus, the judge who was a murderer could not be tried until impeached and could not be impeached for committing a murder; such an exegesis does not survive analysis. Goodman either did not know, or failed to recall, that the Constitution does not specify official misconduct and that some of the impeached jurists had been accused of off-duty improprieties, not of activities performed on the bench or directly connected with their judicial function.

The question of whether the conduct under scrutiny had to be an official act was mentioned in Charles Swayne's impeachment trial. Manager James B. Perkins supposed that a judge, in jail for forgery or embezzlement, claimed he could not be impeached for acts committed in his private capacity. If this claim were accepted, Perkins pointed out, the judge "as he marches to perform hard labor . . . will receive . . . his salary as a judge of the United States Court. Such a result shows the absurdity of the position."[22]

On September 15, 1986 the Senate Impeachment Trial Committee began its open, and televised, hearings, which continued for seven days. Judge Claiborne, accompanied by Oscar Goodman and former Senator Howard Cannon, attended. Claiborne restated his position on three points: first, the twelve-member senate panel was unconstitutional; second, the full Senate should hear the evidence supporting his contention that the national government had pursued a relentless vendetta against him; and third, the full Senate ought to consider his claim that material central to his conviction in court had been illegally obtained by agents of the national government. The House managers insisted that evidence presented to the special Senate panel and subsequently to the Senate be limited to the record of the court trial in which Harry E. Claiborne had been convicted of evading part of his income taxes. The managers considered that a line-by-line review of the litigation resulting in the judge's conviction would be wasteful: he had duly been found guilty of a crime, had exhausted all of his appeals, and should be evaluated by the Senate on the basis of these established facts.

The special Senate panel essentially accepted the House managers' position but did agree to hear arguments that witnesses for the judge in his tax evasion trial had been intimidated or coached by federal agents. One such witness, Jerry Watson, who had operated a business in Las Vegas called "Creative Tax Planning," had prepared Judge Claiborne's 1980 tax return. He recounted alleged threats against him by Internal Revenue agents, threats made, he said, unless he desisted from trying to amend his testimony. Watson reported discovering that he had made a mistake in telling the grand jury investigating Judge Claiborne that he did not know that the judge had received $88,000 in legal fees in 1980, fees obviously earned before Claiborne became a judge. Watson subsequently remembered that he had known about the fees and had wired the grand jury of his error in denying having such knowledge. Whereupon, he said, FBI and IRS agents threatened him with prosecution unless he withdrew the amended statement and reaffirmed his original claim that Claiborne had not informed him about the $88,000. Watson reported being asked by the agents whether he understood federal statutes on conspiracy and fraud and knew he might be a target of a grand jury for lying and covering up for Judge Claiborne.[23]

The Senate panel paid little attention to this, or other, evidence of harassment by federal agents. Instead, the panel focused its attention on the two faulty income tax returns. The first incorrect return, 1979, had been prepared by Joseph Wright, Claiborne's accountant for thirty years. It understated his income by $18,700. The judge insisted that he had supplied Wright with all the information about his income and that the accountant had made an error.

Wright noted that the judge, who for many years had had all his bank statements sent directly to Wright's firm, had abruptly ceased doing so. Therefore Wright possessed only the information Claiborne supplied. Unlike most taxpayers who acknowledge examining their returns "under penalties of perjury," Judge Claiborne said he had never seen the 1979 return before it went to the IRS. He readily acknowledged carelessness in tax matters but not willful underpayment; he had relied entirely on his accountant to prepare and submit his return and had no knowledge that it was inaccurate.

The next year Claiborne moved his tax business to Jerry Watson, and the tax return understated the judge's income by $87,900, was incompletely filled out, and was submitted in pencil. Of the 1980 return, the House managers, in a brief filed with the Senate, noted that "A man who had earned a judicial salary of $54,500, who had received $87,900 in legal fees, and who had realized a taxable gain of $214,000 on the sale of his home, reported and paid $1,103 in taxes." The managers termed Claiborne's attempted explanation of the return "not worthy of belief."[24]

Jerry Watson's testimony before the trial committee did nothing to justify the faulty and extraordinary 1980 return. His tangled and bumbling description of his procedure in preparing it did not exemplify professional accounting practices. Nor did Judge Claiborne's subsequent expression of total reliance on his tax preparer—"I was totally a hundred percent sucked in by this man"—account for Watson's creating a false return favorable to his client but unbeknown to that client. As Warren Rudman (Republican, New Hampshire) commented to Watson, the Senate could not be expected to believe that a man in the accounting business "independent of the client, sat down and constructed a wholly artificial series of transactions resulting in a loss." Dennis De Concini (Democrat, Arizona) called Watson "the most reprehensible witness I have ever seen come before the Senate."[25] The antic testimony on the two tax matters had not convinced the trial jury and would not persuade the Senate that Claiborne was a hapless and trusting victim, fallen under the control of careless tax preparers. The judge may well have been, as he said, inattentive in these instances, but even his detractors acknowledged his intelligence and energy.

The impeachment committee ended its seven days of hearings on September 23, 1986, and two weeks later the Senate met as a Court of Impeachment to decide on Harry E. Claiborne's guilt or innocence. The Senate in the 99th Congress contained fifty-three Republicans and forty-seven Democrats, a 53 percent majority for the

Republicans but neither a favorable nor unfavorable factor in Democrat Claiborne's trial.

The first matter presented to the full Senate was a motion by Oscar Goodman to postpone the trial until Claiborne's request to the Ninth Circuit Court of Appeals for reconsideration of his conviction in federal district court had been acted upon. Goodman told the Senate that important testimony had not been admitted at the judge's trial: development of the vendetta theme and discussion of the alleged burglary of Claiborne's home. Manager Henry J. Hyde (Republican, Illinois) replied that Claiborne had had a fair trial and had exhausted all appeals; hence, his efforts to delay the Senate trial should not be allowed.[26]

Next, Goodman moved to have the Senate special impeachment committee declared unconstitutional, thereby providing for the entire Senate to hear the witnesses and evaluate their reliability and conduct. Of this motion Manager William J. Hughes (Democrat, New Jersey) noted that creation of a special impeachment committee was "a wise, prudent, and constitutional delegation of authority," and that Claiborne was reaching in all directions in an effort to postpone the trial.[27]

The third motion made on Judge Claiborne's behalf asked the Senate to designate the phrase, "beyond a reasonable doubt," as the standard of proof in the trial. Manager Robert Kastenmeier (Democrat, Wisconsin) replied that past impeachment trials had set the standard as "preponderance of evidence"; he noted that a Senate trial was not a criminal proceeding, but one simply to decide whether Claiborne should be removed from office.[28]

The Senate by voice vote defeated Claiborne's motion to postpone the trial, whereupon Managers Fish and Rodino summarized the evidence pointing to conviction.[29] They described Harry E. Claiborne's evasion of taxes as willful, intentional, and fraudulent. Respecting Article 3, conviction in trial court as sufficient ground for a Senate verdict of guilty, Congressman Rodino argued that the converse should not be inferred: acquittal at a court trial would provide a defense against conviction under impeachment. This possibility concerned several senators who were thinking about Judge Alcee L. Hastings, acquitted in 1983 in a trial for soliciting a bribe but recommended for impeachment in 1986 by the Eleventh Circuit Court of Appeals and later by the Judicial Conference. Rodino was asked if Senate conviction of Claiborne based on his having been convicted of a felony in a court trial would "set a precedent that a judgment of acquittal on a felony is a complete defense" in an impeachment trial. He replied that it would not, because "the Senate, as the body that is the trier of the impeachment, must consider the impeachment on the basis of the facts before it."[30]

The trial concluded with summary statements by Oscar Goodman and Judge Claiborne. Goodman called attention to the judge's high standing as a jurist and repeated his arguments that the full Senate should hear the witnesses, that no proof of willful misconduct had been put in evidence, and that Claiborne provided the only example of an impeached official being "charged with a situation outside of his judicial function," an inaccurate declaration, as mentioned earlier.[31]

Judge Claiborne told the Senate that he had been unable to present his evidence of being a victim of government misconduct in any forum, that he had been a hardworking and dedicated jurist, and that the independence of the judiciary was threatened by "young Turks in the Justice Department" who had become "headhunters" to gain publicity.[32] He had disregarded urgings from supporters that he resign, he said, because he could not walk away from a situation in which he was not guilty of anything.

Following an hour of closed session on October 7, the Senate voted on the respondent's motion to accept the phrase "beyond a reasonable doubt" as the standard of proof. The vote was seventy-three to seventeen against adoption; the seventeen no votes were cast by ten Democrats and seven Republicans.[33] Thus, on the second of Claiborne's motions, as on the one to delay the trial, his position did not prevail.

The next day, the Senate met in closed session for nearly three hours. It then took the only public action for that day by defeating Judge Claiborne's third motion: a request that the full Senate hear the witnesses who had appeared before the special panel. Sixty-one senators voted against the motion, thirty-two in favor.[34] The thirty-two supporting the judge's position included twenty Democrats and twelve Republicans.

On the last day of the trial, October 9, the Senate again met in closed session, this time for nearly five hours. It then voted on the four articles of impeachment.[35] On Article 1, underpayment of income tax in 1979, the vote was eighty-seven guilty, ten not guilty; senators voting not guilty included five Democrats and five Republicans. On Article 2, concerning Judge Claiborne's 1980 tax return, ninety senators voted for conviction, seven against; four Democrats and three Republicans cast the no votes. Article 3, proposing a guilty finding because Claiborne had been convicted in court, proved to be the only article not receiving a two-thirds guilty vote. Forty-six senators favored adoption and seventeen senators, five Democrats and twelve Republicans, rejected adoption; thirty-five senators voted present. The fourth article charged Claiborne with betrayal of public trust and of bringing disrepute on the federal judiciary. The Senate found him guilty by a vote of eighty-nine to eight; four Republicans and four Democrats comprised the senators voting not guilty.

Therefore, on three of the four articles Harry Claiborne was found guilty by far more than the two-thirds needed for conviction and was convicted on Article 3 by a substantial majority, 86 percent of those voting, but not constituting the requisite two-thirds of the senators present. Upon conclusion of the vote, the Senate ordered "that the said Harry E. Claiborne be, and he is hereby removed from office."[36]

The vote on Article 3 deserves particular notice. Several senators feared the consequences of accepting that article if it could be interpreted as establishing that conviction in court mandated conviction in an impeachment trial. Two problems might arise from such an interpretation. First, the Senate could be ceding its unique role in impeachment to the judiciary. Second, despite Congressman Rodino's argument to the contrary, a vote upholding Article 3 might be viewed as establishing a reverse precedent: a court trial resulting in a verdict of innocent precludes, or constitutes an argument against, a Senate finding of guilty. This second point aroused concerns about the status of Judge Hastings, acquitted in court on a bribery charge, as noted, and headed for impeachment; Hastings could be expected to argue that his acquittal should be decisive proof of innocence in an impeachment trial.

Harry E. Claiborne's conviction was unequivocal, showing no partisan or geographic characteristics. Senators voting not guilty on one or more articles, or expressing only qualified support for the verdict, stated, variously, that (1) Claiborne had made negligent, not willful, errors on his income taxes; (2) he should have been subjected to a civil, not criminal, action for underreporting his income taxes; (3) the possible, and unexamined, overreaching of government agents to catch the judge tainted the proceedings; and (4) the full Senate should have heard the witnesses, not relied on the testimony presented to the twelve-member hearing panel. But no senators advanced an argument that Judge Claiborne was innocent, and only a handful cast a not guilty vote on the basis of reasons just noted.

These observations are based on the statements filed by eighteen senators, twelve Democrats and six Republicans, at conclusion of the trial.[37] Only three senators—Daniel J. Evans (Republican, Washington), Orrin G. Hatch (Republican, Utah), and David Pryor (Democrat, Arkansas)—voted not guilty on all four articles. Therefore, the magnitude of Harry E. Claiborne's conviction is exceeded only by that of West H. Humphreys's. The Senate gave no consideration to permanent disqualification of Claiborne, undoubtedly because no expectation existed that he would be appointed to, or run for, a national office at some future time.

Given Judge Claiborne's conviction in court; the rejection of his many appeals; the disavowals of his conduct by the Judicial Conference, the American Judicature Society, and prominent public figures; his impeachment by unanimous vote of the House of Representatives; and, finally, his being found guilty by a staggering 92 percent vote in the Senate, why did he still continue his efforts to have his court conviction overturned? The most solemn attempt to deal with this question has produced no solid answers.

Although the vindication he had hoped for at an impeachment trial had completely failed, the judge continued to press for reversal of his court conviction. Such a reversal could be expected to clear his name but not permit him to resume his judgeship or secure a federal pension. The years of seeking to overturn his conviction and the expenditures of money in that cause can be understood only as the effort of a man who viewed himself as unjustly treated by the system he was sworn to uphold. This appraisal falls short when measured against the record, but it is the only one that makes sense. Otherwise, Harry E. Claiborne had been flying in the face of crushing evidence against him, and of significant public and professional repudiation of his position.

The best explanation of Claiborne's persistence seems to be that he considered himself innocent of willful misconduct. He acknowledged that he had underpaid his taxes, but he claimed that the underpayments occurred through accountants' mistakes, not by any intention on his part to defraud the government. The inadequate income tax payment should have been a subject of civil, not criminal, action, Claiborne argued, and added that he had been convicted on evidence secured by a burglary of his home. Furthermore, he said, the trial court had not permitted introduction of proof alleged to show prejudice and misconduct by agents of the federal government. For these reasons, Judge Claiborne felt badly used.

302

Post-impeachment trial activities on Claiborne's behalf included continuing to press the Ninth Circuit Court of Appeals for reconsideration of his conviction in federal district court. The circuit court, in a three to zero ruling, rejected the appeal on March 22, 1989. Prior to that ruling, the United States Parole Commission had voted unanimously to deny the judge's request for immediate parole. The commission said that Claiborne had breached the public's trust by submitting "fraudulent tax returns."[38]

On May 18, 1988, the Nevada Supreme Court ruled that Claiborne, who had completed his prison term, could resume practicing law in the state.[39] In reaching this decision the court suspended operation of its rule (SCR111) that requires a disciplinary hearing conducted by the state bar on matters concerning suspension or disbarment of an attorney. The reason for suspending the rule, the court stated, arose from the fact that the court had conducted its own extensive examination of all material relevant to Harry E. Claiborne's trials and appeals. State bar officials were unwilling to study this voluminous review and, instead, proposed hiring an outside investigator. The court rejected the proposal as too time-consuming. It pointed out that the state bar was empowered only to make a nonbinding recommendation to the Nevada Supreme Court, a body already satisfied that its own exhaustive study of the case demonstrated that Claiborne was entitled to resume the practice of law. Another unusual aspect of the decision concerns the Nevada Supreme Court's reliance on dissenting opinions of the Ninth Circuit Court of Appeals and on minority opinions of senators in the impeachment trial. Not once did the court cite a circuit court majority opinion or a majority position of senators involved in the impeachment trial.

Whatever its unusual characteristics, the court's ruling is the most complete presentation of Claiborne's position that can be found in any single source. In a summary sympathetic to the judge's contentions, the court reviewed the conduct of federal agents (the vendetta theme), the federal government's dubious reliance on the testimony of Joseph Conforte as a witness against the judge, the rebuffs Claiborne encountered in his court trials in trying to present evidence of governmental misconduct, and the absence of proof of *willful* failure to pay his income taxes in full. The Nevada Supreme Court's appraisal of Judge Claiborne's experience led it to conclude that "questionable investigative and prosecutorial motivations, as well as anomalous and arguably unfair practices and procedures pervade the record of this matter from its inception. . . . In light of the above we decline to impose additional punishment upon respondent Claiborne."[40]

Harry E. Claiborne also applied for readmission to practice before the federal courts. His application was denied in September 1988; the ruling included a proviso that he could not reapply for admission for a year. His second application, December 1989, was approved, and Claiborne was readmitted to practice in federal courts.

Judge Claiborne occupies an eccentric position in impeachment history; his case is unique in some respects and unusual in others. Claiborne's involvement in the impeachment process reveals his participation to be something of an anomaly when compared with the history and habits of earlier impeachments and trials.

The unique aspects of the judge's experience began with the fact that no other target of impeachment had been convicted of a crime for which he was currently imprisoned. In nearly two hundred years, the Senate had never before been presented with a trial record as part of its evaluation of an officer's performance. Whether a trial transcript would be conclusive in any subsequent impeachment trial is not plainly established from the Claiborne example. The judge's criminal record certainly proved to be the key element in his conviction, but the Senate shied away from a pronouncement that court conviction in itself formed an absolute ground for impeachment and a subsequent finding of guilty by the senate. The question of whether a life-tenured jurist is *entitled* to be impeached before he is tried in a court of law deserves close attention. That question has current and, I suspect, ongoing significance, and it will be considered in the Epilogue.

Other unique attributes of the Claiborne example include Senate delay in accepting the articles; employment of a special Senate investigating panel; the highest attendance at a trial, with ninety-eight Senators present, ninety-seven voting; the only instance before 1986 of a subsequently impeached official claiming that he could not be tried in court unless he had been impeached; and the only allegation by an impeached officer that the government had waged a relentless government vendetta against him. None of the eleven preceding trials displayed any of these characteristics.

Judge Claiborne's case also reveals certain qualities that, although not unique, are rare in impeachment history. Along with just one other impeached officer, he shares three aspects of the procedure: (1) unanimous impeachment by the House of Representatives, shared with Secretary of War Belknap; (2) impeachment by a House in which his own party composed the majority, a characteristic of Judge Swayne's impeachment; and (3) prosecution by a board of managers composed of a majority of his own party, also a quality of Swayne's impeachment.[41] Another unusual aspect of the Claiborne experience concerns the relatively brief time Congress spent on investigating and trying him: just four months for the whole procedure, including a trial consuming only portions of three days. Judge Claiborne's trial is exceeded in brevity only by that of Judge Humphreys, whose trial took a mere half day.

In at least two other respects Harry E. Claiborne's association with impeachment is out of the ordinary. Neither the House of Representatives nor the Senate displayed partisan attitudes either for or against the judge; his fellow Democrats did not support him or point out mitigating circumstances accounting for his conduct. Many of the preceding impeachments and trials reveal noticeable, often controlling, partisanship. The other unusual quality concerns the scant, and fleeting, references to earlier Senate impeachment trials. Claiborne proved to be so singular a subject that the trial records of his predecessors did not supply useful material to his attorneys, nor did the managers need to rely on any such historical support in demonstrating the judge's culpability.

Had Judge Claiborne resigned, past experiences indicate that Congress would not have proceeded against him; he would then have been an obscure footnote instead of a major figure in impeachment history. Comments by several representatives and senators involved in Claiborne's case support the thesis that resignation would have halted further congressional action; so also does the history of the effect of past resignations in stopping proceedings. Congress has shown more concern for the first prong of the process, removal from office, than for the second, disqualification from obtaining any further federal post.

Two constitutional amendments were proposed as a consequence of Harry E. Claiborne's misconduct. Senator Strom Thurmond (Republican, South Carolina), stating that it was an "unacceptable quirk" and "outrageous that the time and energies of Congress are spent on this tedious and unwarranted process," proposed that any officer appointed by the president and confirmed by the Senate and who was convicted of a felony would forfeit office.[42] Senator De Concini also proposed an amendment; it too provided for automatic forfeiture upon a felony conviction and added a section empowering the Supreme Court to discipline judges.[43] Nothing came of these potential amendments, and neither would have reached any of the eleven officers whose impeachment trials preceded Claiborne's.

An encompassing description of "good behavior" is needed, including such defects as alcoholism, absenteeism, or senility—problems besetting jurists far more commonly than does criminality.

Claiborne's case may prove of enduring significance by tightening future Senate appraisals of judgeship nominees. Senators may look less intently at a nominee's political connections and more intently at the character, temperament, and judicial qualities of such nominee. If it had no other consequence, the example of Harry E. Claiborne would be of permanent importance in underlining the value of the impeachment mechanism. It is the only device for reaching delinquent federal judges, who, immune from dismissal and immune from being voted out of office, can, unless they die or resign, be ousted only by employment of that mechanism.

Epilogue

Is [impeachment] not designed as a method of *National Inquest* into the conduct of public men? If this be the design of it, who can so properly be the inquisitors for the nation as the representatives of the nation themselves?
—Alexander Hamilton

Since my completion of this study, the Senate has tried and convicted two federal district judges, Alcee L. Hastings and Walter L. Nixon, Jr. Their convictions occurred within a three-week period in October 1989; never before had there been so short an interval between trials. Their misconduct, and that of their immediately impeached predecessor Harry E. Claiborne in 1986, suggests that the shoddy practices afflicting the executive and legislative branches in the 1980s also occurred in the judicial branch.[1] The decay of conventional standards of personal and political behavior in that decade indicates either a decline in the morality of public officers or a sharper scrutiny of political performance than had previously existed.

To whatever cause one attributes the downhill slide in ethical conduct that became notorious in the 1980s, it can be noted with respect to judicial performance that no other decade in United States history produced three impeachments and three trials. In two hundred years the United States has impeached and tried one senator, one president, one cabinet officer, and eleven jurists, including Judges Hastings and Nixon. All trials in the twentieth century have concerned judges, and all seven convictions have been of judges. These facts provide convincing evidence of where the problem of impeachment lies and will continue to lie until Congress, forced to recognize the peculiar situation that life tenure confers upon federal judges, faces the task of activating the good behavior clause, or, as some scholars have proposed, places the power to remove judges in the hands of the judiciary. I do not believe that Congress can delegate its removal power. But the rash of trials in the 1980s may lead to an enactment changing the procedure. If it came in the form of a proposed constitutional amendment, Congress would be acknowledging what I believe to be correct: the Constitution places the power of removing judges exclusively in the legislative branch, and a statute would not suffice to divest it of that power.

Another unresolved matter besets application of the impeachment process: Can a life-tenured judge be subject to court trial before being impeached? This question did not arise in an impeachment until 1986, when Harry E. Claiborne, who had been tried in court, found guilty, and sentenced to prison, was impeached and tried. And the experiences of Judges Alcee L. Hastings and Walter L. Nixon, Jr., in 1989 swiftly revived the question, because both had been tried in court prior to their Senate trials.

In addition, Judge Nixon, like Judge Claiborne, was in prison when he was tried in the Senate. Imprisonment obviously removes a judge from office and hence raises a profound constitutional question, Can a life-tenured jurist be ousted from his post, even if temporarily, by court decision rather than by legislative action, the method of removal established in the Constitution?[2] The underlying, and bizarre, moral question also deserves attention: Could a committed felon, having served his sentence, resume his judicial post? Before examining the difficulties arising because of court trials of judges prior to their impeachment, it is necessary to describe conduct of Hastings and Nixon that brought them first to court and then to the bar of the Senate.

Alcee L. Hastings, appointed a federal district judge for the southern district of Florida in 1979 by Jimmy Carter, became the first black federal judge in that state. He achieved notoriety soon after ascending the bench. In 1981 a federal grand jury indicted him and his long-time friend William Borders of bribery, conspiracy, and obstruction of justice for soliciting a $150,000 bribe designed to mitigate the sentences of two felons, the Romano brothers, convicted in Hastings's court. Borders was found guilty in March 1982; his conviction was upheld on appeal.[3]

The FBI engineered and financed the scheme by which William Borders was trapped. He was arrested upon taking money from an employee of the FBI, money ostensibly being paid because Borders had persuaded Judge Hastings to reduce the two felons' sentences. Although clearly the victim of a "sting," Borders was eminently entrappable and not simply caught up in an action alien to his nature. He did not implicate Judge Hastings as a co-conspirator in his court trial and subsequently went to jail for contempt of Congress for refusing to testify in the judge's Senate trial. Thus, if both men were involved in the bribery plot, Borders proved to be a very loyal friend.

Alcee L. Hastings's court trial took place a year after Borders had been convicted. The two trials had been separated because Hastings sought to prevent being tried until he had been impeached, an argument that was rejected.[4] In February 1983 a jury acquitted the judge of the charges levied against him.[5]

It is difficult to understand how Hastings could have been found innocent and Borders found guilty in their trials. The success of the bribery depended upon favorable action by the sentencing judge, namely Alcee L. Hastings, who had reduced the sentences of the two felons at the very time when Borders was, if unwittingly, trafficking with the FBI. There would have been no sting and no story had Hastings not made a change in the felons' sentences.

Following complaints that Judge Hastings had secured a not guilty verdict by lying and submitting false evidence at his jury trial, the Eleventh Circuit Court of Appeals, under authority of the Judicial Conduct Act, undertook an investigation of the trial and the circumstances leading to it. The investigation, continuing for three years, resulted in a unanimous recommendation to the Judicial Conference that the judge's conduct might warrant impeachment.[6] The conference concurred and sent the recommendation to the House of Representatives on March 17, 1987.[7] After a sixteen-month investigation, the House voted 413 to 3 to impeach the judge and adopted seventeen articles of impeachment—the greatest number ever brought against an officer.

Article 1 charged Alcee L. Hastings with conspiring with William Borders to obtain $150,000 for reducing the jail sentence of the Romano brothers. Articles 2 through 15 described the judge as lying and submitting false evidence in his jury trial. Article 16 alleged that Hastings had revealed confidential information about a government wiretap to a person involved in the surveillance. Article 17, a cumulative article summarizing all the preceding charges, added that the actions of Alcee L. Hastings had undermined public confidence in the judiciary.[8]

The Senate decided to employ the special committee procedure used for the first time in Harry E. Claiborne's trial to hear evidence for and against Judge Hastings. Like Claiborne, Hastings tried, without success, to force the full Senate to listen to all the testimony. Thus, the trials of the 1980s probably established that a special Senate hearing committee would become an accepted feature of impeachment trial practices.

The twelve-member Senate Impeachment Trial Committee, six Democrats and six Republicans, met from July 10 to August 3, 1989 and heard evidence from an extraordinary assortment of characters. The acknowledged actors in the bribery drama included

William Borders, who had solicited and received a bribe; Mafia figures, including the Romano brothers; career criminals, one of whom became an FBI informant and the direct cause of Borders's arrest; and an ex-FBI agent who impersonated one of the Romano brothers and taped the proceedings with Borders.

Borders had initiated the bribery scheme by having the Romano brothers informed that he controlled Judge Hastings and could get the judge to reduce the brothers' jail sentences if they paid Borders $150,000. After an elaborate scheme had been devised and carried out to demonstrate to the brothers that Borders had control over Hastings, they seemingly agreed to make such a payment, *seemingly*, because the former FBI agent representing himself to Borders as one of the Romanos was actually making, as well as recording, all the arrangements.

Judge Hastings did modify the sentences of the Romano brothers and did reduce the amount of the forfeiture of their property. Soon thereafter, the agent masquerading as one of the Romanos paid the agreed-upon bribe to William Borders. The FBI apprehended Borders as he left with the money. Judge Hastings, then in Washington, D.C., where the payoff took place, learned of Borders's arrest soon after it occurred and also learned that the FBI wanted to talk with him. But Hastings promptly left Washington by a circuitous route and returned to Florida, where the FBI located him on the evening of Borders's arrest. Hastings explained that his failure to return calls to the FBI and his abrupt departure from Washington were based on concern for his mother, who had become hysterical upon learning of Borders's situation and her son's possible connection with his friend's arrest. His hasty leave-taking was also based, Hastings explained to the FBI, on his belief that he could make a stronger defense against allegations while on his own turf. He denied any connection with a bribery plot.[9]

The special Senate committee hearings opened with a statement by the House managers, four Democrats and two Republicans, detailing the case against Hastings, following which Hasting's attorney summarized the arguments supporting the judge's position.[10] The managers called twenty-six witnesses and the respondent called twenty-nine.

Appearing in his own defense, Judge Hastings explained that he had made misstatements in his jury trial but, contrary to the managers' claim, he had not lied. Nor, as alleged in Article 16, had he disclosed any information about a government wiretap. He recounted his extensive dealings with William Borders and claimed they were entirely unrelated to any bribery arrangements.[11]

But the managers produced evidence of numerous telephone calls and meetings between Borders and Judge Hastings that corresponded to key events during the hatching and completing of the bribery scheme. The evidence was documented by records of the telephone company and airlines and by the judge himself. Also, contacts between the judge and Borders corresponded closely to developments in the plot as recorded by the FBI agent who impersonated one of the Romano brothers. Because Judge Hastings was expected to, and did, reduce the Romanos' jail sentences and forfeiture of property, the presumption was strong that he did so because Borders reported to him that the bribe arrangements had been agreed to and the money would be paid.

The House managers also succeeded in demonstrating that Judge Hastings's acquittal in court had been obtained by false testimony, and they documented the instances in which the judge had lied.[12] The documents supported the managers' contention that Hastings had a corrupt relationship with William Borders and had connived with him to solicit a bribe.

Hastings's core argument as presented to the Senate committee concerned the fact that, six years earlier, a jury had found him innocent of the same charges now being brought before the committee; the Senate, Hastings insisted, was obliged to respect the jury system and honor that verdict. Furthermore, his court trial had taken place close to the time at which his alleged crimes had been committed. The jury heard testimony while the events surrounding the crimes remained fresh in the witnesses' minds, and consequently determined that Judge Hastings had not been a participant in the bribery scheme of which his friend William Borders had been convicted. The Senate now would have no such opportunity because of the death of some of the witnesses and the fogging of memory of the survivors.

The House managers responded with the following statement, in which the Senate subsequently concurred: "It is the position of the House of Representatives that Judge Hastings' acquittal is, in fact of no consequence in this case. . . . To defer to a jury verdict in effect places in the hands of the Judicial Branch what is clearly a legislative function. Moreover, in this case, to defer to the acquittal would be tantamount to accepting a jury verdict obtained by fraud."[13]

Hastings further claimed, again unsuccessfully, that the Senate trial subjected him to double jeopardy because he had already been tried on the same charges in a court of law. The managers argued that an impeachment trial has no elements of a criminal trial, but is simply a civil test of whether the accused is fit to be continued in office. The Senate could not imprison or fine a convicted officer, nor could a jury remove an officer from his post; therefore, the judge was not a victim of double jeopardy. This position was later accepted by the Senate.

The trial committee filed its report on October 2, 1989, and the trial opened on October 18 before the full Senate. Each side had been granted two hours to review its case. In their review, the managers pointed out that William Borders had been found guilty of soliciting and receiving a bribe, an object contingent upon cooperative action by Judge Hastings. The judge, tried essentially on the same counts, had been found innocent. Such an outcome could have been achieved only by fabricated evidence and false testimony, the managers claimed. They recounted the number of meetings and telephone calls between Borders and Hastings during the conspiracy period and argued that no transactions between the two men other than arranging the bribe could account for the number or nature of the exchanges.[14]

The respondent's summary focused on the length and intensity of the investigation of his conduct and the failure to uncover any direct proof of his presumed wrongdoing. All the evidence presented against him had been circumstantial.[15] Restatements were also set forth of Hastings's position concerning double jeopardy and the need to defer to the trial jury's verdict.

The Senate voted on October 29, 1989 and convicted the judge of eight of the first nine articles, those accusing him of conspiring with William Borders and lying about the conspiracy at his court trial.[16] On Article 1, accusing Judge Hastings of reducing the sentence of the Romano brothers in exchange for $150,000, the Senate voted sixty-nine guilty, twenty-six not guilty. Thirty-five Republicans and thirty-four Democrats comprised those voting guilty. Twenty-one Democrats and five Republicans found Judge Hastings not guilty, a result indicating some partisan Democratic support for their fellow Democrat.

Article 9 received the largest vote recorded against Hastings, seventy guilty to twenty-five not guilty. Thirty-six Democrats and thirty-four Republicans voted guilty, and nineteen Democrats and six Republicans voted not guilty. As also demonstrated in the vote on Article 1, Democrats showed somewhat less appetite for convicting Hastings than did Republicans; 65 percent of the Democrats voted guilty on Article 9 compared with 85 percent of the Republicans.

The Senate did not vote on Articles 10 through 15, a unique event in impeachment history but sensible because the judge had already been convicted.[17] Article 16, charging Judge Hastings with disclosing information about a government wiretap, secured no guilty votes; the Senate cleared him by a vote of zero to ninety-five.

On the cumulative Article 17, the Senate voted sixty to thirty-five to convict, short of the two-thirds vote necessary for a finding of guilty. The article repeated the descriptions of Alcee L. Hastings's corrupt dealings with William Borders, his repeated false testimony at his jury trial, and his improper disclosure of confidential information.

Use of a cumulative article has a history, and a malign one in my opinion, in preceding trials. However, only in the trial of Halsted L. Ritter in 1936 did use of such an article result in a verdict of guilty. The Senate failed to convict Ritter on any specific allegations; nevertheless, it convicted him on a final article recounting all the charges on none of which had it been able to find him guilty by the requisite two-thirds vote. Failure to convict on any one of several alleged misdeeds should, I believe, preclude a guilty finding on a cumulative list of those misdeeds.

The House managers in Judge Hastings's trial explained their use of a cumulative article by stating that the Senate had "recognized that an omnibus article is a separate and important basis for removing a corrupt official from public life in an impeachment proceeding." That conclusion stretches the record; only Judge Ritter's trial depended on a cumulative article to secure conviction and removal from office.[18]

Some senators who voted not guilty in Hastings's trial expressed dissatisfaction with the failure to connect the judge directly with the bribery or with any of the money secured thereby. Two senators commented on an unusual aspect of Hastings's experience, an aspect peripherally observable in Harry E. Claiborne's case: executive department initiation of an investigation leading to impeachment and trial. Terry Sanford (Democrat, North Carolina) said the judge had been involved in "a sting operation set up by the FBI," and that a case against him has not been proved. Brock Adams (Democrat, Washington) observed that "the FBI broke the case [by arresting William Borders] before the sting money was distributed, and therefore we will never know whether the money was to remain with Mr. Borders or go to Judge Hastings."[19]

Alcee L. Hastings enters impeachment annals as the first impeached officer to have been tried in court and found innocent, the second to have been tried before being impeached, the first to be impeached on recommendation of the Judicial Conference, the first black to be a subject of impeachment procedure, and the first jurist to be impeached on a charge dealing squarely with his conduct as a judge.

Hastings also is the first convicted federal officer to announce his candidacy for public office upon being relieved of his post by the Senate. On October 23, 1989 he filed for governor of Florida. "Negative celebrity brings one into the fray the same as positive celebrity does," Hastings noted, "I'm at least well-known."[20]

Two weeks after it had convicted Alcee L. Hastings, the Senate, on November 3, 1989, convicted another federal district judge, Walter L. Nixon, Jr. Nixon had been appointed to the federal district court of the southern district of Mississippi in 1968 by Lyndon B. Johnson. Thus, when he came before the Senate, he had served on the bench for twenty-one years.

Judge Nixon had been convicted in February 1986 of lying to a grand jury; he was sentenced to five years in prison.[21] The perjuries arose from the judge's denial that he had talked to the district attorney in an effort to secure favorable treatment for an acknowledged drug smuggler. The smuggler was the son of a wealthy oilman, Wiley Fairchild, who earlier had arranged an unusual and lucrative oil investment for Judge Nixon. The allegation that the judge's efforts on the son's behalf stemmed from gratitude for the profitable business deal was not plainly established at Nixon's trial, but the jury found him guilty of lying about his activities in the matter.

Two years after the trial, in March 1988, the Judicial Conference asked the House of Representatives to consider impeaching Walter L. Nixon, Jr., a second instance of an impeachment initiated by the judiciary, Judge Hastings's providing the first instance. Following a one-year investigation of Nixon's conduct as revealed in his court trial and after hearing testimony of witnesses for and against the judge, the House Judiciary Committee's Subcommittee on Civil and Constitutional Rights recommended that he be impeached; the full committee adopted the proposal on April 25, 1989. The House of Representatives acted swiftly on the Judiciary Committee's recommendation and impeached Walter L. Nixon, Jr., by unanimous vote, 417 to zero, on May 10, 1989.[22] It selected five managers, three

Democrats and two Republicans, to develop the case and prosecute it before the Senate.

Nixon had performed no judicial duties since August 1985 but continued to receive his $89,500 salary; he announced his intention to resume his seat on the bench after he had served his sentence. These facts displeased several congressmen and attracted negative observations from various commentators.

The case against Judge Nixon centered on two perjurious statements for which he had been convicted in his court trial. Over the objections of Nixon's attorney, the trial transcript had been admitted as evidence in his Senate trial.[23]

The instances of Nixon's lying became the first two impeachment articles. Article 1 detailed the judge's appearance before the grand jury, which was investigating his business dealings with Wiley Fairchild and his involvement in the criminal prosecution of Fairchild's son for drug smuggling. It accused Nixon of false testimony in denying that he had discussed the drug case with the district attorney; the attorney testified at Nixon's jury trial that the judge had interceded in Fairchild's son's behalf and that his intervention had caused the case to be shelved.

Article 2 asserted that Judge Nixon lied when he told the grand jury that he had nothing to do with the drug-smuggling case, "never handled any part of it, never had a thing to do with it at all, and never talked to anyone, State or Federal prosecutor or judge, that in any way influenced anybody."[24]

The third and final article, essentially cumulative, set down fourteen specific false statements by the judge that related to the first two articles and added that he had brought discredit on the federal court system.

The Senate continued its practice of employing a special hearing committee. The Impeachment Trial Committee for Nixon, six Democrats and six Republicans, held evidentiary hearings from September 7 through September 13, 1989.[25]

The proceedings began with an opening statement by Don Edwards (Democrat, California), speaking for the House managers. He reviewed the details of Judge Nixon's relations with Wiley Fairchild and said that the judge felt obliged to help the son with his legal problem because of the profitable business deal Fairchild had arranged for Nixon's benefit. The help consisted of calling upon the district attorney and putting in "a good word" for the son. The district attorney, "knowing that Judge Nixon was interested in more investments with Wiley Fairchild ... agreed to sweep [his son's drug smuggling] case under the rug."[26]

The judge's activities, according to the managers, were known to the district attorney, Wiley Fairchild, and Fairchild's lawyer. All three had testified at Nixon's court trial and had said that he intervened in the drug-smuggling case. When the three men appeared at the Senate trial, their collective testimony, the managers asserted, "will show that Judge Nixon lied to the interviewers [the FBI] and to the grand jury."[27]

Following Congressman Edwards's introduction, Nixon's attorney surveyed the case from the respondent's point of view. He described the judge's fine reputation as a lawyer and jurist and said that Nixon became a target of the Justice Department because of his ruling against the government in a land condemnation case. The testimony of the district attorney and of Wiley Fairchild that Nixon had intervened in the drug case had been secured by government intimidation, according to the respondent. "Give us Judge Nixon or you got big trouble, you're going to get indicted or we're going after you. [Both men] cut deals." Nixon's attorney also reminded the Senate committee that the judge had voluntarily agreed to be interviewed by the FBI and had demanded to appear before the grand jury. "These are not the furtive actions of a cover-up," the attorney pointed out, but "the outraged actions of somebody ... who knows he's innocent of any wrongdoing."[28]

After the introductory statements, the two sides presented their witnesses—four for the managers, six for the respondent. The unusual paucity of witnesses can probably be attributed to the incorporation of Nixon's trial record into the Senate record. The four men who appeared for the managers described their knowledge of Judge Nixon's involvement with Wiley Fairchild respecting the oil lease and the judge's alleged efforts to help Fairchild's son solve his legal problems.[29] When cross-examined, these witnesses acknowledged the high regard the legal community held for Judge Nixon. One of the managers' witnesses said that the judge's having mentioned the drug-smuggling case to the district attorney was legal and appropriate, but that his lying about doing so caught him in a trap that led to his court conviction and impeachment.

The first five of the respondent's witnesses spoke of Nixon's reputation for truthfulness and his skill as a judge; the sixth witness was Walter L. Nixon, Jr., himself.[30] The judge spoke of his professional life and said that the charge of lying had no foundation. He had not knowingly said anything false but had not recalled certain conversations when he testified before the grand jury because they were trivial. He denied making any effort to help Fairchild's son with his drug case.

The managers' summation included a statement that the House of Representatives had not relied on Nixon's court conviction nor on the recommendation of the Judicial Conference; instead, it based its case on its own exhaustive investigation. The respondent's concluding remarks repeated that nothing the judge did had been illegal and that no evidence existed that he had knowingly testified untruthfully.

The Senate Impeachment Trial Committee filed its report on October 16, 1989, and the full Senate met on November 1; each side had been allowed one and one-half hours to review its case. The managers, summarizing the accusations against Judge Nixon, said that his conviction by a jury had been justified and insisted that his conduct warranted removal from office.[31] The respondent's summary asserted that the judge had been selectively targeted by overzealous prosecutors who were displeased with one of his decisions, that the government had encouraged his accusers to lie, and that he forthrightly denied having perjured himself or having been involved in any way in the drug case settlement.[32]

The following day the Senate met in secret session for six hours to consider its course in the Nixon matter; on November 3, it voted.[33] On Article 1, accusing the judge of discussing the drug case with the district attorney and denying that he had done so, the vote was eighty-nine guilty, eight not guilty. Article 2 also concerned the drug-smuggling matter. It charged the judge with saying, untruthfully, that he had never talked with anyone or tried to influence anyone about the case; the Senate convicted Judge Nixon on Article 2 by a vote of seventy-eight to nineteen. The Senate did not convict Nixon on the potpourri article. The vote on Article 3, fifty-seven guilty and forty not guilty, did not meet the two-thirds majority required for conviction. No significant party or regional loyalty is reflected in the conviction of Walter L. Nixon, Jr. Only three of his fellow Democrats voted not guilty on Article 1, as did five Republicans.

Nixon was paroled soon after his conviction by the Senate, having served just under two years of his five-year prison sentence. In August 1990 he was arrested for carrying a gun while hunting wild turkeys in a field seeded with grain. Carrying a gun violated his parole, and seeding a field to attract wildfowl violated Mississippi law.

317

These events seemed unlikely to further his efforts to have his license to practice law restored.

Both Hastings and Nixon were impeached by a House of Representatives controlled by Democrats and convicted by a Senate with a Democratic majority. Neither example revealed any significant party-centered support or antagonism. The nonpartisan attributes of their experiences are unusual compared with earlier impeachments and trials.

All three impeachments in the decade of the 1980s concerned judges who had been tried in court. The key constitutional issue arising from these experiences is, as noted earlier, whether impeachment of a life-tenured jurist must precede a court trial. Several senators in the course of the three trials noted that the Senate should not consider itself bound by a trial court's decision. Such a decision did not create a precedent for an impeachment trial, they insisted. True enough, but the court decisions did provide a record, one that the Senate considered.

Judges Claiborne and Nixon were, as mentioned, in prison during their Senate trials. They could not as imprisoned felons perform their judicial duties and had therefore been effectively deprived of office by a judicial, not a legislative, act.

The Constitution states that "Judgment in cases of impeachment shall not extend further than to removal from office, and disqualification to hold and enjoy any office of honor, trust, or profit under the United States; but the party convicted shall nevertheless be liable and subject to indictment, trial, judgment and punishment, according to law."[34] This clause plainly prevents any valid claim of double jeopardy by an official found guilty under the impeachment provisions who is subsequently tried in court, an event that has never occurred. It also shows that impeachment extends only to removal from office, not to punishment as handed down by courts of law.

However, does "the party convicted" mean that the official must have been subject to impeachment before he can be tried in court? The logic of the language suggests a "yes" answer to the question. Although this proposition is clearly arguable, if it is agreed that imprisonment takes a judge away form his post by a method not prescribed by the Constitution, courts are, if inadvertently, usurping a legislative function.[35]

The problem of court trial before impeachment did not become an issue until raised by Judge Otto Kerner in 1973. In his case the court ruled that a federal judge could be tried in court before being impeached.[36] The same decision was reached in *U.S. v. Hastings*[37] and *U.S. v. Claiborne*.[38] In all three instances the United States Supreme Court denied certiorari. In addition to ruling that federal judges can be tried without having first been impeached, the court in Claiborne's case specifically rejected the argument that imprisonment is equivalent to removal from office.[39]

William Rawle, noted attorney and constitutional scholar, observed more than a hundred years before the question of court trial preceding impeachment became an issue that "the ordinary tribunals . . . are not precluded either before or after an impeachment from taking cognizance of . . . official delinquency."[40] No one will quarrel with the statement that court trial following impeachment is authorized, but court trial before impeachment remains arguable. Despite Rawle and all court rulings to date, I believe that the words "the party convicted" establish that a life-tenured jurist must be impeached before he can be tried in court.

Curiously, in three impeachment trials a contrary position was advanced: that court trial must precede impeachment. Attorneys for Senator William Blount (1799), Secretary of War William Belknap (1876), and Judge Charles Swayne (1905) argued, unsuccessfully, that a court trial must come before an impeachment trial. However, according to extant interpretation, but clearly debatable, the Constitution, in providing a trial following impeachment and conviction, does not prohibit a court trial before the officer has been impeached. Either impeachment or a court trial may come first, and neither procedure precludes the other.

Despite the Constitutional Convention's focus on creating a procedure to curb executive excesses, impeachment has evolved into a nearly exclusive process for gauging judicial misconduct. In fact, all seven officials convicted under the impeachment provisions from 1799 to 1989 have been judges, and no executive officer has been impeached since Secretary of War Belknap in 1876. Therefore, if Congress is going to give any serious attention to improving the mechanism, it should focus on jurists, the only members of the national government not subject to rejection at the polls or dismissal by a superior officer.

Until recently, criminality has not figured conspicuously as a basis for bringing charges of judicial misconduct. Alcoholism, absenteeism, senility, and violation of canons of judicial ethics have been problems besetting judges far more commonly than has criminal misconduct. But these afflictions prove difficult, probably impossible, to classify as high crimes or misdemeanors. An enactment by

Congress defining "good behavior" would not essentially change any part of the process for impeaching and trying judges nor would it infringe upon judicial independence, but it would clarify the problem encountered in many impeachment trials of employing the term "good behavior" when it has never been defined.

Evidence accrued from the trials supports a conclusion that the impeachment mechanism makes a significant contribution to good government. In the absence of that mechanism Judges Claiborne and Nixon could have served their prison terms and resumed their seats on the bench, an outcome too grotesque for serious contemplation.

Also, the threat of impeachment caused several presumably defective judges to resign. Resignation need not technically stop an impeachment, but experience shows that it will; Secretary Belknap is the solitary exception to this custom. Congress loses interest in a dishonorable public servant once he has left office; additionally, the Senate has rarely invoked, or even considered, the second facet of the impeachment procedure: permanent disqualification from holding a position with the national government.

The twelve federal officers whose trials are appraised here, plus the two briefly surveyed in this chapter, indulged, as the record brings out, in criminal activities, or gave evidence of possessing flaws unfitting them to retain their posts, or had become unpopular with dominant political or business forces. To allude again to Edward Gibbon's terminology, they fall into a category of crimes, or follies, or misfortunes.

Five officers—Senator William Blount, Secretary of War William W. Belknap, Judge Harry E. Claiborne, Judge Alcee L. Hastings, and Judge Walter L. Nixon, Jr.—comprise the first category.[41] They committed crimes for which they could have been, or were, convicted in court.

Five officers, all judges, belong in the second category: unfitness to remain in office because of breaches of judicial propriety or chronic inability or unwillingness to perform their duties. I place the alcoholic John Pickering, the overbearing Samuel Chase, the absconded West H. Humphreys, and the abusers of office Charles Swayne and Robert W. Archbald as examples of ill-performing officials. Of this group, Chase and Swayne escaped conviction by the Senate.

The four officers in the "misfortune" category include three jurists and one president, all targets of powerful political or business interests. The Senate did not convict James H. Peck and Harold

Louderback, and it narrowly exonerated Andrew Johnson. Only Halsted L. Ritter of this group was found guilty, a judgment bringing no luster to the saga of impeachment because the Senate convicted him only on a cumulative article, not on any precise charge. All men in the "misfortune" category were political orphans, unsupported by the dominant forces of their time.

Certain generalizations about the impeachment mechanism emerge from a review of the trials. Partisanship, as mentioned, has been a significant aspect of the history of impeachment. Andrew Johnson is the stellar example of a party-centered impeachment and trial. Except for Judges Humphreys, Claiborne, Hastings, and Nixon, in whose trials no party commitments can be discerned, the cases of the respondents show some elements of party backing or party repudiation. This observation is unsurprising, given the purpose and practice of impeachment and trial, and given the fact that even such a political pariah as President Johnson had performed in a fashion that dispassionate observers considered questionable and worthy of investigation. Charges levied against each officer, then, had a basis in fact; the charges were not rooted just in partisan antagonism, but in real or suspected abuse of power.

It must be recorded also that faced with a grossly misbehaving officer, the House of Representatives can put partisanship entirely aside. This fact is demonstrated in the cases of Secretary Belknap, Judge Claiborne, and Judge Nixon, all of whom the House impeached unanimously. The Senate also showed itself capable of disregarding party identification. Although it found Belknap not guilty because of want of jurisdiction, only three senators voted him innocent of the charges leveled in the impeachment articles; his brother Republicans made slight effort to explain or defend his conduct. The verdict in Claiborne's case revealed a 90 percent vote for conviction in a Senate made up of 47 percent of his fellow Democrats. Nixon was convicted by a 90 percent vote in a Senate composed of a 57 percent majority of his party, Democratic. Democrat Alcee L. Hastings was impeached 413 to 5 by a House composed of 262 Democrats and 173 Republicans; the Senate, with a Democratic majority, convicted Hastings by a 72 percent vote. These examples should dispel any notion that party loyalty, although a recognizable feature in many impeachments and trials, presents an insurmountable obstacle to use of the mechanism, either to investigate or to evaluate a member of the majority party.

The trials do not provide a solid answer to the question of what constitutes "high crimes and misdemeanors." The phrase is generally interpreted as extending to misconduct not necessarily criminal. This position finds support, for example, in the trial of Robert W. Archbald in 1913. The Senate, perforce recognizing that the House of Representatives had not charged the judge with committing any criminal offenses, nevertheless found that his soliciting and acquiring favors from railroad companies transgressed both judicial ethics and anyone's concept of good behavior, whether defined or not. The Senate not only convicted Archbald but also disqualified him from ever again holding any national office. It appears logically and historically accurate to accept the interpretation that the phrase "high crimes and misdemeanors" extends to acts not necessarily indictable in court, but this interpretation cannot be claimed as universally accepted.

Another aspect of the process concerns the question of whether the official must be found guilty of willful misconduct. Proof of volitional malperformance has not been a requirement in the trials. The respondents' attorneys have usually argued that failure of the managers to demonstrate knowing misbehavior by their clients should lead to a verdict of innocent. But in several instances the Senate has not viewed proof of deliberate misconduct as essential to conviction. For example, Harry E. Claiborne's counsel leaned heavily on the claim that no evidence existed of intentional avoidance of proper income tax reporting on the judge's part. This argument did not influence the senators. They appeared to look at the consequences of the accused's actions, not at the intention with which he undertook them. Although not in the realm of certainty, a good case can be made, based on past Senate habits, that proof of willful bad behavior is not a requirement for conviction in an impeachment trial.

Recurring frequently in the trials has been the argument of the respondents' attorneys that unless the conduct complained of arose in pursuit of official duties it was not impeachable. Again, Harry E. Claiborne is the major example of this facet of the process. Obviously, he did not cheat on his income taxes as part of his judicial duties, but the Senate found him guilty by a convincing majority. Support for the position that the questioned behavior need not be performed in the suspect's official role may also be located in the trials of William Blount, Robert W. Archbald, Charles Swayne, and Walter L. Nixon, Jr.

Impeached officers have displayed persisting misconduct; only James H. Peck came before the Senate accused of just one misdeed. All the other trials have concerned several alleged malperformances, set down in articles ranging in number from four to seventeen. It is fair to assume that the Peck trial was an aberration and that, ordinarily, the House of Representatives will act only when it discovers a pattern of questionable conduct by an officer whose behavior had made him an object of impeachment.

My analysis of the history of impeachment trials discloses that the targeted officials shared the following characteristics: (1) they were generally alienated from the political mainstream; (2) they performed in an unacceptable fashion, not necessarily criminal or willful and not necessarily while performing their official duties; (3) they engaged in repeated misconduct; (4) they were males; (5) they belonged mainly to the judicial branch, entirely so in the twentieth century; and (6) they evaded impeachment, trial, or both by resigning. Three additional characteristics emerged only in the 1980s: (1) initiation of the procedure by executive and judicial action, possibly signifying abdication by Congress of its heretofore exclusive role in originating impeachments; (2) conducting an impeachment trial of an officer already tried in a court of law, a practice sanctioned by all court challenges; and (3) employment of a special Senate committee to hear evidence and report to the full Senate prior to trial.

The results of employing the impeachment procedure have not in every instance been admired, and precedents emerging from the trials are tenuous and debatable. But it can be recognized that the process has been and will continue to be of great value, not only for its often successful use but also for the fact that the threat of its employment has rid the nation of many defective officeholders who resigned when about to be investigated, about to be impeached, or about to be tried. Impeachment has been the major method of insuring accountability of life-tenured federal judges whose malperformances have made them the cardinal objects of the mechanism. The impeachment provisions of the Constitution have served to protect the public by bringing about, in one way or another, the ouster of officials engaged in betraying their trust.

Appendix

Constitutional Provisions on Impeachment

Article I, section 2, clause 5   The House of Representatives . . . shall have the sole power of impeachment.

section 3, clause 6   The Senate shall have the sole power to try all impeachments. When sitting for that purpose, they shall be on oath or affirmation. When the President of the United States is tried, the Chief Justice shall preside; and no person shall be convicted without the concurrence of two thirds of the members present.

clause 7   Judgment in cases of impeachment shall not extend further than to removal from office, and disqualification to hold and enjoy any office of honor, trust, or profit under the United States; but the party convicted shall nevertheless be liable and subject to indictment, trial, judgment, and punishment, according to law.

Article II, section 2, clause 1   [The President] shall have power to grant reprieves and pardons for offenses against the United States, except in cases of impeachment.

section 4   The President, Vice President and all civil officers of the United States, shall be removed from office on impeachment for, and

	conviction of, treason, bribery, or other high crimes and misdemeanors.
Article III, section 1	[Federal judges] shall hold their offices during good behavior. (Not an impeachment provision, but a feature in several impeachment trials.)
section 2, clause 3	The trial of all crimes, except in cases of impeachment, shall be by jury.

Notes

INTRODUCTION

1. *Judges of the United States* (Washington, D.C.: Government Printing Office, 1983), p. 126. For information on Delahay's association with Abraham Lincoln, see John G. Clark, "Mark W. Delahay: Peripatetic Politician," *The Kansas Historical Quarterly* 25 (Autumn 1959): 301–12.
2. *Congressional Globe,* 42d Cong., 3d sess., pp. 1899, 1900.
3. *Hinds' Precedents of the House of Representatives of the United States,* 5 vols. (Washington, D.C.: Government Printing Office, 1907), 3: 1010, sec. 2505.
4. *Congressional Record,* 69th Cong., 1st sess., pp. 6280–88, 6585–6608, 6643–69, 6705–37.
5. *Proceedings of the United States Senate in the Trial of Impeachment of George W. English,* Senate Document 177, 69th Cong., 2d sess., p. 25.
6. Ibid., p. 93.
7. The details included in the articles as adopted by the Judiciary Committee may be found in House of Representatives, *Impeachment of Richard M. Nixon, President of the United States,* Report no. 93–1305, 93d Cong., 2d sess., pp. 1–4, hereafter, *Nixon Impeachment Report.*
8. For the text of the pardon and other material on the Nixon presidency, see A. Stephen Boyan, Jr., *Constitutional Aspects of Watergate: Documents and Materials,* 6 vols. (Dobbs Ferry: Oceana Publications, 1976–86), 5:6.
9. House of Representatives, *Hearings of the Committee on the Judiciary,* 93d Cong., 2d sess., 1974, pp. 329–31, 445–47, 488–89.
10. *U.S. v. Nixon,* 418 U.S. 683 (1974).
11. *Nixon Impeachment Report,* p. 499.
12. See Joseph Borkin, *The Corrupt Judge* (New York: Clarkson N. Potter, 1962), pp. 219–58; Carlos J. Moorhead, quoted in *Hearings Before the Subcommittee on Courts, Civil Liberties and the Administration of Justice of the House Judiciary Committee,* 99th Cong., 2d sess., June 19, 1986, p. 4; and *Hinds' Precedents,* pp. 981–1034.

CHAPTER 1

1. For example, Senator Howell T. Heflin and Congressman Robert W. Kastenmeier had bills before the 101st Congress in 1990 to place

removal of judges in the hands of the judicial branch. See also Burke Shartel, "Federal Judges: Appointment, Supervision, and Removal—Some Possibilities Under the Constitution," *Michigan Law Review* 28 (1930): 870; Phillip B. Kurland, "The Constitution and the Tenure of Federal Judges: Some Notes from History," *University of Chicago Law Review* 36 (1969): 665; Sam J. Ervin, Jr., "Separation of Powers: Judicial Independence," *Law and Contemporary Problems* 35 (1970): 108; and Raoul Berger, *Impeachment: The Constitutional Problems* (Cambridge: Harvard University Press, 1973), chapter 4. For a valuable review of these matters, available to me only after this work was completed, see *Kentucky Law Journal* 76 (1987–88): 633–859.

Of this problem, Chief Judge Alfred T. Goodwin of the Ninth Circuit Court of Appeals wrote: "I still think impeachment . . . is the best way to maintain the quality without losing the independence of the judiciary. Any system of expedient and expeditious removal from office . . . short of impeachment could become an invitation to politically inspired purging of judges. . . . The slow, painstaking and deliberate design of impeachment . . . is probably necessary to preserve both the independence and the quality of the federal judiciary." Letter to author, December 17, 1990.

Congress passed the *Judicial Discipline and Removal Reform Act of 1990* (104 Stat.5122), an act containing two provisions of significance to the matters under consideration. The first states that the Judicial Conference, without needing to conduct its own investigation, may report to the House of Representatives that it should consider impeachment of a judge convicted of a felony who has exhausted all means of review of that conviction. To date, January 1991, Judge Harry E. Claiborne and Judge Walter L. Nixon, Jr. would be subject to this requirement.

The second provision, and one with far more potential impact, establishes a commission to study problems of discipline and removal of life-tenured judges. The thirteen-member commission is charged with evaluating alternatives to "current arrangements," including those that would require amendment of the Constitution. Its recommendations are to be submitted to Congress, the chief justice, and the president.

2. Peter Charles Hoffer and N. E. H. Hull, *Impeachment in America, 1635–1805* (New Haven: Yale University Press, 1984), p. xi; see also pp. 3–106, passim.

3. *The Federalist* (New York: Modern Library, 1937); Jonathan Elliot, *The Debates in the Several State Conventions on the Adoption of the Constitution*, 5 vols. (Philadelphia: J. B. Lippincott, 1896); Max Farrand, *The Records of the Federal Convention of 1787*, 4 vols. (New Haven: Yale University Press, 1911); Gaillard Hunt, ed., *Writings of James Madison*, 9 vols. (New York: G. P. Putnam's Sons, 1900–1910); Joseph Story, *Commentaries on the Constitution of the United States*, 2 vols. (Boston:

Little, Brown, 1905). Also valuable are Hoffer and Hull, *Impeachment*, pp. 107–90, passim; Raoul Berger, *Impeachment: The Constitutional Problems* (Cambridge: Harvard University Press, 1973), chapters 1 and 2; Office of Legal Council, Department of Justice, *Legal Aspects of Impeachment: An Overview*, February 1974, particularly Appendix 1, "The Concept of Impeachable Offense," and Appendix 2, "History of Provisions of the Constitution Relating to Impeachment"; A. Stephen Boyan, Jr., *Constitutional Aspects of Watergate: Documents and Materials*, 6 vols. (Dobbs Ferry: Oceana Publications, 1976–86), 1:401–73; and Charles L. Black, Jr., *Impeachment: A Handbook* (New Haven: Yale University Press, 1974), pp. 27–41, 49–52.

4. Berger, *Impeachment*, p. 62.
5. See Glenn R. Winters, ed., *Handbook for Judges* (Chicago: American Judicature Society, 1975), pp. 254–69.
6. Lack of good behavior was cited in the cases of Judges John Pickering, West H. Humphreys, Charles Swayne, Robert W. Archbald, George W. English, Harold Louderback, and Halsted L. Ritter. Raoul Berger argues for judicial removal of erring judges under the "good behavior" clause; he also appraises competing beliefs that only legislative removal is authorized by the Constitution. Berger, *Impeachment*, pp. 122–80.
7. The Judicial Councils Reform and Judicial Conduct and Disability Act, Public Law 96–458, 28 U.S.C. sec. 372. In 1986, 312 new complaints were filed, and 218, some of them holdovers, were dismissed as frivolous or related to the merits of a decision. United States Courts, *Annual Report of the Director of the Administrative Office*, 1986, p. 88. For a discussion of the act, see Stephen B. Burbank, "Procedural Rulemaking under the Judicial Councils Reform and Judicial Conduct and Disability Act of 1980," *University of Pennsylvania Law Review* 131 (1982): 283. For a discussion of the problems of correcting improper judicial behavior before passage of this act, see Berger, *Impeachment*, pp. 122–80, and Joseph Borkin, *The Corrupt Judge* (New York: Clarkson N. Potter, 1962), pp. 189–210.
8. When the Judiciary Committee failed to secure House approval for impeaching Andrew Johnson, the House assigned the task to the Reconstruction Committee, which succeeded in gaining adoption of a resolution to impeach the president.
9. The House had also employed a catchall article in the impeachments of Judges Robert W. Archbald, George W. English, and Harold Louderback, but in none of these instances did the dubious device affect the outcome; English resigned before trial.
10. See *Ritter v. U.S.* (84 Court of Claims 293, 1936). The Supreme Court denied a review of this case (300 U.S. 668, 1936).
11. Belknap resigned on the day the House impeached him; action was continued, and his trial in the Senate resulted in a not guilty verdict based on the assumption of most senators that they lacked jurisdiction to try a *former* officeholder.

CHAPTER 2

1. The Jeffersonians were often called Democratic-Republicans, Republicans, and, occasionally, Democrats. It was not until Andrew Jackson's administration that the title *Democratic party* became fixed. The opposition party was variously called Federalist, National Republican, and Whig; it finally became Republican in James Buchanan's administration, with a brief period as Union during Abraham Lincoln's second campaign for the presidency.

2. Information on Blount's pre-impeachment career is taken from William H. Masterson, *William Blount* (Baton Rouge: Louisiana State University Press, 1954), passim.

3. Francis Wharton, *State Trials of the United States* (New York: Burt Franklin, 1849, repr. 1970), pp. 317–21. Wharton (1820–89) was an authority on criminal law; in addition to his legal eminence he was a professor, clergyman, writer, and adviser to the State Department. Cobbett, the well-known British journalist and reformer, lived in the United States at the time of the Blount affair.

4. 5 *Annals of Congress*, 1797–1799, 1: col. 449. Sitgreaves was subsequently elected a manager for Blount's trial but resigned from the House of Representatives before the trial began. He had accepted appointment as commissioner to Great Britain to confer about British claims against the United States.

5. Ibid., cols. 449–50.

6. Ibid., col. 453. Dana, later elected a manager for Blount's trial, served in the House of Representatives from 1797 to 1810, and in the Senate from 1812 to 1821.

7. Ibid., cols. 459, 461–62, 40, 43.

8. Ingersoll had been a delegate to the Continental Congress from Pennsylvania, a member of the Constitutional Convention, and attorney general of Pennsylvania. Dallas, a successful lawyer and writer, was appointed district attorney for eastern Pennsylvania by President Jefferson and served as secretary of the Treasury under President Madison. Wharton, *State Trials*, pp. 30–31n. Charles Warren called Dallas "the most violent Republican of all lawyers at the Bar." Charles Warren, *The Supreme Court in United States History*, 2 vols., rev. ed. (Boston: Little, Brown, 1922, 1926), 1: 298.

9. 5 *Annals of Congress*, 1797–1799, 1: cols. 38, 41.

10. Ibid., col. 43. For other materials on Blount's duplicity as later revealed in British, French, and United States State Department records, see Frederick Jackson Turner, ed., "Documents on the Blount Conspiracy, 1795–1797," *American Historical Review* 10 (April 1905): 574–606.

11. 5 *Annals of Congress*, 1797–1799, 1: cols. 43–44.

12. Ibid., cols. 951, 948–49.

13. Ibid., col. 951.

14. Wharton, *State Trials*, quoting *Jefferson Correspondence*, 3:376 n. 315. Dumas Malone records that Jefferson became sympathetic toward Blount as a fellow Republican who might be a victim of partisan persecution. Jefferson said that he saw "nothing in the mode of proceeding by impeachment but the most formidable weapon for the purposes of a dominant faction that was ever contrived." Dumas Malone, *Jefferson and His Time*, 6 vols. (Boston: Little, Brown, 1948–81), 3:362. Jefferson himself used the "formidable weapon" to the advantage of his own party when the Republicans controlled the national government.

15. 5 *Annals of Congress* 1797–1799, 3: cols. 2472–2473.

16. The trial is recorded in 5 *Annals of Congress* 1797–1799, 2: cols. 2247–2416.

17. This amendment provides speedy and public trial by an impartial jury in all criminal prosecutions. Actually, the Blount attorneys referred to the amendment as the *Eighth*. The "Bill of Rights" as originally presented was composed of twelve amendments; the first two were not ratified, so the present Sixth Amendment would be in the eighth position on the list as it came from the Congress in 1789. (1 *Annals of Congress* 1789, pp. 88, 913; 1 stat. 97). The Constitution exempts impeachment from the requirement of trial by jury, Article III, section 2, clause 3. Raoul Berger argues that the Sixth Amendment provision for trial by jury in all criminal prosecutions shows that impeachment should be regarded as a removal procedure, not a criminal trial. Raoul Berger, *Impeachment: The Constitutional Problems* (Cambridge: Harvard University Press, 1973), pp. 81–83.

18. Wharton, *State Trials*, p. 263.

19. Ibid., p. 282.

20. Ibid., p. 302.

21. See Peter Charles Hoffer and N. E. H. Hull, *Impeachment in America, 1635–1805* (New Haven: Yale University Press, 1984), especially pp. 151–63.

22. Wharton, *State Trials*, p. 265.

23. Ibid., pp. 265–66.

24. Ibid., pp. 275–76.

25. Ibid., p. 292.

26. Found in Alex. J. Simpson, Jr., *A Treatise on Federal Impeachments* (Philadelphia: Law Ass'n., 1916), p. 58.

27. Wharton, *State Trials*, p. 313.

28. 5 *Annals of Congress* 1797–99, 2: col. 2318.

29. Ibid., col. 2319.

30. Ibid.

31. Hoffer and Hull, *Impeachment in America*, pp. 162, 163.

32. The West's taste in heroes and in politics was reaffirmed a few years later when Aaron Burr, under indictment in New York and New Jersey for killing Alexander Hamilton, was lionized in Nashville and New

Orleans following the end of his term as vice president. Francis Wharton noted a similarity between Blount and Burr; he observed that "both Blount and Burr were men of long political experience and tact, and gifted in an eminent degree with the art of winning and attaching adherents. Both aimed at the erection of an independent ultramontane confederacy." Wharton, *State Trials*, p. 318.

33. Ibid., p. 321. Marcus J. Wright uses exactly the same quotation, attributing it to a "writer, evidently a political opponent" of Blount, *Some Account of the Life and Services of William Blount* (Washington, D.C.: E. J. Gray, 1884), p. 135. This book is unflaggingly pro-Blount and lacks the depth and analysis of the Masterson, *William Blount*, or Wharton, *State Trials*, treatments of Blount and his career.

34. See Joseph Borkin, *The Corrupt Judge* (New York: Clarkson N. Potter, 1962) pp. 219–58; and *Hearings Before the Subcommittee on Courts, Civil Liberties, and the Administration of Justice of the House Judiciary Committee*, 99th Cong., 2d sess., June 19, 1986, p. 4.

CHAPTER 3

1. *Dictionary of American Biography*, 22 vols. (New York: Charles Scribner's Sons, 1934), 14: 563–64.

2. Ohio's admission to the Union in 1803 had increased the size of the Senate to thirty-four.

3. Dumas Malone, *Jefferson and His Time*, 6 vols. (Boston: Little, Brown, 1948–81), 4:458, 116.

4. William Plumer, *William Plumer's Memorandum of Proceedings in the United States Senate, 1803–1807*, ed. Everett Somerville Brown (New York: Macmillan, 1923), p. 101. Plumer was a delegate to the New Hampshire Constitutional Convention, a United States senator, and governor of New Hampshire.

5. Malone, *Jefferson*, 4:461.

6. Lynn W. Turner, "The Impeachment of John Pickering," *American Historical Review* 54 (1949): 490.

7. 7 *Annals of Congress*, 2d sess., 1802–1803, col. 460. Gallatin fought in the Revolutionary War, was a member of the House of Representatives (1798–1801), served as secretary of the treasury (1801–14) under both Presidents Jefferson and Madison, and undertook several foreign assignments after leaving the cabinet.

8. Ibid., col. 642.

9. 8 *Annals of Congress*, 1st sess., 1803–1804, cols. 319–22, 796. Six of the managers in the Pickering trial would also be managers in the trial of Samuel Chase (1804–5): John Boyle, George W. Campbell, Peter Early, Joseph H. Nicholson, John Randolph, and Caesar A. Rodney.

10. *Extracts from the Journal of the United States Senate in All Cases of Impeachment presented by the House of Representatives, 1798–1904.*

62d Cong., 2d sess., Document 876, vol. 32, p. 21, hereafter, *Sen. Doc. 876.*

11. Plumer, *Memorandum*, p. 97.
12. John Quincy Adams, *Memoirs*, ed. Charles Francis Adams, 12 vols. (Philadelphia: J. B. Lippincott, 1874), 1:283.
13. Plumer, *Memorandum*, p. 100. At a later date (1807) Jefferson said that he would "take no more pleasure in hanging a madman than in impeaching poor lunatic Judge John Pickering." Fawn M. Brodie, *Thomas Jefferson: An Intimate History* (New York: W. W. Norton, 1974), p. 408.
14. 8 *Annals of Congress*, 1st sess., 1803–1804, col. 362.
15. Adams, *Memoirs*, 1:299.
16. Plumer, *Memorandum*, p. 156.
17. Ibid., p. 163. Curiously, in groping for an answer to Pickering's problem, no senator mentioned Alexander Hamilton's opinion that "insanity, without any formal or express provision, may be safely pronounced to be a virtual disqualification [for a judge remaining in office]." *The Federalist*, no. 79 (New York: Modern Library, 1937), p. 514.
18. 8 *Annals of Congress*, 1st sess., 1803–1804, col. 333.
19. Ibid.
20. Ibid., cols. 328–29.
21. Ibid., col. 336; the depositions are recorded in cols. 334–42.
22. Ibid., cols. 343–45.
23. Ibid., cols. 345–53.
24. Plumer, *Memorandum*, pp. 178–79.
25. 8 *Annals of Congress*, 1st sess., 1803–1804, col. 362.
26. *Sen. Doc. 876*, 32:32.
27. 8 *Annals of Congress*, 1st sess., 1803–1804, col. 363.
28. Ibid., cols. 364–66.
29. Ibid., col. 366.
30. Adams, *Memoirs*, 1:309.
31. 8 *Annals of Congress*, 1st sess., 1803–1804, col. 366.
32. Ibid., col. 368. The three senators who had voted for Pickering's impeachment in the House and afterward voted for his conviction in the Senate were Israel Smith (Vermont), John Smith (New York), and Samuel Smith (Maryland). Although John Smith asked to be excused from voting, his name appears among the nineteen who voted guilty.
33. Raoul Berger, *Impeachment: The Constitutional Problems* (Cambridge: Harvard University Press, 1973), p. 186.
34. For efforts to remove judges by means other than impeachment see Tydings Bill, 1506, 91st Cong., 1st sess., 1969; and H.R. 146, 77th Cong., 1st sess., 1941–1942, Report no. 921. In the latter attempt to deal with the problem of removal of a judge, the point was made that "It is a governmental absurdity that the cumbersome machinery of impeachment must be resorted to in order to process the ouster of a district or circuit judge" (p. 2). Senator Strom Thurmond (Republican, South Carolina) made a similar comment in 1986, following conviction of Judge Harry

Claiborne, saying it was "outrageous that the time and energies of Congress are spent on this tedious and unwarranted process." *Hearings Before the Subcommittee on the Constitution,* Senate, 99th Cong., 2d sess., Serial no. J, 99–126, p. 7. Nothing came of these, or other, efforts to modify the procedure.

35. Plumer, *Memorandum,* p. 101.
36. Malone, *Jefferson,* 4:463.
37. *Trial of Samuel Chase,* 2 vols. (New York: DaCapo Press, 1970), 2:256.
38. *Trial of Andrew Johnson,* 2 vols. (New York: DaCapo Press, 1970), 2:270.
39. Malone, *Jefferson,* 4:458.
40. For a review of the Pickering case and the tensions between Republicans and Federalists, see Peter Charles Hoffer and N. E. H. Hull, *Impeachment in America, 1635–1805* (New Haven: Yale University Press, 1984), pp. 207–20.

CHAPTER 4

1. *Dictionary of American Biography,* 22 vols. (New York: Charles Scribner's Sons, 1931), 4:34–37.
2. Dumas Malone, *Jefferson and His Time,* 6 vols. (Boston: Little, Brown, 1948–81), 4:465. See also James Haw et al., *Stormy Patriot: The Life of Samuel Chase* (Baltimore: Maryland Historical Society, 1980), pp. 103–9; and Peter Charles Hoffer and N. E. H. Hull, *Impeachment in American, 1635–1805* (New Haven: Yale University Press, 1984), pp. 228–30.
3. The Alien and Sedition Acts (1798) were passed by the Federalists during a period of threatened war with France; the Sedition Act was designed to punish those who conspired, or even spoke, against the administration or Congress.
4. Francis Wharton, *State Trials of the United States* (New York: Burt Franklin, 1849, repr. 1970), pp. 46–47.
5. Wharton, *State Trials,* p. 42.
6. Charles Warren, *The Supreme Court in United States History,* 2 vols. (Boston: Little, Brown, 1922, 1926), 1:273.
7. Albert J. Beveridge, *The Life of John Marshall,* 3 vols. (Boston: Houghton Mifflin, 1919), 3:169.
8. Warren, *Supreme Court,* 1:286.
9. Lynn W. Turner, *William Plumer of New Hampshire* (Chapel Hill: University of North Carolina Press, 1962), p. 156.
10. Beveridge, *John Marshall,* 3:160. Dumas Malone, however, noted that the belief that Marshall was the real target was "warranted by nothing he himself [Jefferson] or his ministers said," although statements of some of his supporters made the claim credible. Malone, *Jefferson,* 4:469–70. For an appraisal of Republican intentions toward Federalist

jurists in Pennsylvania as exemplified in the impeachment of Judge Addison, see Hoffer and Hull, *Impeachment,* pp. 191–205.

11. Malone, *Jefferson,* 4:116.

12. John Quincy Adams, *Memoirs,* 12 vols., ed. Charles Francis Adams (Philadelphia: J. B. Lippincott, 1874), 1:322.

13. *Trial of Samuel Chase,* 2 vols. (New York: DaCapo Press, 1970), 1:2–3, hereafter, *Trial.*

14. *Trial,* 1:3–4. Only four Republicans were among the thirty-two congressmen who voted against adopting the resolution to impeach.

15. Warren, *Supreme Court,* 1:281–82 n1.

16. Like William Blount's counsel, the House managers cited the *Eighth* Amendment; it is clear in both cases that the Sixth Amendment was meant. Chase noted the error in his opening reply, *Trial,* 1:26.

17. *Trial,* 1:5. Fries was subsequently pardoned by President John Adams, who thought Fries's conduct was threatening and highhanded but feared that to construe as treason "every sudden, ignorant, inconsiderable heat among a part of the people wrought up by political dispute" would be very dangerous. Page Smith, *John Adams,* 2 vols. (Garden City: Doubleday, 1962), 2:1003.

18. Smith, *John Adams,* pp. 5–6. The Callender trial is reported in Wharton, *State Trials,* pp. 688–721. President Jefferson pardoned Callender and all others imprisoned under the Sedition Act as soon as he became president.

19. Ibid.

20. Both of Fries's trials are recorded in Wharton, *State Trials,* pp. 458–648.

21. Fawn M. Brodie, *Thomas Jefferson: An Intimate History* (New York: W. W. Norton, 1974), p. 315.

22. Wharton, *State Trials.,* p. 690. Before Chase's impeachment, Callender drowned, possibly a suicide.

23. James Morton Smith, "Sedition in the Old Dominion," *Journal of Southern History* 20 (May 1954):158.

24. Burr wrote to his son-in-law following Chase's trial, "In New York I am to be disfranchised, and in New Jersey hanged. Having substantial objections to both, I shall not, for the present, hazard either, but shall seek another country." James Parton, *The Life and Times of Aaron Burr* (New York: Mason Brothers, 1858, repr. New York: Johnson Reprint, 1967), p. 379.

25. *Trial,* 1:14.

26. Ibid., 1:18.

27. Luther Martin would, in addition, be counsel for Aaron Burr in the latter's treason trial. Martin's excessive drinking was well known. Five years after the Chase trial he appeared before Justice Chase in a drunken condition. Chase reproved Martin for prostituting his talents, and Martin said: "Sir, I never prostituted my talents except when I defended you and Colonel Burr, a couple of the greatest rascals in the world." Paul S.

Clarkson and R. Samuel Jett, *Luther Martin of Maryland* (Baltimore: Johns Hopkins Press, 1970), p. 280. Robert Goodloe Harper had participated in all of the federal impeachments, acting as a manager against William Blount, a spokesman for John Pickering, and now a counsel for Samuel Chase. Joseph Hopkinson, associated with Daniel Webster in the Dartmouth College case, served as a Federalist in the House of Representatives from 1815 to 1819. Philip Barton Key, a Federalist congressman (1807–13), fought with the British during the Revolution. Charles Lee, appointed attorney general by President Washington shortly before the end of his term as president, served in that post throughout John Adams's administration; he joined Luther Martin as defense counsel for Aaron Burr.

28. *Trial*, 1:47–48.
29. Ibid., 1:7.
30. Ibid., 1:95–96; also, Exhibit 8, *Trial*, appendix, 2:v–viii, 95.
31. Ibid., 1:96.
32. Ibid., 1:102–3.
33. Ibid., 1:124.
34. Hay, subsequently a prosecutor in Aaron Burr's treason trial, was referred to as "the plodding and conscientious but not overly brilliant son-in-law of James Monroe. He was politically and personally devoted to Jefferson." Clarkson and Jett, *Luther Martin*, p. 246.
35. *Trial*, 1:181, 183.
36. Ibid., 1:194.
37. Ibid., 1:240.
38. Ibid., 1:194.
39. Ibid., 1:289.
40. Ibid., 1:214.
41. Ibid., 1:217.
42. Harper was disliked by the Republicans because he had abandoned that party to become a Federalist; he served as House floor leader during John Adams's administration. Lynn W. Turner has described him as "brilliant, pompous, insolent," "The Impeachment of John Pickering," *American Historical Review* 54 (1949): 497.
43. *Trial*, 1:225.
44. Ibid., 1:228.
45. Ibid., 1:231.
46. Ibid., 1:244.
47. Ibid., 1:257, 258.
48. William Plumer, *William Plumer's Memorandum of Proceedings in the United States Senate, 1803–1807*, ed. Everett Somerville Brown (New York: Macmillan, 1923), p. 291.
49. *Trial*, 1:267.
50. Ibid.
51. Ibid., 1:294–95.
52. Ibid., 1:305–6.

53. Ibid., 1:307.
54. Ibid., 1:317.
55. Ibid., 1:345.
56. Ibid., 1:346–47.
57. Ibid., 1:350, 354.
58. Ibid., 1:4.
59. Ibid., 1:25.
60. Ibid., 1:121, 130. Wirt, Nicholas, and Hay had been Callender's attorneys.
61. Henry Adams, *John Randolph* (Boston: Houghton, Mifflin, 1896), p. 141.
62. *Trial*, 2:136.
63. Ibid., 2:177.
64. Ibid., 2:213.
65. Ibid., 2:216. Wirt would be chief counsel for James H. Peck in the latter's impeachment trial that followed Chase's twenty-five years later, a prosecutor in the treason trial of Aaron Burr, and attorney general under presidents James Monroe and John Quincy Adams.
66. Plumer, *Memorandum*, p. 300.
67. *Trial*, 2:250.
68. Ibid., 2:255.
69. Ibid.
70. Ibid., 2:257.
71. Ibid., 2:317.
72. Ibid., 2:327.
73. Ibid., 2:330.
74. Ibid., 2:332.
75. Ibid., 2:335.
76. Beveridge, *John Marshall*, 3:207.
77. *Trial*, 2:365.
78. Ibid., 2:448–49.
79. Beveridge, *John Marshall*, 3:174–75; Malone, *Jefferson*, 4:471.
80. *Trial*, 2:452. This position had a brief resuscitation following Judge Claiborne's trial in 1986.
81. Ibid.
82. Beveridge, *John Marshall*, 3:581.
83. Adams, *Memoirs*, 1:359; Plumer, *Memorandum*, p. 302.
84. Ibid., p. 308.
85. *Trial*, 2:492.
86. Adams, *Memoirs*, 1:364.
87. 8 *Annals of Congress*, 2d sess., 1805, p. 1213.
88. Plumer, *Memorandum*, p. 311.
89. Adams, *Memoirs*, 1:365.
90. For a discussion of the Yazoo controversy and its final resolution in *Fletcher v. Peck* (6 Cranch 87, 1810) see C. Peter Magrath, *Yazoo, Law and Politics in the New Republic* (Providence: Brown University Press, 1966).

CHAPTER 5

1. The term *Democrat* had become common for the Jacksonians by this time; however, not all "Democrats" were Jackson supporters or legatees of Jefferson. The National-Republicans and Federalists, later Whigs, were the opposition. But party labels and party loyalties were far from fixed at this time. See Roy F. Nichols, *The Invention of the American Political Parties* (New York: Macmillan, 1967).

2. Louis Houck, *A History of Missouri*, 3 vols. (Chicago: R. R. Donnelley and Sons, 1908), 3:21.

3. Rene Auguste Chouteau was a founder of St. Louis in 1764. His descendants were prominent in the economic, political, and social circles of the state in the period of the land claim cases.

4. J. F. Darby, *Personal Recollections* (St. Louis: G. I. Jones, 1880), p. 13.

5. Reviewed in *Soulard's Heirs v. the United States*, 10 Peters 100 (1836): 100–102.

6. Summarized in Arthur J. Stansbury, *Report of the Trial of James H. Peck* (Boston: Hilliard, Gray, 1833), p. 12, hereafter, *Trial*.

7. *Trial*, pp. 33–34.

8. Ibid., pp. 50–51.

9. Ibid., p. 3.

10. Ibid., p. 50.

11. Ibid., pp. 50, 23.

12. Ibid., pp. 33–34.

13. Ibid., p. 100.

14. Ibid., p. 86.

15. John Quincy Adams recorded a conversation with Chief Justice John Marshall in 1830, after *Soulard* had been appealed and before the Supreme Court ruled on the matter. Marshall asked Adams if the Spanish government could supply authentic copies of land grants because "the Supreme Court had before them questions upon the validity of large land-grants in Missouri, and were much perplexed to ascertain the authenticity of the titles." Adams thought the copies could not be supplied and told Marshall that much fraud and bribery had occurred. He added that the mere request for records might cause more fabrications. John Quincy Adams, *Memoirs*, 12 vols., ed. Charles Francis Adams (Philadelphia: J. B. Lippincott, 1874), 8:200.

16. *Trial*, p. 5. Scott and Benton split when Scott supported John Quincy Adams in 1825 despite Benton's insistence that the voters of Missouri demonstrably preferred Andrew Jackson and that Congressman Scott ought to vote in accordance with his state's wishes when the disputed presidential election of 1824 was decided by the House of Representatives. Scott voted for Adams.

17. Buchanan had an extensive public career. He fought in the War of 1812, served as a state assemblyman, was a member of the United States House of Representatives (1821–31), appointed minister to Russia by

President Jackson and to Great Britain by President Pierce, elected as a Democrat to the Senate serving from 1834 to 1845, appointed secretary of state under President Polk, and elected fifteenth president of the United States (1857–61).

18. *Trial*, p. 6.
19. Ibid., p. 15; the entire statement is printed on pp. 11–45.
20. Ibid., p. 14.
21. Ibid., p. 16.
22. Ibid., p. 20. Four years later, in 1836, the Supreme Court gave its opinion. It overruled Judge Peck and granted all land claimed by the Soulard heirs except that which had become property of the United States. *Soulard v. United States*, 10 Peters 100 (1836). Between Peck's ruling and its reversal Congress had passed an act (1832) that admitted the validity of all the inchoate land claims. Thomas Hart Benton, *Thirty Years' View*, 2 vols. (New York: D. Appleton, 1854), 1:280.
23. Benton, *Thirty Years' View*, p. 45.
24. Ibid., pp. 45–46.
25. Ibid., pp. 46–47.
26. See Charles Warren, *The Supreme Court in United States History*, 2 vols. (Boston: Little, Brown, 1922, 1926), 1:652–85.
27. In the Blount, Pickering, and Chase trials, the Senate called itself the High Court of Impeachments; in the Peck, Humphreys, and Johnson trials, the High Court of Impeachment. Ten years later Tyler would become a target of impeachment:

> By repeated use of his veto power and his appointing and removal powers, Tyler completely frustrated the legislative program of the Whig party. . . . A committee headed by former president John Quincy Adams, then a member of the House, reported that Tyler's misconduct deserved impeachment, but failed to recommend the process because of the lack of votes to convict in the Senate. The House accepted the report by a majority of 100 to 80, thus implying that Tyler was impeachable. When nine formal articles of impeachment were presented, however, the House defeated a motion to appoint a committee to investigate, again, because of expected failure of conviction in the Senate.

C. Vann Woodward, ed., *Responses of the Presidents to Charges of Misconduct* (New York: Delacorte Press, 1974), p. xxiv.
28. *Trial*, pp. 51, 52.
29. Wirt, a prominent lawyer, was attorney general of the United States from 1817 to 1829 under Presidents James Monroe and John Quincy Adams. He had been counsel for James Callender in the latter's trial before Justice Chase and prosecutor in the treason trial of Aaron Burr.
30. *Trial*, p. 62.
31. Ibid., p. 82.
32. Ibid.

33. Ibid., p. 83.
34. Ibid., p. 85.
35. Ibid., pp. 93, 101.
36. Ibid., p. 102.
37. Ibid.
38. Ibid., p. 116.
39. Ibid., p. 164. The quotation is from the testimony of Arthur L. Magenis, an attorney for Lawless at the contempt hearing.
40. Geyer, destined to defeat Thomas Hart Benton in the 1850 Senate race, served in the Senate from 1851 to 1857; he would serve as the slave-owner's counsel in the Dred Scott case.
41. *Trial*, p. 175.
42. Ibid., p. 170.
43. Darby, *Recollections*, pp. 170–71.
44. *Trial*, p. 285.
45. Ibid., p. 190.
46. Ibid.
47. Ibid., p. 211. Pettis won election to the House of Representatives in 1828 with Thomas Hart Benton's endorsement.
48. Ibid., p. 205.
49. Ibid., p. 198.
50. Ibid., p. 305.
51. Ibid., pp. 308, 310.
52. Ibid., p. 324.
53. Ibid., p. 328.
54. Ibid., p. 485. William Wirt's speech was printed as an appendix to the *Trial of James H. Peck* because it was not received by the printer in time to be included in its proper place in the record; hence, the page numbers are misleading because they are higher than the page numbers of the managers' rebuttal, which actually followed Wirt's summary.
55. Ibid., p. 543.
56. Ibid., p. 528.
57. Ibid., p. 544.
58. Ibid., p. 552.
59. Ibid., p. 427.
60. Ibid., p. 429.
61. Ibid., p. 473.
62. One of those voting not guilty was Littleton W. Tazwell (Democrat, Virginia), whose father had cast the lone Senate vote against expelling William Blount. Only one senator, Samuel Smith (Democrat, Maryland), had previously acted as a national impeachment judge. Smith voted guilty in the trials of John Pickering, Samuel Chase, and James H. Peck.
63. Adams, *Memoirs*, 8:306.
64. *Trial*, p. 474.

65. 4 stat. 487, March 2, 1831; subsequently replaced by 36 stat. 1163, March 3, 1911. The replacement retains the requirements of Buchanan's law.

66. Charles B. Davis, "Judge James Hawkins Peck," *Missouri Historical Review* 27 (October 1932): 14–15.

CHAPTER 6

1. Biographical information on the Humphreys family was found in Frederick Humphreys, *The Humphreys Family in America* (New York: Humphreys Print, 1883), pp. 1043–48.

2. Oliver P. Temple, *Notable Men of Tennessee, from 1833 to 1875, Their Times and Their Contemporaries* (New York: Cosmopolitan Press, 1912), pp. 35–36.

3. *House Report No. 44*, 37th Cong., 2d sess., p. 1. Maynard, a supporter of the Union, was elected to three Congresses as a member of the American party (1857–63). When Tennessee reentered the Union, he served as a Republican in the House of Representatives (1866–75).

4. The *Globe* merely reports that the impeachment resolution "was agreed to." *Congressional Globe*, 37th Cong., 2d sess., pt. 3, p. 1966, hereafter, *Globe*.

5. Grow, a congressman from Pennsylvania, was elected as a Free-Soil Democrat and subsequently reelected as a Republican.

6. Hamlin served in the House of Representatives (1843–47) and in the Senate (1848–57) as a Democrat. He became a Republican in 1856, and was elected governor of Maine as that party's candidate. After his term as Lincoln's vice president (1861–65), he served again in the Senate (1869–81).

7. *Globe*, 37th Cong., 2d sess., pt. 4, p. 2042.

8. Ibid., p. 2943.

9. Ibid.

10. Ibid., pt. 3, p. 1966.

11. Ibid., pt. 4, p. 2946.

12. Ibid., p. 2947.

13. Ibid.

14. Ibid., p. 2948. Brownlow, sometimes called the "fighting parson," subsequently served as governor of Tennessee (1865–69) and as a Republican senator from Tennessee (1869–75). He was succeeded in the Senate by his longtime foe Andrew Johnson. Brownlow's public life is described by his friend and political ally Oliver P. Temple in *Notable Men of Tennessee*, pp. 271–356.

15. Ibid., p. 2949.

16. Votes on the articles are listed in *Globe*, pt. 4, pp. 2949–50. Henry S. Lane (Republican, Indiana) came in after the vote had been taken; he

was recorded at a later time and voted guilty on every article. Hence, the total on Part 2 of Article 6, listed in the *Globe* as *eleven* guilty, became *twelve* following Senator Lane's tardy vote.

17. *Globe*, pt. 4, p. 2951. Both Trumbull and Grimes would later disappoint their Republican allies by voting Andrew Johnson not guilty in his impeachment trial.

18. Ibid., p. 2953.

19. Ibid.

20. Humphreys, *Humphreys Family*, p. 1047.

CHAPTER 7

1. The terms *radical* and *moderate* designate commonly opposing views on Reconstruction policy. Moderate Republicans (Secretary of State William Seward and Senators James Grimes, William Fessenden, John Sherman, and James R. Doolittle, for examples) generally sought prompt restoration of the former Confederate states, opposed confiscation of rebel property, were wary of or opposed to black suffrage, and favored states rights and noninterference in internal state governance. Radical Republicans (Senators Charles Sumner and Benjamin Wade, Congressmen Benjamin Butler and Thaddeus Stevens, for examples) favored an active policy to secure black legal and political equality, complete restructuring of the southern states, and exertion of national power to assure that former rebels did not reassume control in the South. For a thorough analysis of the positions of the moderates and the radicals, see Michael Les Benedict, *A Compromise of Principle* (New York: W. W. Norton, 1974).

2. Ulysses S. Grant, *Personal Memoirs of U.S. Grant*, 2 vols. (New York: Charles L. Webster, 1886), 2:510.

3. Edward McPherson, *The Political History of the United States of America during the Period of Reconstruction*, 2d ed. (Washington, D.C.: Solomons and Chapman, 1875), p. 45. McPherson was clerk of the House of Representatives during the Civil War and Reconstruction periods.

4. McPherson, *Political History*, p. 62.

5. All biographers of Johnson describe the inaugural performance in similar fashion. Lincoln said that Johnson had made a bad slip at the inauguration but was not a drunkard; Hannibal Hamlin, outgoing vice president, who had supplied Johnson with the liquor he requested at the inaugural ceremony, said that Johnson was a sober man. Lately Thomas, *The First President Johnson* (New York: William Morrow, 1968), p. 103.

6. This question was not definitely answered until the Supreme Court decision *Texas v. White* (7 Wall, [74 U.S.] 700, 1869). Chief Justice Salmon P. Chase, in an oft-quoted pronouncement, held that "The

Constitution, in all its provisions, looks to an indestructible Union, composed of indestructible States. When, therefore, Texas became one of the United States, she entered into an indissoluble relationship" (725–26).

7. Johnson's amnesty proclamation, printed in McPherson, *Political History*, pp. 9–10, was much like Lincoln's. It exempted from amnesty high Confederate civil or military officers, those who had resigned from federal posts to serve the South, and any rebel worth $20,000. Johnson added the last exemption, but he also stated that he would receive applications for pardons from the exempted groups, who began in great numbers to ask for, and get, their pardons from the president. By May 1866, Johnson had pardoned about twenty-one thousand former Confederates who fell within the "exempt" classification. John Hope Franklin, *Reconstruction After the Civil War* (Chicago: University of Chicago Press, 1961), p. 34.

8. Article I, section 3.

9. McPherson, *Political History*, p. 55.

10. Ibid., p. 134.

11. Ibid., pp. 176–77. The act had passed 22 to 10 in the Senate and 112 to 41 in the House; it was repassed over Johnson's veto 35 to 11 in the Senate and 138 to 40 in the House.

12. Benjamin P. Thomas and Harold M. Hyman, *Stanton: The Life and Times of Lincoln's Secretary of War* (New York: Alfred A. Knopf, 1962), p. 526.

13. McPherson, *Political History*, p. 187. Benjamin Perley Poore, Washington correspondent for the *Boston Journal* and other papers, described Ashley as "a man of the lightest mental calibre and most insufficient capacity, he constituted himself the chief impeacher, and assumed a position that should have been held by a strong-nerved, deep-sighted, able man." *Perley's Reminiscences of Sixty Years in the National Metropolis*, 2 vols. (Philadelphia: Hubbard Brothers, 1886), 2:202.

14. *Congressional Globe*, 39th Cong., 2d sess., pt. 1, p. 320, hereafter, *Globe*.

15. McPherson, *Political History*, pp. 264–65.

16. Thomas and Hyman, *Stanton*, p. 560.

17. McPherson, *Political History*, pp. 282–92.

18. Ibid., p. 287. The general, already being talked about as a presidential candidate, may have been warned by the radical Republicans to detach himself from any association with the embattled president.

19. James G. Blaine, *Twenty Years of Congress: From Lincoln to Garfield*, 2 vols. (Norwich: Henry Bell Publishing, 1886), 2:350.

20. Hans L. Trefousse, *Impeachment of a President* (Knoxville: University of Tennessee Press, 1975), p. 70.

21. The House assigned impeachment activities to the Reconstruction Committee because the Judiciary Committee had failed to secure a House vote favoring Johnson's impeachment.

22. *Globe*, 40th Cong. 2d sess., pt. 2, p. 1400; *Trial of Andrew Johnson* 3 vols. (New York: DaCapo Press, 1970), 1:2, hereafter, *Trial*.

23. Four congressmen—Samuel Cary (Ohio), Julius Hotchkiss (Connecticut), Charles E. Phelps (Maryland), and Thomas E. Stewart (New York), all of whom voted against the impeachment—are variously listed as Independent Republican, Unionist, Conservative Republican, or in Hotchkiss's case as Republican. These affiliations might seem to deny the all-party vote, but do not. I am greatly indebted to Michael Les Benedict (letter of May 12, 1978) for pointing out that all of these men were identified with the pro-Johnson forces and became Democrats, caucused with the Democrats, or were at least in no significant respect identified with the Republicans. Stewart is a possible exception to the solid party vote. Although he was elected as a conservative (pro-Johnson) Republican, he voted for the Republican candidate (Colfax) for speaker. *Globe*, 40th Cong., 1st sess., p. 4.

24. Benedict, *Compromise*, pp. 27–28, 91, 214, 245.

25. George S. Boutwell, *Reminiscences of Sixty Years in Public Affairs*, 2 vols. (New York: Greenwood Press, 1968), 2:10. For a study of Stevens's extensive political career, see Fawn M. Brodie, *Thaddeus Stevens: Scourge of the South* (New York: W. W. Norton, 1959).

26. Butler started his political life as a Democrat and supported Jefferson Davis for that party's presidential nomination in 1860; Butler said, "I voted fifty-seven times for the nomination of Jefferson Davis," an oft-quoted boast frequently used against him. Clement Eaton, *Jefferson Davis* (New York: Free Press, 1977), p. 116. For a thorough study of Butler's life, see Hans L. Trefousse, *Ben Butler: The South Called Him Beast!* (New York: Twayne Publishers, 1957).

27. Curtis dissented in the Dred Scott case and resigned from the Court soon after that decision. Evarts was subsequently attorney general under Johnson for eight months from 1868 to 1869; secretary of state, (1877–81) in Rutherford B. Hayes's administration; and a United States senator, (1885–91).

28. *Trial*, 1:4, 6–10.

29. Ibid., 1:11.

30. Benedict, *Compromise*, p. 28; Benedict's classification system is detailed on pp. 28–29.

31. The Tennessee legislature supported the impeachment, and all but one of the Tennessee congressmen (Isaac R. Hawkins) had voted for it in the House. The two senators from Tennessee—Andrew Johnson's son-in-law David Patterson, a Democrat, and Joseph Fowler, a Republican—both voted Johnson not guilty when the vote was taken at the end of the trial. Fowler, usually associated with the radicals, was denounced by them as a "nineteenth-century Judas" when he voted for acquittal. Stanley J. Folmsbee, Robert E. Corlew, and Enoch L. Mitchell, *Tennessee: A Short History* (Knoxville: University of Tennessee Press, 1964), p. 360.

32. *Trial*, 3:360–88. References were also made concerning the actual structure of the Senate during an impeachment. Was it the Senate trying an impeachment or a court trying an impeachment?
33. Ibid., 3:388–401. Wade did not vote at all during the trial but did vote Johnson guilty at the trial's end.
34. *Trial*, 1:19–20.
35. Ibid., 1:36. Only Davis's colleague from Kentucky, Thomas C. McCreery, a Democrat, joined him in the yes column.
36. Ibid., pp. 6–10.
37. Congress repealed the act in 1887. In *Myers v. United States* (272 U.S. 52, 1926) the Supreme Court rejected the principle on which the act was based.
38. *Trial*, 1:8.
39. Ibid., 1:37–68.
40. Ibid., 1:82.
41. Ibid., 1:87–147.
42. Ibid., 1:698.
43. *Trial*, 2:324.
44. *Trial*, 1:88.
45. *Trial*, 3:249.
46. *Trial*, 1:409.
47. Ibid., 1:115, 117.
48. Ibid., 1:175–86.
49. Ibid., 1:185. The Senate adopted this rule by a vote of thirty-one to nineteen (p. 186). All twelve Democrats voted yes; they were joined by nineteen Republicans.
50. Ibid., 1:187–88. Chase gave only one other casting vote in the trial, and that on a motion to adjourn (p. 276).
51. Ibid., for examples, 1:210–11, 431–32, 439–49.
52. Ibid., 1:439.
53. Ibid., 1:281–351.
54. Ibid., 1:327.
55. Ibid., 1:351–71, 375–97, 537–97, 653–63, 729–36.
56. Benedict, in *The Impeachment and Trial of Andrew Johnson* (New York: W. W. Norton & Company, 1973), pp. 162–64, questions the correctness of the lists presented by both sides.
57. *Trial*, 1:377–414.
58. Ibid., 1:386.
59. Ibid., 1:404.
60. Ibid., 1:405–7.
61. *Trial*, 2:326.
62. This act divided the rebel states into five military districts to be commanded by a general appointed by the president and authorized to protect "all persons in their rights of person and property, to suppress insurrection, disorder, and violence" and to institute military tribunals

when necessary. For the text of the act and of the supplemental act of the 40th Congress, see McPherson, *Political History*, pp. 191–94. The bill had been repassed over Johnson's veto 138 to 51 in the House and 38 to 10 in the Senate; all ten no votes in the Senate were cast by Democrats. Ibid., p. 173.

63. *Trial*, 3:217. Henry Wilson (Massachusetts) was elected vice president in Grant's second administration; he died in midterm (1875).
64. Ibid., 3:257.
65. Ibid., 3:318.
66. *Trial*, 2:111.
67. *Trial*, 1:470.
68. Ibid., 1:460–508, 517–31.
69. Ibid., 1:701. The vote was twenty-six to eighteen. All ten Democrats who voted, joined by eight Republicans, favored admitting the testimony.
70. Ibid., 1:629.
71. Ibid., 1:631–32.
72. Found in Robert B. Warden, *An Account of the Private Life and Public Services of Salmon Portland Chase* (Cincinnati: Wilstach, Baldwin, 1874), p. 685.
73. *Trial*, 2:14–67.
74. Ibid., 2:66–67.
75. Ibid., 2:116–17.
76. Ibid., 2:297.
77. *Trial*, 1:90.
78. *Trial*, 2:152–53.
79. Ibid., 2:178.
80. Ibid., 2:219–30. "Mr. Manager Stevens read a portion of his argument standing at the Secretary's desk; but after proceeding a few minutes, being too feeble to stand, obtained permission to take a seat, and having read nearly half an hour from a chair until his voice became almost too weak to be heard, handed over his manuscript to Mr. Manager Butler, who concluded the reading." Ibid., 2:230.
81. Ibid., 2:209.
82. *Trial*, 1:364. President Johnson's communications to the Senate concerning Stanton's suspension and the Grant and Thomas appointments are reprinted on pp. 148–54 and 155–57.
83. *Trial*, 2:226.
84. Ibid., 2:228.
85. Ibid.
86. Ibid., 2:230.
87. Ibid., 2:233–34.
88. Ibid., 2:251–52.
89. Ibid., 2:271.
90. Ibid., 2:300.
91. Ibid., 2:391.

92. Ibid., 2:409.
93. Ibid., 2:469.
94. Ibid., 2:486–87.
95. Ibid., 2:489.
96. Ibid., 2:498.
97. McPherson *Political History*, pp. 263, 264. Stanton subsequently campaigned for Grant, was appointed by him to the Supreme Court in 1869, and was promptly confirmed by the Senate. He died on December 20, 1869, before joining the Court.
98. *Globe*, 40th Cong., 2d sess., p. 3786.
99. Ibid., p. 4474.
100. James A. Garfield, a Republican member of the House of Representatives (1863–80), said that Wade was "a man of violent passions, extreme opinions, and narrow views . . . a grossly profane, coarse nature who is surrounded by the worst and most violent elements in the Republican party." Found in Benedict, *Impeachment*, pp. 134–35.
101. James G. Blaine observed that "Contrary to the etiquette of the occasion, the incoming President was not escorted to the Capitol by his predecessor [because] Grant had conceived so intense a dislike of Johnson . . . that he would not officially recognize his predecessor, even so far as to drive from the White House to the Capitol in the same carriage." Blaine, *Twenty Years*, 2:422–23.
102. President Grant let it be known "that if Johnson were elected he would consider it a 'personal insult'." Folmsbee et al., *Tennessee*, p. 379.
103. Edmund G. Ross, *History of the Impeachment of Andrew Johnson* (Santa Fe: 1896, repr. New York: Burt Franklin, 1964), p. 173.
104. David Frost, *"I Gave Them a Sword": Behind the Scenes of the Nixon Interviews* (New York: William Morrow, 1978), p. 183.

CHAPTER 8

1. Judge West H. Humphreys's impeachment in 1862 may also have been unanimous, but the *Congressional Globe* reported only that the resolution "was agreed to." *Congressional Globe*, 37th Cong., 2d sess., pt. 3, p. 1966.
2. As reported by his friend and neighbor Ralph P. Lowe when he was testifying for Belknap in the latter's impeachment trial. *Proceedings of the Senate, Sitting for the Trial of William W. Belknap* (Washington, D.C.: Government Printing Office, 1876), p. 266, hereafter, *Trial*.
3. The Mrs. Belknap referred to here was actually Belknap's second wife. She was, however, the first of the two Mrs. Belknaps involved in the scandal that caused Belknap's impeachment and is referred to throughout the chapter as the first Mrs. Belknap.
4. Ben: Perley Poore, *Perley's Reminiscenses of Sixty Years in the National Metropolis*, 2 vols. (Philadelphia: Hubbard Brothers, 1886),

2:308. Poore was a journalist with a broad exposure to national affairs and to the major political figures of the period.

5. *Trial*, pp. 225, 338.

6. Ibid., p. 238.

7. This summary is based on Report no. 186, *Report of Committees*, 44th Cong., 1st sess., 1875–76.

8. *Trial*, pp. 304, 250.

9. A portion of the *Tribune* account is reprinted in *Trial*, pp. 185–86.

10. Allan Nevins, *Hamilton Fish, the Inner History of the Grant Administration*, rev. ed., 2 vols. (New York: Frederick Ungar, 1957), 2:804–6.

11. George S. Boutwell, *Reminiscences of Sixty Years in Public Service*, 2 vols. (New York: Greenwood Press, 1968), 2:231. Boutwell had been a manager in the Johnson trial and served as Grant's secretary of the treasury (1869–73). He was a senator at the time of Belknap's impeachment and trial.

12. William B. Hesseltine, *Ulysses S. Grant, Politician* (New York: Frederick Ungar, 1935), p. 266.

13. *Trial*, p. iii.

14. Ibid., p. 2, part of Article 3.

15. Ibid., pp. 306–13, passim.

16. Ibid., p. 6.

17. Ibid., p. 9.

18. Ibid., pp. 245-51, 254-55.

19. Ibid., p. 340.

20. Ibid., pp. 10–11. The nays were evenly divided between the major parties, six Republicans and six Democrats; the Anti-Monopolist, Newton Booth, made the thirteenth no vote.

21. Ibid., p. 11.

22. The 1876 election between Republican Rutherford B. Hayes and Democrat Samuel J. Tilden marked the resurgence of the Democratic party in national politics and resulted in the controversial election of Hayes by one electoral vote although Tilden had received 264,000 more popular votes then Hayes.

23. *Trial*, p. 14.

24. A demurrer alleges that even if the facts should be admitted, they are insufficient for the case to go forward. See Henry Campbell Black, *Black's Law Dictionary*, 5th ed. (St. Paul: West Publishing, 1979), p. 389; *Trial*, p. 26.

25. *Trial*, pp. 28–31.

26. Ibid., p. 30.

27. Ibid., pp. 36, 37. Both of Blount's attorneys were involved in the formative years of the nation, and Ingersoll had been a member of the Constitutional Convention. Thus, their comments deserve attention respecting the scope of the impeachment provisions.

28. Ibid., p. 42.

29. Ibid., p. 55.
30. Ibid., p. 63.
31. Ibid., p. 71.
32. Ibid., p. 294
33. Ibid., p. 59.
34. Ibid., p. 69.
35. Ibid., p. 76.
36. Contrary to Carpenter's assumption, four senators, three Republicans and the Anti-Monopolist, Booth, voted against accepting jurisdiction but found Belknap guilty at the end of the trial.
37. *Trial*, p. 181.
38. Ibid., p. 190.
39. Ibid., p. 193.
40. Ibid., p. 207.
41. Ibid., p. 220.
42. See Marvin E. Kroeker, *Great Plains Command, William B. Hazen in the Frontier West* (Norman: University of Oklahoma Press, 1976) for a study of Hazen's career and his relations with Belknap.
43. *Trial*, p. 228-30, passim.
44. Kroeker, *Great Plains*, p. 112.
45. *Trial*, p. 276.
46. Hancock, a prominent Union general, became the Democratic nominee for president in 1880; he lost the election to James A. Garfield by 9,500 votes of more than nine million votes cast.
47. *Trial*, p. 289.
48. Ibid., p. 293.
49. Ibid., p. 294.
50. Ibid., p. 300.
51. Ibid., p. 308.
52. When Matthew Carpenter was delivering the final defense argument, Senator Howe (Union Republican, New York) asked him about this discrepancy. Carpenter stated that Marsh had applied for a post in August 1870 but did not receive an appointment until after his care of Mrs. Belknap had endeared him to the secretary. Ibid., pp. 324–25.
53. Ibid., p. 316.
54. Ibid., p. 318.
55. Ibid.
56. Ibid., p. 327.
57. Ibid., p. 322.
58. Ibid., p. 339.
59. Ibid., pp. 343–57.
60. The three who voted Belknap innocent were Simon B. Conover (Florida), John J. Patterson (South Carolina), and George Wright (Iowa).
61. *Trial*, pp. 358–65.
62. Ibid., pp. 359, 365.

63. Ibid.
64. *Reports of Committees,* 44th Cong., 1st sess., 1875–76, Report no. 791, pp. 1–2.
65. Ulysses S. Grant 3d, *Ulysses S. Grant, Warrior and Statesman* (New York: William Morrow, 1969), p. 339. The author commented that the Grant family believed Belknap to be innocent.
66. Elliott Coues, ed., *Forty Years a Fur Trader on the Upper Missouri: The Personal Narrative of Charles Larpenteur, 1833–1872,* 2 vols. (New York: Francis P. Harper, 1898), 2:393n. Coues was a naturalist, historian, and army physician.

CHAPTER 9

1. *Proceedings in the Senate of the United States in the Matter of the Impeachment of Charles Swayne, Judge of the United States in and for the Northern District of Florida,* Senate Document, no. 194, 58th Cong., 3d sess. (Washington, D.C.: Government Printing Office, 1905), p. 61, hereafter, *Trial.* In 1893 the Florida legislature had unanimously passed a resolution denouncing Swayne as corrupt and demanding his impeachment. The House took no action on this request. *Congressional Record,* 58th Cong., 3d sess., vol. 39, pt. 1, pp. 247, 1023.
2. *Revised Statutes of the United States,* 2d ed. (1978), Title 13, ch. 2, sec. 551, p. 93; 28 USC sec. 134(b), 1976.
3. *Trial,* p. 61.
4. *Who's Who in America,* 1897–1942, 1:1209.
5. *Congressional Record,* vol. 39, pt. 1, p. 980.
6. Ibid.
7. Ibid., p. 1044.
8. Ibid., p. 925.
9. Ibid., pp. 214–49.
10. Ibid., pp. 248, 277. House of Representatives, *Report No. 1905,* 58th Cong., 2d sess., March 25, 1904. The three Republican dissenters were Charles E. Littlefield (Maine), Richard W. Parker (New Jersey), and James N. Gillett of California, subsequently elected governor of that state.
11. *Congressional Record,* vol. 39, pt. 1, p. 1054; and pt. 2, pp. 1057–58.
12. Frye became presiding officer when the assassination of William McKinley in 1901 elevated Vice-President Theodore Roosevelt to the presidency.
13. *Trial,* p. 18. The 1905 Senate did not concern itself over titles as had earlier Senates—it was referred to as a "court" throughout Swayne's trial.
14. Ibid., p. 37.
15. Swayne originally sentenced the two men to ten days' imprisonment, a $100 fine, and two years' disbarment. He was told by an attorney

present in the court that he could not disbar for contempt, and by Judge Don A. Pardee, when the cases came before the circuit court on appeal, that he could punish with fine or imprisonment but not both. See *Trial*, pp. 252, 286.

16. Provided by an act of 1896, 29 stat. 451, allowing "reasonable expenses . . . not to exceed $10 per day."

17. *Trial*, pp. 64–65.

18. Ibid., pp. 67–68. Later in the trial, John M. Thurston, one of Swayne's lawyers, disproved the allegation that Judge Swayne's use of the car had in any real degree depleted the railroad's assets. He demonstrated that the railroad did not rent the private car and did not have reciprocal arrangements with other lines for hauling each other's private cars. *Trial*, pp. 183–87, passim.

19. Ibid., p. 69.

20. House of Representatives, *Report No. 1905*, pp. 2, 5; also *Congressional Record*, vol. 39, pt. 1, p. 217.

21. *Trial*, p. 122. The witness, J. Emmett Wolfe, was former United States attorney for the northern district of Florida.

22. Ibid., p. 146. This was a voice vote; hence there is no record of how each senator voted.

23. *Congressional Record*, vol. 39, pt. 1, p. 215.

24. *Trial*, p. 199. The first vote, concerning attorneys' complaints about Swayne's absences from his districts, was not recorded.

25. Ibid., p. 290.

26. Ibid., p. 286.

27. Ibid., p. 319.

28. Ibid., p. 346.

29. Ibid., p. 372; the survey is recorded on pp. 373–416. The scholar was identified as Hannis Taylor, a prominent Alabama and later Washington, D.C., attorney and a prolific, if not always reliable, writer on legal and constitutional matters (see 18 D.A.B. 366). His identity as author of the brief used in Swayne's trial was revealed by Augustus Worthington, chief counsel for Robert W. Archbald in the latter's impeachment trial. *Proceedings in the Trial of Impeachment of Robert W. Archbald*, 62d Cong., 3d sess., 1912–13, vol. 17, p. 1533.

30. *Constitution*, Article I, section 3, clause 2. In 1984 Harry Claiborne, a federal district judge in Nevada on trial for filing false income tax returns, attempted to reverse the arguments of Blount's, Belknap's, and Swayne's attorneys by claiming he could not be a subject of a court trial until he had been impeached and tried. The argument failed as it had also in the case of Vice President Spiro T. Agnew in 1973.

31. *Trial*, pp. 457–77.

32. Ibid., pp. 516–34.

33. Ibid., p. 543.

34. Ibid., pp. 546–47.

35. Ibid., p. 566.

36. Ibid., p. 569.
37. Ibid., p. 594.
38. Ibid., p. 601.
39. Ibid., p. 602.
40. Ibid., p. 604.
41. Ibid., p. 615.
42. Ibid., p. 623.
43. Ibid., p. 667.
44. Ibid., p. 673.
45. Ibid., p. 672.
46. Ibid., p. 676.
47. Ibid., p. 680.
48. Jacobus Ten Broek reports that O'Neal had hired lawyers to lobby the impeachment resolution before the Florida legislature. "Partisan Politics and Federal Judgeship Impeachment since 1903," *Minnesota Law Review* 23 (1938–39): 185, 187n.14.
49. *Trial*, pp. 693–715.
50. Ibid., p. 699.
51. Ibid., p. 700.
52. Ibid., p. 712.
53. Ibid., pp. 716–25.
54. *Congressional Record*, vol. 39, pt. 4, p. 3988.
55. The five non–Southern Democrats were William A. Clark (Montana), Paris Gibson (Montana), Francis G. Newlands (Nevada), Thomas M. Patterson (Colorado), and Henry M. Teller (Colorado).
56. *Trial*, p. 713.

CHAPTER 10

1. *Who Was Who in America, 1897–1942* (Chicago: A. N. Marquis, 1942), 1:29.
2. *Proceedings in the Trial of Impeachment of Robert W. Archbald*, vols. 16, 17, 18, 62d Cong., 3d sess., 1912–13 (Washington, D.C.: Government Printing Office, 1913), 16:113; 18:1234, hereafter, *Trial*.
3. *Trial*, 18:1778. The Commerce Court had a short and ineffective existence; Congress abolished it in 1913.
4. Ibid., 16:702–3.
5. Ibid., 18:1682.
6. Ibid., 18:1793–94. Republican John Richard Farr, like Archbald a resident of Pennsylvania, cast the only vote against impeachment.
7. Ibid., 16:5–11.
8. Ibid., 16:44–59, 61–62.
9. Ibid., 16:92.
10. Ibid., 16:96. Simpson, a member of the Philadelphia bar, subsequently published *A Treatise on Federal Impeachments* (Philadelphia: Law

Association, 1916). The first sixty pages of the book set forth the brief Simpson prepared, but did not use, for the Archbald trial.

11. A culm dump is the byproduct of anthracite mining operations in which retrievable quantities of coal remain.
12. *Trial*, 16:5.
13. See *Trial*, 17:1424–25, for a summary of some states' procedures.
14. *Trial*, 16:110, 111.
15. Ibid., 16:143.
16. Ibid., 16:159, 165.
17. Ibid., 16:214–40; 255–62.
18. Ibid., 16:271–77.
19. Ibid., 16:281.
20. Ibid., 16:280.
21. Ibid., 16:336–55. This witness did not appear in person. His testimony before the Judiciary Committee was inserted in the trial record.
22. Ibid., 16:437.
23. Ibid., 16:718–19.
24. Ibid., 16:624.
25. Ibid., 16:789–99.
26. The forty-seventh, and final, prosecution witness appeared in rebuttal at the end of the trial, *Trial*, 17:1385.
27. *Trial*, 16:459, 937.
28. Ibid., 16:875–944.
29. Ibid., 16:907. The case was *Hill, Keizer and Company v. Stetler, Atlantic Reporter* 13 (1888):306.
30. Ibid. 16:908.
31. A female witness in Charles Swayne's trial, "too nervous to appear in person," had reported by deposition.
32. *Trial*, 16:971.
33. Ibid., 16:951.
34. Ibid., 16:1015.
35. Ibid., 17:1230–34.
36. Ibid., 17:1296.
37. Ibid., 17:1246.
38. Ibid., 17:1343–44.
39. Ibid., 17:1267.
40. Ibid., 17:1398–1417.
41. Ibid., 17:1426, 1439.
42. Ibid., 17:1465.
43. Ibid., 17:1479.
44. Ibid., 17:1504–05.
45. Ibid., 17:1518.
46. Ibid., 17:1538.
47. Ibid., 17:1577.
48. Ibid., 17:1585–86.
49. Ibid., 17:1597.

50. Ibid., 17:1600.
51. Ibid., 17:1614.
52. Simpson, *Treatise*, p. 67.
53. *Trial*, 17:1642.
54. Such an anomaly did not occur until 1936, in Judge Halsted L. Ritter's impeachment trial.
55. *Trial*, 17:1623.
56. Ibid., 17:1624.
57. Ibid., 17:1626. The sixty guilty votes were cast by thirty-three Republicans and twenty-seven Democrats. Two Democrats and nine Republicans comprised the eleven-member group finding Archbald innocent.
58. Ibid., 17:1628. The guilty votes were cast by twenty-four Republicans and twenty-eight Democrats. Eighteen Republicans joined by two Democrats (Thomas Paynter, Kentucky and Claude Swanson, Virginia) voted not guilty.
59. Ibid., 17:1630. The six not guilty votes came from five Republicans and one Democrat, Thomas H. Paynter.
60. Ibid., 17:1645–47. The vote on Article 13 was the lowest recorded in the trial. Those voting guilty included twenty-one Republicans and twenty-one Democrats; voting not guilty were fifteen Republicans and five Democrats.
61. The vote on Article 2 was forty-six guilty, twenty-five not guilty. *Trial*, 17:1626. On the other accusation of misconduct as a circuit court judge, that of attempting to induce the Lehigh Valley Coal Company to buy a tract of land (Article 6), the vote was twenty-four guilty, forty-five not guilty. Sixteen Republicans and eight Democrats cast the guilty votes.
62. *Trial*, 17:1650–78, passim.
63. Ibid., 17:1649. Absent or not voting were eleven Democrats and nine Republicans, of whom all but three had been excused.
64. Ibid., 17:1650.
65. Ibid., 17:1658–78, passim.
66. *Congressional Record*, 69th Cong., 1st sess., p. 6715.
67. *Trial*, 17:1658.
68. Ibid., 17:1659.
69. Cited in the House of Representatives debate on the impeachment of George W. English. *Congressional Record*, 69th Cong., 1st sess., p. 6713.
70. The convictions of Judges Alcee L. Hastings and Walter L. Nixon, Jr., both Democrats, in 1989 were also obtained in a Senate in which Democrats held a majority; their trials are summarized in the Epilogue.

CHAPTER 11

1. *Who's Who in America, 1932–1933* (Chicago: A. N. Marquis, 1934), 17:1449.

2. *Proceedings of the United States Senate in the Trial of Impeachment of Harold Louderback, United States District Judge of the Northern District of California,* 72d Cong., 2d sess., 73d Cong., 1st sess., Document 73, serial 9746, p. 88, hereafter, *Trial.*
3. *Congressional Record,* 72d Cong., 1st sess., vol. 75, pt. 11, p. 12470.
4. Ibid., 2d sess., vol. 76, pt. 5, p. 4922.
5. Ibid., p. 4913.
6. Ibid., p. 4923.
7. Ibid., pp. 4916–25.
8. Ibid., p. 4924.
9. Ibid., p. 4925.
10. *Trial,* pp. 171, 195.
11. Joseph Borkin, *The Corrupt Judge* (New York: Clarkson N. Potter, 1962), p. 13.
12. *Trial,* pp. 23, 24.
13. Ibid., pp. 4–9.
14. His brother, George D. Louderback, was professor of geology at the University of California and dean of the school's College of Letters and Science. Giving a false address when registering to vote is a felony, but the managers did not directly raise this point in their arguments during the trial.
15. The receiver's attorney, Samuel Shortridge, Jr., was the son of Samuel Shortridge (Republican, California), who served in the Senate from 1921 to 1933. Senator Shortridge had nominated Harold Louderback for the federal judgeship. *San Francisco Chronicle,* March 22, 1928, p. 4.
16. *Trial,* p. 6.
17. Ibid., p. 8.
18. Ibid., pp. 10–11.
19. Senator Johnson had not supported Louderback's appointment to be a federal district judge (*San Francisco Chronicle,* March 22, 1928, p. 4) and probably felt that his objectivity might be questioned should he serve in the trial.
20. *Trial,* p. 17.
21. Ibid., pp. 14–18.
22. Ibid., pp. 31–50.
23. Ibid., p. 33.
24. Ibid., p. 37. The contradiction is found in *Trial,* p. 738.
25. Ibid., p. 44.
26. Ibid., pp. 50–51.
27. Ibid., pp. 58–65.
28. Ibid., p. 65. The first four articles accused Louderback of misbehavior and of being guilty of a misdemeanor in office.
29. Ibid., pp. 66–75.
30. Ibid., p. 87.
31. Ibid., p. 96.

32. Ibid., p. 137.
33. Ibid., pp. 797–98; statement made by Walter H. Linforth.
34. Ibid., p. 150.
35. Ibid., p. 187.
36. Ibid., p. 195.
37. Ibid., p. 204.
38. Ibid., pp. 213–388.
39. Ibid., pp. 222–23.
40. Ibid., p. 235.
41. Ibid., p. 336.
42. Ibid., p. 341.
43. Ibid., p. 253.
44. Ibid., p. 247; the exhibits may be found on pp. 294–329.
45. Ibid., pp. 549–50.
46. Ibid., pp. 714–62.
47. Ibid., p. 738. The Louderbacks' domestic problems surfaced in May 1931, when the judge spent a six-week vacation in Japan without his wife. Asked whether she planned to sue him for divorce as had been widely rumored, she replied that she had no intention of divorcing "the husband I have helped all the way through life, the husband to whom I have been married twenty-seven years." *San Francisco Chronicle*, May 13, 1931, p. 4.
48. *Trial*, p. 741.
49. Ibid., p. 753.
50. Ibid., p. 628.
51. Ibid., p. 771.
52. Ibid., p. 772.
53. Ibid., p. 792.
54. Ibid., p. 784.
55. Ibid., p. 788.
56. Ibid., pp. 796–97.
57. Ibid., p. 797–98. The attorneys constituted the firm of Heller, Ehrmann, White, and McAuliffe, the attorneys for the stock exchange. McAuliffe had been vice president of the San Francisco Bar Association and was, at the time of the trial, its president; the complaint against Louderback was initiated by the bar association.
58. Ibid., p. 802.
59. Ibid., p. 814.
60. Ibid., p. 815.
61. Ibid., pp. 816–17.
62. Ibid., p. 819.
63. Ibid., p. 825–27.
64. Ibid., pp. 827–29.
65. Ibid., pp. 829–30.
66. Ibid., pp. 830–31.
67. Ibid., pp. 831–36.

68. Ibid., p. 837.
69. Ibid., p. 841.
70. Ibid., pp. 838–39.
71. Ibid., p. 838.
72. Ibid., p. 841.
73. *San Francisco Chronicle,* December 12, 1941, p. 15.
74. *Time,* March 13, 1936, p. 18. Found in Raoul Berger, *Impeachment: The Constitutional Problems* (Cambridge: Harvard University Press, 1973), p. 167, n. 199.

CHAPTER 12

1. *The National Cyclopedia of American Biography* (New York: James T. White, 1961), 43:549–50. Halsted Ritter's sister was Mary Ritter Beard, a well-known historian in her own right and collaborator with her husband, Charles A. Beard, on several books on American civilization.
2. *Proceedings of the United States Senate in the Trial of Impeachment of Halsted L. Ritter, United States District Judge for the Southern District of Florida.* (Washington, D.C.: Government Printing Office, 1936), p. 88, hereafter, *Trial.*
3. Robert Sherrod, "Impeachment Then: Trial by the Senate," *Washington Post,* April 7, 1974. p. C1.
4. Jacobus Ten Broek, "Partisan Politics and Federal Judgeship Impeachment since 1903," *Minnesota Law Review* 23 (1938–39): 185.
5. *Congressional Record,* 74th Cong., 2d sess., pp. 6685–86.
6. Ibid., p. 3069.
7. Ibid., p. 3088.
8. Ibid., p. 3089.
9. Ibid., p. 3083.
10. Ibid., pp. 3091–92.
11. *Trial,* p. 1.
12. Ibid., p. 6.
13. Ibid., p. 10.
14. 28 USCA 373. Articles 4, 5, 6, and 7 were amended, see *Trial,* pp. 32–36; the description in the text is of the articles as finally presented.
15. *Trial,* pp. 34–36.
16. Ibid., p. 40.
17. Ibid., p. 42.
18. Ibid., p. 50. Senator Backman's use of "duplicity" does not mean hypocrisy or deception but is a legalism for pleading two or more matters in the same count.
19. Ibid., pp. 53–76.
20. Ibid., pp. 89, 90, 91.
21. Ibid., p. 132.

22. Ibid., p. 138.
23. Ibid., pp. 178–80.
24. Ibid., p. 420.
25. Ibid., pp. 494–506.
26. Ibid., p. 495.
27. Ibid., p. 497.
28. Ibid., p. 501.
29. Ibid., p. 502.
30. Ibid., p. 504.
31. Ibid., p. 506.
32. Ibid., p. 516.
33. Ibid., pp. 535–40.
34. Ibid., p. 538.
35. Ibid., p. 539.
36. Ibid., p. 540.
37. Ibid., p. 563.
38. Ibid., p. 574.
39. Ibid., p. 584–85.
40. Ibid., p. 607.
41. Ibid.
42. Ibid., p. 617.
43. Ibid., p. 612.
44. Ibid., p. 638.
45. *New York Times*, April 18, 1936, p. 1.
46. *Trial*, p. 644.
47. Ibid., pp. 644–45. Following Ritter's trial, Congress gave serious consideration to establishing a new procedure for evaluating and removing judges—Senate Bill 4527, and House Resolution 2271, 74th Cong., 2d sess., 1936. Congress took no action on these measures; they would essentially authorize the judiciary to decide if "good behavior" had been violated.
48. Ibid., p. 658.
49. Ibid., p. 648.
50. Ibid., p. 657.
51. Ibid., p. 663.
52. *New York Times*, April 22, 1936, p. 22.
53. *Ritter v. U.S.*, 84 Court of Claims 293, 1936, p. 295. The Supreme Court denied a review of this case, 300 U.S. 668 (1936).

Chapter 13

1. Quoted in *Hearings Before the Senate Impeachment Trial Committee*, 99th Cong., 2d sess., pt. 1, p. 1140, hereafter, *Trial Committee*.

2. David Frost, *"I Gave Them a Sword": Behind the Scenes of the Nixon Interviews* (New York: William Morrow, 1978), p. 292. See also Clark R. Mollenhoff, *The Man Who Pardoned Nixon* (New York: St. Martin's Press, 1976), pp. 57–59; and Richard Nixon, *RN: The Memoirs of Richard Nixon* (New York: Grosset and Dunlap, 1978), pp. 912–18, 922–23.

3. *U.S. v. Claiborne,* 727 F.2d 842 (1984); 469 U.S. 829 (1984).

4. *U.S. v. Claiborne,* 765 F.2d 784 (1985) affirmed the judge's court conviction; the Supreme Court declined review of this decision, 475 U.S. 1120 (1986). In *U.S. v. Claiborne,* 790 F.2d 1355 (1986) the 9th Circuit denied a stay of execution of the judge's jail sentence and rejected the argument that a jurist cannot be imprisoned prior to impeachment and removal from office.

5. *Markup of House Resolution 461,* 99th Cong., 2d sess., serial 11, p. 7, hereafter, *Markup.*

6. Ibid., p. 17.

7. *Reno Gazette-Journal,* June 13, 1986, p. 5C.

8. Ibid., May 17, 1986, p. 1A.

9. *San Francisco Chronicle,* June 20, 1986, p. 16.

10. *Reno Gazette-Journal,* August 7, 1985, p. 1C.

11. *Impeachment of Judge Harry E. Claiborne,* 99th Cong., 2d sess., H.R. 461, Doc. 99–688, p. 3.

12. *Markup,* passim.

13. *Reports of the Proceedings of the Judicial Conference of the United States.* Administrative Office of the United States Courts (Washington, D.C.: Government Printing Office, 1986), pp. 41–43, 92. This was the first time the conference had acted under the authority of the Judicial Conduct and Disability Act. The Judicial Conference, a supervisory body of the federal judiciary, is composed of the chief justice of the United States, the thirteen chief judges of the courts of appeal, and twelve district judges.

14. *Reno Gazette-Journal,* July 8, 1986, p. 1C.

15. *Congressional Record,* 99th Cong., 2d sess., vol. 132, no. 95, p. 4721.

16. Ibid., pp. 4713, 4716–18.

17. *Reno Gazette-Journal,* August 4, 1986, p. 1C.

18. *Procedure and Guidelines for Impeachment Trials in the United States Senate,* rev. ed., 99th Cong., 2d sess., Doc. 99–33, rule 3.

19. *Reno Gazette-Journal,* August 4, 1986, p. 3C.

20. *Trial Committee,* pt. 1, p. 77.

21. Ibid., p. 80.

22. *Congressional Record,* 58th Cong., 3d sess., p. 3246.

23. *Trial Committee,* pp. 714, 718, 1084–85.

24. *Proceedings of the United States Senate in the Impeachment Trial of Harry E. Claiborne* (Washington, D.C.: Government Printing Office, 1987), Sen. Doc. 99–48, p. 37, hereafter, *Proceedings.*

25. *Trial Committee,* pp. 366–84; also *Addendum to Trial Committee,* pp. 1032, 1046, 1070, 2133–44. The transcript has Claiborne saying he was *not* "totally sucked in," but one of his attorneys has confirmed that the text is correct in stating that the judge claimed total confidence in Watson. William J. Raggio to author, June 27, 1987.
26. *Congressional Record,* 99th Cong., 2d sess., no. 137, pp. 15482–485.
27. Ibid., pp. 15485–487.
28. Ibid., p. 15490.
29. Ibid., pp. 15491–496.
30. *Proceedings,* p. 123. The House impeached Judge Hastings on August 4, 1988. The Senate convicted him of perjury and conspiracy on October 20, 1989 by a vote of sixty-nine to twenty-six. Hastings is the first officer found guilty by the Senate after he had been acquitted in a criminal trial (Epilogue).
31. *Congressional Record,* 99th Cong., no. 137, pp. 15496–505.
32. Ibid., p. 15504.
33. Ibid., p. 15507.
34. Ibid., no. 138, p. 15557. Claiborne filed suit in the district court in Washington, D.C., for a temporary restraining order based on the claim that the special trial committee and the refusal of the full Senate to hear witnesses were both unconstitutional. *Harry E. Claiborne v. United States Senate, et al.* (86–2780, October 8, 1986). The motion was denied, as were subsequent appeals to the Court of Appeals and to the Supreme Court. *Proceedings,* pp. 157–288
35. Ibid., no. 139, pp. 15759–762
36. Ibid., p. 15762
37. *Proceedings,* pp. 301–72
38. *Reno Gazette-Journal,* January 22, 1987, p. 1A.
39. *State Bar of Nevada v. Harry Eugene Claiborne,* 104 *Nev.,* 115, 756 P 2d. 464, 1988.
40. Ibid., 113.
41. The vote to impeach Judge West H. Humphreys was probably also unanimous, but the *Congressional Globe,* 37th Cong., 2d sess., pt. 3, p. 1966 reports only that the resolution "was agreed to."
42. *Hearings Before the Subcommittee on the Constitution of the Committee on the Judiciary, United States Senate,* 99th Cong., 2d sess., Serial no. J, 99–126, p. 7. Judge Walter L. Nixon, Jr., of Mississippi was convicted of perjury in 1986 and sentenced to five years in prison. The House impeached him unanimously on May 10, 1988, and the Senate convicted him November 3, 1989 by a vote of eighty-nine to eight. Like Judge Claiborne, Nixon was in prison when impeached and tried; both men would have been subject to Senator Thurmond's proposed amendment had it been in effect when they were impeached. Nixon's impeachment is referred to in the Epilogue.
43. Ibid., pp. 5–6.

Epilogue

1. Federal district judge Robert Aguilar (California) was indicted in 1989 for conspiracy, obstruction of justice, and leaking wiretap information. Appointed by Jimmy Carter in 1980, Aguilar, like Claiborne, Hastings, and Nixon, was a subject of a Justice Department investigation. He was convicted in August 1990 of the wiretap charge and of lying to the FBI. In February 1991, federal district judge Robert F. Collins (Louisiana), appointed to the bench in 1978 by President Carter, was indicted for bribery, obstruction of justice, and conspiracy; he was convicted of those charges in June 1991. Collins provides another instance of questionable judicial conduct in recent years—five federal judges indicted in seven years.

   In July 1991, Judge Nixon appealed his impeachment conviction on the ground that a committee, not the Senate, had heard the evidence against him. The court ruled that the sole power to try impeachments rests with the Senate; there is no recourse to courts from an impeachment conviction. Judge Hastings also challenged his Senate conviction in July 1991. He claimed that his acquittal in criminal court precluded being found guilty by the Senate.

2. On this question, see Robert S. Catz, "Removal of Federal Judges by Imprisonment," 18 *Rutgers Law Review* 103, 1986.

3. *United States v. Borders,* 693 F. 2d 1318 (1982).

4. *United States v. Hastings,* 681 F. 2d 706 (1982).

5. *United States v. Hastings,* No. 81–596–CrE79, District Court of the United States for the Southern District of Florida, 1983.

6. The Judicial Conference had also recommended that Judge Harry E. Claiborne be subject to such an inquiry, but his impeachment had already been undertaken when the House of Representatives received the recommendation. Judge Hastings unsuccessfully challenged the constitutionality of the Judicial Conduct Act, *Hastings v. Judicial Conference of the United States* (829 F. 2d 91, 1987) under the authority of which he was being investigated. An earlier case, *Chandler v. Judicial Council of the Tenth Circuit* (398 U.S. 74, 1970) had upheld a judge's being deprived of his docket by order of the Judicial Council of his circuit.

7. *Procedure for the Impeachment Trial of U.S. District Judge Alcee L. Hastings,* 101st Cong., 1st sess., Y 1.1/5: 101–1, pp. 4–5.

8. *Report of the Impeachment Trial Committee on the Articles Against Judge Alcee L. Hastings,* Senate Report 101–156, 101st Cong., 1st sess., pp. 151–60.

9. *Post Trial Memorandum of the House of Representatives,* Y 4.J 88/ 1:1M 7/15, September 15, 1989, p. 37, hereafter, *Memorandum.*

10. *Hearings Before the Senate Impeachment Trial Committee,* 101st Cong., 1st sess., Y 4 IM 7/2: 5, Hrg., 101–94, pt. 2A, pp. 2–18.

11. Ibid., pt. 2B, pp. 2209–491.

12. *Memorandum,* pp. 47–49, 96–128.

13. Ibid., p. 170.
14. *Congressional Record*, 101st Cong., 1st sess., vol. 135, no. 141, pp. 13618–626.
15. Ibid., pp. 13626–636.
16. Ibid., no. 143, pp. 13783–788.
17. These articles concerned various telephone calls relating to Hastings's sudden departure from Washington, D.C. when he learned that Borders had been arrested.
18. *Memorandum*, p. 160. The Senate found Judge Robert W. Archbald guilty on a cumulative article in 1913, but it had convicted him on five specific articles prior to the final article, making the vote on the latter superfluous.
19. *Congressional Record*, 101st Cong., 1st sess, vol. 135, no. 143, p. 13809; no. 147. p. 14203. The FBI had responded to criticism of its immediate arrest of Borders by stating that it (1) expected Borders to become a co-operative witness against Hastings because Borders had been caught committing a crime; (2) feared for the safety of the agent who had impersonated one of the Romano brothers and wanted to terminate the arrangement; and (3) had no expectation that Borders would set off with the money to share it with Judge Hastings because they believed that a more sophisticated system of distributing the bribe would be employed.
20. *San Francisco Chronicle*, October 24, 1989, p. A19.
21. His conviction was upheld on appeal. *U.S. v. Nixon*, 816 F. 2d 1022 (1987).
22. *Congressional Record*, 101st Cong., 1st sess., vol. 135, no. 151, p. 14495. Thus, Nixon joined Secretary Belknap, Judge Claiborne, and probably Judge Humphreys, as receivers of a unanimous House vote to impeach.
23. *Hearings Before the Senate Impeachment Trial Committee*, 101st Cong., 1st sess, S. Hrg. 101–247, pt. 4A: Y4.1M, 712:S. Hrg, hereafter, *Hearings*,
24. *Impeachment of Judge Walter L. Nixon, Jr.*, 101st Cong., 1st sess., Senate Document 101–17, pp. 22–23.
25. *Hearings*, pt. 2.
26. Ibid., pp. 2–6.
27. Ibid., p. 5.
28. Ibid., pp. 6–16.
29. Ibid., pp. 17–195.
30. Ibid., pp. 204–317.
31. *Congressional Record*, 101st Cong., 1st sess, vol. 135, no. 151, pp. 14495–502.
32. Ibid., pp. 14505–513.
33. Ibid., no. 153, pp. 14633–636. The Senate also voted, prior to its impeachment vote, to deny Nixon's request for trial before the full Senate (90 to 7, p. 14634), and to deny dismissal of Article 3 as redundant, complex, and confusing (63 to 34, pp. 14634–35).
34. Article I, section 3, clause 7.

35. For a discussion of the matters considered here, see Melissa H. Maxman, "In Defense of the Constitution's Judicial Impeachment Standard," *Michigan Law Review* 86 (1987):420.

36. *United States v. Isaacs*, 493 F. 2d 1124 (1974). Kerner was convicted in court; he resigned his judgeship on July 25, 1974 soon after his conviction. No action to impeach him was undertaken.

37. 681 F. 2d 706 (1982).

38. 727 F. 2d 842 (1984).

39. Ibid., 846.

40. William Rawle, *A View of the Constitution of the United States of America* (Philadelphia: H. C. Carey and I. Lea, 1825), p. 204.

41. Judges Swayne, Archbald, and English might also have violated the law, but pre- or post-impeachment legal action against them is less clearly demonstrable than in the cases of Blount, Belknap, Claiborne, Hastings, or Nixon.

Bibliography

Documents

5 *Annals of Congress*, 1797–99. (Impeachment and trial of William Blount.)

7 *Annals of Congress*, 2d sess., 1802–1803; 8 *Annals of Congress*, 1st sess., 1803–1804, Sen. Doc. 876, Vol. 32. (Impeachment and trial of John Pickering.)

Biographical Directory of the American Congress, 1774–1971. Washington, D.C.: Government Printing Office, 1971.

Boyan, A. Stephen, Jr., comp. and ed. *Constitutional Aspects of Watergate, Documents and Materials.* 6 vols. Dobbs Ferry: Oceana Publications, 1976–86.

Cannon, Clarence. *Cannon's Precedents of the House of Representatives of the United States.* 3 vols. Washington, D.C.: Government Printing Office, 1935.

37 *Congressional Globe*, 2d sess., pts. 3 and 4, 1861–1862. (Impeachment and trial of West H. Humphreys.)

Department of Justice. *Legal Aspects of Impeachment: An Overview.* Washington, D.C.: Government Printing Office, 1974.

Dictionary of American Biography. 22 vols. New York: Charles Scribner's Sons, 1934.

Elliot, Jonathan. *The Debates in the Several State Conventions on the Adoption of the Constitution.* 5 vols. Philadelphia: J. B. Lippincott, 1896.

Farrand, Max, ed. *The Records of the Federal Convention of 1787.* 4 vols. New Haven: Yale University Press, 1911.

The Federalist. New York: Modern Library, 1937.

Hinds, Asher C. *Hinds' Precedents of the House of Representatives of the United States.* 5 vols. Washington, D.C.: Government Printing Office, 1907.

Judges of the United States. Washington, D.C.: Government Printing Office, 1983.

McPherson, Edward. *The Political History of the United States during the Great Rebellion.* New York: D. Appleton, 1864.

——— . *The Political History of the United States of America during the Period of Reconstruction,* 2d ed. Washington: Solomons and Chapman, 1875.

National Cyclopedia of American Biography. 75 vols. New York: James T. White, 1961.

Stansbury, Arthur J. *Report of the Trial of James H. Peck.* Boston: Hilliard, Gray, 1833.

Trial of Andrew Johnson. 2 vols. New York: DaCapo Press, 1970.

Trial of Samuel Chase. 2 vols. New York: DaCapo Press, 1970.

U.S. Congress. House. Committee on the Judiciary. *Comparison of Passages, Transcripts of Eight Recorded Presidential Conversations.* 93d Cong., 2d sess., July 1974.

——. *Hearing Before the Subcommittee on Courts, Civil Liberties, and the Administration of Justice of the Committee on the Judiciary.* 99th Cong., 2d sess., June 19, 1986. (Impeachment of Harry E. Claiborne).

——. *Hearings of the Committee on the Judiciary.* 93d Congress, 2d sess., 1974. (Impeachment of Richard M. Nixon.)

——. *Impeachment of Judge Harry E. Claiborne.* 99th Cong., 2d sess., 1986. House Resolution 461, Doc. 99–688.

——. Committee on the Judiciary. *Impeachment of Richard M. Nixon, President of the United States.* 93d Cong., 2d sess., 1974. Report no. 93–1305.

——. Committee on the Judiciary. *Impeachment, Selected Materials.* 93d Cong., 1st sess., 1973. (Impeachment of Richard M. Nixon.)

——. Committee on Expenditures in the War Department. *Reports of Committees.* 44th Cong., 1st sess., 1875–76, nos. 186, 791. (Impeachment of William W. Belknap.)

U.S. Congress. Senate. *Extracts from the Journal of the United States Senate in All Cases of Impeachment, 1798–1904.* 62d Cong., 2d sess., Doc. 876, Vol. 32.

——. *Hearings Before the Committee on the Judiciary.* 96th Cong., 1st sess., 1979. Serial 96–21.

——. *Hearings Before the Senate Impeachment Trial Committee.* 99th Cong., 2d sess., 1986. Doc. 99–812.

——. *Hearings Before the Senate Impeachment Trial Committee.* 101st Cong., 1st sess., 1989. Y4Im 7/215; *Congressional Record.* 101st Cong., 1st sess., 1989. Vol. 135. (Trial of Alcee L. Hastings.)

——. *Hearings Before the Senate Impeachment Trial Committee.* 101st Cong., 1st sess., 1989. Y4Im 712; *Congressional Record,* 101st Cong., 1st sess., 1989. Vol. 135. (Trial of Walter L. Nixon, Jr.)

——. Committee on Rules and Administration. *Miscellaneous Documents.* 93d Cong., 2d sess., 1974.

——. *Procedure and Guidelines for Impeachment Trials in the United States Senate.* Rev. ed. 99th Cong., 2d sess., 1986.

——. *Proceedings in the Senate of the United States in the Matter of the Impeachment of Charles Swayne.* 58th Cong., 3d sess., 1904–5. Doc 194.

——. *Proceedings in the Trial of Impeachment of Robert W. Archbald.* 62d Cong., 3d sess., 1912–13. Docs. 16, 17, and 18.

——. *Proceedings of the United States Senate in the Impeachment Trial of Harry E. Claiborne, a Judge of the United States District Court for the District of Nevada.* 99th Cong., 2d sess., 1986. Doc. 48.

——— . *Proceedings of the United States Senate in the Trial of Harold Louderback, United States District Judge for the Northern District of California.* 72d Cong., 2d sess., 73d Congress, 1st sess., 1933. Doc. 73.

——— . *Proceedings of the United States Senate in the Trial of Impeachment of George W. English.* 69th Cong., 2d sess., 1926. Doc. 177.

——— . *Proceedings of the United States Senate in the Trial of Impeachment of Halsted L. Ritter, United States District Judge for the Southern District of Florida.* 74th Cong., 2d sess., 1936. Doc. 200.

——— . *Proceedings of the Senate, Sitting for the Trial of William W. Belknap.* 44th Cong., 1st sess., 1876. Vol. 4, pt. 7.

United State Courts, *Annual Report of the Director of the Administrative Office.* Washington, D.C.: Government Printing Office, 1986.

Books

Abraham, Henry J. *Justices and Presidents.* New York: Penguin Books, 1975.

Adams, Henry. *John Randolph.* Boston: Houghton Mifflin, 1896.

Adams, John Quincy. *Memoirs.* Edited by Charles Francis Adams. 12 vols. Philadelphia: J. B. Lippincott, 1874.

Badeau, Adam. *Grant in Peace, from Appomattox to Mount McGregor.* Freeport: Books for Libraries Press, 1971.

Bay, W. V. N. *Reminiscences of the Bench and Bar of Missouri.* St. Louis: F. H. Thomas, 1878.

Belknap, Michael R., ed. *American Political Trials.* Westport: Greenwood Press, 1981.

Benedict, Michael Les. *A Compromise of Principle.* New York: W. W. Norton, 1974.

——— . *The Fruits of Victory: Alternatives in Restoring the Union, 1865–1877.* Philadelphia: J. B. Lippincott, 1975.

——— . *The Impeachment and Trial of Andrew Johnson.* New York: W. W. Norton, 1973.

Benton, Thomas Hart. *Thirty Years' View; or, A History of the Working of the American Government for Thirty Years, from 1820 to 1850.* 2 vols. New York: D. Appleton, 1854.

Berger, Raoul. *Executive Privilege: A Constitutional Myth.* Cambridge: Harvard University Press, 1974.

——— . *Impeachment: The Constitutional Problems.* Cambridge: Harvard University Press, 1973.

Beveridge, Albert J. *The Life of John Marshall.* 3 vols. Boston: Houghton Mifflin, 1919.

Billon, Frederic L. *Annals of St. Louis, in Its Territorial Days.* St. Louis: Nixon-Jones Printing, 1888.

Black, Charles L., Jr. *Impeachment: A Handbook.* New Haven: Yale University Press, 1974.

Black, Henry Campbell. *Black's Law Dictionary*, 5th ed. St. Paul: West Publishing, 1979.

Blaine, James G. *Twenty Years of Congress: From Lincoln to Garfield*. 2 vols. Norwich: Henry Bell Publishing, 1886.

Borden, Morton. *The Federalism of James A. Bayard*. New York: Columbia University Press, 1955.

Borkin, Joseph. *The Corrupt Judge*. New York: Clarkson N. Potter, 1962.

Boutwell, George S. *Reminiscences of Sixty Years in Public Affairs*. 2 vols. New York: Greenwood Press, 1968.

Brant, Irving. *Impeachment, Trials and Errors*. New York: Knopf, 1973.

Brock, W. R. *An American Crisis, Congress and Reconstruction 1865–1867*. New York: St. Martin's Press, 1963.

Brodie, Fawn M. *Thaddeus Stevens: Scourge of the South*. New York: W. W. Norton, 1966.

———. *Thomas Jefferson: An Intimate History*. New York: W. W. Norton, 1974.

Buchanan, James. *The Works of James Buchanan*. Edited by John Bassett Moore. 12 vols. Philadelphia: J. B. Lippincott, 1911.

Chambers, William Nisbet. *Old Bullion Benton, Senator from the New West*. Boston: Little, Brown, 1956.

Clarkson, Paul S., and R. Samuel Jett. *Luther Martin of Maryland*. Baltimore: Johns Hopkins Press, 1970.

Collier, Christopher, and James Lincoln Collier. *Decision in Philadelphia: The Constitutional Convention of 1787*. New York: Random House, 1986.

Coolidge, Louis A. *Ulysses S. Grant*. Boston: Houghton Mifflin, 1917.

Coues, Elliott, ed. *Forty Years a Fur Trader on the Upper Missouri: The Personal Narrative of Charles Larpenteur, 1833–1872*. 2 vols. New York: Francis P. Harper, 1898.

Cox, Lawanda, and John H. Cox. *Politics Principle, and Prejudice 1865–1866*. New York: Free Press of Glencoe, 1963.

Darby, J. F. *Personal Recollections*. St. Louis: G. I. Jones, 1880.

Dauer, Manning J. *The Adams Federalists*. Baltimore: John Hopkins Press, 1953.

Dewitt, David Miller. *The Impeachment and Trial of Andrew Johnson*. 1903. Reprint. New York: Russell and Russell, 1967.

Drew, Elizabeth. *Washington Journal: The Events of 1973–1974*. New York: Vintage Books, 1976.

Dunning, William Archibald. *Essays on the Civil War and Reconstruction*. New York: Harper and Row, 1965.

Eaton, Clement. *Jefferson Davis*. New York: Free Press, 1977.

Ehrlich, Walter. *Presidential Impeachment, an American Dilemma*. St. Charles, Mo.: Forum Press, 1974.

Fairman, Charles. *History of the Supreme Court of the United States*. New York: Vol. 6, pt. 1. Macmillan, 1971.

368

Fields, Howard. *High Crimes and Misdemeanors.* New York: W. W. Norton, 1978.

Fischer, David Hackett. *The Revolution of American Conservatism.* New York: Harper and Row, 1965.

Folmsbee, Stanley J., Robert E. Corlew, and Enoch L. Mitchell. *Tennessee, a Short History.* Knoxville: University of Tennessee Press, 1969.

Franklin, John Hope. *Reconstruction After the Civil War.* Chicago: University of Chicago Press, 1961.

Friedman, Leon, and Fred L. Israel. *The Justices of the United States Supreme Court 1789–1969,* 4 vols. New York: Chelsea House, 1969; Vol. 5, 1978.

Frost, David. *"I Gave Them a Sword": Behind the Scenes of the Nixon Interviews.* New York: William Morrow, 1978.

Geis, Gilbert, and Robert F. Meier, eds. *White-Collar Crime.* Rev. ed. New York: Free Press, 1977.

Grant, Julia Dent. *The Personal Memoirs of Julia Dent Grant.* Edited by John Y. Simon. New York: G. P. Putnam's Sons, 1975.

Grant, U. S. *Personal Memoirs of U. S. Grant.* 2 vols. New York: Charles L. Webster, 1885.

Grant, Ulysses S., 3d. *Ulysses S. Grant: Warrior and Statesman.* New York: William Morrow, 1969.

Haines, Charles Grove. *The Role of the Supreme Court in American Government and Politics, 1789–1835.* 2 vols. Berkeley: University of California Press, 1944.

Hall, Clifton R. *Andrew Johnson, Military Governor of Tennessee.* Princeton: Princeton University Press, 1916.

Harris, Joseph P. *The Advice and Consent of the Senate.* Berkeley: University of California Press, 1953.

Haw, James et al. *Stormy Patriot: The Life of Samuel Chase.* Baltimore, Maryland Historical Society, 1980.

Haynes, George H. *The Senate of the United States.* 2 vols. New York: Russell and Russell, 1960.

Hesseltine, William B. *Ulysses S. Grant, Politician.* New York: Frederick Ungar, 1935.

Hildreth, Richard. *The History of the United States of America.* 6 vols. New York: Harper and Brothers, 1851.

Hoffer, Peter Charles, and N. E. H. Hull. *Impeachment in America, 1635–1805.* New Haven: Yale University Press, 1984.

Houck, Louis. *A History of Missouri.* 3 vols. Chicago: R. R. Donnelley and Sons, 1908.

Humphreys, Frederick. *The Humphreys Family in America.* New York: Humphreys Print, 1883.

Hyman, Harold, ed. *The Radical Republicans and Reconstruction, 1861–1870.* Indianapolis: Bobbs-Merrill, 1967.

Kennedy, John P. *Memoirs of the Life of William Wirt.* 2 vols. Philadelphia: Lea and Blanchard, 1849.

Kirk, Russell. *John Randolph of Roanoke*. Chicago: Henry Regnery, 1964.

Kroeker, Marvin E. *Great Plains Command, William B. Hazen in the Frontier West*. Norman: University of Oklahoma Press, 1976.

Kutler, Stanley I. *Judicial Power and Reconstruction Politics*. Chicago: University of Chicago Press, 1968.

Labovitz, John R. *Presidential Impeachment*. New Haven: Yale University Press, 1978.

Levy, Leonard W. *Against the Law: The Nixon Court and Criminal Justice*. New York: Harper and Row, 1974.

Lomask, Milton. *Andrew Johnson: President on Trial*. New York: Farrar, Straus and Cudahy, 1960.

McDonald, Forrest. *Novus Ordo Seclorum, the Intellectual Origins of the Constitution*, Lawrence: University Press of Kansas, 1985.

McKitrick, Eric L. *Andrew Johnson and Reconstruction*. Chicago: University of Chicago Press, 1960.

Maclay, William. *The Journal of William Maclay*. New York: Frederick Ungar, 1890.

Madison, James. *Writings of James Madison*, 9 vols. Edited by Gaillard Hunt. New York: G. P. Putnam's Sons, 1900–1910.

Magrath, C. Peter. *Yazoo, Law and Politics in the New Republic*. Providence: Brown University Press, 1966.

Malone, Dumas. *Jefferson and His Time*, 6 vols. Boston: Little, Brown, 1948–81.

Mantell, Martin E. *Johnson, Grant, and the Politics of Reconstruction*. New York: Columbia University Press, 1973.

Masterson, William H. *William Blount*. Baton Rouge: Louisiana State University Press, 1954.

Miller, Merle. *Plain Speaking: An Oral Biography of Harry S. Truman*. New York: Berkeley Publishing, 1973.

Milton, George Fort. *The Age of Hate, Andrew Johnson and the Radicals*. Hamden: Archon Books, 1965.

Mollenhoff, Clark R. *The Man Who Pardoned Nixon*. New York: St. Martin's Press, 1976.

Morison, Samuel Eliot. *The Oxford History of the American People*. New York: Oxford University Press, 1965.

Myers, Gustavus. *History of the Supreme Court of the United States*. 1912. Reprint. New York: Burt Franklin, 1968.

Nevins, Allan. *Hamilton Fish, the Inner History of the Grant Administration*, rev. ed. 2 vols. New York: Frederick Ungar Publishing, 1957.

Nichols, Roy F. *The Invention of the American Political Parties*. New York: Macmillan, 1967.

Nixon, Richard. *RN: The Memoirs of Richard Nixon*. New York: Grosset and Dunlap, 1978.

Oates, Stephen B. *With Malice Toward None*. New York: Harper and Row, 1977.

Parmet, Herbert S., and Marie B. Hecht. *Aaron Burr: Portrait of an Ambitious Man.* New York: Macmillan, 1967.

Parton, James. *The Life and Times of Aaron Burr.* New York: Mason Brothers, 1858; New York: Johnson Reprint, 1967.

Pessen, Edward. *Jacksonian America: Society, Personality, and Politics.* Homewood, Ill.: Dorsey Press, 1969.

Plumer, William. *William Plumer's Memorandum of Proceedings in the United States Senate, 1803–1807.* Edited by Everett Somerville Brown. New York: Macmillan, 1923.

Poore, Ben: Perley. *Perley's Reminiscences of Sixty Years in the National Metropolis.* 2 vols. Philadelphia: Hubbard Brothers, 1886.

Rawle, William. *A View of the Constitution of the United States of America.* Philadelphia: H. Carey and I. Lea, 1825.

Roske, Ralph J. *His Own Counsel: The Life and Times of Lyman Trumbull.* Reno: University of Nevada Press, 1979.

Ross, Edmund G. *History of the Impeachment of Andrew Johnson, President of the United States by the House of Representatives, and His Trial by the Senate for High Crimes and Misdemeanors in Office, 1868.* New York: Burt Franklin, 1964.

Sanderson, John. *Biography of the Signers to the Declaration of Independence,* 2d ed. 5 vols. Philadelphia: W. Brown and C. Peters, 1828.

Schlesinger, Arthur M., Jr. *The Age of Jackson.* Boston: Little, Brown, 1946.

———, ed. *The Coming to Power, Critical Presidential Elections in American History.* New York: Chelsea House, 1971.

Schnapper, M. B., ed. *Conscience of the Nation.* Washington, D.C.: Public Affairs Press, 1974.

———, ed. *Presidential Impeachment: A Documentary Overview.* Washington, D.C.: Public Affairs Press, 1974.

Simon, James F. *In His Own Image: The Supreme Court in Richard Nixon's America.* New York: David McKay, 1973.

Simpson, Alex. J., Jr. *A Treatise on Federal Impeachments.* Philadelphia: Law Ass'n., 1916.

Smith, Gene. *High Crimes and Misdemeanors: The Impeachment and Trial of Andrew Johnson.* New York: William Morrow, 1977.

Smith, Page. *John Adams.* 2 vols. Garden City: Doubleday, 1962.

Story, Joseph. *Commentaries on the Constitution of the United States.* 2 vols. Boston: Little, Brown, 1905.

Stryker, Lloyd Paul. *Andrew Johnson: A Study in Courage.* New York: Macmillan, 1936.

Taylor, Tim. *The Book of Presidents.* New York: Arno Press, 1972.

Temple, Oliver P. *Notable Men of Tennessee, from 1833 to 1875, Their Times and Their Contemporaries.* New York: Cosmopolitan Press, 1912.

Thomas, Benjamin P., and Harold M. Hyman. *Stanton: The Life and Times of Lincoln's Secretary of War.* New York: Alfred A. Knopf, 1962.

Thomas, Lately. *The First President Johnson*. New York: William Morrow, 1968.

Trefousse, Hans Louis. *Ben Butler: The South Called Him Beast!* New York: Twayne Publishers, 1957.

——— . *Impeachment of a President*. Knoxville: University of Tennessee Press, 1975.

——— . *Reconstruction: America's First Effort at Racial Democracy*. New York: Van Nostrand Reinhold, 1971.

Turner, Lynn W. *William Plumer of New Hampshire*. Chapel Hill: University of North Carolina Press, 1962.

Warden, Robert V. *An Account of the Private Life and Public Services of Salmon Portland Chase*. Cincinnati: Wilstack, Baldwin, 1874.

Warren, Charles. *The Making of the Constitution*. New York: Barnes and Noble, 1928.

——— . *The Supreme Court in United States History*, rev. ed. 2 vols. Boston: Little, Brown, 1926.

Wharton, Francis. *State Trials of the United States*. 1849. Reprint. New York: Burt Franklin, 1970.

Wharton, Helen Elizabeth (Ashurst). *Francis Wharton, a Memoir*. Philadelphia: n.p., 1896.

White, Horace. *The Life of Lyman Trumbull*. Boston: Houghton Mifflin, 1913.

Who Was Who in America, 1897–1942. Chicago: A. N. Marquis, 1942.

Wilson, James. *Works*. Edited by Robert G. McCloskey. 2 vols. Cambridge: Harvard University Press, 1967.

Winston, Robert W. *Andrew Johnson, Plebian and Patriot*. New York: Barnes and Noble, 1928.

Winters, Glenn R., ed. *Handbook for Judges*, Chicago: American Judicature Society, 1975.

Woodward, C. Vann, ed. *Responses of the Presidents to Charges of Misconduct*. New York: Delacourt Press, 1974.

Wright, Marcus J. *Some Account of the Life and Services of William Blount*. Washington, D.C.: E. J. Gray, 1884.

PERIODICALS

Bender, Paul, "The Techniques of Subtle Erosion." *Harper's*, December 1972, pp. 18–32.

Berger, Raoul. "Impeachment: An Instrument of Regeneration." *Harper's*, January 1974, pp. 14–22.

——— . "The Grand Inquest of the Nation." *Harper's*, October 1973, pp. 12–23.

Brodie, Fawn M. "The Presidential Hero: Reality of Illusion." *Halcyon, a Journal of the Humanities* (Nevada Humanities Committee), 1981, pp. 1–16.

Burbank, Stephen B. "Procedural Rulemaking Under the Judicial Councils Reform and Judicial Conduct and Disability Act of 1980." *University of Pennsylvania Law Review* 131 (1982): 283.

Bushnell, Eleanore. "The Impeachment and Trial of James H. Peck." *Missouri Historical Review*, January 1980, pp. 137–65.

———. "Judge Harry E. Claiborne and the Federal Impeachment Process." *Nevada Historical Society Quarterly*, Winter 1989, pp. 235–60.

———. "One of Twelve: The Nevada Impreachment Connection." *Nevada Historical Society Quarterly*, Spring 1983, pp. 3–12.

Catz, Robert S. "Removal of Federal Judges by Imprisonment." *Rutgers Law Review* 18 (1986): 103.

Clark, John G. "Mark W. Delahay: Peripatetic Politician." *Kansas Historical Quarterly*, Autumn 1959, pp. 301–12.

Clark, Tom C. "Judicial Self-Regulation and Its Potential." *Law and Contemporary Problems* 35 (1970): 37.

Congressional Quarterly. "Guide to the Congress of the United States." 1971.

———. "Impeachment and the United States Congress." March 1974.

Davis, Charles B. "Judge James Hawkins Peck." *Missouri Historical Review*, October 1932, pp. 3–20.

Ervin, Sam J., Jr. "Separation of Powers: Judicial Independence." *Law and Contemporary Problems* 35 (1970): 108.

Feerick, John D. "Impeaching Federal Judges: A Study of the Constitutional Provisions." *Fordham Law Review* 39 (1970): 15.

Havens, Murray Clark, and Dixie Mercer McNeil. "Presidents, Impeachability, and Political Accountability." *Presidential Studies Quarterly* 8, no. 1 (1978): 5–18.

Hoffer, Peter C., and N. E. H. Hull. "The First American Impeachments." *William and Mary Quarterly*, October 1978, pp. 653–67.

———. "Power and Precedent in the Creation of an American Impeachment Tradition: The Eighteenth-Century Colonial Record." *William and Mary Quarterly*, January 1979, pp. 51–77.

Hollowman, John H. III. "The Judicial Reform Act: History, Analysis, and Comment." *Law and Contemporary Problems* 35 (1970): 128.

Kaufman, Irving R. "Chilling Judicial Independence." *Yale Law Journal* 88 (1979): 681.

———. "Lions or Jackals: The Function of a Code of Judicial Ethics." *Law and Contemporary Problems* 35 (1970): 3.

———. "Unnecessary and Improper: The Judicial Councils Reform and Judicial Conduct and Disability Act." *Yale Law Journal* 94 (1985): 1117.

Kurland, Phillip B. "The Constitution and the Tenure of Federal Judges: Some Notes from History." *University of Chicago Law Review* 36 (1969): 665.

Maxman, Melissa H. "In Defense of the Constitution's Judicial Impeachment Standard." *Michigan Law Review* 86 (1987): 420.

Miller, Arthur Selwyn. "Public Confidence in the Judiciary: Some Notes and Reflections." *Law and Contemporary Problems* 35 (1970): 69.

Otis, Merrill E. "A Proposed Tribunal: Is It Constitutional?" *University of Kansas City Law Review* 7 (1938): 3.

Pritchett, Herman. "Johnson Case Gave Impeachment a Bad Name." *Los Angeles Times,* July 29, 1974, pt. 2, p. 7.

Shartel, Burke. "Federal Judges: Appointment, Supervision and Removal—Some Possibilities Under the Constitution." *Michigan Law Review* 28 (1930): 870.

Sherrod, Robert. "Impeachment Then: Trial by the Senate." *Washington Post,* April 7, 1974, p. C1.

Smith, James Morton. "Sedition in the Old Dominion." *Journal of Southern History* 20 (May 1954): 157–82.

Stathis, Stephen W. "Nixon, Watergate, and American Foreign Policy." *Presidential Studies Quarterly* 13, no. 1 (1983): 129–43.

Stolz, Preble. "Disciplining Federal Judges: Is Impeachment Hopeless?" *California Law Review* 57 (1969): 659.

Stone, I. F. "Impeachment." *New York Review of Books,* June 28, 1973, pp. 12–19.

Ten Broek, Jacobus. "Partisan Politics and Federal Judgeship Impeachment since 1903." *Minnesota Law Review* 23 (1938–39): 185.

Turner, Frederick Jackson, ed. "Documents on the Blount Conspiracy, 1795–1797." *American Historical Review* 10 (April 1905): 574–606.

Turner, Lynn W. "The Impeachment of John Pickering." *American Historical Review* 54 (1949): 485–507.

Wills, Garry. "The Impeachment Man." *Atlantic,* May 1974, pp. 79–84.

Index

Adams, John: and Federalist bench, 25; and documents against Blount, 27

Adams, John Quincy: in Pickering trial, 46–48; on removal of judges, 59; on partisanship in Peck trial, 111–12; referred to in Belknap trial, 176

Agnew, Spiro T., 37, 290–91

Archbald, Robert W.: pre-impeachment career of, 217–18; complaint against to ICC, 218; articles of impeachment against, 218–19, 221–22; composition of House in impeachment of, 219; managers in trial of, 219; cumulative article in trial of, 219, 237; composition of Senate in trial of, 220; response of, to impeachment articles, 220; problem of charges against, in former office, 222, 238–39; and good behavior, 233; and coal dump transactions, 223–26 passim; witnesses against, 223–28; and Boland brothers' rate problems, 226–27; and secret letter charge, 227; and promissory notes, 227, 228; trial witnesses for, 228–32; testimony of, 230–32; summary of managers' case against, 232–33, 235–36; summary of case for, 233–35; Senate vote in trial of, 237–38; disqualification of, 239; central questions arising in trial of, 240–42; good behavior in trial of, 241–42; mentioned, 12, 17

Ashley, James M., and Johnson impeachment, 134–35, 343 n13

Austin, Warren, 284

Barton, David, 91

Bayard, James A., 32, 34, 84

Belknap, William W.: unanimous impeachment of, 165; composition of Senate in trial of, 165, 169; pre-impeachment career of, 165–66; dealings with Caleb Marsh, 166–86 passim; dealings with John Evans, 166–85 passim; Grant accepts resignation of, 167, 168; managers in trial of, 169; bribery in trial of, 170, 180–81; impeachment articles against, 170; attorneys representing, 170–71; and Senate jurisdiction over, 171, 173–76, 186–88; arguments on disqualification in trial of, 175; managers' case against, 177–80; witnesses for, 180; summary of case for, 180–85; summary of case against, 182–86 passim; Senate vote in trial of, 186; and effect of resignation of, 187–88; post-impeachment career of, 189; mentioned, 16, 38

Benton, Thomas Hart, 91, 92, 96, 103–4

Bingham, John A., 117, 137–56 passim

Black, Jeremiah S., 170, 175, 176, 177, 183–84

Blair, Montgomery, 170–71, 175, 180–82

Blount, William: party divisions in trial of, 25–26, 30–31, 36; pre-impeachment career of, 26–27; composition of House in impeachment of, 27; Senate investigations of, 28–29; Senate expulsion of, 29; composition of Senate in trial of, 29; articles of impeachment against, 29–30; managers in trial of, 30; and jury trial, 31; failure to appear at trial, 31; attorneys for, 31; case for, 31–35; and civil officer argument, 32–36 passim; and exemption of Congress from impeachment, 32–40 passim; case against, 32–35; Senate decision on, 35–36; post-impeachment activities of, 37; mentioned, 16, 161, 173–74

Boland, William P.: report against Archbald by, 218–33 passim

Boutwell, George S., 130–58 passim
Borders, William: in Hastings case, 308–13 passim
Bribery: in Belknap trial, 170, 180–81
Browning, Gordon, 247, 260–61
Brownlow, William G., 120–21
Buchanan, James, 96–112 passim, 338 n17
Burger, Warren, 294
Burr, Aaron, 47, 63, 85, 290, 331–32 n32, 335 n24
Butler, Benjamin F., 130–55 passim

Callender, James: in Chase trial, 58–85 passim
Campbell, George W., 75
Cannon, Howard W., 290, 296
Carey, James, 27, 28, 29
Carpenter, Matthew H., 170, 175, 177, 178–79, 184–85
Chase, Salmon P., 25, 139, 144–45, 150
Chase, Samuel: pre-impeachment career of, 57–58; and Sedition Act, 58; campaigns for John Adams, 58; appraisals of, 58–59; composition of Congress in trial of, 59; and Fries trial, 60, 61–62, 64, 67–84 passim; impeached, 60; managers in trial of, 60; articles of impeachment against, 60–63; and Callender trial, 62–63, 64–65, 68–88 passim; response of to impeachment articles, 63–67; attorneys for, 64; claims willful and criminal misconduct required for impeachment, 64; and Baltimore grand jury speech, 66, 69–70, 72–73; managers' case against, 67–70; summary of case for, 70–73; comparison of managers' and respondent's case, 73–74; summary of case against, 74–76, 82–84; summary of case for, 76–82; Senate vote on, 84–86; and post-impeachment actions of manager, 86; consideration of Republicans' failure to convict, 86–88; mentioned, 12, 25
Chauvin, L. Stanley, 292
Claiborne, Harry E.: and court trial before impeachment, 1, 289–90, 299–300, 301, 351 n30; and income tax, 289, 297–98; pre-impeachment career

of, 290; court trial of, 290–92; attorney for, 292; seeks impeachment trial, 292–93; composition of House in impeachment of, 293; articles of impeachment against, 293; unanimous vote to impeach, 294; defense of, 294; House criticism of, 294–95; managers in trial of, 295; Senate panel for review of charges against, 295; defense of, 295–300 passim; composition of Senate in trial of, 298–99; case against, 299–300; testimony of, in impeachment trial, 300; Senate vote in trial of, 300–301; statements of senators following trial of, 301–2; post-impeachment activities of, 302–4; and Nevada Supreme Court, 303–4; constitutional amendments proposed after trial of, 305; mentioned, 11–12, 23, 37, 38
Clark, Christopher, 76
Clayton, Henry D., 192, 193, 198–99, 207, 218–19, 223, 235–36
Clymer, Hiester, 169, 171–72, 179–80, 188
Cocke, William, 46, 85, 86
Congress: sole power to impeach and try, 9–10; exemption of members of, from impeachment, 28, 32–40 passim
Contempt of court: Buchanan's bill on, 112
Cooper, Thomas: in Chase trial, 58–85 passim
Court trial before impeachment. See Claiborne, Hastings, Walter Nixon, passim
Cumulative article in impeachment trials: 21–22, 219, 237, 249, 251–52, 273, 282–84, 313, 329 n9
Curtis, Benjamin R., 138–48 passim

Dallas, Alexander J., 28, 31, 33, 34, 173
Dana, Samuel, 28
Davis, John W., 219, 233
Dayton, Jonathan, 51
De Armond, David A., 193, 199–200, 210–11
Delahay, Mark W.: impeachment of, 1–2; effect of resignation of, 9; mentioned, 38

Disqualification following impeachment trial, 6–7, 17, 29, 32–34, 122–23, 175, 181, 239, 283
Double jeopardy in Hastings trial, 311–12
Douglass, Frederick, 132

Early, Peter, 50, 60, 74–75
Edwards, Don, 315–16
English, George W.: impeachment of, 2–4; effect of resignation of, 9; mentioned, 38
Evans, John S.: and payments to Belknaps, 166–85 passim
Evarts, William M., 138–56 passim

Fairchild, Wiley: in Walter Nixon trial, 314, 315, 316
Federalist judiciary; Jeffersonians frustration with, 25, 43–45, 54–55, 58–59, 88
Fish, Hamilton, 294, 299
Foot, Solomon, 118, 123
Ford, Gerald, 5, 155
Free speech: in impeachment trials, 102, 106, 147
Freedom of press: in Peck trial, 101, 102, 106, 110

Giles, William B., 59
Good behavior: never defined, 10, 20; in Peck trial, 99; in Pickering trial, 47, 48, 53–54; in Humphreys trial, 124; in Archbald trial, 223–42; in Louderback trial, 264; in Ritter trial, 284; need for definition of, 307, 319–20; in Constitution, 326, 329 n6
Goodman, Oscar, 292–300 passim
Goodwin, Alfred T., 328 n1
Grant, Ulysses S.: on Johnson as military governor, 129; appointed ad interim secretary of war, 135; friction of, with Johnson, 136–37; accepts Belknap's resignation, 167–68; and knowledge of Belknap's misconduct, 168
Groesbeck, William S., 138–53 passim
Grow, Galusha, 117
"Guilty as charged": in Pickering trial, 51–52

Hanley, James M., 250, 252–53, 254–55, 256
Harper, Robert Goodloe, 33, 34, 35, 47, 49, 50, 64, 70–71, 80–82
Hastings, Alcee L.: indicted by grand jury, 308; target of Justice Department, 308–9; House impeachment vote, 309; articles against, 309; Judicial Conference in impeachment of, 309; evidence against, 309–11; special Senate committee in trial of, 309–12; testifies in own trial, 310; acquittal at court trial, 311; and double jeopardy claim, 311–12; Senate trial of, 312; summary of case for, 312; summary of case against, 312; Senate conviction of, 312–13; cumulative article against, 313; place of, in impeachment history, 314; post-impeachment activity, 314, 361 n1
Higgins, Anthony, 194, 200–201, 204, 207–8
High crimes and misdemeanors: lack of definition of, 18–20; analysis of use of, 321–22
Hoar, George F., 169, 174–75
Hobbs, Sam, 272, 273, 275, 276, 280–81
Hoffman, Carl T., 273, 274
Hopkinson, Joseph, 64, 76
Howland, Leonard P., 219, 233
Humphreys, West H.: no defense for, in impeachment trial, 115; Senate composition in trial of, 115–16; pre-impeachment career of, 116; on Confederacy, 116–17; managers in trial of, 117; composition of House in impeachment of, 117; articles of impeachment against, 117–18; "good behavior" clause in trial of, 118, 124; managers' case against, 118–19; treason referred to in trial of, 119; witnesses against, 119–21; Senate vote on, 121–23; disqualification vote on, 122–23; post-impeachment activities of, 123; mentioned, 17

Impeachment: frequent causes for, 7; rare use of, 9, 22; prevalence of judges in, 9, 307, 319; procedures for in Congress, 10, 21–22; partisanship in, 12–13, 39, 52, 54, 111–12, 212–13, 321; precedents in, trials, 13–18; constitutional requirements for, 18–20, Appendix; value of, 22–23, 323; legislators and, 28; universal applicability of, 34; insanity as ground for, 43–55 passim, 333 n17; analysis of value of, 320, 323; criminal conduct not required for, 322; official misconduct not required for, 322; willful misconduct not required for, 322

Jefferson, Thomas: confronted with all-Federalist bench, 25, 43–44; on impeachability of senators, 30–31; on Pickering's conduct, 47; on removal of judges, 54; on partisanship in impeachments, 331 n14; on Pickering, 333 n13
Jenks, George A., 169, 174, 183
Johnson, Andrew: appraisals of, 127–28; pre-impeachment career of, 128; views South as oppressed, 129; and Lincoln's Reconstruction plan, 128–29; major issues dividing, from Congress, 129–34; and black suffrage, 132; and 1866 congressional campaign, 132–33; on lack of southern representation in Congress, 132; vetoes of, 133–34; and Tenure of Office Act, 133–57 passim; impeachment resolution against, 134–36; suspends Stanton, 135; House defeats impeachment resolution against, 135–36; friction of, with Ulysses S. Grant, 136–37; composition of House in impeachment of, 137; impeached by House, 137; managers in trial of, 137; attorneys for, in trial, 138; core problems in trial of, 138–39; composition of Senate in trial of, 139; articles of impeachment against, 140–41; and Reconstruction acts, 141–57 passim; response of, to impeachment articles, 142; campaign speeches of, 145–56 passim; and removal power, 146; Article 11 in trial of, 147–48; and veto of Tenure Act, 149–50; managers' objections to testimony in trial of, 149, 150; summary of manag-

ers' case in trial of, 150–51, 152–55; 156; summary of case for, 151–52, 155–57; and use of Tenure Act, 152–54; Senate vote in trial of, 156; "recusants" in trial of, 157–58; and reasons for managers' defeat in trial of, 159; post-trial career of, 160; impeachment themes in trial of, 160–61; amnesty proclamation of, 343 n7
Judges: court trial before impeachment of, 137–38, 308, 318–19; prevalence of, in impeachments, 9, 191, 319; efforts to modify impeachment procedures of, 9–10, 86, 305, 327 n1, 333 n34, 358 n47; see also Good behavior; life tenure and impeachment, 53; imprisonment of, ruled not removal, 319
Judicial Conference: and Claiborne impeachment, 294; and Hastings impeachment, 309; and Walter Nixon impeachment, 314, 359 n13, 361 n6
Judicial Councils Reform and Judicial Conduct and Disability Act, 20–21, 329 n7, 359 n13, 361 n6
Judicial Discipline and Removal Reform Act (1990), 328 n1
Justice Department: initiates impeachment of Claiborne, 290–91; Hastings, 308; Walter Nixon, 314

Kerner, Otto, 318–19
Key, Philip Barton, 64, 76–77

Lapham, Elbridge, 169, 182–83
Lawless, Luke E.: as antagonist in Peck trial, 91–112 passim
Leake, W. S. (Sam), 250–62 passim
Lee, Charles, 64, 77
Legislators: impeachability of, 27–28, 39–40
Linforth, Walter H., 250, 253, 254, 258, 261–62
Logan, George, 48
Logan, John A., 137–50 passim
Lord, Scott, 169–71, 185–86
Louderback, Harold: effect of New Deal in case of, 245; unique aspects in trial of, 245; pre-impeachment career of, 245–46; Judiciary Committee vote

against impeachment of, 246; debate on impeachment of, 246–47; House vote to impeach, 247; composition of House in impeachment of, 247; managers in trial of, 247; articles of impeachment against, 247–49; composition of Senate in trial of, 249; and cumulative article, 249, 251–52; attorneys for, 250; reply of, to articles, 250–51; opening statements in trial of, 252–53; witnesses against, 253–57; witnesses for, 257–59; testimony of, 258–59; managers' summation in trial of, 260–61, 262–63; summation of case for, 261–62; vote in trial of, 263–64; good behavior in trial of, 264; appraisal of, 264–65; post-impeachment career of, 265

Lynde, William P., 169, 177–78, 182

Marsh, Caleb P., 166–85 passim
Marshall, John: as target of Jeffersonians, 59, 334 n10; witness for Chase, 71–72
Martin, Luther, 64, 72, 77–79
Maynard, Horace, 117
McDuffie, George, 96, 98, 100–102
McMahon, John A., 169–78
Meredith, Jonathan, 99–100, 102, 104, 107
Montgomery, John, 69–73

Nelson Thomas A. R., 138–52 passim
Nicholson, Joseph H., 45, 49, 50, 60, 82–83
Nixon, Richard M.: near-impeachment of, 5–6; mentioned, 23; and claim of legality of presidential acts, 162
Nixon, Walter L., Jr.: convicted in court, 314; and Judicial Conference, 314; impeachment vote on, 314; articles of impeachment against, 315; and special Senate trial committee, 315; arguments against, 315, 316–17; arguments for, 316–17; Senate vote on, 317; post-impeachment activities of, 317–18, 361 n1, 362 n22
Norris, George W., 219, 228, 249, 280

Olmsted, Marlin E., 193–97, 205–6

Palmer, Henry W., 193, 194, 195–97, 199
Pardee, Don A., 191–92
Peck, James H.: pre-impeachment career of, 91; land policies and impeachment of, 92; ruling of, in Soulard case, 92–93; sentences Lawless for "A Citizen" letter, 93; and "A Citizen" letter, 93–95; impeachment resolutions against, 96; response to impeachment resolution, 96–97; composition of House in impeachment of, 98; House vote on impeachment, 98; composition of Senate in trial of, 98; managers in trial of, 98; hostility to courts as factor in impeachment of, 98; article of impeachment against, 99; response to article of impeachment, 99–100; witnesses against, 102–4; summary of case against, 105–6, 108–9; case for, 104–5, 107–8, 110; Senate decision on, 111–12; partisanship in trial of, 111–12; mentioned, 16, 39
Perkins, James B., 193, 198, 206–7, 296
Perkins, Randolph, 273, 275
Peters, Richard, 58, 62
Pickering, John: pre-impeachment career of, 43; disabilities of, 43; composition of House in impeachment of, 45; managers in trial of, 45; articles of impeachment against, 45–66; doubts about impeachability of, 46; and insanity plea, 47–48; Senate vote to accept insanity plea of, 48–49; son Jacob's description of afflictions of, 49–50; presentation of witnesses detailing his condition, 50; motion to have testimony of, 51; and "guilty as charged" device, 51–52; guilty vote on, 52; partisan positions in vote on, 52; mentioned, 12, 25, 106, 109
Plumer, William, 47, 48, 50, 54, 72
Powers, Samuel L., 193, 207

Randolph, John, 59–60, 67, 83–84, 86
Rankin, A. L., 271–81 passim
Rawle, William, 27, 319
Resignation: effect of, on impeachment, 1–7 passim, 11, 38–39, 165, 187–88

Ritter, Halsted L.: pre-impeachment career of, 269–70; and New Deal, 269, 285–86; investigation of (1933), 270–71; House debate on impeachment of, 271–72; composition of House in impeachment of, 272; House decision to impeach, 272; articles of impeachment against, 273; managers in trial of, 273; attorneys for, 273; response of, to articles, 274–75; witnesses against, 275–77; testifies in trial, 277–80; managers' summation in trial of, 280–82; summation for, in trial, 281; composition of Senate in trial of, 282; Senate vote on, 282–83; cumulative article in trial of, 282–84; "good behavior" in trial of, 284; reasons for impeachment of, 285–86; appeals to Court of Claims, 287

Rodino, Peter, 293, 299, 301

Rodney, Caesar Augustus, 47, 83

Scott, John, 96

Senate: special impeachment trial committee of, 295, 296–98, 309–12, 315, 323

Sewall, Samuel, 31

Simpson, Alexander J., 220, 233–34, 236–37

Sitgreaves, Samuel, 27–28, 39

Soulard, Antoine: court case of, 92, 93, 95, 98

Spencer, Ambrose, 98, 105–6

Stanbery, Henry, 138–56 passim

Stanton, Edwin M.: and Johnson impeachment, 124–58 passim

Sterling, John A., 219, 230, 231, 232

Stevens, Thaddeus, 129–58 passim

Storrs, Henry R., 98, 108

Strong, Addison G., 250–65 passim

Sumner, Charles, 129–48 passim

Sumners, Hatton W., 246, 247, 252, 262–63, 265, 266, 272, 273, 274, 279, 281–82

Swayne, Charles: Florida legislature recommends inquiry of, 191; pre-impeachment career of, 191–92; composition of House in impeachment of, 192; House vote in impeachment of, 193; managers in trial of, 193–94; articles against, 194; attorneys for, 194; composition of Senate in trial of, 194; reply of, to impeachment articles, 194–95; testimony of witnesses against, 197–200; main points of managers against, 200; testimony of witnesses for, 200–205; impeachment precedents in trial of, 201–2; main points favoring position of, 204–5; summary of case against, 205–7, 210–11; summary of case for, 207–10; Senate vote on, 212–13; partisanship in trial of, 212–13; mentioned, 12, 38

Tenure of Office Act: and Johnson impeachment, 133–59 passim

Thurston, John M., 194–95, 200, 201, 202–4, 205, 208–10

Train, Charles R., 117, 118–19

Trumbull, Lyman, 122–23

Tyler, John, 99, 399 n27

Wade, Benjamin F.: in Johnson trial, 130, 139, 159, 161, 347 n100

Walsh, Frank P., 273, 276, 279, 281

Washington, George: appointed all-Federalist bench, 25, 57

Webb, Edwin Y., 219, 223–24, 227, 232–33

Wickliffe, Charles A., 98, 106

Williams, Thomas, 137–55 passim

Wirt, William, 99, 107–8

Worthington, Augustus, 220, 224–25, 234–35

About the Author

ELEANORE BUSHNELL, professor of political science emeritus at the University of Nevada, has published books and articles on impeachment and on reapportionment. Her nonacademic activities include serving on the Rhodes Scholarship Committee, the National Endowment for the Humanities, and the Nevada Commission on Judicial Discipline.